# Republics, Nations and Tribes

# Republics, Nations and Tribes

MARTIN THOM

**VERSO**
London · New York

For the Helsinki Citizens' Assembly

First published by Verso 1995
© Martin Thom 1995
All rights reserved

**Verso**
UK: 6 Meard Street, London W1V 3HR
USA: 180 Varick Street, New York NY 10014-4606

Verso is the imprint of New Left Books

ISBN 1–85984–920–2
ISBN 1–85984–020–5 (pbk)

**British Library Cataloguing in Publication Data**
A catalogue record for this book is available from the British Library

**Library of Congress Cataloging-in-Publication Data**
A catalog record for this book is available from the Library of Congress

Typeset by York House Typographic Ltd, London
Printed in Great Britain by Biddles Ltd, London and King's Lynn

# Contents

Again, shall we say that while the race of inhabitants remains the same, the city is also the same, although the citizens are always dying and being born, as we call rivers and fountains the same, although the water is always flowing away and more coming? Or shall we say that the generations of men, like the rivers, are the same, but that the state changes? For, since the state is a partnership of citizens in a constitution, when the form of the government changes, and becomes different, then it may be supposed that the state is no longer the same, just as a tragic differs from a comic chorus, although the members of both may be identical.

Aristotle, *The Politics*

# Preface

This book was researched in five different libraries, and I wish therefore to thank the librarians and staff at the British Library, in London; at the Library of the British School in Rome; at the Brotherton Library, the University of Leeds; at the London Library, in St James's Square, London; and at the University Library, Cambridge. Michael Baynham, Rose Elgar, Timothy Jenkins, Ian Patterson, Ewan Smith, Deborah Thom and Nigel Wheale kindly read parts of an earlier draft, and I am most grateful to them. I also owe much to the writings of Sergio Moravia, Sebastiano Timpanaro and Franco Venturi. This said, my greatest debt is to Gareth Stedman-Jones, who commented at length on the second version of the book. I alone must answer, however, for any errors of fact or interpretation. Finally, I would like to thank Malcolm Imrie at Verso for help and encouragement offered over the years.

Martin Thom

# Introduction

Although this book is primarily a study of nascent European nationalism, the wording of my title is intended to warn the reader that I am also concerned with the impact of the principle of nationality upon both classical scholarship and ethnology. For scrutiny of changing perceptions of the ancient way of life of the indigenous peoples of the Americas reveals a momentous alteration, late in the eighteenth and early in the nineteenth century, in the value accorded to such forms of liberty.

I maintain that, during the years of transition between the Enlightenment and Romanticism, a high wall was raised between ancient and modern liberty, assembled, so to speak, out of the rubble from the Bastille. At the same time, the noble savage, after centuries of shadow service, was given notice to quit the European imagination. A shift in the balance of classical scholarship was thus accompanied by the fading of an infatuation with a primordial, sylvan liberty, so that modern ethnology, so delicately balanced between estrangement from and identification with the object of its enquiry, was born just as the Plutarchian legend of a heroic, republican Rome was, by many though not by all, laid to rest. I seek to establish this connection, and to account for it, in the first two parts of my book.

The dismantling of ideal images of an ancient republican liberty was followed, however, by the staging of other tableaux of collective origin. The writings of Boulainvilliers, Du Bos, Giannone, Montesquieu, Muratori, Sainte-Palaye and Vico testify to the intense interest shown by both *érudits* and *philosophes* in the fifth and sixth centuries AD, and by their very existence belie the notion that the eighteenth-century mind was 'unhistorical'. What took place, then, in the first three decades of the nineteenth century was not so much an empirical discovery of early medieval sources, for publicists like François Guizot and Augustin Thierry could not, to begin with, match the scholarship of the Benedictines of St Maur, but a transfer of value from the ancient city to the barbarian tribe, from Rome to the Germanic peoples whose invasions and subsequent patterns of settlement were thought to have determined

1

the contours of Christian Europe. Not only was the *philosophe* historians' indictment of the early Church rejected, but in addition the merely
formal notion, most pithily expressed by John Locke, that 'in the
beginning, all the world was America', was swept aside by substantive
claims regarding a stubborn, deep-rooted identity, variously called Indo-
European or Indo-Germanic. The celebrated discovery of structural
links between Sanskrit, Greek and Latin towards the end of the eighteenth century served to reinforce this great change; to consider the
prehistory of Europe as at once Germanic and Indian became at last a
commonplace. Thus, in 1871, Henry Maine came very close indeed to
saying that, in the beginning, all the world was India.[1]

So radical a recasting seemed to herald a golden age in archaeology,
ethnology, comparative linguistics, comparative mythology, folklore,
jurisprudence and history, and yet the human sciences bore the ghostly
traces of a divine cargo, since fervent sifting of a but lately erased set of
values fostered the illusion that, through the mere fact of speaking,
occupying a territory or having ancestors, the bereft might inhabit them
still. The transience of cities, a self-evident fact for Aristotle (as my
epigraph demonstrates), for Machiavelli or for Rousseau, had ceased to
count for much in a world that took its measure from redemptive
languages, stocked lands and immortal corporations. Far from being
lost, Troy was indeed on the Troad, if Schliemann had looked on the face
of Agamemnon, and in the 1880s and 1890s the revealed depths of
ancient Rome threatened to outshine the modern capital, just then a vast
building-site, of united Italy. The Indo-Germanic, though by definition
tied to the purportedly massive migrations of tribal peoples, thus promoted the illusion of organic continuity, to the detriment of rival
accounts of the lateral diffusion of artefacts, institutions or lexical items.
To use terms current in the first half of the nineteenth century, the native
was favoured over the dative.

In order to spell out the above argument, I have studied the writings of
a number of key thinkers and publicists, each of whom has been
described as both an heir of the Enlightenment and as a forerunner of
Romanticism. Born in the second half of the eighteenth century, arriving
at adulthood even as the old regime was hastening towards its end, such
transitional figures as Pierre-Jean-George Cabanis, René-François de
Chateaubriand, Benjamin Constant, Vincenzo Cuoco, Claude Fauriel,
Johann Gottlieb Fichte, Wilhelm von Humboldt, Alessandro Manzoni,
Georg Barthold Niebuhr, Jean-Claude-Léonard Simonde de Sismondi,
August-Wilhelm von Schlegel, Friedrich von Schlegel, Germaine de
Staël and Constantin-François Volney testify, in the altering texture and
pattern of their innermost belief, to the yielding of a world of cities to a
world of nations. Their lives, it could be said, span the years between the

Encyclopédie and the generation of 1830. My narrative begins in Thermidorian Paris, but I close with a chapter devoted to the cultural and historiographical controversies that raged in Restoration Milan, and which provide a perhaps unrivalled opportunity to study in fine detail the transition from Enlightenment to Romanticism. My book therefore ends with a thumbnail account of the thought of Carlo Cattaneo, a Lombard polymath who, throughout the Risorgimento, defended Enlightenment values and remained loyal to the principle of confederation, and to the subsumed, occluded liberty of cities. The constellation of terms derived from *foedus*, or treaty, has long been a source of confusion, and I would stress, by way of preliminary explanation, that the nation-state has been shadowed throughout its history by the union of states, or confederation, a fact which the characteristic teleologies of nationalist belief tend to mask. Yet for every Bodin there is an Althusius, for every Hobbes a Pufendorf. To summon up a world of cities, alongside or even transecting a world of nations, is thus by itself to shed light upon the principle of nationality.

Most of the fourteen writers and publicists listed above were either *idéologues* or else members, central or peripheral as the case may be, of the Coppet Circle, described by Stendhal in 1816 as 'the States General of European opinion'.[2] Both milieux allow us to study forms of thought in transition, and in transmission across frontiers, but both have also been gravely misrepresented. Party spirit was certainly much to blame for this state of affairs, yet account should also be taken of the moral turmoil into which those who survived the Terror were thrown. Thus, the critic Sainte-Beuve once observed that 'the republicans of the year III', as he termed them, were never able to complete the systematic treatises they had dreamed of writing, because the times were too unsettled for the composition of a second *Spirit of the Laws*.[3] It is certainly true that Sismondi had wished to emulate Montesquieu in the domain of politics, that Constant had hoped to do as much for both politics and religion, and that Madame de Staël had likewise planned to identify, not prescribe, the laws of literature. It is also the case that those works that saw the light two or three years after Thermidor and the fall of Robespierre were characterized both by an excessive 'spirit of system' and by a sometimes heartrending anguish. Thus Chateaubriand, in his *Essai Historique* of 1797, missed no occasion to draw a parallel, however far-fetched, between a prominent figure in revolutionary France and a statesman or demagogue from classical Athens, Carthage, Rome or Sparta, and yet, against the grain of this preposterous system, there ran passages of excoriating disillusion. In the course of the year III, Madame de Staël herself planned a systematic treatise, in two parts, the prospectus for which was contained in the introduction to *De l'Influence des Passions sur le Bonheur des Individus et des Nations*. Her treatise, like Chateaubriand's bizarre construction, was marked by an intensely personal, even confessional tone, and by an undefended agony of spirit.

A generation in shock, haunted by catastrophe, produced its synoptic studies too late, or mislaid them or failed to complete them. For example, Constant had already written thirty-seven chapters of *De l'Esprit des Religions* by September 1794, when he first met Staël, and yet this, the project closest to his heart, only saw publication three decades later, as *De la Religion* (1824–31) and *Du Polythéisme Romain* (1833).[4] Likewise, Claude Fauriel, one of the most influential of the *idéologues*, mislaid his draft history of Stoicism, a work much praised by all those who knew something of it, and never finished his ambitious history of southern Gaul. Yet some publicists righted themselves under the Consulate and the Empire, and produced full-scale treatises answering to the mood of the times. For example, Sismondi's manuscript *Recherches sur les Constitutions des Peuples Libres*, completed in 1796, may fairly be regarded as a trial run for the celebrated history of the Italian communes, published in 1807–18. In 1821, the first three volumes of his *Histoire des Français*, a work of original scholarship which belongs on the same shelf as the researches of Guizot and Thierry, were widely acclaimed. Another fully achieved and altogether timely work was Niebuhr's *Römische Geschichte*, delivered as a course of lectures at the University of Berlin, in 1810–11, published first in 1811–12, and again, in drastically altered form, in 1826–28. Yet if this celebrated book was so thoroughly eclipsed by Mommsen's monumental history of Rome, published in 1854–56, it was in part because the latter was a far more compelling narrative. This fact is not without its ironies, for Niebuhr's book was at once a denial and an endorsement of Livian providentialism, both a philological destruction and a poetic rehabilitation of epic truth.

Since the human sciences are dyed with colours registered at the proof stage of the age of nations, a modern reader finds it hard to see anything but a gain for knowledge in the great alterations of the late eighteenth and early nineteenth centuries. It was then, after all, that the much-reiterated call for a 'science of man' led to the foundation of the Société des Observateurs de l'Homme, and of the Académie Celtique, which are generally held to mark the inauguration of modern ethnology and folklore studies respectively. Nor would I deny that many of our notions of social history, or even of history from below, stem from the new approaches pioneered under the First Empire and during the Restoration, and consolidated after the July Revolution. Augustin Thierry's clarion call still has the power to move us:

The history of France as it has been written by modern writers is not the true history of the country, the national, the popular history; this history is still buried in the dust of contemporary chronicles . . . The best part of our annals, the most serious, the most instructive, remains to be written; we lack a history of citizens, a history of subjects, a history of the people.[5]

Given the clarity of this demand, it would seem perverse to deplore the fact that scholars wrenched their gaze away from the horizon of classical Antiquity, or from the errant abstractions of an imagined counter-Europe, and touched their cold foreheads to the earth, or to regret that ears were bent to catch, not Ciceronian cadences in the forum, but the murmuring of diverse streams of language received and given in all humility by the peoples.

Whatever the gains, the transfer entailed great losses. Quite simply, the city, in fact as in imagination, was obscured by the nation. Rousseau may sometimes have regarded the social contract as an actual occurrence (an oath sworn by an assembled people), and at other times as merely notional, whereas Kant insisted that it was no more than an idea of reason, but both thinkers allowed that it was the foundation of right. In the age of nations, however, most look past assembly or universal declaration to an aboriginal authority, be it the ancestral dead, the native land or the mother tongue. Yet to live and die for such primordial unities is to fall for what was once a sweet, and is now a bitter, illusion. In Europe, at any rate, toponomastics, the science of place names, offers no comfort to the self-appointed singers of a single, earthed tribe, since a hill may be remembered in one language, a ford in a second, a salt-works in a third. As for dialect maps, the distribution of ancient and minute phonological shifts may move us, but in the shallows of present time they justify nothing. The case I make here is therefore not vitiated, I think, by those scholars who, surveying whole millennia, have produced accounts of 'nations before nationalism', or of 'the ethnic origins of nations'.[6]

If throughout this book I have descried within the eighteenth century (and before) an age of cities, and within the nineteenth century (and since) an age of nations, it is in order to highlight the fact that the tradition of classical republicanism presupposed one conception of the upholding of human lives in concert, the principle of nationality quite another. It may at first appear woefully inexact to speak of an age of cities where the historical record bears witness to the consolidation of great monarchies, in a climate of reason of state, and to the theory and practice of absolutism; where the small state of Western Europe, the *Kleinstaat*, was in manifest and terminal decline; and where, in the early stages of the French Revolution, protestations of republican faith were rare. Nonetheless, the image of the city, like that of tribal lands of dissidence, persisted as a source of value, even or perhaps especially where it was most strenuously denied. Before doctrines of progress and perfectibility were fully secured against the notion that civilizations were condemned to cycles of glory and decadence, city and tribe continued to serve, even at times in the writings of some who had embraced a stadial theory of society, as Utopian guarantees. Conversely, the age of nations, which we still inhabit and endure, had arrived when the Stoic hierarchy of duties was overturned, when the theory of natural right was supplanted by that of *Volksgeist*, or the spirit of the people, and when love of accustomed land and language, either or both providentially guaranteed, replaced love of fellow citizens.

As Peter Gay has shown, no sect of late Antiquity enjoyed greater prestige among the thinkers of the European Enlightenment than did Roman Stoicism.[7] What the *philosophes* found to admire in Cicero or Seneca was a wholehearted commitment to the earthly, not the heavenly city, and a readiness nonetheless to renounce the vanities of this world if justice were at issue. Although Cato of Utica was accorded much honour in Dante's *Purgatorio*, since in 1300 there existed a tradition of natural law which for centuries had been both Stoic and Christian, it had always been necessary to tread with care upon the common ground between the two belief systems, each of which is characterized, as Ernst Troeltsch demonstrated, by an extreme individualism and an equally unconfined universalism. Where, for example, Montesquieu in Paris or secure at La Brède, risked asserting equal ethical status for Christianity and for Roman Stoicism, Vico, in Naples, had to be more circumspect. Both the Stoics and the Epicureans, he said, had denied providence, the former binding themselves to fate and an inexorable chain of cause and effect, the latter abandoning themselves to chance and to a blind concourse of atoms. Both sects had neglected the extraordinary providence of 'the omnipotent, wise and beneficent will of the best and wisest God'.[8] Enlightenment discussion of these matters tended in fact to turn upon a sometimes casuistical use of the distinction, derived from Bossuet, between ordinary providence, where the writ of Stoic natural law might safely be allowed to run, and an extraordinary providence, through which the will of God was paramount. It is clear, then, that the relation between Christianity and Stoicism was of crucial importance, both in the Enlightenment and during the transition to Romanticism. As Troeltsch observed, 'in spite of the theism of Stoicism, the elements of primitive and underlying pantheism reappear continually', this aspect allowing the boldest of the *philosophes* to throw open a door to Epicurean and Lucretian speculations.[9] For those who believed that the operations of Stoic natural law, notwithstanding its long-established alliance with Christian ethics, precluded any reference to the will and authority of

God, it was nature, and not the annals of human history, that was saturated with divine providence.

When, however, the Enlightenment fell into crisis, and was harshly judged for its impiety, value ceased to inhere in either great souls or nature, and became instead a thread drawn through historical time. Not all of those studied in the present book reneged, like Hegel, upon Roman Stoicism, but where they did so, pride was replaced by humility in the list of virtues. A Pantheon of Plutarchian *grands âmes*, responding to assembly and to the earthly city, was supplanted by a flock of Christian souls ascending to God and to the heavenly city. This change need not of itself have made nations the imagined subjects of a redeemed history, for identification with the origin of value was at the same time an identification with all other human members of Creation. Yet once divine authority was again allowed to have had a hand in every stage of the historical process, the way was open to a sacralization of an elect people, and to a corresponding demonization of those stamped by canon law as *populi estranei*. Even as the fame of Rousseau, who had sung both city and solitude, was eclipsed, a world-renouncing concept of the person, and therefore of liberty, was replaced by a world-inhabiting concept, a transformation in values exemplified by the case of Fichte.

As the dedication of this book to the Helsinki Citizens' Assembly does, I hope, make clear, I write from the conviction that before the age of nations there was an age of cities, and that after the age of nations there could be, if there is not a pandemonium of 'ethnic cleansing' instead, a new age of cities, in which regional assemblies, freed of the terminal claims of providence, could answer in all clarity to the rightful demands of cosmopolis. In the third part of my study, I therefore show how the Enlightenment cosmopolitan concept of liberty, law and confederation was challenged in the Napoleonic period and the Restoration by a providential vision of the tribe- or word-nation. Machiavelli became the prophet of the strong state, not of the free city, and Bossuet was restored to favour.

In advancing such claims, I am obviously vulnerable to the charge of having misrepresented the historiography of the Restoration, which was characterized, at least in the voluminous researches of Guizot, Sismondi and Thierry, by a celebration of both city and nation. A sceptical reader might, after all, object that the militant articles, essays and books of the period 1820–22, far from obscuring the free city, turned upon the heroic struggles of a handful of twelfth-century communes and upon a rejection, by the same token, of legitimation in terms of Frankish liberties. As Thierry observed, in the celebrated letter already quoted: 'In a truly national history . . . France would feature with its various cities and populations, which would appear before us as so many collective beings endowed with will and action.'[10] Moreover, later thinkers, among them Carlo Cattaneo, Friedrich Engels and Karl Marx, used his researches in order to sustain a vision of the free city, and yet to transcend it, in the promise of future confederation or of communism. However, Thierry, in his protracted historiographical dispute with the Ultras, had given too many hostages to his adversaries. By countering the prescriptive rights of a warrior aristocracy with the thronged time and haunted territory of the Gauls, he was plainly both defending the imperilled gains of the Revolution and championing a recognizably modern notion of social history. Yet in the shift from the transience of cities to the eternity of nations, or, in other terms, from the civic to the social, time and the land were rendered sacred. Through a curious reversal of seventeenth-century historical Pyrrhonism, all the dead were now honoured as martyrs, all graves were shrines, all objects were numinous, and no words were lost. This sacralized notion of social identity, which favoured the separated destiny of the peoples over their lateral interrelation, was not shared by those who remained unreservedly loyal to the Enlightenment. One may grasp the nature of this divergence by contrasting Jules Michelet's concept of the passage in the French Revolution from federation to unity, mystically embodied in Paris, with Cattaneo's commitment to the subsistence of free cities within any national movement. This contrast was still more marked where the history of ancient Rome was concerned, since Michelet accepted the Christian view, rejected by Machiavelli, Montesquieu and Rousseau, that the city had served as an instrument of the divine will, establishing a military and political unity as a precondition for a higher moral and spiritual life. He even went so far as to vest in France the 'extraordinary' providence which, in the *New Science*, had watched over the Hebrew people. Such theologico-political primacies, commonplace in Metternichian Europe, were altogether alien to Cattaneo, though not, I think, to his friend and foil, Giuseppe Ferrari, resident then in Paris, an admirer of Michelet and on good terms with many in Victor Cousin's circle.

By elaborating upon seemingly slight divergences between thinkers and publicists who set out with much the same intellectual baggage, I have tried to demonstrate that, in the transition between an age of cities and an age of nations, the belief system of nationalism was not a conceptual prison, sociologically determined even in its most intricate details. Those at mortal risk in Sarajevo who, even as I write, defend against all the odds an ideal of multi-ethnic and multi-cultural society, insist that the war destroying their city is not a war between three tribes, and yet so enduring is the myth of the tribe-nation that the image constantly returns. The same myth may be discerned in the writings of nineteenth-century publicists and historians who had ostensibly rejected racist arguments, and who allowed that neither blood nor language nor territory are necessary criteria for a national identity. If, therefore, I have referred in the same breath to the word-nation and to the tribe-nation, it is in order to show that an appeal to divine providence informs both celebrations of diversity and invocations of continuity. For example, Michelet, in a state of exaltation after the July Revolution, the apotheosis of the people, claimed that France, being blessed with a greater geographical diversity than any other country in Europe, had achieved a correspondingly more complete fusion of races. His fatherland, then, was the bearer of the *verbe sociale*, and its Declaration of Rights of Man and the Citizen was a social revelation, complementing and carrying forward the moral word of Christ. Paris and France would found the general city of humankind. Germany, Michelet went on, was a race, but France a nation.[11] The perplexing thing about such fervent celebrations of diversity, which have remained a feature of French scholarship up until the present day, is that they are voiced by the citizens of a state that pursued, at an earlier date and with greater efficiency than elsewhere, a policy of relentless centralization. Under pressure, therefore, its historians have set the cult of diversity to one side, and discerned, beneath the universal promise of the word-nation, the consoling ground of the tribe-nation.[12]

Oscillation between visions of general redemption and a clinging to specific lineages is not peculiar to France, however, but is a characteristic feature of the thought-forms of the age of nations. In the narrative of, for example, Friedrich Meinecke, the German nation has an imagined ethnic substance and, beyond the generalizing fact of civic assembly, a pure and unassimilated tribe subsists, much as it had done in the accounts written a hundred years before by Fichte, Niebuhr and the Schlegel brothers.[13] There is something of the same quality to Benedetto Croce's invocations of 'the organic development of the peoples', as I show in my final chapter. It may smack of antiquarianism to frame the historical moment of my study with theoretical works from early this century, but the closing of the gap between liberal and reactionary nationalist movements in the era of high imperialism is the sternest reminder we can have of the moral and political dangers of our own times.

Before embarking upon my narrative, I wish to add some clarification regarding the scope of the present enquiry. In geographical terms, my account has its centre in France, or even in Paris, and is carried outwards from there by the Emigration and by the armies of the Grande Nation. When, therefore, I discuss late Enlightenment perceptions of America or of Germany, I consider them from the viewpoint of *Europe Française*. It would be possible to compose a still larger tableau, and to tell a similar

story – with slight adjustments to the chronology – from, say, Philadelphia or Weimar. Paris might then itself be seen from a distance, through
the eyes of Benjamin Franklin or Wilhelm von Humboldt. A recursive
method of this sort, by which the observers are themselves observed, has
been deployed to great effect by Franco Venturi. In Part IV I shift the
scene to the Italian peninsula or, more specifically, to Restoration Milan,
in order to rehearse the crisis of the Enlightenment and the genesis of
Romanticism in another context. Although I cannot hope to match
Venturi's cosmopolitan erudition, I have tried by this means to offer a
more rounded picture of the cultural and political legacy of the *idéologues* and of the Coppet Circle.

# PART I

# The Last of the Romans

Who can be the general of such a vast multitude, or who the herald, unless he have the voice of Stentor?

Aristotle, *The Politics*

# Passion, Pity and the Last of the Romans

## The Terror

From September 1793 to July 1794, the Terror raged in France. Under the rule of the Committee of Public Safety, atrocities were perpetrated in the name of revolutionary virtue, sometimes ratified by judicial procedures, no matter how travestied or cursory. Horror, as much as terror, had become the order of the day, and the slaughter in Paris was matched by summary executions and massacres in Nantes, Lyons, Arras and Toulon, each authorized by representatives on mission, by local popular societies or by revolutionary tribunals. Because the Terror was precipitated by a deputation of commissioners from the forty-eight sections, and from the Jacobin Club, who came before the Convention on 5 September, it has also become irrevocably associated with the political alliance forged between the sans-culottes, the network of clubs and the Montagnard deputies aligned with Robespierre. As readers of *A Tale of Two Cities* will recall, representations of this notorious event have rarely been without an element of social fear.

Sometimes the victims were enemies in the most generalized sense of the Revolution; they belonged, simply, to a proscribed category, be it former aristocrat or refractory priest. Thus, at Nantes, on the night of 26–27 Brumaire year II, Carrier was responsible for the *noyade*, or mass drowning, of some ninety such priests in the river Loire, an event reported in the regime's official gazette, the *Moniteur*.[1] Sometimes the death-dealing had not been indiscriminate but directed at named factions, the Girondins in 1793, the Hébertists and Dantonists in the spring of 1794. The emergency measures had been introduced as an instrument of state policy in the most desperate of circumstances, in a country encircled by hostile armies, and many were at the time convinced that the scaffolds within France had fired the courage of the revolutionary forces at the frontier.[2] The demeanour of the ragged foot soldiers at Valmy had astonished Europe. By the same token, as victory followed victory, in the summer of 1794, the Terror subsided. Robespierre was defeated and destroyed by those who feared that they would be the next to die, by those who had always been opposed to the slaughter at home but who had cowered in silence on the benches of the Convention, and in part also by those who wished to persevere with the same policies.

With hindsight, even some who had been proscribed or imprisoned by the revolutionary committees admitted that the dictatorship, and with it the Terror, had saved France. For example, Jacques Bailleul, a Girondin, allowed in 1818 that the men of the year II had not meant to do wrong, and that they had merely wished to defend their country against both domestic and foreign enemies.[3] If victims, nursing real injuries and real grievances, could forgive their adversaries, it is not surprising to find that, by 1837, Thomas Carlyle, in a highly theatrical alteration of frame, could scale down the bloodshed by contrasting the lamentable fate of 'the speaking thousands' with that of 'the dumb millions', those who had already died and those who were yet to die in the famines in Ireland.[4]

In a recent study of the historiography of the French Revolution, Eric Hobsbawm has argued that, if Guizot, Mignet and Thierry refused to condemn even that passage of time which, in liberal terms, was altogether indefensible, namely, the Montagnard dictatorship of 1793–94, it was because the White Terror of 1816, the fragile balance of power in France between 1816 and 1820, and the triumph of the Ultras, the reactionaries, after 1822, had left them in no doubt that, should there have been a complete return to the old regime, nothing less than another revolution, with its attendant turmoil and suffering, would have been needed to reverse it. For this reason, the liberal historians of the Restoration no longer felt able to draw a clear line between Mirabeau and Robespierre, or between 1789 and the year II.[5] Consequently, the entire unfurled Revolution was construed as the act of collective liberation of a class, the bourgeoisie, which had first laid claim to its freedom, despite the resistance of both barons and monarch, in the twelfth century.[6]

*Echoes of the Marseillaise* is a rejoinder to the revisionist historians, among them François Furet, who regret that the revolutionary process was not abruptly checked in 1789 or in 1790, and a constitutional monarchy consolidated. Hobsbawm does not attend to the lived detail of the phenomena with which I am concerned here, namely, the emergence, out of and against a classical republican idiom, of modern concepts of the nation, chiefly because he quite plausibly draws the notion of bourgeois revolution across the Consulate, the First Empire, the Restoration and the July Monarchy.[7] Yet contemporary responses to the Terror, returning obsessively to the place of virtue or passion in earthly cities, merit close scrutiny. Hobsbawm does in fact quote from one such response, a pamphlet by Benjamin Constant, in which he called upon his contemporaries to 'yield to the necessity' which swept them along, and to 'cease to ignore the march of society'.[8] This sentiment is in stark contrast, Hobsbawm points out, to the viewpoint of the revisionist historians, who now argue, against the grain of informed opinion throughout the nineteenth century and the first half of the twentieth century, that the Revolution was not an event of epochal importance.[9] In support of Hobsbawm's argument, I would add that Constant and Staël, to name but two moderate republicans in Thermidorian and Directorial Paris, had been much impressed by the sheer scale of the event that they lived through or observed in horror from a distance, and much exercised also by the pathological nature, as they saw it, of the Terror. Addressing the Convention, in the year III, their associate, Boissy d'Anglas, declared that France had lived six centuries in as many years, and voiced the hope, as if to end a Shakespearean tragedy with an ashen but consoling quatrain, that they might all profit from their ordeal by a gain in wisdom.[10] As a fellow traveller of the *idéologues*, Staël believed that history was governed by rules which the human mind could fathom and, faced with the irrational nature of much that was done under the Jacobin republic of virtue, had no choice but to argue that such hecatombs lay 'outside of nature, and beyond crime; and . . . no combination could lead one either to foresee or to account for such atrocities; this chance convergence of every kind of moral monstrosity is an unprecedented accident that will not recur for thousands of centuries'.[11]

There was in short a loss of innocence at this moment in European history, which was then likened by almost all to Saint Bartholomew's Eve, and now by many to other atrocities – more terrible, less terrible, who is to say, in our own century of innocents massacred in great numbers?[12] The most nightmarish and the most celebrated image of the horror was of the river Loire, dyed blood-red from Saumur to Nantes.[13] This shocking scene was known to all of France at the time of Carrier's trial, and no doubt many pondered the fate of Nantes as they returned to their churches in the course of 1795 and 1796. Those who knew the *Henriade* would perhaps have thought also of Voltaire's evocation of 'terrified seas'. We should therefore give due weight, notwithstanding Hobsbawm's remarks, to the horror felt by those who had lost friends or family in the course of the Revolution, and take care not to exaggerate the degree to which liberals (or, to be precise, future liberals) regarded the Terror as a historical necessity. Benjamin Constant is a case in point. He had warned moderates that, if they failed to rally to the imperilled Directorial Republic, they would risk fanning the embers of Jacobinism. He went on to describe how, in a battle, a serried line of soldiers might halt and divide, to reveal 'a formidable artillery piece', which 'unleashes terror and death upon the pale enemy', yet he had never meant to insinuate that the Directory would resort to Terror as an instrument of policy.[14] Adrien de Lezay-Marnésia, a Thermidorian and a friend of Madame de Staël, countered with the provocative claim that the republican principle and Terror were synonymous, and that all republics were founded upon bloodshed and upon the raising of scaffolds in city squares.[15] In reply, Constant insisted that the Terror had only been implemented after 31 May and 2 June 1793, that is to say, after the Girondins had been routed and destroyed. Lezay-Marnésia had referred in his pamphlet to the history of Rome, as related by Livy, and had argued that the city had been founded by brigands (as if republican France had been founded by sans-culottes). But, Constant retorted, Livy had in fact stated that it was the monarchy that had been founded by brigands, and that it was a full 250 years later that such men '[who were] undisciplined and incapable of liberty, gave way to a generation more civilised in its mores, more elevated in its sentiments, and more moral in its principles'. In this fashion, Constant was able to clear moderate republicans of blame for the atrocities committed in the year II, and so to distinguish between Condorcet and Vergniaud, the austere and honourable founders of the Republic, and the terrorists and the demagogues.[16]

Moderate republicans were in fact as much disturbed by the savagery of counter-revolutionary reprisals as they had been by the excesses perpetrated under the Montagnard dictatorship, and they urged respect for judicial and constitutional forms. When royalist gangs were taking revenge upon the Jacobins in Lyons, Marie-Joseph Chénier, an *idéologue* and the brother of André Chénier, the executed poet, compared the bloody deeds of the Company of Jesus to a whole range of atrocities, both religious and political: the proscriptions of Marius and Sulla in Rome, the Sicilian Vespers, the Albigensian Crusade, Saint Bartholomew's Eve and the Terror. All such killings, Chénier warned the Convention, had been done in the name of the public good but, if due legal process were flouted, it would not be saved but ruined. The murderers in Lyons would have it that the Terrorists were being brought to trial too slowly, but 'such was the language of the heroes of 2 September [those responsible for the September Massacres] . . . '.[17] By making royalist and Jacobin atrocities into mirror images of each other, the republicans of the year III hoped to heal wounds, and to found a social order in which politics would be free of the spirit of fanaticism. Passions, curbed, should yield to calculation, but also to mercy, a quality of the heart and a pure expression of the moral sense, without which man would be but a wolf to man. If the civil wars of the 1560s and 1570s were the obvious precedent for recent events in France, beyond a second Saint

Bartholomew's Eve there would have to be, for reparation, another Henry IV. This was to be the task of the Directory, while the *idéologues* Constant and Staël were to be the *politiques* of their day. A 'heroic forgetting' was required.[18]

A plea for clemency was well and good, yet all who honoured the memory of Condorcet, who had died in 1793, were appalled by the many miscarriages of justice that had tarnished the annals of the Revolution. Try as they might to plant the standard of right beside one particular date in the revolutionary calendar, waves of blood would seem to wash it away. The loss of innocence could not be masked, and even the most revered days within the new measure of time fell away towards the dark at one hour or another. For, since the opening of the States General, there had been so many atrocities that memoirs seem in retrospect to paint the light of that May morning all the more brightly in order to lift the shadows that later overtook France, as if hope had only been released for a season from the underworld. Consider, for example, the deaths of the Marquis de Launay, of Foulon de Doué and of Bertier de Sauvigny (all in July 1789), or those occurring during the Great Fear (July–August 1789), or the killing of members of the Royal Bodyguard during the October Days (5–6 October 1789), or the *journeé* of 10 August and the slaughter of the Swiss Guard, or the September Massacres or, finally, the Great Terror.

The publicists of the late Enlightenment had been greatly preoccupied by individual rights, and Voltaire himself had campaigned for long years on behalf of victims of injustice (for example, Jean Calas, a Protestant merchant tried and executed in 1762). The struggle to rid France's judicial system of its most barbaric features was as a consequence of crucial importance in the early stages of the Revolution. Those who revered the Habeas Corpus Act, if not the actual operation of criminal justice in England, or who had read Cesare Beccaria's *Dei Delitti e delle Pene*, were naturally delighted by the reforms enacted by the National Assembly, in particular the abolition of torture and of *lettres de cachet*. A concern for individual liberty and for freedom of conscience, reflected in the campaign against the slave trade and in the legislation of the late 1780s on behalf of both Protestants and Jews, also lay at the heart of Rousseau's thought, for nothing, he said, could justify the death of an innocent man.

What then did readers of Voltaire or of Rousseau think of the murders of Foulon de Doué or of Bertier de Savigny, both victims of an enraged crowd? The initial response of many in the Third Estate was not so markedly different from that of Barnave. 'Is this blood then so pure', he had asked the National Assembly, 'that one should so regret the shedding of it?'[19] Madame Roland had agreed, and so, to begin with, had

Gilbert Romme, a fervent Rousseauist and the recently elected representative for the Third Estate in Riom, in the Puy de Dômes. Indeed, on July 1789, he wrote in the coldest terms of the summary execution of the two men.[20] Two or three days later, however, he had changed his mind. No matter how guilty Foulon and Bertier had been, their deaths were more terrible than anything perpetrated under Nero or Caligula; regular courts should be constituted to try the crime of *lèse-nation*, and everything possible should be done to ensure respect for 'the religion of the laws', and to keep such 'bloody souls' at bay.[21] However, as I argue below, the notion of a religion of the laws was open to a variety of different interpretations.

Another follower of Rousseau, Chateaubriand, had seen the heads of Foulon and Bertier, stuck on pikes and with straw stuffed into their mouths. He had dashed to the window, or so he recalled in his memoirs, and harangued the crowd: 'Is this what you mean by liberty?'[22] Convinced by Lamoignon de Malesherbes, the loyal friend of Rousseau, that the social order had descended into anarchy, Chateaubriand embarked a few months later for America, in the hope that he might follow in the footsteps of the authentic 'man of nature'.

The Voltaireans were of a like mind. Thus, a fragment by Condorcet featured Philodemus, a moderate, and Demagoras, a demagogue. To set such a narrative in Greece was to voice the fear that Paris would more nearly resemble a feverish, frivolous Athens than Rome in all its solemnity. Where the people, led astray by orators, had resorted to violence, Philodemus did not seek to excuse it, or to point to the crimes committed by its victims; he did not, Condorcet observed, 'ask if the blood that had been shed was so pure'. This reference to Barnave's chilling outburst was followed by an invocation of 'the majesty of the violated laws, and the outraged laws of nature'. To point the contrast, Demagoras – who, as the title of the fragment indicates, was Marat – hailed a gang of brigands as 'the good people', and recognized their actions as a legitimate expression of popular sovereignty.[23]

In the nineteenth century, historians in the liberal or moderate republican camp would continue, despite their retrospective identification with the insurgent Third Estate, to draw a distinction between those who, like Condorcet, had honoured the majesty of the laws, and those who had connived in riot and massacre. Mignet, for example, spoke of the Girondins' 'aversion for violent measures'.[24] Falling victim to the *journées* of 31 May and 2 June 1793, the latter had left the Convention before the Montagnard Terror, and could apparently be taken at their word when they proclaimed their abhorrence of popular violence and their commitment to the principle that the national representation was sacrosanct. So it was that the Thermidorians built their image of the Republic around the wronged Girondins, who were, Thibaudeau observed, 'the dividing line between light and shadow'.[25] Closer examination of the Girondin press at the time of the September Massacres has, however, shown that figures such as Gorsas, Mercier, Condorcet and Roland offered, in their journalism, no real criticism of the atrocities perpetrated in the prisons. Only later, after the battle of Valmy had secured France's frontiers, did the Girondins denounce the massacres, holding their Montagnard rivals responsible for them.[26]

The Girondins wished to tame the passions and hoped to reduce a turbulent world to reason. They were nonetheless prepared, where necessary, to construe popular violence as sublime. Thus Roland, in his letter of 3 September to the Legislative Assembly, had written: 'I know that revolutions are not calculated by the ordinary rules . . . The wrath of the people and the movement are comparable to the action of a torrent which overturns obstacles which no other power could ever have destroyed.'[27] More generally, the Girondins would seem to have accepted the truth of Machiavelli's dictum that the achievement of *gran cose* might in exceptional circumstances require terrible deeds.[28] This reasoning, embraced by Gabriel Naudé in the sixteenth century to justify the original Saint Bartholomew's Eve, has been used to render less scandalous the many occasions since then upon which shimmering ends have veiled bloody means. For *virtù*, in *The Prince*, is an efficacious grappling with the pure force of *fortuna*, let virtues be what they may. One can plausibly argue that it was the October Days that drove Louis XVI to ratify the Declaration of Rights of Man and the Citizen, imparting, one might add, a little more haste to his pen, and it may equally be claimed that it was the Montagnard dictatorship that, though not itself socialist, carried European political thought from the lofty but abstract humanitarianism of 1789 to the embryonic social democracy of 1793–94. Marx and Engels, faced with the slaughter perpetrated by General Cavaignac in the course of the June Days, showed no hesitation in modelling a proletarian revolution upon the bourgeois revolution, or a dictatorship of the proletariat upon a dictatorship of the bourgeoisie, for utilitarian justifications of the one could obviously be applied with still more cogency to the other.[29]

The contrary view has been advanced by many commentators, both in our own day and during the nineteenth century. Thus, in a book written long after the events described, Alessandro Manzoni, a poet and novelist on intimate terms with many of the moderate republicans who survived the storms of the Revolution, argued that the Terror had in fact begun in July 1789, since lynch law had then caused the death of innocent individuals.[30] Yet in the immediate aftermath of Thermidor, and for some years afterwards, anyone who made such an observation would have been presumed to be, quite simply, a counter-revolutionary. Constant, for example, warned against the tendency of the Ultras to follow the thread of their hatred back step by step, so that representatives of the Third Estate would already be regicides in June 1789.[31] Likewise Thibaudeau, writing after the Restoration, noted that enemies of the Revolution dated the Terror to the first lynching to have occurred after the capture of the Bastille. He observed that, when a nation broke its chains, it was certainly the case that fear entered the hearts of those who had fettered it, but while a great number had trembled under a despotism, now it was only a minority. At no time in the Revolution had there been a complete absence of fear, but a distinction should be made, Thibaudeau argued, between such a situation and that which prevailed after 31 May 1793, when the whole nation was in its grip.[32]

The very identity of the Revolution, and that of social order, had thus seemed to turn upon the use of violence. The right of resistance to oppression was enshrined in the Declaration of Rights of 1789, but the sanguinary uprisings that had taken place since then had left many representatives anxious as to the form that such resistance ought properly to take. Thus, the Girondins had specified that 'men united in society ought to have a *legal* means to resist oppression', and in their draft Constitution, the work of Condorcet, referenda featured. The context in which these arguments were aired, in the spring of 1793, was one of furious animosity between the Montagnards and the Girondins, with Robespierre leading the former inexorably towards a political alliance with the Paris Commune and the radicalized sans-culottes in the sections. Thus, on 15 April, a deputation from thirty-three sections, with the sanction of the Jacobin Club and the Commune, had called for the exclusion of twenty-two Girondin deputies from the Convention; at some point between 18 and 20 April, the Montagnards came to an agreement with the Paris radicals over the need for price controls; and, on 24 April, Robespierre called for significant restrictions on property rights. A British historian, M.J. Sydenham, has insisted that the Girondins were not a party at all, however much their nineteenth-century apologists may have fostered the notion that they were. Out of the two hundred or so who have been accorded the title, Sydenham reckons that no more than fourteen or fifteen, and probably as few as seven or eight, deserve it.[33] Nonetheless, a significant number of those within the core group played a prominent part in debates over the right of resistance, each of them advancing a recognizably Girondin line of argument. Gensonné, Louvet, Salle and Vergniaud each called, then, for legal means of resistance, warned of the oppression originating in 'partial authorities', that is, the Commune and the sections, and expressed the fear that a people that had acquired the habit of insurrection would be prey to intriguers. Yet, as Sydenham notes, individual Girondins continued to break ranks even at the most critical moments in the struggle with Robespierre, and 22 April was no exception. Lasource, who had clashed violently with Robespierre on more than one occasion in the course of the previous year, judged the article redundant, on the grounds that 'the sentiment of insurrection is stronger than anything; it dares to cross any barrier'. This, curiously enough, was the exalted idiom of Robespierre himself:

> I judge it altogether ridiculous to define the cases of oppression, and I assert that it is altogether impossible for you, in any circumstance whatsoever, to say what my sensibility is . . . [Murmurs from a great number of benches] . . . Who among you deems himself capable of confining within its right barriers the sensibility of citizens, of placing limits to it, and of anticipating circumstances in which the people, finding its laws intolerable, will resist? Can you not see that this depends above all on each individual; and do you not fear that this means of resistance . . . might be the very thing to prevent the people from rising up . . .

The compromise wording arrived at that same day had half a Girondin and half a Montagnard soul, with legal means being counterbalanced by a definition of insurrection as the holiest of duties, but it was the latter that would prevail on 31 May and 2 June.[34]


## The republic of virtue

Rousseau once declared that, if he had had to choose the place of his birth, he would have chosen

> a society of which the dimensions were limited by the extent of human faculties, that is to say, by the possibility of being well-governed; a society where everyone was equal to his job so that no one was obliged to commit to others the functions which belonged to him; a state where, every individual being acquainted with every other, neither the dark manoeuvres of vice nor the modesty of virtue was concealed from public gaze and judgement, a state where the delectable habit of meeting and knowing one another made love of country a love of fellow citizens rather than love for land.[35]

This vision of the free city, combining features of Calvinist Geneva and of Plutarchian Rome, had exerted a profound influence upon Montagnards such as Robespierre and Saint-Just, and upon the Jacobin Clubs in 1793–94.[36] Yet the nightmarish picture of Nantes painted by witnesses at Carrier's trial suggested that a wholly transparent social order, in which one might not only be a 'suspect' but even be 'suspected of being a suspect', was in reality a dance of death. If the inspection of citizens' hearts culminated in massacres, would it not be better to go, in a fallen world, masked?

The attempt had, however, been made to restore a way of life in which there was no distinction between public and private spheres, and in which the morality of citizens was subject to general scrutiny. The Genevan Consistory or the Roman Censorship therefore fascinated all those republicans who believed that, for want of such exceptional magistracies, right would not be shielded from passion. Thus Lanthénas, a Girondin, in a tract hostile to the Montagnards, called for 'the solemn establishment of a public morality, and of a censorship serving to return errant citizens to it'.[37] It was, nonetheless, the Jacobin Clubs that actually tried to implement this programme, intensifying their criticism of drunkenness, gambling and prostitution, as outward displays of loyalty to the regenerated nation, whether in dress, in documentation (the *certificats de civisme*) or in speech, became compulsory. At Nancy, the Club came very close to introducing a censor, while the revolutionary regimes in Geneva and Naples introduced councils or tribunals of mores.[38]

The code of morality embraced by radical sans-culottes in the year II was perforce invoked by those Montagnards who attended the Jacobin Clubs regularly. 'It is far more important to render poverty honourable', Robespierre declared on 10 May 1793, 'than to proscribe opulence.'[39] To be frugal, to dress simply, and to follow a regular routine was to embody an honourable *médiocrité*, to be an example to one's fellow citizens. Retrospective accounts suggest that citizens stood, therefore, full in the glare of an undivided social authority, yet modest clothes and humble dwellings were thought to offer, paradoxically enough, a sort of privacy.[40] A hut, come what might, was quieter than a palace. Madame de Staël was once denounced in the Convention for her assiduous wining and dining of representatives, her accuser remarking that good republicans dined not at salons but at home with their families, and yet it was she who would give prominence to the distinction, so central to the theory of ancient and modern liberty, between the private and the public spheres.[41] The point is that the simplicity of authentic republican mores was designed to render a life wholly transparent, and the narrating of the virtues in a republic, an act achieved most effectively through festivals, was meant to produce a regulation of the moral economy, so that each individual story would not veer off towards the opposite extremes of luxury and penury.

Gilbert Romme burned with just such a neo-Stoic enthusiasm for the public narration of virtuous deeds yet, by contrast with others in the year II, he kept a balance between the judgement of the assembled people and the tribunal of the reasoning mind and conscience. In an undated bulletin, signed on behalf of the Comité d'Instruction Publique, Romme wrote of the need to broadcast 'seeds of republican virtues, through the publication of those noble deeds which are performed daily amongst us'. 'We invite you', he went on,

> to collect . . . in the dwellings, the workshops and the battalions of the Republic, those deeds which most deserve to be transmitted as examples; . . . for the most useful virtues have almost always emanated from such places . . . The narrating of fine actions ought to be as simple as the virtue which gives birth to them. This collection . . . will be the first elementary book to be placed before the children of the fatherland; at the same time it will furnish materials for history.[42]

In chapter 2 I show how far moderate republicans retreated, after Thermidor, from a republican pedagogy of this sort. It was indeed in a climate of chill disillusion that Romme, recognizing that republican liberty as he understood it had ended, chose to emulate Cato of Utica and to teach France the last lesson it was in his power to teach, namely, how to die.

For historians and militants within the Third International, the Jacobins of 1793–94 were model bourgeois revolutionaries, whose example might usefully be followed by socialists under the altered circumstances of the new century. Conversely, those unequivocally hostile to socialism have tended to treat Jacobinism as a sort of mass illusion, psychological or rhetorical or both. These critics jeer at the constant invocation of classical precedent, the implication being that any and every reference to an exemplary deed or utterance in the distant past betrays an at best misguided, at worst pernicious antiquarianism. Harold Parker's valuable enquiry into the classical education of the revolutionaries has sometimes been deployed with this purpose in mind, yet the central claim made by the critics of Jacobinism regarding the damage done by Plutarchian tableaux does not bear close scrutiny.[43] Babeuf, for example, though steeped in classical Antiquity, was never so deluded as to suppose that he was actually in Rome and a tribune of the plebs. He merely recognized that there was a sufficient likeness between republican Rome and revolutionary Paris for him to employ, though never uncritically, ancient concepts for modern tasks.[44] Marx's grasp of this elementary point was far superior to that of many who have written in the last twenty years on the rhetoric of Jacobinism. So savage has the backlash been, however, that one would not expect a good word to be said again for the Jacobins. Yet Alasdair MacIntyre, a moral philosopher whose stance is usually described as communitarian, has shown that, whereas the Anglo-Scottish Enlightenment could not muster a full list of the virtues, and could do little more than pit a (Stoic) self-command and a (Christian) altruism against the raging egoism of the passions, the revolutionary clubs seemed to call for a revival of the Aristotelian notion of the complete, narrated life, the precondition for a frank parade of human value in the round.[45]

Not content with setting a feral cat among ruffed pigeons, MacIntyre then ran his own lynx eye across the drawing-rooms of Highbury, Mansfield Park and Bath, bringing into ostensibly bizarre conjunction the clubs of revolutionary Paris and the 'two inches of ivory' upon which Jane Austen worked.[46] Nonetheless, if one grants that her novels attempt, despite the countervailing operations of the wide world, a resurrection of the Aristotelian notion of the virtues, one may discern in them a preoccupation with the righteousness of assembly and a despair, even a horror, at the falling away of persons, when hearts are not open and brave, into isolate sorrow. It would be folly to press MacIntyre's case too far here, or to spell out how it is that a censorship of mores haunts some of Jane Austen's novels, not least because in chapter 4 I bring the terms of this argument to a less wistful conclusion.[47] Yet the temporal coincidence between the decisive formulation of the doctrine of the liberty of the Ancients and Moderns and the first draft of *Pride and Prejudice* is worth remarking upon, for the simple reason that it rescues the debate from the furnace of the Terror and restores it to its proper shape. Rather than defining Robespierre, for example, in terms of a future totalitarianism, whether of the Left or of the Right, we draw him to scale only if, setting aside the matter of genealogy or legitimation, we place him in the company of like-minded contemporaries. Robert R. Palmer thus makes an illuminating comparison between John Adams, at least in the years 1774–76, and Robespierre, and argues that a shared commitment to 'the moral republic' could have led the former, in different circumstances, down as bloody a path as the latter.[48]

Socialist values in the next century will in part rest upon the concept of relative (not absolute) equality, which classical republicanism presupposed, and which unregulated capitalism tramples underfoot. The truth of this is borne out daily within what Galbraith has called 'the culture of contentment', where those at their ease reap the whirlwind twice over, once in the simple acts (crime) of those who have all but nothing, and once in the more shadowy but no less real recoil in their own hearts. The wheel of the virtues cannot turn in an order from which the lynchpin of justice has been removed. In this regard, the reconstruction of republics in America and in France, after 1786–87 and after Thermidor, remains of momentous significance to us all.[49]

## The last of the Romans

The winter of 1794–95 was the most severe of the whole century, with chronic bread shortages and, in many areas, famine; the labouring poor suffered more terribly than at any other time in the history of modern France.[50] Even the *Messager du Soir*, a paper not known for its democratic sympathies, recorded that 'in the streets you see only pale and emaciated faces, on which are etched pain, exhaustion, hunger and misery'.[51] With the lifting of the Maximum, the price of bread had climbed 1,300 per cent in the space of a few months, and the poor could simply not afford it. On the brink of starvation, they rose twice in open rebellion, once in Germinal (1 April 1795), once in Prairial (20–23 May 1795). If Georges Lefebvre dubbed the latter, the most considerable of all the *journées*, 'the end of the Revolution', it was because the surviving Montagnards inside the Convention never again made common cause with the *bras nus*.[52] Prairial was the fire in which the Constitution of the year III was forged.

The uprising was precipitated by the printing and distribution of a pamphlet calling for the overthrow of the executive, for the release of those imprisoned after the previous insurrection, for bread and for the restoration of the Constitution of 1793. At five o'clock in the morning, on 1 Prairial, the tocsin sounded in the Faubourgs Saint-Antoine and Saint-Marceau; with the slogan 'bread and the Constitution of 1793' pinned to their clothes, the armed insurgents swarmed into the Convention at half past three that same afternoon. In the ensuing skirmish, the deputy Féraud – mistaken for Fréron, the prominent Thermidorian and ringleader of the *muscadins* – was shot, and his head stuck on a pike. In a macabre scene, Boissy d'Anglas, acting president of the Convention and subsequently one of the chief architects of the Constitution of the year III, saluted the head of the murdered representative. Under the July Monarchy, painters were invited to immortalize this celebrated gesture, which marked the triumph of liberalism over proletarian anarchy. The winning entry, by Delacroix, is now in the Musée de Bordeaux.[53]

A number of Jacobins once prominent in the sections had certainly played a part in the planning of the uprising, but preparations cannot have been as elaborate as some retrospective accounts suggested. With the later Conspiracy of the Equals in the forefront of their minds, Babeuf, Buonarroti and Levasseur thus cast some of the Montagnard deputies as conspirators, although evidence for this is scanty.[54] In fact, the Thermidorians of the Right deliberately allowed the stalemate to drag on, in the hope that the 'last Montagnards' would be drawn. This gamble was rewarded, for at last Rühl spoke, to the applause of the insurgents, of implementing the Constitution of 1793. These few words were enough to condemn him; he died by his own hand nine days later.[55] By the time the session had been reopened, at around seven o'clock in the evening, National Guardsmen from the more affluent quarters had already been summoned by the besieged Thermidorians. Romme and Soubrany then compromised themselves also, by calling for the release of the jailed patriots; for one type of bread, the 'bread of equality', to be available to all; for the Committee of Public Safety to be abolished, and, most rashly, for the sections to be in permanent session. Two armed columns entered the chamber and dispersed the rioters at around half past eleven; warrants were issued for the arrest of thirteen Montagnards at two or three o'clock in the morning. Tallien expressed the hope that they would all be dead before the sun had risen again.[56]

The ensuing repression was on an unprecedentedly large scale. On 4 Prairial, National Guardsmen, for the most part jeunesse dorée, put down the Faubourg Saint-Antoine, and it was plain to observers, Benjamin Constant among them, that they were witnessing the triumph of the principle of property.[57] A military tribunal was hurriedly created, and the sections purged. Three thousand to four thousand persons were arrested and disarmed, and well over a quarter of their number were incarcerated. In its panic, the Convention resorted to novel techniques of repression, rounding up not specific individuals but whole categories, for example, members of the revolutionary committees, of the sections or of other popular institutions.[58] These new methods, later perfected by Fouché, destroyed the popular movement in Paris.

The military commission passed sentence on thirty-six persons, among them the gendarmes who had made common cause with the insurgents. The condemned deputies, held in the Fort du Taureau, resolved to follow Rühl's example and to win for themselves the honour of heroic suicide. In a desperate attempt to cheat the executioner, they passed two daggers and a pair of scissors from hand to hand as they left the courtroom. Goujon, Romme and Duquesnoy died instantly; Soubrany, mortally wounded, perished before he reached the scaffold. Only Duroy and Bourbotte failed in this atrocious fashion to place their liberty in high relief. Who, then, were the last of the Montagnards, and why were they known as the last of the Romans?[59]

After the popular insurrection of 4 and 5 September 1793, through which the Terror became 'the order of the day', the Montagnard deputies had made ever more concessions to their political allies, the sans-culottes organized in sociétés populaires and sociétés fraternelles, and in the general assemblies of the Paris sections. The majority of the sans-culottes favoured small-scale units of production or distribution (peasant small-holdings, artisanal workshops and small shops), and believed that personal labour was the real basis of property rights. They were deeply suspicious of the larger manufactures, which were flourishing under wartime conditions, of wealthier merchants, monopolists and profiteers, and vaunted their own 'honorable médiocrité'. In Rousseau's writings they found a mirror for their own anxieties and longings, for he too feared the advent of new forms of machinery, the concentration of industrial enterprises and the division of labour: 'in everything depending on human industry, it is essential . . . to proscribe every machine and every invention which might shorten labour, reduce the number of workers and produce the same result with less trouble'.[60] The sans-culottes in Paris, disturbed at the prospect of joining the ranks of the propertyless, exerted pressure on the Montagnard Convention in the course of the year II, their chief preoccupation being to guarantee their subsistence through the regulation of the economy (the Maximum), to limit the size of personal fortunes by making an equal division of inheritances obligatory, to introduce the sale of national properties in small lots, and to restrict the number of workshops that anyone might possess.[61] Some aspects of this programme met with the approval of members of the Great Committee of Public Safety, notably Billaud-Varenne, Robespierre and Saint-Just, and the most dramatic expression of this apparent convergence of conviction and interest, the Ventôse Decrees, called for the confiscation of the property of suspects and its redistribution to patriots. The socialist nature of the decrees, so firmly maintained by Mathiez, may now be disputed, but the Ventôse crisis clearly was, as Soboul has declared, 'the crucial point in the relations between revolutionary government and sans-culottes, Robespierrists and the popular movement'.[62] There had been a parting of the ways between the Committee of Public Safety and the radicalized populace. The martyrs of Prairial, by contrast, were unable to choose; they were stranded, as Gilbert Romme said in his final defence, 'between two abysses'.

There was, on the one hand, the spirit of Thermidor, manifest in the salons, in the demeanour of the most corrupt and compromised of the former Terrorists (Fréron, Rovère, Tallien) and in their strident and disdainful repudiation of republican mores. The Convention had lost the *dignitas* of the senate at Rome, and would not now recover it. Choudieu, one of the last of the Montagnards, contrasted the ambitious and cynical proconsuls, contracting marriage alliances with çi-devant aristocrats and amassing private fortunes, with those who had been hounded after the Germinal uprising, and who, 'accustomed to living in an honourable mediocrity, . . . have not exchanged the humble roof of their fathers for palaces . . . [and] do not insult public misery with insolent display'.[63] This remark reflects very exactly the frame of mind of the Prairial martyrs, who had returned from their work as representatives on mission with an enhanced reputation for moral rectitude, and who sympathized deeply with the plight of the labouring poor.[64]

If, on the other hand, Goujon, Romme and Soubrany looked past the galleries in the Convention and fixed their gaze upon the insurgents from the faubourgs, their estrangement was no less complete. I noted Romme's second, more considered response to the murder of Foulon and of Bertier above, and there is every reason to suppose that the killing of Féraud sickened him quite as much. After his arrest, Romme recalled the insurrection: 'I saw in the mêlée some intent on crime. I saw others driven by need and asking in good faith for bread and for the Constitution [of 1793]. To the former, justice owes all its rigours; does not humanity owe a helping hand to the latter?'[65] Some historians have argued that, because Romme spoke of a 'monstrous horde' and of 'cannibals', deploying a lexicon that a Thermidorian of the Centre (such as Boissy d'Anglas) would later use, the moral and political divergences between the last of the Montagnards and their adversaries were not of great significance.[66] It is true that, being committed to 'the religion of the laws', Romme baulked at the view of Robespierre that the authority of the Committee of Public Safety was *legibus solutus*, or absolute. In his opinion, the Convention, and not the Committees or the Jacobin Club, was the government of the sovereign people, and it was therefore with complete sincerity that he wrote that his words and deeds on 1 Prairial had been designed to uphold 'that authority which is the exclusive preserve of the national representation . . . '.[67] Yet if Romme and his fellows were not Robespierrists, they were hardly Tallienists either, and the spectacle of laws without virtues distressed them as much as the trampling underfoot of due legal process by a tyranny had done.[68] Indeed, their concern for the labouring masses, and for the peasantry in particular, is beyond dispute. Romme's Sundays were often spent expounding the new laws, and he also wrote agricultural manuals and launched schemes (backed by Soubrany) for the loan of seed to hard-pressed peasant farmers.[69] Involvement with the *Feuille Villageoise*, the most important revolutionary journal distributed in rural areas, was complemented by work on the republican calendar, whose new (or, more accurately, ancient–modern) months were scored as trumpet-blasts for the ears of the primary producers.

Romme, though hostile to revolutionary vandalism and sceptical of communal schools on the Spartan model, had embraced the neo-Stoic view that a legislator's life should serve as a sort of lesson to his fellow citizens.[70] Placed between a senate, so to speak, that had reneged upon this principle and a populace in the grip of destructive passions, he had now to withdraw from the disordered city and, if need be, from life itself. He would follow the example of Marcus Brutus on the battlefield at Philippi and meet his death in the Roman manner, leaving it to the tribunal of history to judge him. 'I have done my duty', he declared, 'my body belongs to my judges; my soul is independent and calm in the midst of my memories.'[71] Soubrany, Goujon and Bourbotte were likewise indebted to Epictetus, a Stoic philosopher, for the wording of their last declarations. 'If I had merely to defend a [bodily] existence', wrote Soubrany, 'I would calmly abandon what remains of it to events . . . but I could not sacrifice my reputation with the same Stoicism, for I cannot be so indifferent to the judgement which my contemporaries and posterity will pass upon my memory.'[72] 'My life', Goujon stated, 'is in the hands of men, it is the plaything of their passions; my memory does not belong to them, but to posterity; it is the inheritance of just men of all times, [and] of sensitive and generous hearts.'[73] Bourbotte, for his part, apostrophized Cato of Utica, the Roman who had best exemplified heroic virtue as seen against the backdrop of a republic from which mores had long since fled.[74] These doomed men carried an image of the fatherland in their hearts, and their suicides were conceived and enacted as the final act in a Senecan tragedy. A number of other revolutionaries, Chamfort among them, had affirmed their liberty in this fashion, at once denying the Thermidorian Convention the right to bring them to trial, and restating the neo-Stoic belief that a government without virtue was no better than a tyranny.

If Montagnard rhetoric had seemed to echo, as Georg Büchner well understood, through vast, empty spaces, it was because those who had, in Saint-Just's phrase, anchored themselves to the future, belonged to the age of cities.[75] As loyal disciples of Rousseau, they were committed to a cyclical vision of liberty, derived in the main from Polybius, and were reconciled to the fact that the city was by its nature transient. Though Sparta and Rome had miraculously remained free for many generations, they too, like all other creations of 'perfected art', could not last forever. The same might be said of republican France. Another 'revolution', another turn of the wheel of fortune, and the city-nation might be restored to liberty.

Even as the last of the Romans were preparing to meet their deaths, the two chief architects of the doctrine of the liberty of the Ancients and Moderns, Benjamin Constant and Madame de Staël, entered Paris.

# 2

# Word and City

During the Prairial uprising, the insurgents called upon the Convention to reinstate the Constitution of 1793, a document that had remained a dead letter while France's borders were threatened by hostile armies. Many representatives were privately appalled at the idea of implementing a document that gave so much latitude to the clubs and to the right of insurrection, but few dared, given the ambiguities of the times, to challenge it directly or even to demand that it be replaced by the Girondin Constitution, drafted by Condorcet. However, the events of Germinal and of Prairial provided the excuse for wiping the slate clean.

The chief authors of the draft submitted to the Convention in the summer of 1795 were Daunou, known for his courageous challenge to the principle of Terror, and Boissy d'Anglas, honoured for his defiance of the sans-culottes at the time of the Prairial insurrection, and their primary concern was to forestall any return to the more democratic aspects of Montagnard policy. Indeed, the majority of the new constitutional committee were moderates, among them Lanjuinais, La Revellière-Lépeaux and Thibaudeau, at least some of whom covertly favoured the restoration of monarchy. With the arrest, on 12 Ventôse, of three prominent members of the Montagnard Committee of Public Safety, Boissy d'Anglas deemed it safe to unleash a savage attack on the demagogues, denouncing their exploitation of the passions of the people.[1] He was Protestant, a friend of Benjamin Constant and a habitué of Madame de Staël's salon on the Rue du Bac, and it is therefore not at all surprising to find echoes in his speeches of her treatise on the passions, particularly in the chapters on ambition, vanity and party spirit. Conversely, Staël indubitably had a hand in the drafting of the Constitution of the year III.[2]

Almost all the speakers in the ensuing debate warned of the dangers of a single chamber, a feature of the much-admired Pennsylvanian constitution of 1776, and then of the Montagnard and Girondin constitutions.[3] Whereas in 1789 the Constituent Assembly had decided against an upper chamber, fearing that it would perpetuate the power of the hereditary nobility, in 1795 the only representative to voice a similar objection was Alexandre Deleyre, a friend of Rousseau and a regicide, who described bicameralism as a Trojan horse, and an upper chamber as a 'seedbed of aristocracy', which would guarantee the ultimate triumph of England over revolutionary France.[4] If Deleyre's warnings went unheeded, it was in part because moderate Thermidorians were convinced that the hereditary aristocracy had been destroyed, either by the anti-feudal legislation of the night of 4 August 1789, or by the Emigration and the Terror, and that it no longer posed a threat to republican social order. Advocates of the new constitution spoke unabashedly of 'government by the best' or of 'natural aristocracy', and thus pitted against the direct democracy celebrated in certain interpretations of Rousseau a version of Montesquieu which was, so to speak, structural rather than historical. In other terms, they did not reintroduce the discredited notion of 'mixed government', whereby the various orders of a hierarchized society were at once represented and balanced, but rather sought to create a division of powers. Boissy d'Anglas referred in passing to the experience of the American colonists, noting that most of the states had in fact divided their legislatures and that even Pennsylvania had in the end followed suit. The creation of an upper chamber in France need not result in the creation of a peerage: 'A chamber of hereditary peers is the result of feudal pride, serving to preserve the privileges of the great and to defend the authority of the throne, whereas our Council of Elders is designed to prevent the return of a monarchy.' The Council of 500 was to be the thought and imagination of the Republic, the Council of Elders its reason.[5]

A series of obstacles would be placed between the two legislative bodies and the populace. Both the Girondin draft (by Condorcet) and the Jacobin Constitution of 1793 had featured six thousand primary assemblies in virtually constant session, but Boissy d'Anglas was adamant that such incessant debating would distract labourers from their duties in the fields.[6] By 1795 those on the more moderate benches of the Convention were prepared to forego their enthusiasms of 1789 and 1790, and to endorse social and economic inequality, for the Terror, and the challenge mounted to the principle of private property, had deeply disturbed them. Boissy d'Anglas thus insisted that 'the people' was simply 'the sum of all men born on the soil of France'. Of this people, a part owned property, whether through inheritance, through purchase or through their own efforts; the other part laboured to acquire such property themselves. Although there were many gradations between the two conditions, the rich and the poor, the few and the many, were interdependent. Boissy d'Anglas then analysed the moral characteristics

of the well-to-do, who had more education, more talent and more
refinement, but 'a greater tendency towards pride, domination and
selfishness', and of the poor, who had more simplicity, more frankness
and purer mores but also 'a dangerous tendency towards bitterness,
mistrust and anger, and so towards the excesses which only too often
follow from them'.[7] So it was that moderate republicans, constant in their
criticism of the aristocracy since 1788–89, now closed ranks against the
labouring classes. In 1791 Volney had celebrated the moral dignity, and
therefore the intellectual capacities, of 'all those who, by useful labours,
keep and feed society'. Utility had long been the criterion by which a
parasitical nobility might be judged. By contrast, in the *Leçons d'Histoire*, delivered early in 1795, Volney made it clear that those whose days
were taken up with earning a subsistence could not retain, and indeed
had no use for 'all purely scholarly and speculative notions . . . .'.[8] Under
the Directorial republic, a system of suffrage in two stages would
disqualify all but thirty thousand notables from real or effective
participation, as electors, in the political process.[9]

It was further argued that, while a country ruled by property-owners
was within the social order, one in which the propertyless held sway was
within the state of nature. This argument was a recapitulation of the
debates staged in the Convention in April and May 1793, although now
the signs were, so to speak, reversed. Thus, during the lengthy discussions surrounding the recast Declaration of the Rights of Man and the
Citizen, Robespierre had proposed that property, like liberty, entailed a
degree of reciprocity. For, if the enjoyment of liberty was limited by the
need to respect the liberty of others, so too should rights to property be
restricted by the need to respect the rights of others. The slave-owner,
whose ships were floating coffins, had no right to his cargo of human
souls.[10] Robespierre therefore inserted an article into the Declaration
specifying that the right to property could prejudice 'neither the safety,
nor the liberty, nor the existence, nor the property of our fellows'.[11] In
practice, as he went on to explain, this principle would take the form of
progressive taxation, not agrarian law, which he dismissed as chimerical.
Nonetheless, the political legacy, real or imagined, of the Ventôse
Decrees, and the defiant use of Robespierre's name as a rallying-cry by
Babeuf, had left moderate republicans with a deep suspicion towards the
Montagnard tradition. For Boissy d'Anglas, therefore, the state of
nature was a condition of barbarity and crime, of which the Terror was
the paramount example. It was no longer acceptable to invoke a space
beyond social being, to which one might flee, for the year II seemed, to
the horrified survivors, death's own kingdom.

The right of insurrection, of such crucial importance to the Conventionnels, was therefore omitted from the preamble to the Constitution of

the year III, and with its disappearance the state of nature lost much of its leverage upon the socius. For example, Jean Mailhe, who had played so prominent a part in the trial of Louis XVI, sustained the distinction between nature and the social order, but plainly valued the former state less highly than either Rousseau or Diderot had done:

> We shall continue to distinguish between the rights and the duties of man and the citizen; one is man in the state of nature; one is man and citizen in the social state. In the state of nature, man is independent, but this independence is the very thing that occasions his unhappiness, for, since in this state the passions acknowledge no curb, each is by turns tyrant and victim of weakness and of strength.[12]

Mailhe was concerned with the second part of the *Discourse on the Origins of Inequality*, not with the first, for the state of nature alluded to here is the Hobbesian condition established by the bad contract, the cycle of anarchy and despotism. Whereas Staël would continue to insist for some time to come that a world untouched by pity – the world, she said, of Marat and of Robespierre – could not be the state of nature, since Rousseau had remarked upon the primordial operation of both pity and self-love, Mailhe here maintained that the Terror was indeed the state of nature. During the first half of the nineteenth century, a consensus would emerge in Europe that, as Jacques Bailleul remarked in the course of this same debate, no one had any choice but to be in society, for each was in essence a social being. However, before the advent of sociology and the consolidation of Humboldtian or proto-Whorfian assumptions regarding the isomorphism of soul, language and community, the state of nature had subsisted as a primordial zone of experience to which a person might, in casting off citizenship, have recourse.

A striking instance of such invocations of a state of nature is supplied by the case of the Massachusetts towns west of the Connecticut River, which were in a state of almost perpetual rebellion against the constituted authorities in the 1770s and 1780s. As Gordon Wood has observed:

> Shays's uprising in 1786 was only the climactic episode in one long insurrection, where the dissolution of government and the state of nature became an everyday fact of life. Indeed, it was as if all the imaginings of political philosophers for centuries were being lived out in a matter of years in the hills of New England.[13]

Although reference was certainly made there to the notion that the earth had once been and, in cases of dire necessity, should again revert to being, a positive community of goods, the impoverished and indebted small farmers of western Massachusetts justified their repeated closure of the law courts in terms of the American Revolution itself.[14] For, with the Declaration of Independence, the contract between ruler and people was perforce dissolved, as it had been in England in 1688. In an interesting treatment of this question, T.W. Tate has observed that the colonists relied very heavily upon Locke's *Second Treatise*, and therefore upon the notion of a double contract. In Locke's opinion, a people first of all consents, through a compact, to unite in a society, and then, by means of a contract, chooses a government. Although the Americans sometimes spoke of dissolving contracts and of returning to a state of nature, Tate is adamant that they almost invariably had the social contract, not the original compact, in mind. Having allowed for the towns of western Massachusetts and, in addition, for those settlers with secessionist ambitions in western Vermont, he therefore concludes that the social contract served a none too radical function in late eighteenth-century America.[15] There is nothing controversial about the claim that the Lockean double contract, because it guarantees individual property rights, has generally proved a less subversive concept than has the social contract of Rousseau.[16] What is more open to question is the assertion that the natural law tradition of Locke has exerted a more fundamental influence upon American culture than has the classical republicanism of Machiavelli and of his followers, Rousseau among them.[17]

I cannot address the larger debate here, and wish merely to explain that, no matter how startling it may seem, late eighteenth-century concepts of secession, exile and suicide were all predicated upon such a domain of natural liberty, and that the later obliteration of imagined lines of flight, whether to the Mons Sacer in ancient Rome, to a frontier or to another world, was followed not merely by the creation of a science of society but, in addition, by the consolidation of a confining principle of nationality. Where nature, the repository of value, had glimmered in the wastes beyond artificial, and therefore not incorruptible, cities, the nineteenth century witnessed its slow relocation within the body politic, which thereby acquired an ontological guarantee. In the process, the union of states, or confederation, was increasingly viewed as a transitional stage on the way, first to the federal state, and then to the unitary state.[18] Movement seemed to be all towards a national incorporation. It is hard to say just when the principle of confederation was overwhelmed, for one can find exceptions to the rule, but the 1860s and 1870s were plainly a turning-point in both the Old and the New World. Through the Sonderbund war, which had set canton against canton, Switzerland had already, some years before, become a federal state. Italy witnessed the military and political triumph of Piedmont, a solution to the Risorgimento which, in Carlo Cattaneo's opinion, was no better than a 'royal

conquest', and which represented a historical defeat for Lombard traditions of confederation. Likewise, in Germany, the bizarrely heteroge-
neous Bund had been replaced, first by the North German Bund and
then by the German Empire, self-evidently an expression of Prussian
hegemony. In each case, force of arms had sealed the fate of small states
which, being subsumed, descended to regional or even municipal status.
Some have argued that the United States of America had already
become a federal state, as distinct from a union of states, in 1789, with
the promulgation of the Constitution, but this was not truly the case, as I
argue in chapter 6. A graphic demonstration of this point is supplied by
the fact that the troops of the secessionist states were immediately
accorded the status of belligerents, rather than rebels, by the Union, as if
their actions were governed by international, not constitutional law.[19]
The linked motifs of nature, frontier, virtue and secession survived even
the catastrophe of civil war, and make of American culture something of
a special case. *The Confidence Man*, for example, could hardly have been
written in the Old World, and, if one were to take the *Fidèle*, Melville's
riverboat of masked souls, from the Mississippi, one might perhaps
relaunch it on the Amazon or the Orinoco, but never on the Rhine. By
way of preparation for this larger argument, which unfolds throughout
the book, I propose now to consider three Thermidorian responses to the
earthly city of the Jacobins.

## A turncoat *philosophe*

Although Robespierre had fallen in July 1794, it was not until December
that public opinion in Thermidorian France had tilted away from Jacobinism.[20] Revulsion, however, at the atrocities perpetrated by Le Bon at
Arras, and by Carrier at Nantes, helped to hasten the general shift in
mood and perception. On 8 December, most of the surviving Girondins
were rehabilitated; eight days later Carrier was executed. That winter
also witnessed an alteration in the mores of revolutionary France, as
gangs of royalist youths ransacked the Paris clubs. Above the Marseillaise, the Réveil du Peuple was more and more heard, and salons,
shadow-haunted during the Terror, opened their doors again.

On 31 December 1794, Jean-François La Harpe, released from prison
shortly after Thermidor, delivered the most venomous attack yet heard
on the Montagnard dictatorship. On the occasion of the reopening of the
Lycée Royale, known since the previous year as the Lycée Républicaine,
his chosen theme was Vandalism, and the audience was gripped, he later
recalled, '[by] a sort of sombre and anxious silence which still resembled
terror'. A protégé of Voltaire, a critic and dramatist notorious for his

impiety and anti-clerical rancour, La Harpe had recovered his faith while behind bars. Armed with his new but no less virulent convictions, he masked as best he could his complicity in some of the iniquities of the year II. He expressed the bitterest revulsion for the sans-culottes of the faubourgs; recalling the inauguration of the Lycée, he described the 'brigands'' grotesque garb, their crude tone and brutal language, their improprieties, their wild and staring eyes, and he observed with contempt how they cast 'glances at once stupid and threatening upon scientific instruments whose names they did not even know . . . '. Outspoken though La Harpe was at the turn of the year, the ambiguities of Thermidor were such that the *idéologues* could still regard him as one of their own. Garat, for example, asked him to lecture at the Ecole Normale. This illusion was to be all too swiftly shattered.[21]

In La Harpe's opinion the Montagnard dictatorship had been sustained by an unprecedented torrent of speeches, pamphlets and handbills, so relentless and concentrated as to sweep all reason from its path.[22] Like many Thermidorians of the Centre or of the Right, he was horrified by the new and more radical use of the term 'equality', and opposed to the levelling vision of some Jacobins or Hébertists a hierarchical society of orders:

> whereas, in a free state, the citizens are ordinarily placed in terms of their talents and their virtues, here one was to be raised up because of one's perversity and baseness. Everything that belonged to the last rank in human nature then rose to the first rank in the state.[23]

In short, the free republics of Antiquity had been founded upon a stable system of ranks. This was to agree with Rousseau, who, as I show in chapter 3, ascribed the final collapse of the Roman republic to the recruitment by Marius and Sulla of *proletarii* and *capite censi*, that is, of those traditionally having no right to bear arms. If, therefore, La Harpe sought to reclaim ancient liberty from the Jacobin usurpers, it was because there was no intrinsic contradiction between classical republicanism and the principle of hierarchy.

As the most prominent advocate in old-regime Paris of a classicism whose models derived from the age of Louis XIV, La Harpe conceived of the history of literature in terms of a sequence of nigh-miraculous formal perfections of style, expressions of *convenance* reflecting equally finished social orders. So committed was he to this conception, later to be challenged by Madame de Staël, that the turncoat *philosophe* could not imagine a theatre that outshone that of Corneille and Racine. The Roman tragedies of Voltaire, however, anatomized in lectures at the Lycée Républicaine in 1797, could at least bear comparison with the works of the masters, not least because they obeyed the sacrosanct rules of classical drama.

Having set Voltaire's Roman plays in the context of his journey to England, where Addison's *Cato* was then all the rage, La Harpe gave a brief description of the opening scene of *Brutus*, in which, he said, there breathed 'the first energy of a nascent republic, this sentiment of a liberty so powerful when it is enlightened, so dear when its object is real, so respectable when it is the outcome of a general desire.'[24] How then should one interpret his apparent sympathies for Rome, declared by him to be, notwithstanding his own bitter hostility towards Jacobinism, a 'sanctuary of liberty'? Is one to suppose that he remained a sincere republican in 1796 and 1797, or even in 1794 and 1795? From Constant's brilliant and scornful portrait of him at the time of the Germinal elections, and from the sentence of exile passed upon him after the *coup d'état* of 18 Fructidor, it is plain that those still loyal to the Directorial republic did not believe him to be so.[25] With good cause, as it turns out, for historians have since discovered that the journal edited by La Harpe and Fontanes during this period was the recipient of covert funding from England.[26]

We may go some way towards accounting for the difficulty we have in interpreting La Harpe's lectures if we reflect upon the ambiguity attaching to the term 'republic' in eighteenth-century theory. Thus, for both Rousseau and Montesquieu, the term 'republican' had a twofold meaning. On the one hand, it referred to a form of government. A monarchy was rule by one, and aristocracy rule by the few, so a republic was rule by the many. On the other hand, all three forms might be termed republican, that is to say, committed to the public good or under the rule of law; they could all, by the same token, cease to be well ordered and sink into either anarchy or despotism. 'Any state which is ruled by law', declared Rousseau, 'I call a "republic", whatever the form of its constitution; for then, and then alone does the public interest govern, and then alone is the "public thing" – the *res publica* – a reality. Every legitimate government is republican . . . '. In order to banish any lingering doubts, Rousseau appended a note, observing that by 'legitimate government' he meant not only an aristocracy or a democracy but 'any government directed by the general will, which is the law'. For a government to be legitimate, it could not be united with the sovereign but had rather to serve as its ministry. This being the case, even monarchies could be republics.[27] Indeed, the exemplary status enjoyed by the English political system for so much of the eighteenth century was in no way undermined by the fact that it featured a mixed system of government. To combine so perfectly the one, the few and the many, and thus to blend the principles of monarchy, aristocracy and democracy was to forestall the ineluctable decline of the body politic by ensuring that laws, not individual wills, had the upper hand.

Although in other contexts La Harpe was prepared to damn Voltaire as a *philosophe*, his mentor's austere vision of an anti-despotic, republican Rome could serve as a reproach to the Jacobins. Like Vittorio Alfieri, who had written plays treating of the heroic deeds of Lucius Junius and Marcus Brutus, or like Vincenzo Monti, the author of a *Caius Gracchus*, La Harpe therefore believed that the Revolution had usurped the insignia of a classical tradition in order to impart a spurious decorum to atrocity.[28] It should be borne in mind that Voltaire, the author of *Brutus*, of *The Death of Caesar*, and of *Rome Saved*, had later rallied upon several occasions to the defence of individuals who had fallen foul of arbitrary legal authority, and that such campaigns, conducted with equal vigour and tenacity by Condorcet and Brissot in the 1770s and 1780s, took the English principle of *habeas corpus* as a yardstick. The Constituent Assembly had done much to eliminate such injustices, but who could doubt that, after the enactment and implementation of the law of 22 Prairial, the Revolution had lost its way?

We learn something more of La Harpe's treatment of these issues during the Thermidorian Reaction from a glancing reference in his address of 31 December 1794 to a performance of Marie-Joseph Ché- nier's *Caius Gracchus*. In October 1793, Albitte, a Montagnard repre- sentative on mission just returned from the south of France, had interrupted the tragedy at the point at which Caius Gracchus, the tribune of the plebs, knowing that the plebeians were about to rise up and 'liquidate' the senate, had pleaded for 'laws, not blood'. Furious at the applause given to this line, which could be taken for a criticism of the Terror, Albitte had rounded upon the audience, thus showing scant respect, La Harpe observed in retrospect, for 'hommes assemblés'.[29] What did La Harpe mean by this reference? On the day of the perform- ance, 6 October 1793, Chénier, Condorcet, Daunou and Sieyes, being reckoned guilty of the crime of federalism, had been dropped from the Comité d'Instruction Publique. To condemn Albitte's intervention, a year or so later, was certainly to align oneself with the Girondins and the *idéologues*, and to lend support to their policies, not least because the uproar had led indirectly to a stricter regime in the Paris theatres. Yet it is worth pointing out too that *Caius Gracchus* was itself a curiously ambiguous work, each claque finding sentiments to applaud. Thus, at the first performance, on 9 February 1792, the sixty or more bravoes hired by Marie Antoinette to barrack the tragedy had ended up cheering 'laws, not blood', or the patrician arguments of the Consul, Opimius. There was certainly little in the text to please Babeuf, for agrarian law was defined as the confiscation and redistribution of émigré property, but nothing more.[30]

There were many, in the aftermath of the Robespierrist republic of virtue, who did not so much question the terms of such an ethics of chaste display as protest at its misappropriation.[31] La Harpe himself, in his discussion of Voltaire's tragedies, repeatedly stated what a Roman was, and what a Roman did, as if no further explanation were required. *Brutus* had been performed in Paris, in 1790, when Voltaire's prestige was at its height, but it had been banned under the Montagnard dictatorship. Furthermore, when *The Death of Caesar* was revived in 1792, an additional scene was tacked on at the end. Here La Harpe, who had not scrupled to reshape his own *Virginia* in a similar fashion, came to the crux of the matter, deploring the fact that Brutus and Cassius

> spoke to the Roman people using the language of the French Jacobins, and spewed out *philosophical* invectives against the gods and the priests, that is to say, sacrilegious impieties in the presence of the most religious people on earth, who, without a doubt would have torn to pieces whoever dared to declare themselves . . . the enemy of the gods and of religion.[32]

To appreciate the significance of this note, one needs to recall that many Thermidorians' revulsion at the Terror was prompted as much by the dechristianization movement as by the scale of the slaughter. Just as Niebuhr would later draw comparisons between the stout-hearted peasants of free Ditmarsh and the citizens of the early Roman republic, so too here La Harpe was able to equate Roman with French piety.

Because La Harpe's pamphlets and lectures have sometimes been considered an unbiased source for historians curious to learn what Jacobin rhetoric really was, I should add that his anxiety about a foaming excess of speech expressed a disquiet at the idea that everyone, of whatever station or rank, might be entitled to formulate public utterances. His tenacious classicism, like that of Fontanes or Rivarol, was therefore in part driven by a wish to restore the damaged authority of the priesthood. Moderate in tone though the passages quoted above may seem, on many occasions La Harpe embraced the view, made famous by Joseph de Maistre, that the Revolution had been a punitive lesson given to an impious, and so treacherous, people by a vengeful god.[33] The perfidy evidently lay in wresting speech, with all its highly structured forms and occasions, from privileged mediators, and ascribing it, through the Declaration of Rights of Man and of the Citizen, to a potentially unlimited number of persons. As Jacques Rancière has remarked, with reference not to French Jacobins but to the London Corresponding Society, this was indeed a heresy.[34]

## Volney at the Ecole Normale

The Directorial Republic required honourable founders of its own, both
to exorcise the shade of the martyred king and to obscure the bloody
figures of Marat and Robespierre. Lucius Junius Brutus and Marcus
Brutus therefore remained of paramount importance in official republican circles. For proof of this, one need merely recall that the terms of the
Bologna Armistice, agreed in June 1796, gave the Army of Italy the right
to seize the celebrated busts of both figures from the Capitoline Museum
in Rome and to ship them to Paris. Of the many treasures confiscated by
General Bonaparte upon that occasion, these were the only two items
mentioned by name.[35] It is clear, then, that moderate republicans did not
seek to sever the values of their republic from those of classical Rome but
aimed, rather, to reaffirm the exemplary status of Lucius Junius Brutus
and Marcus Brutus and to propose Condorcet and Vergniaud as worthy
successors.[36] Furthermore, the establishment of a republic in Rome in
February 1798, and the dethronement and exile of the Pope, was
followed by the most thoroughgoing introduction of Roman titles,
emblems and insignia of the whole revolutionary period. The constitution of 1798, largely Daunou's work, was derided by the Roman populace, who viewed it as a cynical device for ensuring unchecked
despoliation.[37] Madame de Staël judged in retrospect that only the
statues in Rome were republican, but to take this dictum at face value
would be to disregard those Italian patriots, among them Mario Pagano
and Vincenzio Russo, who sought even in such difficult circumstances to
impart some meaning to the evocative names attached to the token
magistracies.[38] Although a poet and critic like Marie-Joseph Chénier
sustained his classical tastes throughout the Directory, the Consulate and
the Empire, most of the *idéologues* were more hostile to that tradition, as
the lectures given by Volney at the Ecole Normale prove.

The new institution had originally been designed to transmit the most
up-to-date pedagogic theories to students drawn from every corner of
France; after attending the appropriate lectures and discussions, they
were to have returned home and trained teachers to work in the Ecoles
Primaires. When this plan was mooted, in June 1794, the Comité
d'Instruction Publique entertained the lofty ambition of attaining universal literacy in France. All children would acquire the rudiments of
reading, writing and arithmetic, while at the same time being formed by a
republican morality. The swift retreat from this programme, plainly
perceptible, as we have seen, in the writings of moderate republicans at
the time, found its most graphic expression in the Ecole Normale, which
Garat recast as an elite institution. The Comité d'Instruction Publique

hoped by means of this unprecedented experiment, in which some of the most eminent scientists of the day were involved, to contribute to the regeneration of France. Although the venture lasted only four months, and was not an outstanding success in practical terms, there is good reason to suppose that it marked a turning-point in the life of many of those who attended, Claude Fauriel among them.[39]

Volney, like many of the *idéologues*, had been thrown into prison in the course of the year II. Exiled to Nice after Thermidor, he was summoned by the Comité d'Instruction Publique to deliver, at very short notice, a course of lectures on historical method. The author of a much-praised account of a journey to Egypt and to Syria, and of the still more celebrated *Ruins of Empires*, Volney was closely associated with the Auteuil Circle and, in 1788, participated in the campaign for the 'doubling' of the representation of the Third Estate, as I explain in chapter 5. Indeed, his pamphlet *La Sentinelle du Peuple* ranked only second in importance to those of Sieyes; subsequently he formed part of Mirabeau's entourage, supplying the great orator with striking phrases and sometimes with entire speeches.

Volney's brief at the Ecole Normale was to define the proper place of history in public education, but, to arrive at a satisfactory definition, he had first to say what the métier of a historian was. The difficulty with historical facts was, Volney declared, that they invariably left 'a margin of uncertainty to opinion and to the most deeply held convictions', and therefore to the passions. Faced with a given testimony, what should one then do? One might believe everything, one might believe nothing, or one might weigh up the evidence. Historical Pyrrhonism was plainly not acceptable to Volney, for it threatened the doctrine of perfectibility. Yet to believe all that one read of the past would be to succumb to a raging fever, which often afflicts those with an 'energetic' temperament, and which, 'acquiring through imitation an infectious intensity, ends up by arousing the convulsions of enthusiasm and the frenzy of fanaticism'. The middle way, advocated by Volney, and by Locke before him, required a sober scrutiny of the evidence, in the light of a calculation of probabilities.[40]

The relation between the certain and the probable had already been considered at length in *The Ruins of Empires*, in which the legislator of humankind puts a series of questions to the peoples of the earth. Agreement was swiftly arrived at wherever reference could be made to the senses, and to the order of nature, and wherever evidence was amenable to testing. When, however, the legislator asked the assembled peoples if the moon were inhabited, or if there were a chasm in the centre of the earth, there was a hubbub, for none could agree. In order for peace to prevail, the legislator declared, *'one must draw a line of demarcation between verifiable and unverifiable objects*, and separate with an unbreachable barrier *the world of fantastical beings* from the world of realities; in other words, one must *remove every civil effect from religious and theological opinions*'. Volney thus believed that prejudices had to be replaced by a rational code, applicable to all men and women everywhere. The legislator in *The Ruins of Empires* was therefore called upon by the assembly to draft a code of natural law.[41]

Volney's distinction between the certainty of the scientists and the probability of the rhetors is at least as old as Aristotle, but its bearing upon republican pedagogy was, in the aftermath of the Terror, by no means self-evident. Cartesians had maintained that the mind of a child was best shaped by logic, by arithmetic and by geometry, but their adversaries had countered by arguing that the young had need of noble examples to emulate and inspiring precepts to ponder. Invention, for a Ciceronian, presupposed a store of topics. Prior to the First Empire, most *idéologues*, even the more 'classicist' among them, would have sided with Descartes. Education, Volney therefore argued, should begin with 'the preliminary notions in the exact sciences, such as mathematics, physics, the state of the heavens and of the terrestrial globe, so that [children] . . . would have their minds furnished with means and terms of comparison, in order to judge the facts that are recounted to them'. More specifically, history ought to nestle within the framework that astronomy and geography provide. The same would be true of ethnology, for Volney now judged celebrations of noble savages out of context to be as worthless, or even as dangerous, as invocations of the moral giants of classical Antiquity.[42]

If Volney or Condorcet, Dupuis or Roucher, used the sky dome to humble earthly empires, it was in order to found a theory of social being and its perfectibility upon the actual origin, despite the book of Genesis, of the universe. The propensity of such thinkers to contemplate the ultimate annihilation of humankind by nature, an eschaton without a presiding judge, was reckoned at best an error, at worst a scandal and a crime by the providentialists of the new century, so thoroughly had Volney's Genius of Liberty been worsted by Chateaubriand's Genius of Christianity.[43] For Condorcet and his immediate followers, however, early cosmogonies and theogonies were merely distorted representations of natural phenomena:

> these gods . . . are merely the *physical powers* of nature, the *elements*, the *winds*, the *stars* and the *meteors*, which have been *personified* by the necessary mechanism of language and of the understanding; . . . their *life*, their *mores*, their *actions*, are merely the play of their *operations*, of their *relations*; and . . . all of their supposed history is merely the description of their phenomena,

traced by the first physicists who observed them, and wrongly interpreted by the vulgar, who did not understand, or by the following generations, who forgot.[44]

Sometimes the *idéologues* would judge sacerdotal physicists more harshly, and accuse them of wilfully misleading the common people with signs and wonders, yet, though the stridency of the recrimination might vary from one writer to another (fading to a resigned acceptance by Benjamin Constant in his later years that human groups cannot help but cage authentic religious sentiment in necessarily transient forms and categories), the general picture remained the same.[45] In order to clear the earth of illusion, for example, spurious chronologies, the revolutionaries dreamed of seeing it as if for the first time. Hence the revolutionary calendar, in place of the Gregorian, the introduction of the year I of Liberty, the Decad, and the new, no longer saintly but now natural-and-technical months.[46] In this profoundly auroral project, in which reason and the heart were in unison, it was possible for admirers of both Locke and Rousseau to agree.

When Volney wrote of the frenzy of fanaticism, he had in mind the blind intolerance of the Terror, and, more particularly, the habit of identifying with illustrious republicans from classical Antiquity, or of treating history as a storehouse of moral precepts. This state of mind had been promoted by Rousseau and it was, in Volney's opinion, pernicious.[47] What was it to a labourer, an artisan or a merchant that Alexander, Attila or Tamburlaine had ever lived, or that Assyria, Carthage or Sparta had ever existed? What could such phantoms have in common with their existence?[48] These rhetorical questions reflect the spirit of the Constitution of the year III, which was taking shape even as Volney was delivering his final lectures. It is perhaps worth noting that exemplary figures were judged by him to endanger the mores of the populace in much the same fashion as the declaration of pure principles had done. In short, one would occasion as much disorder by calling upon an audience to identify with Caius Gracchus as one would by pronouncing that all were equal. Volney's strictures were not solely aimed at the sections, however, but more generally, at the form of classical education established since the Counter-Reformation in Catholic Europe. As young children, he said, we do not really understand Livy or Sallust, Caesar or Tacitus. We may need objects of emulation, but the mores reflected by the Roman historians are not our own. Better, therefore, that the Republic should sponsor the publication of its own elementary books, which would more nearly resemble novels than history.

If the Greek and Roman historians lacked authority, it was because, in Volney's opinion, the oral testimony upon which they had relied was flawed. Such testimony, like that of the priesthoods of early societies, was subject to anamorphic deformation. Like Condorcet, Volney therefore differentiated sharply between cultures with scripts and cultures without, or, as he had argued in *The Ruins of Empires*, between the verifiable and the unverifiable. Even where manuscripts had survived, there was too much scope for individual, partisan mutilation. For want of a large circle of readers and critics, 'it was not public opinion, but the spirit of a faction or coterie which pronounced'. Kinship ties were so important that Greek and Roman authors would preserve their own families' manuscripts down the generations while showing no scruple in destroying those of their rivals. On a still larger scale, the Romans and the Greeks had destroyed each others' books.[49]

Yet Volney was by no means hostile to the practice of ethnography. Indeed, as I show in chapter 5, he welcomed research into the cultures of pre-literate peoples, and his own contributions in this area are recognizably modern. It was precisely because he had prided himself upon being a truly scientific traveller that he so disdained uncorroborated tradition, the shadowy force which had everywhere preceded the noble art of printing. While in Syria, he had remarked upon the paucity of books, and he later observed:

> It is printing which, by making books very common, has spread a more equal sum of knowledge in all classes; it is printing which, by disseminating ideas and discoveries promptly has caused the more rapid development of the arts and the sciences; through printing, all those who concern themselves with them have become an ever-assembled body, which relentlessly pursues the series of the same works; through printing, every writer has become a public orator, who has spoken not only to his own town, but to his nation, and to the whole of Europe. If, in this new form of comitia, he has lost the advantage of declamation and gesture in stirring the passions, he is compensated for that loss by having a more orderly audience, by being able to reason more calmly and by being able to make an impression which is perhaps less vivid but is more lasting. So it has been that only since this epoch has one seen isolated men producing, through the authority of their writings alone, moral revolutions in entire nations, and forming an empire of opinion which has prevailed over that of armed might.[50]

It is significant that the contrast, not spelled out here but implied, between the Roman *populus* assembled in its *comitia*, and a potentially infinite series of readers of an identical printed book in an 'ever-assembled body', should feature in a work published as early as 1785, for it demonstrates that some French Enlightenment publicists had in the pre-revolutionary period made the Anglo-Scottish critique of classical republicanism their own.[51] Others, however, owed a second, conflicting allegiance to Rousseau, the citizen of Geneva.

## A treatise on the passions

For the ardent Rousseauists of the late 1780s, little or no distinction between the author of *Emile* and his books was drawn, since all that he had written had been torn, he said, from the depths of his own heart.[52] Thus, both Staël and Chateaubriand took Rousseau's *grand âme* to be exemplary; they saw a crisis of values, in which sentiment threatened to overwhelm the entrenched prestige of *goût* and *bienséance*, and by and large they welcomed it. When, therefore, the term 'eloquence' is used in the *Lettres sur Rousseau* – and it is, by my reckoning, their leitmotif – no reference to a formal rhetoric is intended.[53] Instead of deploying a system tricked out with terms borrowed from Cicero or Quintilian, Staël had cast a heroic person, a Fabricius or a Cato the Elder, as an unchained vehicle of truth. To reduce authentic sentiment to a system would be, in the terms set by Rousseau's first discourse, after all to welcome the defeat of the values of early republican Rome by the rhetors and sophists of an enslaved Greece. He had in fact damned academic rhetoric out of hand, and his Emile, when speaking, was so well able to transmit 'the movements of his soul' that his 'generous frankness' had an indefinable quality 'more enchanting by far than the artificial eloquence of others; or rather, he alone [was] genuinely eloquent, since he merely [had] to show what he [felt] in order to communicate it to those who were listening'.[54]

Staël acknowledged that Rousseau's style was sometimes in breach of the rules of taste, as construed by several of the most eminent habitués of her mother's salon. Madame Necker had herself warned against the seductive power of Rousseau's eloquence and, as Jean Roussel has convincingly shown, Staël would seem to have established her own identity as a writer in the course of a dispute with her mother over the nature of value. Madame Necker had agreed with Marmontel that *La Nouvelle Héloïse* was an immoral work, and that Rousseau's style enslaved the passions of his readers and led their reason astray.[55] Where the mother preferred the style of Buffon to that of Rousseau, it was precisely the capacity of the latter to express the deepest impulses of his own character that earned the daughter's fervent praise. More generally, the *Lettres* seem to be built upon an identification of their author with Rousseau, and of Rousseau with nature, for, as Staël's cousin was later to observe, 'she wished to be the representative of natural gifts, because her mother had been that of acquired qualities'.[56]

Staël thus found in *Emile* and *La Nouvelle Héloïse* both the purest harmonies and the most farouche discordances, and where Isabelle de Charrière, who had once asked Mozart to set one of her libretti, heard only an aria for voice and mandolin, she caught the infernal braying of trombones.[57] Indeed, much of what she has to say mirrors that point in Rousseau's first discourse at which he rose to fulminate against the urbanity which he had at first seemed to extol. His denunciations in 1749 of taste, politeness and seemliness had established, in the most dramatic terms, an opposition between urbanity and rusticity, between rhetorical ornament and the pure eloquence of a *grand âme*, and between the slavery of courts and the liberty of republican assemblies. 'Perhaps also in a kind of republican spirit', Staël wrote in 1788, 'he does not wish to acknowledge that there are low or lofty terms, actual ranks among words'.[58] She likewise endorsed the vindication of praxis which had given the first discourse its hortatory force, and linked the shade of Rousseau to the effervescent condition of France in the summer and autumn of 1788.[59]

Thus, in the fourth letter, she remarked that 'it was not enough to have demonstrated the rights of men; it was necessary . . . to make them feel how much they should be valued'. A brilliant publicist, such as Buffon, was contrasted with a *grand âme* like Rousseau, who, though he could not transmit all his ideas to all minds, would 'draw his listeners forward by means of his eloquence; it is this that should move and persuade all men equally'. She then contrasted truths of reason with truths of sentiment, noting that access to the former was gradual, to the latter, immediate.[60]

So close had the association between *The Social Contract* and the Montagnard dictatorship of the year II become that it was once believed by historians that the political writings of Rousseau only exerted a belated influence upon the course of the Revolution.[61] Recent scrutiny of the Third Estate pamphleteering of 1788–89, and indeed of the whole period of the Constituent Assembly, has, however, demonstrated that 'the "bible" of the revolutionaries, from the beginning, was not *The Spirit of the Laws*, but *The Social Contract*, and everything which, in Rousseau's political oeuvre, prepares, recapitulates or elaborates upon [it] . . . '.[62] Even in the case of Staël, who had accepted Montesquieu's defence of representation and who shared his attachment to aristocratic values, this observation holds good.

After the Terror, moderates of every stripe would repudiate the revolutionary call for time itself to be accelerated, and they would warn against the dangers of confusing premature with opportune reforms. In addition, a line would be drawn between the space of the heart and the space of the agora. There is a temptation to argue here that the republicans of the year III were merely falling back upon positions established earlier by Enlightenment publicists, yet a glance at David Hume's essays suggests that this was not altogether the case. In 'Of Eloquence', for example, he emphasizes the 'sublime' nature of ancient rhetoric, and remarks upon 'swelling expressions . . . not rejected as wholly monstrous and gigantic'. This is the same art, then, as is practised in the House of Commons, and it could have been perfected even in modern times:

> Had such a cultivated genius for oratory, as Waller's for poetry, arisen, during the civil wars, when liberty began to be fully established, and popular assemblies to enter into all the most material points of government; I am persuaded so illustrious an example would have given a quite different turn to BRITISH eloquence, and made us reach the perfection of the ancient model.[63]

In other writings, as I show in chapter 4, Hume may seem to anticipate the doctrine of the liberty of the Ancients and of the Moderns, but here two worlds are held by Enlightenment classicism in a sort of balance, offering a transfer of qualities across time. Volney had in 1785, as we have seen, set writer against orator, and printed book against *comitia*, in a bid to subsume the ancient city within a vast 'empire of opinion', as wide, indeed, as the world, and yet the motif of actual assembly returned with redoubled force in *The Ruins of Empire*. The same tension between actual and virtual representation, with both being held for a time in a fragile coexistence, may be discerned in Thomas Jefferson's correspondence, as I show in chapter 6, and, more generally, in the changing interpretations of Rousseau advanced in the 1780s and 1790s.

Thus Kant, in 1793, had insisted that the social contract was not an actual occurrence but merely an idea of reason,

> which nonetheless had undoubted practical reality; for it can oblige every legislator to frame his laws in such a way that they could have been produced by the united will of a whole nation, and to regard each subject, in so far as he can claim citizenship, as if he had consented within the general will.[64]

Although Kant accepted the division between state and civil society, and repudiated the right of resistance, some commentators have nonetheless judged his interpretation of Rousseau to be more accurate than any other.[65] *Emile*, they say, subsumes *The Social Contract* and is to be regarded as, so to speak, the frame of a lost human glory. They thus argue that the notion of the education of 'the citizen' had a merely counterfactual value in Rousseau's system, as an image of the good displayed for the edification of 'the man'. In the modern world there would then only be simulacra of laws, not laws as such.[66]

I shall return to this line of argument in other chapters, but here I wish merely to note that, no matter how clear cut Kant's position on the social contract may have been, Rousseau's own account was ambiguous.[67] As historians, we disregard that ambiguity at our peril, for much followed from it. In 1788, there was thus, if only fleetingly, a homology between radiant sentiment and assembled people, and even in his pathos Rousseau was a figure suffused with the still universal qualities of nature and not yet, therefore, an obscured and private soul.[68] It has been said that, of all the treatises of the eighteenth century, *The Social Contract* was well-nigh unique in its proud claim to reconcile the demands of individual and collective happiness.[69] In this regard it was of central importance to the Utopian mood of 1788–89, which is perhaps most easily understood now by those touched by the spirit of 1968. After Thermidor, Staël could only write elegies to the free city (as in certain recessed passages from *Corinne*), or to cantonal democracy in the Alps (as in the Interlaken idyll in *De l'Allemagne*), with all the wistfulness of first love lost. In her first book, however, published on the day that Necker was recalled to office, the passions remained a good. Staël expressed her hopes for the regeneration of France through the convocation of the States General, and her regret that Rousseau himself could not witness 'the imposing spectacle . . . of a great event prepared in advance, in which, for the first time, chance will play no part'.[70] It would nonetheless be mistaken to suppose that her hopes in late 1788 ran even to the form of constitutional monarchy which emerged after 23 June and 14 July 1789.[71] Indeed, she dissolved the shade of Rousseau, guarantor of universal human value, into the figure of Necker, her beloved father, incarnation of a strictly reformist prudence, and clawed back the enraptured sentiments that colour so much of the *Lettres*. After the Terror she was to retreat still further.

*De l'Influence des Passions* was much admired by Madame de Staël's contemporaries. Wilhelm von Humboldt, Schiller and Goethe praised the work highly; it was of great interest, the latter remarked, to see 'how so . . . passionate a nature passed through the grim ordeal of the Revolution, in which she had played so prominent a part, and I may say that, after passing through it, all the qualities left in her are of the most intellectual order'.[72] This acute judgement was echoed by others. Stendhal, for example, though immersed in the writings of Cabanis and Tracy, was nonetheless well able to appreciate the intrinsic worth of a treatise written by 'a passionate soul describing what she has felt'.[73]

The book was begun in the aftermath of the September Massacres, at Juniper Hall in Surrey, and was therefore, first of all, an anguished commentary upon those terrible days and upon 'Robespierre's system'. Secondly, it was a considered response to, and refutation of, a number of works written earlier in the century on the relation between the passions and human happiness, notably by Diderot and Vauvenargues. Thirdly, the book was a heartrending cry of protest at the predicament of those betrayed in love, who were advised to rely upon their own resources, 'independent of fate and above all of the will of men'. Whereas the *Lettres sur Rousseau* had hinted at the promise of love, the new work spoke, in the most direct and autobiographical terms, of the devastation caused by the loss of it: 'alone, in secret, your entire being has passed from life to death. What resource is there in the world that can prevail against such grief?'[74]

One critic has argued that Staël wrote *De l'Influence des Passions* to prove to the Directory, which looked askance at the many monarchists in her circle, that she had no intention of meddling any further in French politics, and to beg for permission to live quietly in Paris.[75] Since all of her other writings derive some of their meaning from their immediate occasion and context, and even when apparently purely literary in scope are invariably political also, it would be foolish to deny such encoded intentions here. It would be still more mistaken, however, to restrict the significance of the treatise unduly.

Staël had at first meant to write one volume upon the happiness of individuals, and a second upon that of nations, in which she proposed

> to examine ancient and modern governments in relation to the influence they have allowed to the natural passions of men combined in political bodies, and to identify the cause of the birth, duration and destruction of governments in the greater or lesser scope they have given to the need for action which exists in every society.[76]

Like many of the surveys written in the aftermath of Thermidor, her second volume was thus intended to provide a comparative account of politics, ancient and modern, and she further specified that part 1 was to be concerned with governments in which passions were suppressed, part 2 with those in which passions were aroused, and part 3 with the nature of small but obscure democratic states. The theoretical framework for this division was plainly taken from Montesquieu, who had distinguished between the nature of a government and its principle, where 'the one is its particular structure, and the other is the human passions that set it in motion'.[77] Monarchies were held to run on honour, despotisms on fear and republics on virtue. In a similar vein, Staël associated the suppression of passions with despotism, and their arousal with both demagogic and military anarchies, and, so as to quash any doubts, she identified the demagogic variety with the Montagnard constitution of 1793.[78]

If Staël never completed her second volume, it was first of all because, as Sainte-Beuve had said, the times were not propitious for the launching of ambitious and systematic treatises. She had declared that she would draw upon evidence from the French Revolution and, in a phrase reminiscent of Montesquieu, from 'the history of all the peoples', and yet the particular horror of the events in Paris overshadows the universalist pretensions of her book. In addition, she was not yet ready for the task she had set herself, which was subsequently realized in part by Benjamin Constant, in an unfinished and unpublished manuscript on the difficulty of founding a republic in a large country, and in part by herself, in *De la Littérature*.[79] Above all, though, the analogy between the happiness of individuals and the happiness of nations had been wrecked upon the reef of the Terror. Staël had written as follows:

> Two works are meant to be comprised within the one: the first studies man in his relation to himself, the second studies man as regards the social relations of all the individuals with each other: there is some analogy between the chief ideas of these two treatises, because a nation presents the character of a man, and because the force of a government should act upon it, just as the power of reason should act upon an individual.[80]

Like Cabanis, Pinel or Volney she could no longer countenance the circuit of passion, imitation and enthusiasm 'electrifying' the free city invoked by Rousseau. More generally it could be said that her failure to complete her task is a symptom of what Gordon Wood, in the context of the American Revolution, described as 'the end of classical politics'.[81] When she watched the three estates process to the States General in May 1789, she had before her eyes the living emblems of what might perhaps have been turned into a mixed government. For, in the latter theory, social classes were directly embodied in political forms, so that fear, virtue and honour were in effect visible. By the time she came to write her Directorial treatises, however, such notions of order and hierarchy in the social world had been destroyed. A nation, being dispersed, could no longer parade as a city, and it was only through the formation of the word- or tribe-nation, predicated upon the replacement of an account of the actual origin of language with a Humboldtian insistence upon its continual recurrence in and through all human beings, that, in the new century, so radiant a relation between individual and collective happiness might be reconstituted.

A cursory reading of Staël's treatise on the passions suggests that a Stoic indifference was aimed at, an elevation of the distraught self above a gladiatorial world. 'I have written', she declared,

> in order to . . . free my faculties from the servitude of sentiments, in order to raise myself to a kind of abstraction, so that I may observe the pain of the soul. I have tried to see whether what is poignant in personal anguish is not shifted a little when we place ourselves as a part of the vast picture of destinies, in which each man is lost in his own century, that century in time and time in the incomprehensible.[82]

The Kantian tone of this declaration does not reflect any direct acquaintance at this stage with *The Critique of Judgement*, but rather a shared sympathy for Roman Stoicism.[83] Condorcet's *Esquisse* would have been a more probable source in 1795–96 and yet, notwithstanding a strong emphasis in Staël's treatise upon social arithmetic, it is addressed to *êtres passionnées*, and is therefore at once a condemnation and a vindication of the passions.

Individual chapters treat love of glory, ambition, vanity, love, gambling, greed, drunkenness, envy, revenge, crime and even party spirit, the majority of these passions being judged to be destructive. Some, being merely physical (gambling, greed, drunkenness), were condemned out of hand; others, being 'unsocial' (envy, revenge, crime, party spirit), were also given short shrift. Yet it was with the discussion of ambition, glory and love that matters became more complex, for Staël neither fully endorsed nor flatly rejected such states. She did, it is true, assert that the moral universe 'belong[ed] to thought' and not, therefore, to passion, but she also intended her treatise to be read by *êtres passionnées* alone. Banally, this may be because real independence from the passions presupposed some direct knowledge of their power to ravage and to destroy. More obscurely, the pursuit of the good was construed as a progressive ascent from embodiment to a spiritualization of being, with the act of study serving as a prefiguration of the world to come.

Earlier in the century, it had been proposed that, if movement were itself a good, desire would be also, and inconstancy an accepted consequence of the fragility of individual identity.[84] A person might, in short, be the passion that assailed them. Vauvenargues, for example, had asserted that 'our passions are not distinct from ourselves; some of them are the whole basis and substance of our soul'.[85] Diderot had likewise insisted that 'only passions, and indeed great passions . . . can elevate the soul to great things. Without them, there would be no more sublime, either in mores or in works; the fine arts would return to their infancy, and virtue would become paltry.'[86] Conceiving of energy as an ubiquitous force in nature, Diderot deplored the suppression of the erotic in human society. Like Holbach and Helvétius, he believed that great passions freed souls from the church – and, crucially, from the tyranny of monastic institutions – and placed the cardinal distinction between mind and body in doubt.[87]

There can be no doubt that Diderot's essentially pagan conception of energy, and his republican ethics, derived from the English Deists in general and from Shaftesbury in particular, exerted a residual influence upon Staël.[88] For she held that the eradication of the passions would lead, as in a despotism, to a sort of moral torpor. She therefore admired extreme manifestations of energy in persons, even though the risk was that such forces transcended good and evil.[89] In her essay on fiction, a trial run for the later treatise, Staël had warned that, for virtue to wage war upon, and to prevail against, the more nefarious passions, it would have itself to be animated or impassioned. Yet if the energy required for the good fight were in essence amoral, how could one guarantee that such a pure force remained within the bounds of the moral order? If, at Juniper Hall, the irregular alliance of Narbonne and Staël gave offence to those in Fanny Burney's circle, this was no doubt because it served as a mirror, in which could be discerned an image of the justifications of inconstancy offered by the *philosophes*, Diderot among them. By the same token, characters such as Frank Churchill, in *Pride and Prejudice*, and Henry Crawford, in *Mansfield Park*, were not merely foils to the virtue of constancy, whether construed in Christian or in Aristotelian terms, but also implied a strictly contemporary reference to the figure of the libertine.[90] In *De l'Allemagne*, composed under the First Empire, Staël would herself condemn unreservedly the notion of desire as animating force, but her call in the essay on fiction for novelists to emulate Richardson and to conjure up Lovelaces of ambition remained altogether in the spirit of Diderot's writings or, one might add, of Da Ponte and Mozart's *Don Giovanni*.[91]

It is also true, however, that as early as 1786–88, the years during which the *Lettres sur Rousseau* were drafted, Staël was, to use Masson's phrase, a parishioner of the Savoyard Vicar.[92] She thus saw Rousseau as one who had broken with the empiricist and at times materialist psychophysiology of the *philosophes*, and who, in order to locate the source of the good, had looked deep into his own soul. A key passage in this regard would be the refutation of Helvétius in *Emile*:

> Everything, they say, is immaterial to us save our own self-interest: and yet it is quite the reverse, for it is the sweetness of friendship, of humanity, which consoles us amidst our troubles; and, even in our pleasures, we would be too much alone and too wretched if we had no one to share them with. If there is

nothing moral in the heart of man, whence derive the transports of admiration for heroic actions, or exalted love for great souls? What connection can there be between such enthusiasm for virtue and our own private interests?[93]

Rousseau's concern with the origin of heroism was echoed by Staël in the *Lettres*, and in the treatise on the passions she defined virtue as the sublime capacity of an individual to find in his or her consciousness the motive for conduct. The opposition between a self-discovered rule and passion recalls Kant's distinction between duty and inclination, but at this date the resemblance very probably derived from a shared debt to Adam Smith, and to *The Theory of Moral Sentiments*. Be that as it may, the conflict was, as Staël saw it, between the radically independent individual, able first to frame and then to follow rules, and those who were under the sway of the passions or, in other terms, between reason and the insidious fascination that a disordered imagination could produce. Yet, speaking more generally, the Coppet Circle, influenced in this regard by Schiller and Humboldt, rejected the rigorism of Kantian ethics.[94]

Although a Stoic indifference features in the treatise on the passions, Staël did not wish an end to enthusiasm. She sought, rather, to establish a moral framework for a republic purged of the twin fanaticisms of 'democracy' and 'royalty', where a combination of humanity and self-command might protect the innocent individual. It seems reasonable, then, to assume that she had read Smith's ethical treatise between 1792 and 1796. In order to say just how she had read it, one needs first to offer a preliminary description. Many contemporaries, like many scholars since, remarked upon Smith's ambition to emulate Hume and to apply the methods of the natural sciences to the domain of morality. One can, for example, point to an almost Newtonian isolation of the principle of sympathy. This was largely, but not exclusively, how Sophie de Condorcet, the widow of the philosopher and an intimate of Cabanis and Fauriel, approached the book. Indeed, she criticized Smith for failing to research the actual origin of sympathy, which she deemed an essential quality of 'every sentient being endowed with a capacity for reflection'.[95] Staël, however, was more concerned, as we have already seen, to bring Smith's naturalist ethics to bear upon her own lists of passions and virtues. She had therefore embraced the distinction, pioneered by Hume, between the 'amiable' and the 'respectable' virtues, between 'the virtues of candid condescension and indulgent humanity' and 'the great, the awful and respectable, the virtues of self-denial, of self-government, of that command of the passions which subjects all the movements of our nature to what our own dignity and honour and the propriety of our own

conduct require'.[96] In her treatise, the former are represented by sentiments located midway between the passions and the resources one finds
within oneself, for example, friendship, filial, paternal or conjugal
tenderness, and religion; the latter by philosophy, study and good works.
In order to cultivate the virtues of humanity, Smith argued, one had to
look at others as one would wish them to look at oneself. In order to
attain to self-command, one needed to scale down all presumption, and
to esteem oneself only as much as, and emphatically no more than,
another might. This scaling down of the self is as perceptible in Staël's
desire to free herself from 'the servitude of sentiments' as it is in Sophie
de Condorcet's claim that her husband had been 'a stranger to all the
passions'.[97] How, in Smith's opinion, did a person achieve such estrangement? And, more important, how are we, from our vantage-point, to
interpret the emergence in the eighteenth century of such a theory of
moral judgement?

Smith derived his ethical theory from Hutcheson and Hume, each of
whom had emphasized the disinterested nature of moral judgements.[98]
Approbation, or disapprobation, was thus defined as the measured
response of a spectator to observed acts. Where Smith's precursors had
been most concerned with judgements pertaining to the deeds of others,
he himself saw that an empirical account of the origins of conscience
might be arrived at if the spectator were, so to speak, introduced into the
tribunal of the self. The theory of the 'impartial spectator' was not
present in Smith's earliest lectures on moral philosophy but emerged,
rather, in the text of *The Theory of Moral Sentiments*, where it gradually
became differentiated from other, less precise terms (for example, 'us',
'mankind', 'other people', 'the company' or 'strangers'). To begin with,
the concept sheds light upon the conduct of third parties, but in its fully
developed form it becomes altogether abstract. Thus, by extrapolation
from judgements applied in the social world by, as it were, bystanders,
we learn to judge our own conduct as if an impartial spectator were
observing it. If that lesson is learned supremely well, the division in our
minds and hearts between such a spectator and our will is elided, so that
in a certain sense we *become* the ideal onlooker we had at an earlier stage
created.[99]

Shortly after the original publication of *The Theory of Moral Sentiments*, in 1759, a friendly critic raised the objection that, if moral
judgement, the ideal spectator within, were so directly a reflection of
popular opinion, the real onlooker without, it was not clear how conscience could ever rise above prejudice. Allowing the objection to be
well-founded, Smith replied that, in his revision of the passage in
question, he had shown both that 'our judgement concerning our own
conduct [has] always a reference to the sentiments of some other being',

and that 'real magnanimity and conscious virtue can support itself under the disapprobation of all mankind'.[100] Provoked into a reexamination of his theory, Smith then remarked upon the self's lived disillusion with *real* bystanders, who are generally biased and partial. Stung by the inaccuracy and injustice of what they say, we imagine an impartial spectator, who supplies us with a wholly inward, truly universal and quasi-divine criterion. Comparison of the various editions of *The Theory of Moral Sentiments* thus reveals a growing distrust of society and a correspondingly enhanced belief in the value of the imagination. Raphael, in support of this claim, refers to Smith's stay in Toulouse in 1764–65, and to the impact upon him of the celebrated case of Jean Calas, a Protestant merchant who had been wrongfully accused of the murder of his son and subsequently tried, charged, tortured and executed. This had been in 1762, but Voltaire's defence of the wronged man had made the case known throughout Europe. A foreign visitor, resident in Toulouse for eighteen months, would have pondered long on the fate of Calas. Smith's thoughts on this matter found expression in a comparison between the outer tribunal of popular opinion and the inner tribunal of conscience. Whereas in the second edition he had stated that the jurisdiction of conscience 'is in a great measure derived from that very tribunal [i.e society], whose decisions it so often and so justly reverses', he wrote in the third edition that 'the jurisdiction of these two tribunals are founded upon principles which, though in some respects resembling and akin are, however, in reality different and distinct'.[101] This was a large concession, but it ought never to be supposed that Smith's account of the operation of sympathy in the human heart, and consequently of the origin of the amiable virtues, ever deviates from a strictly empirical description. Notwithstanding the Christian phrasing of such virtues, the inner voice of duty is not supernaturally derived, as it sometimes is in Rousseau. Staël often voiced Rousseau's claim that to be human at all was to have, and to show, pity, since 'a voice which breaks, an altered face, act directly upon the soul, as sensations do'.[102] If Robespierre and Marat were not touched by the distress of others, it was because they were not human, but animal. Staël was close to the *idéologues* in 1796, the year in which her book on the passions was published, and it is therefore possible to select quotations from it which appear to accord with the viewpoint of Cabanis or Tracy. Yet a distinction ought still to be made between her treatise and, for example, Sophie de Condorcet's letters on sympathy, where we read that 'it is reflection which, at the sight of pain, reminding us that we are the subjects of this life-destroying tyrant, like the being that we see oppressed by him, brings us closer to that being through a movement of emotion and commiseration for our own selves'. 'The sentiment of humanity', she continued, 'is therefore in some sense a seed placed in the depths of man's heart by nature.'[103] It was thus possible to accept Rousseau's reproach to Helvétius, since republican convictions now demanded it, while at the same time defending the description of the origin of value from all spiritualist aberrations.[104] To term pain a life-destroying tyrant, who, by oppressing, inspires a sentiment of radical equality, is to anticipate the cosmology of Leopardi, whose alignment with the *idéologue* tradition I shall have occasion to note in later chapters.

What, then, is the historical significance of the impartial spectator? By 1759, Smith had consolidated his account of the stadial nature of human society.[105] If, however, all human groups were destined to proceed through a sequence of four distinct socio-economic stages, they would, by the same token, have radically different customs and beliefs. Hunting peoples would, for example, compose one sort of poem, pastoral or agricultural peoples quite another. Given a conviction of this sort, the ambition to research a social history of rhetoric, mooted by Smith and Suard but realized by Staël in her *De la Littérature*, followed on naturally.[106] Yet moral judgements had perforce to alter also, from stage to stage. In an essay on Smith's thought in the context of the Scottish Enlightenment, Nicholas Phillipson has thus argued that the intention had never been to propose a general theory of morals, but rather to define one suited to a society with an advanced division of labour.[107] By contrast with earlier times, when a shared ethos could be readily assumed, the spirit of commerce had vested day-to-day social relations with a distressing degree of complexity. It was no longer a matter of conning, glossing and then inhabiting a canon of virtues. Instead, the young persons addressed by Smith and his colleagues in mid-century Scotland were exhorted to acquire by reflection a set of, so to speak, flexible moral skills by which to negotiate the difficulties of the world in which they now found themselves. Indeed, all stadial theorists welcomed the division of labour and the triumph of the commercial spirit, growing inequality being the precondition of the requisite accumulation of capital, and by the same token rejected that strand of classical republicanism which rested upon the possibility of shaming the corrupted in a public place, and thereby restoring the polity as a whole to its first principles. The impartial spectator was to serve those who, arriving in mid-century Glasgow, would be buffeted by crowds that did not in the deepest sense know who they were. The good bystander would stand and stare, and not speak, or else pass by on the other side.

The names of Marcus Brutus and Cato of Utica still feature in *The Theory of Moral Sentiments*, as in the writings of Cabanis or Staël, but the magnificent parade of the virtues, in the presence of the totality of the other citizens, was increasingly seen as a property of an ancient, and now eclipsed, society. The relentless destruction of small city states, obscure rural democracies or of tribal peoples, was accompanied by a theoretical rejection of the classical ideal of the people assembled. Actual assembly could, after all, occasion a delusional multiplication of the passions, as self-command was sacrificed to unreflective sympathy.[108]

To choose Marcus Brutus, not Junius Brutus, and Cato of Utica, not Cato the Censor, was in itself to admit the loss of a fixed moral framework.[109] The drift of the impartial spectator, perceptible in Smith's redrafting of his book, towards abstraction and inwardness, likewise reflects the impossibility of restoring an, as it were, Roman censor to his rightful place at the heart of a society which conceived of itself as dispersed not assembled, divided not whole, and plural not single. The replacement of that hectoring voice of the outer world with a self-spoken but no less demanding inner voice is, I believe, a necessary but not, I would stress, a sufficient condition for the shift from an age of cities to an age of nations. Another symptom of this great transformation was, as I show in chapter 3, the altered status of the prosopopoeia in European literary practice. As Alasdair MacIntyre has argued, the erosion of the fully lived, fully narrated good had left moralists in a world dominated by possessive individualism with a drastically impoverished calculus of the self and the passions. Giotto could hardly have painted Staël's curious list of the virtues, though in its subdivisions one may discern faint traces of Aquinas. Yet, in Smith's case, we still have to do with a republican, who, as MacIntyre remarks, 'had the notion of a public good which is prior to and characterisable independently of the summing of individual desires and interests'.[110] If this were not the case, *The Theory of Moral Sentiments* would not have been so highly esteemed by the *idéologues*.[111]

After Thermidor, the claim was increasingly made in France that the ancient republics had not known individual liberty, and that the Montagnard dictatorship, inspired by Rousseau, was proof of this. To see whether, or to what degree, the charge was justified, I wish now to consider the illumination of Vincennes.

# Rousseau's Rome

## The illumination of Vincennes

In a letter to Lamoignon de Malesherbes, written on 12 January 1762, Rousseau described his original revelation, often known as 'the illumination of Vincennes'. He recalled how, on his way to visit the imprisoned Diderot, he happened to leaf through a copy of the *Mercure de France*, and to read the question posed by the Academy of Dijon:

> Oh Monsieur, if I had ever been able to write a quarter of what I saw and felt under that tree, with what clarity would I have shown all the contradictions of the social system; with what force would I have exposed all the abuses of our institutions, with what simplicity would I have demonstrated that man is naturally good, and that it is by these institutions that men become wicked.[1]

In answer to the question as to whether the restoration of the arts and sciences had served to purify the morals of Europe, Rousseau had drafted a fierce denunciation of the much-vaunted achievements, intellectual, technical and commercial, of the Enlightenment. 'Our minds have been corrupted', he declared, 'in proportion as the arts and sciences have improved'.[2] In later years, Diderot and his circle told the story another way, insisting that Rousseau had at first been in two minds as to how to respond, and that he had been swayed by the mocking observation that argument from the more unfamiliar perspective would distinguish him from the other competitors, and thus earn him the prize. Why ought we to give credence to Rousseau's account, and dismiss those of Diderot, Holbach, La Harpe or Marmontel?[3]

First, so sincere was Rousseau that it is intrinsically improbable that he could have sustained such a charade, in the face of the scornful insinuations of the *philosophes*, for many years. Second, all those who have studied his writings in any depth are agreed that they display a remarkable degree of consistency, both before and after the condemnation in

1762, of *Emile* and *The Social Contract*. It defies belief to suppose that Rousseau could so often have marshalled the elements of his 'system', itself driven by a passionate claim to authenticity, when the central tenet was no more than a bizarre paradox, paraded for the sake of literary ambition alone. It should further be emphasized that the unity of that system is not jeopardized either by the concrete applications of his principles of political right, in the texts written on behalf of the Corsicans and the Polish, or by his last, autobiographical writings.[4] Through his inaugural vision, to be scrutinized in detail below, Rousseau had, as he put it, seen another world and become another man.[5]

For five years, then, Rousseau was in a state of feverish exaltation, as 'all [his] little passions' were 'stifled by an enthusiasm for truth, liberty and virtue'.[6] A close reading of the texts produced in this single period of creative activity reveals the presence in each of key terms, even key phrases, which link one to the other. These crucial formulations, always arrestingly worded, involve fundamental principles, such as equality and liberty. Rousseau had himself asserted that the *Discourse on the Origins of Inequality* enabled him to 'develop completely' the principles advanced in his first discourse and that, in his Preface to *Narcisse*, he 'began to set out [his] principles a little more fully than [he] had done [t]hitherto'.[7] It is true that several pivotal concepts, for example, the opposition between the general will and the will of all, or between sovereignty and government, are absent from the first discourse, which is in fact as defiantly farouche as its author was himself in the early 1750s. I will nonetheless begin my exposition with the inaugural vision that founds that first writing and, consequently, his system. For, when Rousseau spoke with Diderot, later that same day, he read to him the fragment he had written down under the tree, an exalted speech celebrating an imagined episode in the history of Rome:

What would the great soul of Fabricius have felt, if it had been his misfortune to be called back to life, when he saw the pomp and magnificence of that Rome, which his arm had saved from ruin, and his honourable name made more illustrious than all its conquests. 'Ye gods!' he would have said, 'what has become of those thatched roofs and rustic hearths, which were formerly the habitations of temperance and virtue? What fatal splendour has succeeded the ancient Roman simplicity? What is this foreign language, this effeminacy of manners? What is the meaning of these statues, paintings and buildings? Fools, what have you done? You, the lords of the earth, have made yourselves the slaves of the frivolous nations you have subdued. You are governed by rhetoricians, and it has been only to enrich architects, painters, sculptors and stage-players that you have watered Greece and Asia with your blood. Even the spoils of Carthage are the prize of a flute-player. Romans! Romans! make haste to demolish those amphitheatres, break to pieces those statues, burn those paintings; drive from among you those slaves who keep you in subjection, and whose fatal arts are corrupting your morals. Let other hands make themselves illustrious by such vain talents; the only talent worthy of Rome is that of conquering the world and making virtue its ruler. When Cineas took the Roman senate for an assembly of kings, he was not struck by either useless pomp or studied elegance. He heard there none of that futile eloquence, which is now the study and the charm of frivolous orators. What then was the majesty that Cineas beheld? Fellow citizens, he saw the noblest sight that ever existed under heaven, a sight which not all your riches or your arts can show; an assembly of two hundred virtuous men, worthy to command in Rome, and to govern the world.'[8]

The rhetorical device of prosopopoeia, by which a historical figure is represented in the act of delivering a speech that he or she could plausibly have uttered, was one of the most dramatic tricks in the repertoire of the historians of Antiquity, from Thucydides to Livy. Contemporary readers of Rousseau's first discourse had been quick to note the importance of Fabricius, and several reviewers had reproduced the prosopopoeia in full. There could be nothing more thrilling than to call the illustrious dead to witness, and so to advance bolder sentiments than one would risk in one's own person.[9]

A correlation may be made between the device of prosopopoeia and the figure of the great legislator, founder of cities, for both faded with the advent of the age of nations.[10] Being the Fabricius, as it were, of an insurgent Paris, Rousseau himself had become the subject of countless prosopopoeias.[11] If, however, this trope fell into disuse in the first half of the nineteenth century, it was because it had rested upon the increasingly discredited assumption that there was a zone of unconditional liberty between cities, a wilderness across which a rapt lawgiver would pass, or to which a despot would be expelled. With the triumph in Europe of the historical school of law's conception of the spirit of a people, which lent custom (and, crucially, customary law) not merely a dignity but in addition a time-hallowed truth, so radical a passage, flight or secession could barely be imagined. The land had ceased to be a fear stage for the dawn, the meridian and the dusk, and had become instead an immemorial person, a corporation and the inorganic body of the tribe. Once, therefore, the principle of nationality – elevated on the gleaming shields of historical linguistics and a historicist approach to law – had brought the dead, forever murmuring, among the living, a prosopopoeia was no more a possibility than a great lawgiver. I say murmuring, and *forever* murmuring, advisedly, since the new historiography was predicated upon the belief that a historian had the capacity to divine, to one side of the excess of attested utterance of a monarch, the deeper meaning of the lack of

recorded testimonies of a people. At the risk of advancing too paradoxical a formulation, one could put it that Augustin Thierry, for
example, concerned himself more with the silences of the humble than
with the speeches of the great. Yet, viewed from another angle, it was as
if, for the liberal bourgeois historians and their successors, there was
nothing that was not speech, though it took the form of ritual, of
mundane implement or of monument. Every object might then be
redeemed – to employ a religious idiom which is, in this context, wholly
appropriate – in terms of what Marcel Gauchet has called 'the totalising
principle offered by the subjective schema of the nation'.[12] The key
opposition for Thierry was between the contingent fact of conquest, a
brutal act of domination originating from outside, and the necessary fact
of habitation. He therefore mocked the view that liberty came from
elsewhere, through the fiat of the Merovingian kings, and celebrated the
self-willed actions of the communes. The narrative of the dynasties was
discontinuous, that of the people continuous.[13] Augustin Thierry, Ame-
dée Thierry and Mignet in fact nursed the ambition to construct a
seamless chronicle of France, consisting of a sequence of 'naive testimonies . . . interrupted by no philosophical reflection, by no modern
addition', which would therefore be 'the *immediate representation* of the
past which has produced us, our habits, our customs and our civilisation'.[14] Whereas the prosopopoeia served as a torch transmitting light
from one city of transience to another, Thierry's strategies of estrangement, involving, for example, orthographic reform, restored to the
ancestors their authentic ethnographic colour. No Cato the Censor could
vault the abyss of the generations, for his set speech would be absurdly,
not gloriously, rustic. The prosopopoeia still featured in Niebuhr's
history of Rome, but not in that of Michelet. By Mommsen's time, such
tropes had long since ceased to be a part of the repertoire of the serious
historian.

But what had Rousseau seen on the road to Vincennes? A 'veritable
golden age' had been revealed to him, in which there flourished 'societies
of simple, wise and happy men'.[15] Rome 'in the times of its poverty and
ignorance' was therefore but one of a series, for in the first discourse a
number of uncorrupted peoples – the ancient Persians, the Scythians, the
ancient Germans, the mountain Swiss, the American Indians and the
Spartans – put a corrupted Egypt, Greece, Rome and Byzantium to
shame.[16] Asleep beneath an oak tree, Rousseau had been possessed by
the belief that humanity was good, and that it was only its institutions that
had rendered it wicked. Yet the harm was done; there was no way back to
the golden age.

Rousseau later insisted that his intention had never been

to return numerous peoples or large states to their original simplicity, but only to halt, if it were possible, the progress of those whose small size and situation have preserved them from so rapid a march towards the perfection of society and the deterioration of the species . . . he had worked for his fatherland and for small states constituted like it.[17]

Although Rousseau often repeated the distinction advanced here between small and large states, and contrasted the public education of the citizen with a merely 'domestic' education, it is nonetheless possible to identify other passages, hortatory or reproachful in tone, in which the distinction is blurred. Large states might, by some miracle, be restored to the moral condition of small states, 'be born again, so to speak, from [their] own ashes, and leap from the arms of death to regain the vigour of youth'.[18] So it had been in Sparta at the time of Lycurgus, at Rome after the expulsion of the Tarquins, and in Holland and Switzerland after the expulsion of the tyrants. Similar, somewhat apocalyptic passages in *Emile* were interpreted with hindsight as prophecies of the Revolution, even though the latter term carried with it associations of a natural, even cosmic cycle that are unfamiliar to us now.

There seems, then, to be a contradiction in Rousseau's political thought, as if he both did, and did not, believe in the possibility of recovering liberty in states where it had been lost. To resolve this contradiction, we need first of all to admit his profound horror of insurrection. Dangerous enough in a city like Geneva, turmoil was especially to be feared in a large monarchy, for 'once customs are established and prejudices are firmly rooted, it is a vain and risky enterprise to seek to reform them'.[19] Counter-revolutionaries, from *monarchiens* to Ultras, derived a malicious pleasure from demonstrating, in 1789 and 1790, that the status and decrees of the Constituent Assembly were in several respects contrary both in principle and in detail to the stipulations of *The Social Contract*, while moderate patriots, disturbed by the threat to property posed by popular unrest, emphasized Rousseau's dread of civil strife.[20]

Second, commentators have found no difficulty in garnering evidence to substantiate Bertrand de Jouvenel's claim that Rousseau was a 'pessimistic evolutionist', who simply could not believe in a future darkened by the antinomies of civil society, and who therefore placed his trust in uncorrupted enclaves.[21] The debt Marx owed to Rousseau concerned the nature of the relation between liberty and the state or, more properly, the city, and not the question of agency. For Rousseau never conceived of either artisans or peasants as the collective subject of history. Indeed, he seemed almost to lack the concept of the future altogether, and one simply cannot imagine him, like Mercier, dating a text to the year 2440, or, like Condorcet, mapping the kingdom of ends in a tenth and final epoch of human history.[22] This said, Rousseau's deepest sympathies were certainly for the labouring poor or, to be more precise, for those who had fallen victim to the violent upheavals and large-scale transformations of nascent industrial capitalism. From his tramping days he knew what it was to break stone for highways, or to toil, in the most atrocious conditions, deep in the earth.[23] In Paris, which he first visited in 1732, he was horrified by the 'dirty, stinking little streets' and 'ugly black houses' of the Faubourg Saint-Marceau, while five years later, in Montpelier, he remarked upon the stark contrast between 'imposing town houses' and 'miserable hovels filled with mud and smoke', and between the rich and the poor.[24] It seems fair to conclude that, by deliberately assuming the burdens of an artisan's life, and by wearing them as if they were in the eyes of all the world a badge of honour, he had given a voice to the labouring classes.[25]

Rousseau's writings thus express an estrangement from the social order so acute as to merit the anachronistic use of the term 'alienation' to describe it.[26] Already, in his first discourse, he had fulminated against the masked condition of the age, regretting a time when all had been authentic, frank, unadorned. The division between appearance and essence, inauthenticity and authenticity, opacity and transparency informs his whole *oeuvre*, as both Starobinski and Baczko have shown, and lends it a truly corrosive force. Driven by self-interest and not, as formerly, by a love of the common good, each was engaged in a struggle 'to supplant, deceive, betray or destroy each other'; children would dream of an inheritance or merchants wait upon a shipwreck.[27] Rousseau's thunderous accusations sometimes roll on to the horizon, his vision of the triumph of evil being etched so deep as to obscure the detail of social process. At other times, however, he had in mind the fact of primitive accumulation, the consequent destruction of subsistence economies, and the emergence of both 'free' wage-labourer and 'possessive' individual. It is true that the economic development of France lagged behind that of England in the eighteenth century, and that Rousseau was therefore not a witness to upheavals in which, to quote Marx, 'great masses of men are suddenly and forcibly torn from their means of subsistence, and hurled on to the labour market as free, unprotected and rightless proletarians', through 'the expropriation of the agricultural producer, of the peasant from the soil'.[28] Yet, through his contacts with the *philosophes*, he was acquainted with physiocratic doctrine, or with the arguments advanced in England and Scotland for the dissolution of older communal ties by the all-conquering market, and set out expressly to refute them.[29]

Rousseau's response to Enlightenment political economy was cast, however, in an ethical form, being founded upon the cardinal distinction between the self-love of the 'man of nature', and the vanity of the 'man of society'. The former, though tempered by pity, was absolute; the latter, relative, and requiring, therefore, constant comparison between self and other. Due to the ramifying complexity of social relations, each vainly sought to occupy the pre-eminent place in an order that, being sustained by struggle over goods, money or reputation, was the quintessence of disorder.[30] History was, as Lionel Gossman has put it, saturated with evil.[31]

The third comment I would wish to make regarding the perceived contradiction in Rousseau's political thought follows on naturally from Gossman's judgement. If historical time were evil, the very possibility of a just city surviving among a multitude of large states must needs be Utopian. So violent, then, was Rousseau's recoil from the disorder of the world that he seemed at home only in 'chimerae', which were both inversions of existing social relations and, the future being walled up, tableaux of ancient–modern regeneration. Jean Fabre has noted that the draft constitutions for Corsica and for Poland certainly share some of the characteristic features of the eighteenth-century Utopia, namely, a tendency to codify in the minutest detail assemblies, festivals and everyday life. He adds that Rousseau tended to 'create a void around his political institutions, as around Emile's political education, isolating the Corsicans in their Mediterranean, the Valaisans in their mountains, the Poles in their vast plain'.[32] It is true that Rousseau's contemporaries, even where amicably disposed, tended to find his reasoning 'paradoxical' in the extreme, even 'chimerical', that is to say, altogether unconnected to really existing circumstances. Yet, though Rousseau sometimes flaunted the chimerical status of his projects, at other times he denied it, the term itself invariably marking a point of extreme moral and political tension in his writings. As he quite rightly insisted, had he done no more than construct a system, nothing further would have been heard of *The Social Contract*, or rather, it would have been relegated, along with Plato's *Republic* and More's *Utopia*, to 'the land of chimerae'. Rousseau, however, had 'depicted an object that really existed'.[33] As I demonstrate in chapter 6, he did indeed still live in a world containing free cities, weakened but nonetheless defiant in the face of the absolutist monarchies.

Much as Rousseau had wavered in the course of the 1740s, his republican origins were therefore a source of great pride to him.[34] Through Fabricius, he might learn what he, a Genevan, could do for humanity. In summoning an 'inhabitant of some distant country', a 'stranger', it was as if he hoped that a Roman Consul and Censor of the third century BC – as much estranged from the Rome of a later age as he, a citizen of Geneva, was at odds with monarchical France – might offer him a vantage point from which to study European mores ethnographically.[35] Fabricius thus calls to mind the travellers in Montesquieu's *Lettres Persanes*, a work that likewise contains vehement denunciations of despotism and fervent professions of republican faith. Yet the virtuous Roman shade was a more substantial being to Rousseau than ever Uzbeck and Rica had been to Montesquieu. For Fabricius was not simply a representative from an exotic other world, whose ingenuous enquiries shed a glaring light on the iniquities of modern, commercial society, nor, indeed, was he merely an Ancient entrusted with the task of shaming the Moderns, since Rousseau despised mere antiquarianism.[36] Rousseau did not only imagine himself a Roman among Parisians, as Machiavelli, in retirement, had donned a toga and conversed with the heroic dead; he further believed himself to be 'a member of the sovereign', a citizen of Geneva, though residing in an absolute monarchy.

The illumination of Vincennes was thus, for all its ramifications, blindingly simple: Fabricius had reminded him what a city was, a thing that the modern world had all but forgotten.[37] Living in a historical period that was dominated by the arcane procedures of reason of state, by the equally occult powers of the market and of the division of labour, and by the devastation wreaked by mercenary armies, Rousseau had been granted a vision, incarnated in the figure of a virtuous Roman but staged in the adopted city of Calvin, of liberty, equality and confederation.

## Roman virtue

One of the tasks of the historians of classical Antiquity was to propose objects of emulation. As Livy observed:

> what chiefly makes the study of history wholesome and profitable is this, that you behold the lessons of every kind of experience set forth as on a conspicuous monument; from these you may choose for yourself and for your own state what to imitate, from these mark for avoidance what is shameful in the conception and shameful in the result.

Since, in Livy's words, 'there never was a state either greater or more moral, or richer in good examples', why had Rousseau chosen Fabricius to deliver the prosopopoeia, rather than some other virtuous citizen?[38] For the early centuries of the Roman republic could offer Lucius Junius Brutus, who restored liberty to Rome after the tyranny of Tarquin the

Proud, in 509 BC; Gaius Mucius Scaevola, who slew the secretary of Lars
Porsenna, in 508 BC; Horatius Cocles, who defended the bridge across
the Tiber against the Etruscan champions that same year; Cincinnatus,
who was summoned from his farm to become Dictator in 458 BC; Marcus
Manlius Capitolinus, who saved the Capitol in 390 BC; Marcus Attilius
Regulus, who kept his word, not his life; Cato the Elder; Cato of Utica
and many others. Indeed, in Rousseau's *Dernière Réponse*, many such
names feature. 'I admire the Brutuses, the Decii, the Lucretias, the
Virginias and the Scaevolas', Charles Bordes had written, 'but still more
shall I admire a powerful and well-governed state.' To which Rousseau
had retorted, 'a powerful and well-governed state! And so too would I,
truly!', as if to say, without such virtues good government could not be.
After a brief peroration on Lucius Junius Brutus, Rousseau then
observed that 'at the time of Pyrrhus, all Romans were Fabriciuses,
whereas during the reign of Titus he was the only honest man'.[39] Since
the precondition of political liberty was the liberty of each and every
citizen, Fabricius was clearly but one of many witnesses that Rousseau
might have summoned. He could, for example, have called Manius
Curius Dentatus, a Consul in 275 BC and the general responsible for the
final defeat of Pyrrhus in that same year. For, Rousseau observed, just as
Fabricius had refused Pyrrhus's gold, so had Curius Dentatus spurned
the presents of the Samnite ambassadors.[40] Plutarch further records
how, when the latter visited the austere consul, they found him roasting
turnips in the ashes of his fire; other sources state that he ate them from a
wooden dish. When the ambassadors offered him lavish gifts, he refused,
saying that 'he reckoned it more honourable to command those who had
gold, than to have any himself'. Years later, Cato the Censor's estate
stood next to that formerly cultivated by Curius Dentatus and, again
according to Plutarch, he was profoundly impressed by the tiny size of
the holding and by the crude nature of the dwelling, and wondered at the
fact that the first Roman of the time, the man who had tamed the
proudest and most war-like nations of Italy, had continued to work his
land with his own hands.[41]

   Caius Fabricius Luscinus, Consul in 282 and 278 BC, and Censor in 275
BC, was formed in the same mould, then, as Curius Dentatus. In addition,
his censorship was one of the most celebrated in the whole history of
Rome, for he and Quintus Aemilianus Papus had excluded Publius
Cornelius Rufinus from the Senate, on the grounds that he owned ten
pounds of silver plate for use at banquets.[42] I take Fabricius to be as
perfect an example as could be found, though many flanked him, of those
simple, roughly hewn Romans who, in the early centuries of the Republic, sought, in Machiavelli's terms, to return to its first principles. Indeed,
so honoured was he that the Senate waived a prohibition enshrined in the

Twelve Tables, and permitted his burial within the city boundaries.[43] A battle-hardened general, he was neither wealthy nor a member of one of the great patrician houses but a champion, rather, of the small farmers. The backdrop to this image of austere, even harsh Roman virtue was the First and Second Pyrrhic Wars, the period that, according to Livy, was more productive than any other in virtues.[44]

Indeed, Fabricius had himself served on an embassy to Pyrrhus. If this legation was, in Niebuhr's words, 'more celebrated than any other is or will be', it was 'because in it Pyrrhus became acquainted with Fabricius', and 'the difference in the virtue of two noble men, who, belonging to nations entirely different, had no resemblance at all in education, belief, manners and cultivation, is worthy of the most serious attention'.[45] Furthermore, Cineas, the other figure from classical Antiquity named in the prosopopoeia and an honoured confidante and friend of Pyrrhus, was sent to Rome to state his master's terms to the beleaguered city. Since Livy's account of this period of Rome's history is lost, we may assume that, though other, more fragmentary sources have been suggested, Rousseau's portrait of Fabricius is largely drawn from Plutarch's lives of Pyrrhus and of Cato the Censor, for the moral degradation that the resurrected Fabricius discovers in Imperial Rome had already wreaked havoc in Cato's own lifetime. Fabricius therefore stood at the initial point in the cycle of decline of the Roman polity, with Cato the Censor positioned at a stage at which the 'ancienne simplicité', though all but destroyed, was still remembered. During his moral reform, Rousseau undoubtedly identified most closely with the latter, a man who had embarked upon a similar, exemplary ascesis himself. Finally, Cato of Utica and Marcus Brutus, who also feature prominently in Plutarch, represent the lowest point in this *anakuklōsis*, for they carried an image of the fatherland in their hearts, though no such fatherland any longer existed.[46]

As a Greek historian of the first century, Plutarch's abiding concern was with relations between his native land and Rome, his *Lives* therefore being disposed in pairs, a Greek and then a Roman. At a time when it was becoming commonplace for those born in Greece to become senators and consuls, and when Athens and Delphi were held in honour once again, Plutarch wished to press the claims of both worlds. Rousseau, however, though more deeply enamoured of the *Lives* than of any other book – he was as entranced by it, and shed as many tears over it as did Vauvenargues or Alfieri – was always critical of the luxury and corruption of Athens, the prototype of the Paris of the *philosophes*, and championed Sparta and Rome instead.[47]

We may more readily understand the prestige of Fabricius if we bear in mind that, when he held office in Rome, Greek culture had as yet had relatively little impact upon the city. The remarkable reputation that the key embassies of the First and Second Pyrrhic Wars enjoy in the histories derives from the fact that they were thought to represent the first encounter between the two cultures. Cineas, for example, was the very first Greek envoy to appear before the Roman Senate, in the aftermath of Pyrrhus's victory over the Romans. Although the senators had, like Fabricius and Curius Dentatus, rejected the gifts offered to them, a number were on the point of yielding to Cineas's blandishments, when Appius Claudius Caecus (Censor in 312 BC, Consul in 307 BC and 296 BC) was carried into the Senate on a litter. In his celebrated speech, believed to have been the first in Rome ever to be committed to writing, he reminded the Senate of Roman virtue and rebuked the people for their faintheartedness. It is at this point in Plutarch's narrative that we hear Cineas's celebrated remark, quoted in the prosopopoeia, regarding the 'assembly of kings'.[48]

Fabricius's own embassy to Pyrrhus mirrors Cineas's appearance before the Senate. Unmoved by Carthaginian gold, and undaunted by the trumpetings of an elephant, 'un cri effroyable et horrible à merveilles', he was still less impressed by Cineas's philosophy. The conversation at dinner between the two men, which is mentioned by Montesquieu, earns only a glancing reference in Rousseau.[49] Plutarch, whose real sympathies were for a kind of Platonism, roundly condemned the Epicureanism of Cineas, and though, as I have said, Rousseau does not refer to the episode directly, he does observe that the 'seductive and subtle Greeks' had so corrupted the Romans that 'Rome was filled with philosophers and orators, military discipline was neglected, agriculture was held in contempt, men formed sects and forgot their country. To the sacred names of liberty, disinterestedness and obedience to law, succeeded those of Epicurus, Zeno and Arcesilaus.'[50] Cineas thus saw Rome even as it was undergoing momentous changes. No longer a village, not yet a great city, its 'thatched roofs and rustic hearths' were disappearing. Display of the trophies of war had become more brazen, public buildings more magnificent, and roads were often paved. When Curius Dentatus's triumph over Pyrrhus and the Samnites was held in 275 BC, Greek statuary and works of art, fiercely denounced in the prosopopoeia, were introduced into the city for the first time.[51] Cato the Censor's self-appointed task, a generation later, was to recall Rome to its first principles. Plutarch admits that Cato had studied with Nearchus, a Pythagorean philosopher in Tarentum, and that, though he had learned Greek late in life, his writings were embellished with examples taken word for word from the culture whose influence he so resolutely opposed.[52] Rousseau, however, highlights his antipathy to philosophical and rhetorical schools that lacked any anchorage in civic and military virtues: when Carneades, Critolaos and Diogenes came on an embassy to Rome, Cato did his best to send them back as swiftly as possible to Athens.[53]

Rousseau's choice of historical setting for the prosopopoeia had therefore been far from arbitrary. Some have seen Fabricius as but one of a crowd of noble Romans, each of whom would have been disgusted by the turpitude of Imperial Rome. In the first discourse in general, and in the prosopopoeia in particular, 'the ancient Roman simplicity' puts 'useless pomp or studied elegance to shame', yet in Fabricius's day the city really was becoming at once more luxurious and more lettered. Ostentation might soon lie in proffering a wooden platter rather than a silver dish.

## Rousseau's Rome

Montesquieu, a being raised for judgement, had measured the whole span of Roman history, from the earliest days of the Republic to the fall of Byzantium in 1453, and at first glance there is nothing in Rousseau's fiery writings to bear comparison with so lofty, extended and imperious a treatment. Lacking any training in philological method or in the historical study of law, the author of *The Social Contract* had little understanding of, and still less sympathy for, the Empire. Thrilled though he had been by the material aspects of Roman civilization, from the Pont du Gard to the insignia of authority, it is almost impossible to imagine him drawing inspiration, like Edward Gibbon, from the vicissitudes of Imperial coinage. However, no matter how fragmentary and, in scholarly terms, outmoded his account of Rome was, the history of the city was central to the development of his political thought.

Though the voice of Fabricius echoes through the first discourse, the precise nature of Roman liberty was obscured by the many, highly coloured references to other free peoples, both ancient and modern. Rousseau was not slow to grasp the shortcomings of his comparative method and, shortly after winning the Academy of Dijon's prize, declared that it would be better, if one wished to correlate advances in knowledge with changes in mores, to study the history of a single people.[54] Since this is precisely what he seems to have done in *The Social Contract*, it is surely appropriate to treat the passages in that work concerned with the history of Rome as of central, not peripheral importance to the development of his notion of the polis. This editors have shown a marked reluctance to do.[55]

Rousseau attached great importance to the moment at which cities were founded, for it was then that the false contract was annulled and a true contract established. Yet even in the case of Rome, the surviving records of the city's earliest days were little better than fables: 'The name "Rome", which is said to derive from **Romulus**, is really Greek, and it means **force**; the name "Numa" is also Greek and it means law. Is it very probable that the first two kings should have borne before they reigned names so clearly related to what they did?'[56] One could be forgiven for supposing that here Rousseau, like Vico or Niebuhr, doubted the historical existence of individual lawgivers and believed their names to be emblems of social groups, yet these paragraphs probably reflect the historical Pyrrhonism of Beaufort, and are merely token.[57] For Rousseau was persuaded that, in the founding of a city, the genius of a particular individual was of crucial importance; being a work of art, it required a creator who was above or outside the conflict of opposed groups. Special attention should be paid here to the use of the term 'extraordinary':

> The lawgiver is, in every respect, an extraordinary man in the state. Extraordinary not only because of his genius but equally because of his office, which is neither that of the government nor that of the sovreign. The office which gives the republic its constitution has no place in that constitution. It is a special and superior function which has nothing to do with empire over men.[58]

Thus, the lawgiver was not merely a paragon. Since his task was to communicate a vision of order where there was only disorder, he had to stand altogether outside the system of ranks that he was to found. He had, in short, to be almost an apparition from elsewhere, from that margin of liberty, extending between cities, in which so many in the eighteenth century still believed, but of which we, with our nationalist sensibilities, have little or no conception. A clue is supplied by the relation between territory and settlement in a number of Pasolini's films, in part because of his love of the *trecento* and *quattrocento* painters. Rousseau himself had in mind not only Lycurgus, who abdicated his kingship when he gave Sparta laws, but the legislators of the other Greek cities also, the *podestà* of the Italian *comuni*, and even Calvin.[59] It is worth recalling that in late eighteenth-century Italy the rules for the election of the *podestà* sometimes still stipulated that candidates be natives of another city. Gian Domenico Romagnosi, who held office under these terms, is the subject of an extended discussion in my postscript (chapter 10).

The charge generally laid against Rousseau was that he had not accounted for the education of the educator, and that his argument was therefore circular. How did the lawgiver attain to truth in the first place? For Vico, the *verum* arose out of the *certum*, the true out of the certain, and universal precepts owed their origin to earlier, particular applications of law:

> The history of human ideas clearly convicts of their common error all those who, under the influence of the mistaken popular belief in the superlative wisdom of the ancients, have held that Minos, the first lawgiver of the gentile nations, Theseus at Athens, Lycurgus at Sparta, and Romulus and other Kings at Rome established universal laws. For the most ancient laws . . . were each conceived to command or forbid in but a single case.[60]

He was thus more concerned with the slow crystallization of institutions and laws than with the heroic virtues of individuals, and his historiographical scepticism about Fabricius, Curius Dentatus and Mucius Scaevola, whom he mentions by name, is compounded by a moral distaste for their asperities and improprieties.[61] Rousseau too had allowed that 'the art of generalizing one's ideas [was] one of the most difficult, and most belated operations of the human understanding', and that, given the ignorance of the multitude, 'Gods would be needed to give men laws', but resolved the difficulty by accepting, as Vico could not, the quasi-divine status of lawgivers.[62] In this regard, Rousseau added a high Christian gloss to the pagan 'great souls' who, in the accounts given by Montesquieu, Diderot or Helvétius, had founded earthly cities.

However, Rousseau seems to entertain two conflicting versions of the origin of the city. At times, as we have seen, a people is moulded by a quasi-divine legislator, for 'at the birth of societies, the leaders of republics create the institutions'.[63] At other times, a people assembles of its own accord. This is the case with the original formulation of the theory of the social contract, where no mention is made of any lawgiver. There, in order to refute the iusnaturalist justifications of monarchy advanced by Grotius or Barbeyrac, Rousseau paints a picture of the sovereign people effecting its own transformation from 'aggregation' to 'association': 'before considering the act by which a people submits to a king, we ought to scrutinise the act by which people become a people, for that act, being necessarily antecedent to the other, is the real foundation of society'.[64] He further observes that the act by which a people submits to a king 'presupposes public deliberation', and it is clearly tempting to identify such gatherings with the public assemblies of the mountain Swiss, the Macedonians or the Franks. Even in the case of Rome, Montesquieu had emphasized the elective nature of the monarchy, and there are passages in Rousseau that appear to reflect this view.[65] Certainly, at the very beginning of Book 1, Chapter 6 of The Social Contract, the narrative dovetails with that of the discourse on inequality, and describes how, the state of nature having degenerated into a state of war, individual wills attained a sort of unity, and an 'association', 'city', 'republic' or 'body politic' was formed.[66]

The second interpretation seems, however, to be wrecked by the assertion that a 'blind multitude' is not itself capable of framing laws and is, indeed, as the discourse on inequality would make brutally clear, at the mercy of 'imposters'.[67] Hence, Rousseau concludes, the need for a lawgiver. The category 'people' thus floats awkwardly between two, not wholly compatible, meanings. When, for example, in Book 1, Chapter 6, Rousseau had asked what it was that made a people a people, the term meant, as Book 4, Chapters 4–7 confirmed, something akin to *populus Romanus*, since the ordering of Rome stood as a model for all polities. However, in Book 2, Chapters 7–11, a people was a material to be shaped by a quasi-divine lawgiver. It could be argued that Rousseau was looking at the foundation of a free polity by turns from a subjective and an objective point of view. There was after all the same tension in Aristotle, who had asserted both that there existed an immanent impulse towards the formation of a polis, and that 'the man who first constructed such an association was none the less the greatest of benefactors'.[68] Where Rousseau, however, parted company with the entire Aristotelian tradition was in his insistence that no social instinct could be presupposed. This radical refusal of teleology was to issue in paradox. On the one hand, it granted a more complete liberty than the iusnaturalists had in general allowed; on the other, if there was no guarantee that 'the predilection which each man has for himself' would ever be overcome, and a love of order imparted, such an occurrence, against all probability, was perforce miraculous. So liberty was at once given and refused. Or, to phrase it a little differently, the account of the origin of value that Rousseau bequeathed to the nineteenth century was intrinsically ambiguous. In the age of cities, the legislator had been the middle term between humanity and divinity; in the age of nations, his Titanic measures were shrouded in the mists of customary law or social being. As I show in part III, a people ceased to be simply either a collective sovereign assembled in an august place or a material fit to be moulded by a free, if sometimes terrible, intelligence, and became itself a full truth, at once speaking and spoken.

### Romulus, patricians and clients

Convinced that written annals merge imperceptibly with fables, Rousseau favoured a robustly naturalistic treatment of the primitive settlements that precede the great European cities.[69] Like Livy, he saw such settlements as lawless and bandit-infested, and sometimes lent Romulus the attributes of the brigands who surrounded him. Yet a lawgiver, and the first king of Rome, was necessarily at one remove from villainy.[70] Machiavelli had recorded Romulus's ruthlessness, his murder of his brother Remus, and his complicity in the killing of Titus Tatius the Sabine.[71] He acknowledged, however, that the founder of a people had to be prepared to employ extraordinary measures if he were to hold his recalcitrant material to its new form. Armed prophets, he declared, had succeeded where unarmed ones had failed.[72] Rousseau followed Machiavelli, or Montesquieu, so closely that he too held that the founder, or the adroit restorer, of a republic was at times obliged to do things that transcended ordinary morality. He thus referred more than once to Brutus's terrible predicament, after the expulsion of the Tarquins, when he was forced to choose between paternal love and civic duty.

According to Livy, Romulus had drafted a code of laws and founded a mixed form of government, tempering his own authority with that of the senate and the *comitia curiata*.[73] Rousseau likewise revered a virtuous senate, as the prosopopoeia of Fabricius makes plain; respect for the wisdom of the elders was, he believed, an essential feature of a well-ordered society. Rousseau held that there were two kinds of inequality, one natural or physical, the other moral or political, and he set out in his second discourse to account for the disorder of his own time, in which the strong had become servants of the weak, the old of the young, the wise of the foolish, and to explain why 'a handful of people should gorge themselves with superfluities while the hungry multitude goes in want of necessities'.[74] The generation that made the Revolution sometimes took such passages to be a justification for an extreme egalitarianism, and for an enforced redistribution of property; Babeuf, for example, was inspired by them, as I show in chapter 6. Rousseau, however, was opposed to agrarian laws, and spoke of the Gracchi only to condemn them. He did not think it possible to restore natural aristocracy either, since it was a form suited only to simple peoples and was invariably swept aside by growing inequalities of wealth or power; obdurate patterns of inheritance would then favour patrician families and bolster a hereditary aristocracy, in his opinion the very worst sort of government.[75]

Since Rousseau had embraced the view of Machiavelli that Roman liberty had come into existence only gradually, in the course of a series of hard-fought struggles between plebeians and patricians, one may wonder why he took such pains to establish that its basic elements were in existence even at the time of Romulus. A plausible answer would be that, for Rousseau, what was bad in nascent society could be put to good use by means of 'perfected art'. Thus, if measured against a senate of the American forests, the Roman patriciate was plainly a degenerate form but, within the context of a well-ordered society, its underlying principle could serve to guarantee individual liberty.

I will try to clarify this point by means of an excursus on the relation between patron and client. One should understand, first of all, that a client was not a citizen; admitted into the gens through a range of formal procedures, he had no real legal status but was bound in a relation of *fides* to his patron.[76] This relation required obedience, homage and labour on the part of the client, and defence, legal or otherwise, on the part of the patron. Clients provided the bulk of the labour force on the Ager Publicus, but their ownership rights were precarious, and could be revoked at will. Being a part of the gens, they voted with the patricians in the *comitia*. Rousseau commented as follows:

> Romulus, in establishing the curiae, aimed to balance the Senate against the people and balance the people against the Senate, while himself dominating both alike. Under this arrangement he gave the people all the authority of numbers to balance the authority of power and wealth which he left to the patricians. But true to the spirit of the monarchy, he nevertheless gave the great advantage to the patricians, in that they could buy clients to influence numerical majorities. This admirable institution of patrons and clients was a masterpiece of politics and humanity, without which the patriciate, so contrary to the spirit of the Republic, could not have survived. To Rome alone belongs the honour of giving the world this noble example, from which no abuse has ever come, but which has never been followed elsewhere.[77]

It is true that the relation was reciprocal, and that a breach of *fides* on the part of a patron was as devastating in its consequences as an equivalent act on the part of a client but, notwithstanding this reciprocity, both the relation itself, and its effects upon voting in the *comitia*, ought logically to have been anathema to Rousseau.[78] One cannot help but be puzzled as to why a philosopher so committed to the principle of independence should have lauded so complete a dependence.

If, by way of contrast, we turn to Vico's *New Science*, we find that the relation between client and patron is equated with that binding vassal and lord in the Christian Middle Ages. Clients, so the argument goes, had enjoyed no ownership of land until granted bonitary rights by Servius Tullius and then, through the Law of the Twelve Tables, quiritary ownership. Set to work on the Ager Publicus, they had at first been no better than serfs, and indeed Vico believed that the feudal relations of 'returned barbarism' were reminiscent of the heroic commonwealths, archaic Rome among them. Romulus was therefore no Moses but one of a number of founders of cities who, in order to secure a compliant labour force for their fields, opened an asylum; Cadmus had done the same in Thebes, as had Theseus in Athens.[79]

Though Vico had confused clients with plebeians, where the great nineteenth-century historians of ancient Rome would distinguish between them, Niebuhr, Mommsen and Fustel de Coulanges also compared the patron–client relation to vassalage.[80] Marx was likewise convinced that the liberty of the *civis Romanus* rested upon the labour of clients on the Ager Publicus.[81] This being the case, it is hard to grasp just why Rousseau, with his prescient understanding of the destructive effects of modern, commercial society, should have praised so feudal a relation. I show below that the existence of extremes of wealth and poverty, and the capacity of the rich to gain power by buying the votes of the poor, marked in Rousseau's view the descent of a society into terminal disorder. This being so, the patricians' control of their clients' votes ought to have been condemned out of hand. Why then had Rousseau extolled the arrangement, describing it as 'a masterpiece of politics and humanity', instead of identifying it with the grievous state of war preceding the authentic contract?

Several answers are possible. If one were to condescend to Rousseau, as so many do, one could argue that his belief in great legislators was such that he felt obliged to celebrate Romulus's recorded achievements and therefore to take Plutarch at his word when he states that Rome's first king had created the patron–client relation, and that it was a laudable institution.[82] It is true that Rousseau's classical culture was that of an autodidact, derived from the radical artisans he had known as a child in Geneva and therefore all but untouched by the corrosive philological procedures of Northern humanism. Yet the charge of naivety ought always to be a last resort, and in this case it altogether fails to do justice to the elegance of the arguments expounded in *The Social Contract*. A second accusation has been that Rousseau wished quite simply to champion a form of feudalism.[83]

Though there was a hierarchical aspect to his conception of the well-ordered society, as my discussion of the reforms of Servius Tullius will show, it is hard to comprehend how the treatise that inspired the anti-feudal rhetoric of 1789–91 could itself have been a defence of feudalism. I find it more plausible to argue that, since monarchical Rome had collapsed, prior to the expulsion of the Tarquins, into despotism, Rousseau viewed the city, much as he viewed the Europe of his own day, as a place from which liberty had fled. In so desolate a circumstance, the *fides* of the patron–client relation, even though forged in the spirit of the monarchy, might be a shield and a consolation. It was, after all, possible for a 'particular interest' to offer the sort of protection that, in a republic, would be provided by the general will.[84] By the same token, were a revival of liberty among a corrupted people by some miracle to occur, as it had once in Rome, in Sparta, in the United Provinces and in the Swiss cantons, some residue of morality would offer a foothold on a sheer cliff face.[85]

Discussion of Romulus's achievements would rest incomplete if no mention were made of his division of the land. Montesquieu had noted that the Roman army, like the nomadic Scythians, divided their booty equally. So too, he went on to remark, did the founders of ancient republics divide property equally, thus creating a well-ordered society and a powerful army, with each soldier (and farmer) having the same interest in defending the homeland.[86] Rousseau likewise affirmed that the sole source of wealth of a nascent state was its common land, and that Romulus had divided the Ager Publicus into three parts, reserving a third for the payment of magistrates and other officials, a third for the upkeep of priests and for sacred matters, and a third for division among citizens. The condition of the Republic's farmers was then contrasted with that of peasants in France, for the former had plots which, though small, were freehold, whereas the latter were emburdened by crippling taxes and tithes.[87] It was these plots to which the Plutarchian Cato the Censor sought to revert, when Rome had begun its precipitous descent into luxury, and they were reputed to consist of no more than *bina iugera*, that is, two and a half acres. Numa, in Plutarch's account, further consolidated individual property in Rome, both by adding a religious sanction to boundary markers, and by distributing land conquered by Romulus to the poor.[88]

Both Montesquieu and Rousseau, like the classical authorities upon whom they relied, believed that such equality of fortunes could not be easily sustained nor, once undermined, could it be readily restored, for the state was a work of art, enjoying proportion only to the degree that laws or magistracies preserved it from moral harm. In nascent society, however,

the proportion, which nothing maintained, was soon broken; the stronger did more productive work; the more adroit did better work, the more ingenious devised ways of abridging his labour; the farmer had greater need of iron, or the smith greater need of wheat, and with both working equally, the one earned plenty while the other had hardly enough to live on. It is thus that natural inequality merges imperceptibly with artificial inequality, and the differences of men increased by differences of circumstance, make themselves more visible and more permanent in their effects, and begin to influence in the same proportion the destiny of individuals.[89]

One way of forestalling this burgeoning inequality was to guard those moments in the cycle of human existence at which wealth was transmitted from one person to another, that is to say, 'the point not protected by the laws'.[90] Both Montesquieu and Rousseau regarded the Roman laws governing dowries, gifts, inheritances and wills as so many devices for safeguarding equality between persons.[91] To avert corruption, it was sufficient that persons of middling fortune should predominate, for it was on such practitioners of moderation that the laws had most effect.[92] The wealthy might disdain the laws, for they could buy the votes of the needy, and in this regard both rich and poor were a danger to the republic. The general will, the truth of the social order, was therefore perpetually at risk from factions, which were an expression of the individual wills of the rich. The *res publica* was in this sense a 'general association', a public thing endangered by the obscure privacy of sectional associations.

To forestall the emergence of factions, two different methods might be adopted: the Spartan on the one hand, and the Athenian and Roman on the other. Lycurgus's 'unique and sublime invention', Rousseau observed, had been to ban all sectional associations from the state, so allowing citizens complete freedom to make up their own minds.[93] Yet he stood a giant at the gleaming edge of history, his uniqueness being remarked upon by both Machiavelli and Rousseau (especially prior to 1762).[94] If, then, there were to be no sectional associations, as in the early history of societies there had been 'tribes' or 'nations', their number should be increased, so as to ward off inequality. This had in fact been the solution adopted in both Athens and Rome. As Machiavelli had stated:

> some divisions injure republics, while others are beneficial to them. When accompanied by factions and parties they are injurious; but when maintained without them they contribute to their prosperity. The legislator of a republic, since it is impossible to prevent the existence of dissensions, must at least take care to prevent the growth of faction.[95]

This passage is prefaced by the observation, omitted by Rousseau, that 'those who think a republic may be kept in perfect unity of purpose are greatly deceived', and it is thus consonant with the general emphasis in the *Discourses* upon the ultimately fruitful consequences for Rome of turmoil and civil strife. Machiavelli went on to distinguish between two paths to reputation and power, one public and the other private:

> Influence is acquired publicly by winning a battle, taking possession of a territory, fulfilling the duties of an embassy with care and prudence, or by

giving wise counsel attended by a happy result. Private methods are confer-
ring benefits upon individuals, defending them against the magistrates, sup-
porting them with money and raising them to undeserved honours; or with
public games and entertainments gaining the affection of the populace.[96]

Rousseau gave his fullest account of the institutions that debarred such
private routes to honour or influence in his discussion of the sixth king of
Rome, Servius Tullius. But what of the city's second king?

## Numa and the civic oath

All extant sources ascribe the founding of Rome's religious institutions to
Numa Pompilius. Livy, for example, called him 'divini auctor iuris',
while Machiavelli wrote that

> Numa, finding the people ferocious and desiring to reduce them to civil
> obedience conjoined with the arts of peace, turned to religion as the instru-
> ment necessary above all others for the maintenance of a civilized state, and so
> constituted it that there was never for so many centuries so great a fear of God
> as there was in this republic.[97]

If his part in the ultimate triumph of Rome was greater even than that of
Romulus, it was because he had succeeded in instilling in his people a
profound reverence for the act of swearing an oath.[98] Machiavelli then
referred to a number of celebrated occasions upon which Roman citizens, in grave danger, had stayed at their post, being held there by
nothing more substantial than their word. Montesquieu later referred to
this passage, and Rousseau, in the first draft of *The Social Contract*,
defined the oath as one of the guarantees, indeed as the paramount
guarantee, of the commitment of the contractant to the common cause.[99]
It is true that he then conceded that, if set against the brute force that the
general will had entrusted to its executive arm, the mere giving of one's
word was a paltry gesture, and that, sensing the contradiction in his
argument, he omitted this passage from the published version, yet the
oath haunts Rousseau's political thought.[100] As I remarked in chapter 2,
some have accepted Kant's claim that the social contract is entirely a
matter of right, an 'idea of reason', and not of fact, yet the draft
constitution for the island of Corsica had stipulated a general assembly of
the nation, 'each in his own town, borough or parish', at which an oath
would be sworn on the Bible.[101] Union, like submission, could be
enacted in no other fashion. In France, the breach with the monarchy,
and the Third Estate's bid for legitimacy in June 1789, were consolidated

through an oath in the Jeu des Paumes. Likewise, the festivals of federation, and that of 14 July 1790 in particular, created the city-nation through a ritual that culminated in the swearing of an oath on the altar of the fatherland. I would therefore maintain that those who read Rousseau through the writings of the idealist philosophers forget that the city as such, and therefore the fact of assembly, subsisted in his thought as a concrete entity.

More generally, Numa symbolized the precedence generally accorded in the eighteenth century to mores as against laws. For swearing an oath to the fatherland was in effect contracting to love all of its laws, for 'the first of the laws is to respect the laws'.[102] Since only religion could found such respect, Numa was of unrivalled importance to Rome. Once the mores of a people were corrupted, the proliferation of laws served no purpose at all. Indeed, a plethora of laws was, for Rousseau, for Romme or for Saint-Just, proof that a people was lost to liberty.

The great lawgivers of Antiquity had therefore been as much concerned with the embodiment of civic value in rituals or in objects as with revelation or legislation. Rousseau had himself painted Numa as less terrible than the unyielding Lycurgus, but he agreed with Machiavelli that the second king of Rome had been more important than the first, that he had been its true founder, and that he had turned a nest of brigands into an indissoluble body by means of apparently frivolous and superstitious rituals.[103] During the French Revolution, the piety of the citizens of ancient Rome was taken for granted both by the Jacobins and by, for example, La Harpe. What was disputed, rather, was the identity of the 'national' religion.

## The reforms of Servius Tullius

Rousseau regarded the three 'tribes' founded by Romulus, the Ramnenses, the Tatientes and the Luceres, as merely the aggregations of a nascent society, and therefore as sources of disorder. For the third tribe 'grew continuously as more foreigners were recruited, and it soon contained more members than the other two tribes combined'.[104] Given their name, the Luceres were thought by some to have been those who had taken refuge in the asylum of Romulus, a *lucus* or clearing between two groves;[105] at any rate they were in Rousseau's eyes a lawless rabble, later described as the *turba foriensis*, those who swarmed in the forum.[106] Indeed, both Montesquieu and Rousseau believed that the purpose of Servius Tullius's reforms had been to rein in the superstitious multitude, and both reckoned that the Republic was doomed once Marius, in the war with Jugurtha, recruited such vagabonds to serve in his legions.

In order to rectify the imbalance between the Luceres and the other two tribes, in Rousseau's opinion a 'dangerous fault', Servius Tullius altered 'the basis of the division and, in place of the racial distinction, which he abolished, he introduced one based on the district of the town occupied by each of the tribes'. Instead of three tribes, there were then four, each of which was named after and occupied one of the hills of Rome.[107] Alongside the urban tribes, Servius Tullius created fifteen others, known as rustic tribes, 'because they were formed of inhabitants of the country, arranged in so many cantons'.[108] Subsequently, sixteen more tribes were added, making thirty-five in all.

Three points may be made concerning Rousseau's interpretation. To begin with, one should note his belief that the founding of a city entailed the subordination of ethnic ties. A lawgiver had to work a dramatic transformation in the human materials to hand, and there had to be a moment of assembly (and oath-taking), at which natural powers were replaced by an 'artificial and collective body'.[109] The lawgiver established, no matter how fleetingly, a radical equality in which persons as such were mustered. Like Cleisthenes at Athens, Servius Tullius had reordered the city in terms of locality, instead of kinship, and though the true significance of this revolution in social organization was perceived only by Fustel de Coulanges and Morgan, in the second half of the nineteenth century, Rousseau well understood that the state's good and that of the earthed tribe were opposed.

Second, we may begin to grasp the importance for Rousseau of Servius Tullius's creation of the four urban tribes if we recall the polarity between urbanity and rusticity in the first discourse and in the sequence of related polemical writings, and if we bear in mind the frankly rustic attributes of Fabricius, Curius Dentatus or Cato the Censor. Livy, who had ascribed this reform to a much later figure, the censor Quintus Fabius Maximus, made it plain that Roman virtue did not lie with the city tribes: 'partly for the sake of harmony, partly that the elections might not be in the hands of the basest of the people, [he] culled out all the market place mob [*turba foriensis*] and put them into four tribes, which he called "city-tribes"'.[110] Machiavelli saw the importance of this passage, as did Montesquieu, and though Fabius Maximus is not mentioned by name in *The Social Contract*, Rousseau agreed that the long-uncorrupted condition of the city's mores could be ascribed to the division between the urban and the rural tribes, the latter being the undamaged mainspring of the city. When Rousseau wrote here of 'the taste of the early Romans for a country life', he once again had the heroes of Plutarch, and their plots of moderate size, in mind.[111]

Since the country areas were the locii of Roman virtue, the censors would transfer nefarious elements – foreigners, freedmen and those guilty of corruption – to the city tribes. It was when the censors abandoned this practice, and allowed citizens to join whichever tribe they wished, that in Rousseau's opinion the city went into decline.[112] To understand the importance of the censorship, a magistracy so much applauded by the republicans of the year II and so much deplored by Madame de Staël, by Benjamin Constant and by the rank and file of nineteenth-century liberalism, we need to consider Servius Tullius's reforms in greater detail.

From Livy and from Dionysius of Halicarnassus we learn that Servius Tullius had divided the citizens of Rome into five classes, the first owning property to the value of 100,000 *asses*, the second to the value of 75,000 *asses*, the third to the value of 50,000 *asses*, the fourth to the value of 25,000 *asses*, and the fifth to the value of 12,500 *asses* (or, if you follow Livy, 11,000 *asses*).[113] Rousseau noted that the Roman king had 'distributed the whole Roman people into six classes, arranged neither on a personal nor on a residential basis, but according to wealth', and earlier passages in *The Social Contract* make it plain that the reader is meant to applaud such a distribution.[114] Thus, Rousseau had already declared that a republic, though hereditary aristocracy was debarred, should be divided into classes, the members of which would enjoy privileges: 'the law may establish several classes of citizen, and even specify the qualifications which shall give access to those several classes'.[115] Here Rousseau may also have had the classes of his native Geneva in mind.[116]

The census had a military as well as an economic aspect, for under Romulus, Rousseau observed, each of the three tribes had equipped a body of a hundred equites, or knights, called a century. He had further remarked that Servius Tullius doubled the three original centuries of equites and added twelve others. In addition, he had created 193 infantry centuries, divided for the most part into senior and junior. Thus the first, and wealthiest, class supplied 80 centuries, the second 20 centuries, the third 20 centuries, the fourth 20 centuries, and the fifth 30 centuries. In addition, there were two centuries of mechanics, responsible for the building or repair of siege-engines, attached to the first class, and three centuries of horn-blowers or trumpeters attached to the fifth. The military aspect of the system was certainly as evident to Rousseau as it is to us. Niebuhr, writing some forty years later, observed both that the institution of the centuries was 'understood with more certainty and accuracy than any other part of the constitution', and that

> the classes represented an army of infantry, in exact accord with the constitution of the legion; troops of the line, and light-armed soldiers, with their body of reserves, their carpenters, and their band, and even with the baggage-train.

This exact conformity to the frame of the army was peculiar to this institution.[117]

He further noted that the first class held the front line, and that it was because their bodies shielded the other ranks that men of the second, third and fourth classes wore correspondingly less armour.[118] Because the *comitia centuriata* assembled on the Campus Martius, the centurial system had seemed to eighteenth-century commentators to be the people in arms and the incarnation, therefore, of a well-ordered republic.[119] Since the census achieved the miracle, moreover, of masking the fatal division between *città* and *contado*, those who scrutinized Machiavelli's writings were deeply interested in it.[120] Modern authors insist that the centurial system was not itself the people under arms, but rather a reservoir from which men might be called up to serve, or from which financial resources might be extracted.[121] Since the military needs of the city obviously varied from year to year, this interpretation seems entirely plausible. Nonetheless, the centurial system was for Rousseau the embodiment of a citizens' army as opposed to a mercenary force.

To exhaust the significance of Servius Tullius's reforms for eighteenth-century classical republicanism in general, and for Rousseau in particular, a third aspect must be taken into consideration. For the census, and the complex division into centuries, was also informed by a theory of justice. This theory was derived from Greek political thought, and is known as the doctrine of geometrical proportion. Although the census was not mentioned in Rousseau's second discourse, a crucial note in that work – itself more concerned in its closing passages with the history of the Roman Republic than many have realized – refers glancingly to it. Having acknowledged in the body of the text that the creation of a society brought with it inequality, he added that the criteria for the ordering of persons might be wealth, nobility or rank, power or personal merit, and that 'harmony or conflict between these several sorts of distinction is the surest indication of the good or bad constitution of a state'.[122] In a lengthy note, he observed that

> distributive justice would even be opposed to that rigorous equality of the state of nature, even if it were practicable in civil society, and as all the members of the state owe it services proportionate to their talents and their strength, the citizens in turn ought to be honoured and favoured in proportion to their services . . . The ranking of citizens ought . . . to be regulated . . . according to the real services they render to the state.[123]

To take Rousseau's meaning here, one need simply recall Plato and Aristotle's insistence that both rights and duties be in proportion to a citizen's contribution to the polis, and that a distinction therefore be drawn between arithmetical and geometrical (or proportionate) equality. 'Equality', Aristotle declared, 'is of two kinds, numerical and proportional; by the first I mean sameness or equality in number or size; by the second, equality of ratios. For example, the excess of three over two is numerically equal to the excess of two over one; whereas four exceeds two in the same ratio in which two exceeds one, for two is the same part of four that one is of two, namely, the half.'[124] The property census, a universal feature of Greek cities, once they had been reformed, was the most refined expression of the principle outlined by Aristotle, and Greek historians of Rome clearly took it for granted. Dionysius of Halicarnassus, for example, observed that those who owned the most land would by the same token serve in the army more often and pay higher taxes than did those in the lower classes. In return, such men were more highly rewarded.[125]

Modern historians of Ancient Rome have tried to work out the proportions holding between the different classes. Niebuhr, for example, argued that, if the second, third and fourth classes contained eighty centuries, it was because the former together owned property valued at a quarter of that of the latter. The fifth class, with thirty centuries, likewise owned property to the value of three-eighths of that of the first class.[126] The complexities do not end there, however, for the votes of the wealthy counted for more than did those of the poor.[127] Thus, if each century had only a single vote, the political weight of an individual in one of the poorer classes was less than that of a member of the first class. For the second class, though it had centuries in the ratio of 1:4, had numbers in the ratio of 1:3; the third class had numbers in the ratio of 1:2, the fourth class 1:1, and the fifth class 3:1.[128]

Although the nineteenth-century historians of Rome, like Marx, could see the triumphs of the Third Estate prefigured in the struggles of the plebeians with the patricians, the Servian constitution was not, in our sense of the term, democratic.[129] More generally, one may say that Greek and Latin thinkers had some difficulty in accepting the concept of numerical equality. Social relations of production being what they were, it could only be scandalous to posit what Marx called the *Punktualität*, the dot-like isolation of the individual as individual (and wage-labourer).[130] Even the vote of an old man was of more value than that of a young man, a fact that Rousseau applauded.[131]

Livy, Dionysius of Halicarnassus and Cicero each assumed that the purpose of the census was to keep political power in the hands of the propertied. Livy, for example, noted that

the rich . . . were granted special privileges: for manhood suffrage, implying equality of power and of rights, was no longer given promiscuously to all, as had been the practice handed down by Romulus and observed by all the other kings; but gradations were introduced, so that ostensibly no one should be excluded from the suffrage, and yet the power should rest with the leading citizens.[132]

The equites, with their eighteen centuries, voted first, followed by the first class, which consisted of eighty centuries. All the classical authorities agreed that these two groupings by themselves enjoyed a majority, and most emphasized the discrepancy between an appearance that was democratic and a reality that was timocratic.[133] Livy and Dionysius of Halicarnassus had made it perfectly plain that the lowliest citizens, those in the sixth and last class, were wholly disenfranchised, and neither Machiavelli, nor Montesquieu, nor Vico, nor Rousseau shirked this implication. The Servian constitution was in their view aristocratic.[134] Rousseau, for example, would appear to have agreed with Livy that the undemocratic nature of the arrangement had been deliberately masked by Servius Tullius, by giving the system a military form, and by slipping two centuries of armourers into the second class, and two of weapon makers into the fourth class.[135] The crucial point, though, is that members of the sixth class, who belonged almost exclusively to the urban tribes, were not entitled to fight for the republic.[136] This ban, which endured for almost four hundred years, was lifted by Marius, in 107 BC. In the war against Jugurtha, he dispensed with property qualifications and enrolled large numbers of *proletarii* or *capite censi*.[137] From that moment, in the view of both Montesquieu and Rousseau, the Republic was doomed.[138]

In such conditions of terminal disorder, Rome reverted to 'the slough of Romulus', as if 'the freedmen, vagabonds and other mercenaries' who flocked to Marius's standard were as corrupted as those who had taken refuge in the asylum of the city's founder. In this regard, Rousseau belonged, like Vico, to the age of cities, and believed as much as the Neapolitan thinker did in a returned barbarism. Most of those who looked back at the braided city-states from the vantage-point of an increasingly triumphant, national capitalism were by contrast prepared to ascribe the realization of *ius gentium* to the providential powers of the market and so to relinquish Polybian *corsi* and *ricorsi* forever. Rousseau had said of Servius Tullius's creation of the four tribes that 'thus he both corrected an existing inequality and forestalled any future inequality', yet for Marx and Engels, relying upon the researches of Lewis Henry Morgan, the Servian constitution represented the obliteration of the original liberties of the gens.[139]

The founders of communism, in their attempts to present to the world an image of free self-government, invoked both the Rousseauist city, etched upon the memories of the surviving Babouvists and therefore preserved by the oral tradition of early French socialism, and the Germanic village community, the *Markgenossenschaft*. The legacy of classical republicanism was still perceptible in, for example, Marx's polemical writings at the time of the Paris Commune, as Lucio Colletti has shown.[140] In order to paint a convincing picture of the withering away of the state, one could not do better than refer to the free cities of Antiquity, in which the distinction between rulers and ruled seemed to dwindle almost to nothing. However, as we have seen, several classes of inhabitant were denied political rights. Such a city could no more serve as a model for a nineteenth-century democrat than could oligarchical Berne or Geneva. Indeed, Marx and Engels had placed their hope and trust in the proletariat, the *capite censi* of ancient Rome. If, moreover, they seemed almost to mourn the traditional liberties of the Roman gens, it was because a lineage's collective ownership of land could stand as a precedent for communism.[141] Private property and the state were not eternal. Conversely, what had once been the case, in tribal societies the world over, might be again. Thus, for Engels, the *Markgenossenschaft* became a primordial ground of social being and a horizon of universal justice. Rousseau's perfected art of cities by contrast admitted the fragility of willed human constructions, rounded always by the sleep of the just.[142]

Some commentators have argued that the Romantic aspect of the thought of Marx and, more especially, of Engels, is a merit, not a fault, since visions of threatened or destroyed social relations serve the victims of large-scale processes of historical change as at once a consolation and an imaginative resource.[143] Utopians have, after all, to face backwards, sorting ancient fragments into new patterns of resistance. This argument is well and good, but its advocates have then to answer for the disturbing tendency of Romantic thought-forms to drift from Left to Right. Thus, where Marx and Engels, in polemical argument with Hegel, had equated the state with artifice and civil society with nature, the risk arose that *any* putative tribal origin might then function as the telos of a stateless humanity. In celebrating both the Mark and Niebuhr's beloved Ditmarsh, where free peasants subsisted on the redemptive edge of a corrupted history, Engels was straying on to ground already covered by German Romantic thought, as I show in part III.[144] All such conflations of right with origin constitute a betrayal of the Enlightenment, as Kant, for example, understood it, and are haunted by the principle of nationality.

# PART II

# The Eighteenth Century Judged

L'histoire de la vaste mise en accusation des 'lumières' à travers toute l'Europe mériterait d'être écrite.

Roland Mortier, *Le 'Tableau Littéraire de la France au XVIIIe Siècle'*

# The Liberty of the Ancients and the Liberty of the Moderns

The consolidated doctrine regarding the liberty of the Ancients and the liberty of the Moderns has rested throughout its long history upon four linked claims, namely, that the individual had no rights in the city-states of classical Antiquity; that Rousseau had believed this to be the case; that he had then proposed a similar eradication of individual rights in the modern world; and that the Jacobins had scored this *danse funèbre* for the masses. It would be an error, however, to imagine that the dispute has been, or should be, the preserve of classicists or historians of the Ancient World. For no writing on the ancient city has ever been innocent of the burning issues of the day, as Arnaldo Momigliano's magnificent contributions to the historiography of Antiquity have proved time and time again. Conversely, one should not be misled into thinking that the fierceness with which the nature of liberty, ancient and modern, has been contested, is proof of alignments so irreconcilable that some larger truth is wholly lost. I show in the course of the present chapter that each of the above claims is open to question, and that there is much to be learned from testing them. Furthermore, the dispute continually threatens to encroach upon fresh areas of historiographical and theoretical debate, having a bearing upon, for example, the origins of ethnology and sociology and the rise of the nation. For this reason, my discussion of the issue spans several chapters and undergoes a number of surprising metamorphoses.

In the opinion of Benjamin Constant, the first to define the difference between ancient and modern liberty, and to note the absence of individual rights in Antiquity, was Condorcet, and there is no denying the existence of passages in his writings that confirm this impression.[1] Yet such passages, being generally coloured by a rapturous enthusiasm for American liberty, did not preclude an admiration for certain aspects of Roman liberty. Like Machiavelli and Rousseau, Condorcet thus noted the mildness of Roman criminal law, and commented with approbation upon the office of tribune and upon the *ius provocationis*. Harsh though

Roman mores were, he recognized the extraordinarily effective defences that its constitution offered an innocent and persecuted individual.[2] Camille Desmoulins had likewise protested that the lack of clemency shown by the Montagnard dictatorship of the year II was contrary to the spirit of Roman republicanism, even going so far as to urge his former schoolmate, Robespierre, to recall and ponder their early lessons in history and philosophy.[3] It would be an error, in fact, to imagine that Desmoulins was deploying categories that Robespierre either no longer understood or else had rejected, for even in the furious debates of the spring of 1793, the latter had remained committed to the defence of individual rights, as his contributions to the Montagnard constitution prove.

After Thermidor, many moderate republicans continued to invoke ancient liberty but none celebrated it without equivocation, and most, where they called back shades from Rome or Athens, did so in order to denounce Montagnard claims to a virtue whose setting was damaged beyond repair. Jean Debry, a Girondin and a friend of Volney, agreed with Condorcet that the entire body of citizens had only been able to assemble so frequently in Rome because of the existence and expansion of the deplorable institution of slavery, yet he also remarked upon the orderly disposition of those in the *comitia centuriata*, noting that respect for that system had long 'prevented an ambitious tribune from preparing, through the unconsidered enthusiasm of plebiscites, Marius's bloody ascent to the throne, and the annihilation of the republic'.[4] Since Marius had in fact extended the franchise, as I noted in the last chapter, to the poorest citizens of Rome, those whose capital rating was less than eleven thousand *asses*, Debry was both reiterating a classical republican position and combating the levelling egalitarianism of the year II, itself founded upon a specific interpretation of Rousseau, with a hierarchical vision of the social order. It is also characteristic of the mood in the Convention after Thermidor that the tribunate should be associated here with ambition rather than with popular sovereignty, or with the shielding of individuals, through the use of the tribunician veto, from the unlawful violence of the patricians. If Madame de Staël and Benjamin Constant captured that mood so well in their writings, it was because they had a colder eye and yet spoke as if from another, less troubled place.

## Ancient and modern liberty

In her treatise on the passions, Madame de Staël had declared her intention of publishing a second volume, all trace of which was lost until 1885. When this manuscript was published, its editor announced that it was the missing panel from the Thermidorian diptych.[5] However, in a more recent edition, Lucia Omacini has shown that *Des Circonstances Actuelles* was in fact a wholly different book, of less general scope, written in 1798–99 and in direct, polemical response to the *coup d'état* of 18 Fructidor and to the illegalities of 22 Floréal.[6] Nonetheless, both the text itself and the notes which stand at the end of the manuscript – dated by another scholar to 1799–1800, and clearly the yield of research undertaken in preparation for the planned second volume of the treatise on the passions – are of relevance to the present argument.[7]

In the third chapter of *Des Circonstances Actuelles*, the reader is told that between Jacobins and royalists there was an inert mass, concerned above all with public order, a silent majority who wished for nothing more than the chance to enjoy a private, domestic existence. The public opinion of the Moderns was altogether different, therefore, from the assemblies of the Ancients, 'whose every affection and interest was bound up with the destiny of the fatherland'. If the enemy were to win a battle, the land of those defeated would be laid waste, and they themselves would be enslaved, without even the means of transferring their fortune to another country. The destiny of each and every citizen had thus been public and 'subject at every moment to the wills of a people deliberating in the public square'; the 'guarantee of obscurity' did not exist. Conversely, the independence of individual calculations regarding property and trade had meant that the mass of 'peacefully selfish men' could, in the large-scale states of modern times, 'fulfil their destiny apart from public events'.[8]

This pioneering statement contains most of the constituent elements of the theory later fleshed out by Constant, and considered below. What is most striking at first glance is, I think, the notion that citizens should wear masks and be private; that privacy, indeed, was a value. In celebrating a quietness, at one remove from the agora, the republicans of the year III were obviously endorsing the view, first sketched by Adam Smith, that the modest procedures of trade and industry, abetted by the inscrutable effects of the division of labour, had allowed a previously cramped human nature to blossom in a multitude of new forms. Yet horror at the inquisitorial practices of the sections and of the watch committees had driven liberty back into the innermost recesses of the soul, so that a new note, not heard in David Hume's essays, in *The Spirit of the Laws*, in the *Federalist Papers* or in the early writings of Wilhelm von Humboldt, was sounded.[9]

I would further add that, though historians of political thought have generally accepted that nineteenth-century liberalism turned upon invocations of an altogether inward 'sphere of personality which each wishes to preserve as his inviolable asylum', as Staël put it in 1800, they have less often recognized that liberals, in promoting the antinomy of agora and individual and in thereby jettisoning the classical republican tradition, risked replacing the vision of the sovereign people assembled with the providentialist guarantees of the tribe-nation.[10] The larger claim I make here is therefore that, once the liberty of the individual was no longer guaranteed by his or her being an active part of a sovereign assembly – the people had dispersed and only its representatives gathered – the danger arose that it might be thought to inhere in a more general, purportedly ever-present attribute, a race or a language or both. A right of resistance or secession was replaced by a quality of incorporation or inherence. In assessing the dispute over ancient and modern liberty, it should be recognized that, if so many in the eighteenth century could still warm to the ostensibly superceded notion of the primacy of politics, it was not only because the distant suns of Rome, Athens and Sparta were directly above them. In addition, that first glory was reflected in Venice or Genoa, Geneva or Florence, and the doctrine of the liberty of the Ancients and of the Moderns may therefore be seen as a response not only to Jacobinism but also to the annihilation of the *Kleinstaaten*, pale moons though they indubitably were, in the Revolutionary and Napoleonic periods. I give a fuller account of these topics in chapter 6 but I should point out here, for fear of being misinterpreted, that I do not at all regard Enlightenment liberalism as a direct bridge to the tribe-nation. Elie Kedourie's assessment of Kant's thought strikes me as misguided in this respect, for a liberal reservation of rights is, properly understood, incompatible with their exhaustive incorporation by the nation.[11] Indeed, a universal declaration of rights, especially where it is given institutional form, may be viewed as an expression of the right of secession. My intention, then, has not been to derive the tribe-nation from the liberal critique of the city-nation and of direct democracy, but rather to demonstrate that thinkers who had settled accounts with classical republicanism were vulnerable to the allure of Romantic nationalism. This may seem a fine line to draw but, if it can be shown that Staël, for example, fell on one side of it, and Constant, Cabanis or Fauriel on the other, my point is made.

The government of republican Rome, like that of Calvinist Geneva, featured magistracies that were anyway profoundly invasive of the private sphere. Consider, for example, the moral function of the Roman censorship. The censor was empowered to impose a penalty, or *nota*, upon citizens for a wide range of different offences: military misdemeanours, disrespectful behaviour towards magistrates, perjury, theft, neglect of sanctuaries or tombs, excessive cruelty towards slaves, excessive luxury, poor farming methods, maladministration of property, inappropriate marriages, and so on.[12] Anyone guilty of such actions might then forfeit all political rights. The censorship was thus an extraordinary magistracy, which served to restore a disordered society to order by shaming those who had neglected their duties or who had flouted authority. If Rousseau's original illumination had brought forward one such figure, Fabricius, it was because the tradition of classical republican thought told of the drastic reordering of ruined places by heroic individuals, whether censors, tribunes or dictators. To return a city to its first principles was to repeat, in little, the miracle of its foundation.

What liberal critics of Jacobinism, and therefore of Rousseau, objected to in the censorship was its violation of the privacy of individual citizens. If individuality were the highest good, as Constant, Staël and Humboldt each believed, nothing could be more repugnant than an institution that served to render morality uniform.[13] That the censors really had exercised such powers is not in doubt for, as a contemporary historian of ancient Rome has observed, 'the city claimed the right to examine a man's secret acts, on the grounds that virtue is indivisible and that a bad man cannot be a good citizen'.[14] In attacking the Roman censorship and the Athenian ostracism, in the notes at the end of *Des Circonstances Actuelles*, Staël would, like Constant in his *Principes de Politique*, challenge the presumed identity of virtue and citizenship, of city and citizen. Whereas liberty in ancient times, she observed, had 'consisted of whatever ensured the citizens the greatest possible share in the exercise of power', even if one risked sacrificing one's private interests to the common good, 'liberty in modern times consists of whatever guarantees the independence of citizens from the power of the government'.[15]

The classical republics had traced good laws back to a ground of uncorrupted mores, but the large-scale associations, as Staël called them, could no longer direct morality, and had therefore to give more weight to political powers, that is to say, to the state. In place, therefore, of the ethical substance of the polis, liberal publicists accepted the advent of a state that was an alien, coercive force and of a civil society that was, in Kant's phrase, an 'unsociable sociability'.[16] If there has recently been a revival of interest in the republican critique of liberal capitalism, and therefore in the fate of virtue, it is because the last fifteen years have shown just how unsociable such a sociability can be.

## A theorist of modern liberty

Constant was not concerned with the putative origins of human society, but rather with its slow but ineluctable advance towards perfection. His interest in contemporary ethnography deepened during his years in

Göttingen, as his published volumes on religion testify; he was moved by the elementary forms of religious life or of cosmological speculation; he regretted the tendency of progress to render all peoples the same; yet his writings betray little or no enthusiasm for the supposed liberties of tribal groups.[17] 'The origin of the social state', he wrote in 1796, 'is a great enigma, but its advance is simple and uniform. Upon leaving the impenetrable cloud which covers its birth, we see humankind advancing towards equality, upon the debris of institutions of every kind'.[18] The influence of accommodationist theology had led Constant to derive the principle of equality from the founding revelations of Judaeo-Christian religion, and his philosophy of history, like that of Lessing, was predicated upon a cumulative realization of that same principle through the destruction of, in turn, theocracy, slavery, feudalism and, on the night of 4 August 1789, the privileges of the nobility.[19] Since no power on earth could undo these momentous transformations, the counter-revolutionary theorists were mistaken, Constant believed, in supposing that the work of the Constituent Assembly could be reversed, or in descrying in the atrocities of the year II the hand of a wrathful god who had set the destroyers to cutting each other down. It was simply the case that shifting any obstacle on the road to equality required the application of massive forces, which caused havoc; the price paid by Christendom for ridding the Ancient World of slavery had been 'fifteen centuries of degradation and calamities of every kind'.[20]

In a meditation upon the use and misuse of words, Constant therefore differentiated his own position from those of both La Harpe and the Jacobins. No matter how travestied such words as liberty and equality had been during the Revolution, they retained the power to restore authentic values. By employing the term 'form', Constant may in fact have been echoing Pascal's opinion, that external rituals may precipitate inward beliefs. He certainly believed that a true word, even though it were relayed by a clouded soul, could restore the corrupted to goodness, but he warned that the failure to respect the distinction between general and intermediate principles might bring chaos and destruction.[21] For,

> When one casts all of a sudden into the midst of an association of men, a first principle divorced from all the intermediate principles by which it has come down to us and by which it has been adjusted to suit our own situation, one will certainly produce a high degree of disorder; for a principle that is torn from all its surroundings, deprived of all its supports, and flanked by things which are contrary to it, will destroy and overturn.[22]

Since Constant had observed in a private letter that the above formulations would be crystal clear to those who had witnessed recent events in

Paris, there are good grounds for referring back to the debate in the Convention on the Constitution of the year III, in the course of which it was agreed, with very few dissenting voices, that the clause affirming that 'men are born and remain free and equal in rights' should be omitted from the Declaration of Rights.[23] This pure principle was, he judged, abstract, and dangerously destructive if isolated from a number of other, secondary principles (concerning, in particular, the ownership of property).

Nonetheless, Constant subscribed to the principle, valid at all times and in all circumstances, that 'no man can be bound save by laws in which he has had a hand'. He believed, in other words, in popular sovereignty. In a small society, this principle could be applied directly, but where a larger population existed, an intermediate principle came into force, namely, that 'individuals may have a hand in the drafting of laws, either in their own person or through their representatives'.[24]

Another example of the distinction between general and intermediate principles is relevant here: 'The moral principle that holds that telling the truth is a duty, if it were treated in an absolute and isolated manner, would render all society impossible.' Thus, we know in our hearts that telling the truth is a good, but we know with equal certainty that circumstances exist in which we would do better, or less harm, if we were to lie. Kant, for example, had been wrong to claim that, faced with assassins asking whether your friend had taken refuge in your house, it would be a crime to deny it. The paradox is thus that always telling the truth would, in Constant's opinion, destroy society, but rejection of the same principle would just as surely destroy it, by overturning the principles of morality. To resolve the paradox, he observed that it was only our duty to tell the truth to those who had a right to it, and that no one intending to harm another could be said to have such a right. The assassins in Kant's example therefore had no right to the truth.[25]

In the past, students of Constant's thought have tended to situate it in the context of the Restoration, but his political views had in fact attained their more or less definitive form by 1806, and even his later treatises belong essentially to the period of moral and political crisis that followed the death of Robespierre.[26] Rosalie de Constant thus referred to the *Principes de Politique* as 'the history of the Republic and Empire treated philosophically', an accurate enough description.[27] A concern to deprive the state of the right to scrutinize the conscience of a citizen, and a reluctance 'to treat as a crime an uncertainty that some minds cannot help but have', were common to many Thermidorians, but Constant owed a particular intellectual debt to Sieyes for his contributions to the debate on the draft constitution of the year III, which were themselves a rejoinder to Rousseau and a refutation of Jacobinism.[28] Thus, on 2

Thermidor, Sieyes had poured scorn on the notion that there had once been a moment at which the contractants had surrendered all of their rights without reserve to the community:

> When a political association is formed, one does not place in common all the rights that each individual brings to society, all the power of the entire mass of individuals. One only places in common, under the name of public or political power, the least possible, and only what is necessary to maintain each in his rights and duties.

Like Humboldt, with whom he was later to be on good terms, Sieyes saw individuality as both pre-existing and transcending the state. Because the revolutionaries had denied this truth, they had effected a term-for-term transfer of the imagined powers of the absolutist monarch; 'if the sovreignty of mighty kings had been so powerful and so terrible', they had seemed to say, 'the sovreignty of a people ought to be still more so'.[29]

The *Principes de Politique* both contains a long excerpt from the speech quoted above and reiterates a number of its key propositions. The shape of true principles was discernible, Constant argued, even when they had been travestied. Thus, in his account of 'Rousseau's first principle regarding the source of social authority', he acknowledged that the general will was the only legitimate foundation of government which, otherwise, was usurpation. There were, however, two forms of government that were 'essentially, eternally illegitimate, because no association can will them', namely anarchy and despotism. Anarchy was a term employed by the Thermidorians to describe the Terror, and Constant's intention here, as in his Directorial writings, was to highlight the affinities between Montagnards and Ultras, the latter being 'Montagnards de la royauté'.[30] Far from being anarchic, the Committee of Public Safety had been 'the most despotic government which had ever existed on earth', for it had trampled upon each and every guarantee of individual liberty.[31] Constant therefore, like Sieyes, took Rousseau's second principle, namely, the total alienation by associates in the social contract of all their rights to the community, to mean that the general will exercised unlimited authority over individual existence. He further remarked that publicists both before and after Rousseau had advocated a subordination of the individual to the general will. This was as true of Holbach or Mably as it was of Ferrand or Molé, and there were very few exceptions to the rule. To place such disparate and in fact opposed thinkers in the same camp smacks of provocation, and there is no doubt that Constant wished to leave a sting in the mind. Only by admitting a symmetry between the influence of Rousseau and that of Hobbes, and therefore between 'the horrors of Robespierre and the oppression of Caligula', could it be drawn.[32] In the context of the Consulate, Constant sought to warn those rallying to Bonaparte not only that the restoration of monarchy would result in as complete a sacrifice of civil liberties as had occurred under the Montagnard dictatorship, but also that the implementation of such a sacrifice would find its justification and its embellishment in strikingly similar notions of an absolute sovereignty. By way of anticipating lines of argument developed below, I should add that, notwithstanding the very real influence of Hobbes upon Rousseau, Constant here exaggerates the affinities between them, and thereby obscures the concern for individual liberty defiantly expressed in both the *Discourse on Political Economy* and *The Social Contract*.

In the second book of his treatise on politics, Constant defined the principles that ought in his view to supplant misconceived ideas respecting the rightful extent of social authority. Like Sismondi, whose manuscript *Recherches* was in his keeping in 1800–01, Sieyes or Kant, he wished first of all to identify and protect 'a part of human existence which, of necessity, remains individual and independent and which, by right, lies outside of all social competence'.[33] He therefore could not delight in the Greek republics, since they all, with the exception of Athens, 'subjected individuals to a social jurisdiction of an almost unlimited extent'. Even '[in] the heyday of the Roman Republic', he continued, 'the individual was entirely sacrificed to the whole'. In short, 'the Ancients, as Condorcet observes, had no notion of individual rights. Men were, so to speak, merely machines whose laws ruled the mechanisms and directed all the movements'.[34] At the risk of drawing the reader across ground already covered, I will now list the five purported differences between ancient and modern liberty, starting with the crucial fact of scale.

The question of scale was linked to that of the purchase of words upon the soul. Constant had emphasized the moral rewards accruing to citizens, whose power in the ancient city was, as Rousseau had insisted, a reality, manifest in displays of eloquence and in the public staging of events. Thus, Collatinus did not even have to utter a syllable, but merely to expose Lucretia's body in the forum, for the Roman people to see what Sextus Tarquinius had done.[35] If Rousseau, whom Constant plainly has in mind here, had seemed to draw rhetoric back to the immediacy of emblems and to the effervescent union of a festival, and so to dreams of an artless speech as far removed as can be imagined from the formulae of Quintilian, it was because his relation to oratory had been profoundly ambiguous. The austere senators admired by Cineas were an almost Cyclopean wall of silent tradition, destroyed by the elenchi of sophistical Greek rhetors. Constant's view of rhetoric was not simple either, for he seemed to believe both that the modern world, with its vast states, was bereft of eloquence, and that the proper use of speech remained of fundamental importance to the preservation of liberty.

In order to prove that Cicero or Demosthenes would not rise from the grave, Constant noted how inappropriate the oratorical style of Saint-Just had been. As I remarked above, the Rousseauist vision of the free city, where each citizen was by turns subject and sovereign, presupposed a moral community in which words held their value. The fate of Cato of Utica was proof that such circumstances were not eternal, and that at the last great souls could only address their own consciences and the starry heavens, yet even then they might conceive themselves to be, as Saint-Just had put it, 'anchored to the future'. Constant, however, ridiculed the Jacobin orator; he spoke, we are told, in short sentences, in order to rouse 'tired souls'. 'While he seemed to suppose the nation capable of the most painful sacrifices', wrote Constant, 'he acknowledged it, by his style, to be incapable even of paying attention.'[36]

Although Constant reckoned that Jacobinism had been delusion and shrill soliloquy, he did not therefore think that the Moderns would be deprived of rhetoric altogether. Consider in this regard his account of the fateful clash between Greek eloquence and Roman mores.[37] In its early years, Constant observed, Rome had been concerned only with the preservation through war of its liberty, and therefore with a wisdom that was merely practical. However, the conquest of the Greek world had brought slaves into the city, and those that were rhetors or grammarians were entrusted with the education of Roman children. Yet the influence of such men was so slight as to be all but imperceptible, until the famous embassy of Carneades, Critolaos and Diogenes. We saw in the last chapter how Rousseau had lauded Cato the Censor for his harrying of these 'philosophes'. Constant's account was, by contrast, more even-handed, owing something, no doubt, to Bacon's treatment of the same episode in The Advancement of Learning. He began by expressing sympathy for the dignified but doomed attempt of the white-haired senators to stem the tide of corrosive language from Greece, and distaste, too, for the vanity and the verbal ploys of the Athenians. The Romans had never before experienced the 'prodigious flexibility' of speech, and were fascinated by the ability of the sophist Carneades to argue both sides of a question in turn. Yet, as always, Constant insisted that nothing, not even the authority of tradition, could prevent the ultimate triumph of the spirit of free examination. What was false in Greek thought would yield in time to what was true.

If eloquence was necessary to all free states, its purpose in modern times was no longer to spur assemblies into immediate action, but rather to return listeners to a calm meditation upon the truths preserved in forms.[38] The revolutionary word had sought to hasten the advent of universal justice; Constant aimed, rather, to foster prevarication: by recalling the importance of legal guarantees, encroachments of authority upon the individual might be checked.

A second criterion for differentiating between the two kinds of liberty concerned the waging of war. In Antiquity, Constant observed, the world was largely populated by 'small tribal groups, almost without reciprocal relations and disputing small territories by force of arms'.[39] This had remained true of the Spartans and of the Romans, the peoples so much praised by Mably and Rousseau, whereas the Athenians, championed (as were the Phoenicians) by Turgot and Condorcet, more nearly approximated to the condition of modern, commercial society. A city-state might fall in a single battle, and invasion by barbarian hordes was an ever-present threat; the need to marshal the whole body of citizens (and even, in times of emergency, some metics and slaves) therefore required the sacrifice of individual liberty and a more oppressive 'social discipline'.

The spirit of the modern world, however, was for peace, and when wars were fought, peoples were no longer enslaved or the land divided. Although the frontiers of a state might be redrawn, the centre of the national territory was not touched.[40] In such circumstances, individuals resented being impelled as a mass; they hoped, rather, to be defended from the encroachments of authority, the better to prosecute their own individual projects. Liberty rested upon plurality and not, as in earlier times, upon unity.

Third, in Antiquity the majority of peoples were not committed to trade, in part because the compass had not been invented and sea voyages were hazardous, and in part because they were constrained by ritual prohibitions. However, with the substitution of trade for warfare as the paramount activity of modern times, it had become harder for the authorities to inspect the transactions of individuals, and the latter were themselves less tolerant of such encroachments upon their private liberty. Once circulation prevailed over usufruct, wealth became more mobile and social relations less visible. As a consequence, the state was less able to police the transactions of individuals.

Fourth, the institution of slavery, itself the precondition of raised voices in the agora, had imparted a ferocity to the mores of the Ancients. Once one had denied to some the ordinary rights of humanity, one was liable to stifle the sentiment of pity in one's own heart. Even Aristotle had justified study of the art of war in terms of the capture of 'those who . . . deserve to be enslaved'.[41]

Finally, Constant argued that twenty centuries had wrought a fundamental change. Where the Ancients, he observed, had been in the youth of moral life, the Moderns were in its maturity, or even in its old age. One only had to consider the work of the classical poets, imbued as it was with an enthusiasm that was 'true, natural and complete'; modern poets, by contrast, 'always drag behind them an indefinable afterthought, which is born of experience, and which defeats enthusiasm'.[42] Where the Ancients had surrendered to violent impulses, the Moderns would scrutinize their own moral and emotional states, and so not yield to them. The latter were thus condemned to lead a double life, as their coining of the term 'illusion' proved. Ancient philosophers and historians wrote in an exalted spirit, and with complete conviction, whereas the Moderns were accustomed to doubt and to examine. It was for this reason, Constant argued, that we were no longer able to accept a legislator who appeared in the guise of a prophet, and endeavoured to reform a people by means of institutions. These passages on illusion call to mind Constant's novel, *Adolphe*, Cabanis's letter on Homer, and Staël's *De la Littérature*, a work that would in its turn inspire Leopardi's bold meditations on this theme in his *Zibaldone*. Ancient and modern modes of feeling were later driven still further apart by Fustel de Coulanges, who blocked in an Athens and a Rome so primitive as to be altogether beyond emulation, and by his most brilliant pupil, Emile Durkheim. For example, the Roman census, far from being the staging of a citizens' militia, was to Fustel little more than an archaic religious festival (the *lustrum condere*), and the tribunate less an expression of popular sovereignty than a ritual office.[43]

## Constant and Jellinek

Later contributions to the dispute over ancient and modern liberty shed some light upon its essential nature, and it is to these that I now turn. Constant had reiterated his arguments in *The Spirit of Conquest and Usurpation* in 1814, and in the famous lecture delivered at the Athenée Royale in 1819, while Sismondi, another member of the Coppet Circle, had advanced similar distinctions between civil and political liberty in his celebrated history of the Italian republics.[44] In Germany, a growing scepticism towards the *Kleinstaat* and, as I show in chapter 6, towards the republican aspect of the Janus-faced Machiavelli, led many to embrace Constant's thesis. Tittman, for instance, observed in 1822 that 'in modern times, the state is more concerned with the safeguarding of individuals, whereas the Greeks gave greater weight to the safeguarding of the whole, of the constitution, of equality'.[45] In the ensuing years, Stahl and Mohl presented Constant's antithesis between the Ancients and the Moderns in an increasingly stark form, making no mention of the degree of individual liberty enjoyed by citizens in Periclean Athens or of those tendencies in Roman law that served to modify the authority of custom.[46] Finally, in the 1860s, a number of important studies of the topic appeared in France, notably by Laboulaye, the first serious editor of Constant's writings, and by Fustel de Coulanges.

The subtitle of *The Ancient City* declared it to be 'a study of the religion, law and institutions of Greece and Rome', the chief purpose of which was to 'set in a clear light the radical and essential differences which at all times distinguished these ancient peoples from modern societies'. Fustel then noted the baneful influence of classical Antiquity upon European education:

> Having imperfectly observed the institutions of the ancient city, men have dreamed of reviving them among us. They have deceived themselves about the liberty of the ancients, and on this very account liberty among the moderns has been put in peril. The last eighty years have clearly shown that one of the great difficulties which impede the march of modern society is the habit which it has of always keeping Greek and Roman antiquity before its eyes.

If, however, it was no longer possible to imitate the Ancients, it was because our cast of mind, which alters from one century to the next, was no longer the same. 'Man no longer thinks today what he used to think twenty-five centuries ago', Fustel observed, 'and it is for this reason that he is no longer governed as he used to be governed.'[47]

The debt to Constant is obvious, yet Fustel's monograph was also an original contribution to the study of ancient society, acknowledged by leading authorities to be one of the founding texts of both French and British social anthropology.[48] Wherein does its originality lie? Suppose we follow the example of ethnologists of our own century and set aside for the moment Fustel's use of the comparative method, on the grounds that the Indo-Germanic aspect of his thought is not so markedly different from that of, say Theodor Mommsen, Henry Maine or Max Müller. What then strikes us is Fustel's conviction that ancient cities, being centred upon shared worship of tutelary deities at the same altar, were in effect churches. There was therefore no individual liberty:

> The citizen was subordinate in everything, and without any reserve, to the city; he belonged to it body and soul. The religion which had produced the state, and the state which supported the religion, sustained each other, and made but one; these two powers, associated and confounded, formed a power almost superhuman, to which the soul and the body were equally enslaved.[49]

As instances of such oppression, Fustel observed that military service at Rome had lasted until the age of forty-six, and at Athens and Sparta for the whole of one's adult life. He further noted that the ancient city would requisition the personal wealth of citizens whenever it wished; he emphasized the power of moral institutions such as the Roman censorship to encroach upon private life, for example, by fining those who remained too long unmarried, and he passed comment upon sumptuary laws and upon the Athenian ostracism. Such encroachments were best exemplified by the demeanour, much praised by Plutarch and by Rousseau, of the Spartan matrons after the battle of Leuctra. A state able to inspire so cruel a reversal of natural feelings must indeed be omnipotent. This omnipotence was also reflected in a complete control over education, of the sort that Condorcet had deplored, and in a total lack of religious liberty.[50]

One of the first authors to pose a serious and direct challenge to the claim, so widely accepted by nineteenth-century ethnologists, historians and jurists, that the individual had no rights in the city-states of Antiquity, was Georg Jellinek.[51] In his *Allgemeine Staatslehre* the claim is made that modern scholars, in composing their picture of the Greek polis, had drawn on sources that, though Athenian, had proposed the Spartan constitution as a model. Xenophon and Plato, for example, had countered the unbridled democracy of Athens in its decline with the vaunted military discipline of an alien military state.[52] What such partisans of oligarchy wrote was therefore less a reflection of the actual constitution of their city than a vision of a possible future. Even Aristotle had been influenced by the Spartan constitution to some degree, and it was indeed from the *Politics*, selectively treated, that Hegel had derived his view that the Greek polis, as ethical substance, precluded the expression of individual liberty. The good was whatever custom dictated.[53]

Aristotle, like Plato, had denied that there was such a thing as a wholly isolated and self-sufficient individual, but to claim that he had said that there were no spheres of individual liberty distinct from the state was to distort his argument. Jellinek at any rate maintained that the ancient state was not omnipotent, that such spheres had existed, and that historians had lent too much credence to the formulations contained in the *Laws* and the *Republic*, which represent ideal types rather than empirical descriptions.[54] Aristotle's account of the constitution of Athens was first published as late as January 1891, some two years after Fustel de Coulanges's death, and it may in part have been the rediscovery of this text (in the form of the 'London papyrus') that inspired Jellinek to mount a challenge to the view that in Antiquity the state had been everything and the individual nothing.[55] To make sense of this historiographical puzzle, Jellinek drew a contrast between archaic Greece and the period of intense change precipitated by the Persian Wars. As far as the earlier period was concerned, many of Fustel's claims were allowed. Where there was no *ius gentium*, and where those defeated in battle were entirely without rights, the complete identification of citizens with the polis was not to be wondered at. Jellinek also agreed that the polis was at once a religious and a political entity. Where the state was both the work of the gods and their home, to honour it was a citizen's supreme duty. The ancient city had been, just as Fustel said, a church, and there was no ground of belief outside it. In such circumstances, the exposure of ailing or crippled children, the duty of lifelong military service, and of raising a family for the good of the state could all be accounted for, yet such oppressive aspects of the ancient city were, Jellinek insisted, characteristic of early Doric Greece. In the aftermath of the Persian Wars, however, the individual had grown increasingly independent of the state. A number of different schools of philosophy had begun to look beyond a city-state patriotism; the Cynics and the Stoics, in particular, began to conceive of a cosmopolis. Moreover, we know from Aristotle's own contrast between independence and liberty – reiterated by Montesquieu, by Rousseau and even by Saint-Just – that the unquestioning devotion of citizens to the polis could no longer be taken for granted.[56] Jellinek also used Thucydides, and Aristotle, to draw attention to the many rights enjoyed by individuals in law, although other nineteenth-century scholars had insisted that there was no such thing as private law in Periclean Athens.

In one respect, Jellinek's arguments are tautological, and do no more than enlarge upon the somewhat cursory accounts contained in the writings of Turgot, Condorcet, Constant or Fustel de Coulanges, each of whom had remarked upon the processes by which the city of Socrates and Pericles had gradually cast off the shackles of a customary notion of social authority, with the principle of free examination in thought advancing in step with the growing liberty to trade. It is possible, then, to grant that Jellinek's case is well founded but to argue that, although it may serve to correct the detail of Fustel's monograph, it misses the point of Constant's famous lecture.[57]

Benedetto Croce, in a curious little essay on Jellinek's book, put it that Constant had conceived of the liberty of the Moderns in terms of a 'totalità e universalità del sentire e del fare libero'.[58] I take this paraphrase to mean that each and every individual both felt, and was felt by others, to be free, and that as a consequence the inherent tendency of European history was towards liberty. It is certainly true that Constant, in the light of his accommodationist belief in the principle of perfectibility, saw Europe as increasingly under the sway of individuality. Since individuals in their infinite variety, not the state or sacerdotal religion, would carry value forward to the future, in an axiological account owing much (as in Wilhelm von Humboldt's case) to the experience of love, his hope was for an unceasing proliferation of sects. At the last, each person would constitute his or her own church. This conception, which makes schism itself seem eirenic, may rest upon a vision of churches, chapels and meeting-houses of different denominations existing in a single city, as in Philadelphia, a place that would surely have captivated Constant, a child of the Dispersion.[59] He believed that the particular contribution of the Christian religion had been to found the truth that all persons, through the mere fact of being human, were of infinite value, and his stadial theory was therefore, like that of Hegel, conceived in terms of a cumulative equality. Thus, a slave had been regarded in the Ancient World as no better than an object or an animal, but a serf, being in some kind of moral relation to a feudal lord, had been granted a more fully human status.[60] Hegel had likewise contrasted Oriental despotism, where one was free, and Classical Antiquity, where the few were free, with Christian-Germanic society, where all were free.[61] I think that Croce may also have had this famous passage in mind when he wrote of a 'totalità e universalità del sentire e del fare libero'. What is obscured by this phrase, however, is the process by which the notion of *vivere libero*, common to Machiavelli, to Rousseau and to the Jacobins, was surrendered, in the age of nations, to the heavenly city.[62] Conversely, the young Marx's critique of Hegel may be construed as an attempt to replace a merely formal universality with the substantive rights of the free and visible, ancient–modern city.[63]

If, notwithstanding Croce's harsh and intemperate critique, Jellinek's book is still instructive, it is therefore because it serves to remind us that Constant and Fustel, in their accounts of the variety of historically attested forms of liberty, had overstated their case. To vindicate the civil liberty of the Moderns, which flourished under the sign of happiness, they had driven the liberty of the Ancients, and the diffused principle of virtue, so far back in stepped time as to be irrecoverably alien and primitive. Jellinek established on the other hand that the relation between *civis* and *civitas*, or between *politēs* and *polis*, though plain enough to Rousseau, was an exotic mystery to the majority of publicists and ancient historians for over half a century. The agora, formerly celebrated as the radiant unity of an assembled, active and free citizenry, was now imagined as a space subjected to the pitiless glare of an undivided social authority – a sun-people vested with all the attributes of a sun-king – and to the equally cruel actions of an omnipotent state. As the ideas of the historical school of law took hold in Europe, it grew increasingly difficult to conceive of a polis – a unity-in-multiplicity of free and equal citizens, each enjoying the rights of *isonomia* and *isēgoria* – managing its own self-government. In particular, the classical relation of part to whole, of citizen to city, was consistently misconstrued. In a famous passage, Aristotle had written that

> the state is by nature clearly prior to the family and to the individual, since the whole is of necessity prior to the part; for example, if the whole body be destroyed, there will be no foot or hand, except homonymously, as we might speak of a stone hand; for when destroyed the hand will be no better than that.[64]

Both Condorcet and Hegel interpreted statements of this sort to mean that the part in the city-state was really no more than an automatically functioning element of the whole, but closer inspection of the *Politics* reveals Aristotle's deep suspicion of an overly homogeneous social order. Book 2, for example, contains a critique of Plato's enthusiasms for a Spartan regimentation of the state, precisely because there is such a thing as excessive unity: 'the whole cannot be happy unless most, or all, or some of its parts enjoy happiness. In this respect happiness is not like the even principle in numbers, which may exist only in the whole, but in neither of the parts; not so happiness.'[65] It is clear, then, that Aristotle's ideal state was very far from being, in Sieyes's terms, a 're-total'. Indeed, the ancient city was not omnipotent, for its bureaucracy and police were by modern standards minimal.

Durkheim's celebrated distinction between mechanical and organic solidarity, forged in the shadow of Fustel de Coulanges, derives from the theoretical disputes outlined above. For although he, like Maine or Tönnies, conceived of the evolution of human societies as an ascent from solidary community (a lower form) to individualism (a higher form), the division of labour did not produce anomie but a more enduring solidarity, finding concrete expression, it was to be hoped, in a guild socialism. Archaic systems were characterized, Durkheim argued, by near unanimity of religious belief, so that infractions of the repressive law then in force were punished by passionate and violent acts of expiation. Mechanical solidarity both produced 'a general, indeterminate attachment of the individuals to the group', and 'concert[ed] their detailed actions'. This account of wills acting in concert reminds us of Condorcet, who had also used the epithet 'mechanical', and of Constant, a parallel that should not be cause for surprise, since those engaged in a defence of the embattled ideals of the Third Republic saw themselves as the heirs of the *idéologues*. Moreover, Durkheim, like Fustel, deemed it a feature of archaic societies that an assembled people should sit in judgement on a citizen. He therefore redescribed the Rousseauist ideal of a society in which one and all were the equal of Fabricius, noting the outlandish size of the assemblies in which criminal cases were tried in Athens and Rome, and even mentioning in passing the jury system of barbarian Europe. Diffuse sanctions, and therefore a strong form of *conscience collective*, were an index not of popular sovereignty but of a primitive condition. In modern societies, on the other hand, organic solidarity, and with it restitutive law, prevailed; many areas of social life had been rid of the burden of honour and shame.[66]

Where mechanical solidarity still obtained, the *conscience collective* was uniform. Indeed, Durkheim even regarded the existence of strong physical resemblances between the members of early societies as proof of intellectual identity.[67] For he subscribed to the then current hypothesis of an original, undifferentiated horde, within which the principle of resemblance had prevailed, and traced in the subsequent formation of two-, four- or eight-section segmentary systems in acephalous societies a nascent recognition of the principle of difference and an adumbration of the division of labour. Where Fustel, however, had accounted for the social structure of archaic societies in terms of the prior existence of an all-encompassing religion, Durkheim inverted his teacher's explanation, reckoning that so profoundly religious an idiom was a consequence of mechanical solidarity. The more ambitious claim made by Durkheim had been that logical thought itself had a social origin:

> the category of class was at first indistinct from the concept of the human group; it is the rhythm of social life which is at the basis of the category of time; the territory occupied by the society furnished the material for the category of space; it is the collective force which was the prototype of the concept of efficient force, an essential element in the category of causality.[68]

Some passages in Durkheim reflect the Kantian doctrine that there is but one, universal, set of categories, without which thought would be impossible, but others imply a relativist epistemology. The claims quoted above, for example, could be taken to refer to the categories of cause, class, time and space *as such*. Yet social anthropologists, whether in general agreement with Durkheim or not, have tended to view his doctrine as a charter for relativisim. A Durkheimian, like a Wittgensteinian ethnographer, might then, or so the argument runs, treat diverse conceptual frameworks as irreducible one to the other. This interpretation fails, however, to account for Durkheim's ethical and political views.

Immediately prior to the Second World War, Léon Brunschvig observed that 'Nuremberg is religion according to Durkheim, society adoring itself'.[69] Yet, with the rise of anti-Semitism in *fin-de-siècle* Europe, Durkheim had been increasingly concerned to refute the rhapsodes of the tribe-nation, who everywhere identified the final truth of the culture of individuals with the individuality of their culture, and so, unanswerably, with the land and the dead.[70] Whereas Fustel was coopted posthumously (though, in the opinion of many, unjustifiably) by Action Française, Durkheim and his pupils were aligned with the Dreyfusards. This being the case, how is one to account for Brunschvig's accusation? The point is that, as Steven Collins has observed, Durkheim effected a radical separation between two kinds of (previously connected) individualism, methodological and ethical, rejecting the former but embracing the latter.[71] Society, being a priori, wielded a complete authority over the sentient individual, to the extent of being construed as an aspect of nature. Fellow human beings were as much a part of the furniture of the wondrous world as were the sun, the moon, the stars and the life-destroyers – storm, flood, fire, earthquake and volcano. In positing a social origin to the categories, Durkheimian sociology thus betrayed its essentially Restoration origin, for the refusal of methodological individualism was as central to Comte and Bonald as it was to, say, Constant. Yet Durkheim's ethical individualism, like that of Constant, did not require that religion be an illusion without a future, for the triumph of organic solidarity left a cult intact, that of the individual, 'the worship of the personal dignity of the human person'.[72]

It is therefore one of the ironies of intellectual history that Durkheim's description of mechanical solidarity should have played a part, no matter how small, in sustaining the myth of the tribe-nation. Yet one can readily understand how the mistaken idea, fostered by a number of passages in *The Division of Labour*, that segmentary lineage societies were organisms obeying a blind, undifferentiated telos, should have coloured the functionalist ethnology of our own century.[73] However misconceived it may have been to posit a part as the automatically functioning element in a social whole, or to entertain the notion of a complete and, as it were, exhaustive immersion of every single participant in a given ritual, since there can always be individual dissent, dislocation or, more banally, ennui, the views of Radcliffe-Brown guaranteed such misconceptions a surprisingly long life. British social anthropologists, even where they repudiated the cruder sorts of circular, quasi-biological functionalism, tended to produce similarly confining accounts of the imprisonment of grouped persons in a particular conceptual grid. At the limit, the observer's required reverence for a given culture's thought-world, an attitude seemingly predicated upon nothing else but the activity of translation, in fact precluded it. For, to deploy a metalanguage, or so the argument went, would be to betray the conceptually unique world studied. This line of argument was made explicit by Peter Winch, in *The Idea of a Social Science*, a book best understood as a symptom of a remarkably fruitful encounter, in the 1950s, between Wittgensteinian philosophy and social anthropology. Through Winch's application to

ethnographic enquiry of the notion of 'following a rule', the rule being
altogether embedded in a 'form of life', the social scientist was denied the
possibility, as Winch's critics pointed out, of accounting either for
historical change in cosmologies or, more damagingly still, for the
intrinsic ambiguity of concepts.[74]

Yet Durkheim had himself ascribed the attribute of individuality to all
human beings, as had Marcel Mauss. The latter thus distinguished
between 'the sense of "self" ', which he took to be universal, and the
gradually evolving 'notion' or 'concept' of it, as embodied in laws,
religions, customs, social structures and mentalities, which 'has at last
become clear and sharp, in our civilisations (and, in ours, even almost in
our own lifetimes), and not yet in all of them'.[75] These opinions may call
to mind the dispute regarding the liberty of the Ancients and of the
Moderns, but the Durkheimians, like Jellinek, tended to acknowledge
that some individual rights existed in the ancient city. Durkheim, for
example, emphasized just how much the Roman Twelve Tables differed
from the Pentateuch, and Gustave Glotz identified a range of individual
rights in the Greek city-states.[76] Yet members of the Ecole Sociologique
agreed that Christianity had wrought an epochal transformation. Mauss,
for example, judged that 'our own notion of the human person is still
basically the Christian notion', and commented upon 'the transition from
the notion of *persona*', of 'man invested with a status' to the notion of
man as such, a conclusion that tallies with those of Hegel, Croce or
Troeltsch.[77] In recent years, scholars have drawn attention to Mauss and
Durkheim's neglect of Jewish and Hellenistic sources, consideration of
which would indubitably have undermined the supposed uniqueness of
the Christian case. By disregarding the wider cultural context of early
Christianity, it looks very much as if the Durkheimians, notwithstanding
the Jewish origin of many of their number, were influenced, perhaps
unknowingly, by the Restoration notion that it had been the Christian
Revelation that had interposed a caesura between the liberty of the
Ancients and the liberty of the Moderns.[78] Momigliano, for example, has
remarked upon Mauss's omission of any reference to Greek and Hellenistic biography, and has wondered just why a scholar so versed in
classical Antiquity should have made no mention even of Plutarch, who
set the terms for the genre in the West up to and including the eighteenth
century.[79]

In a particularly intriguing contribution to the study of the concept of
the person, Louis Dumont, himself a pupil of Mauss, has remarked upon
the existence of very real affinities between Roman Stoicism, early
Christianity and, in certain respects, early Indian religion. Mauss had in
fact claimed that modern individualism had emerged only gradually,

and, as if to mark the way-stages, had referred fleetingly to the Reformation, to Protestant sects of the seventeenth and eighteenth centuries, to Kant, to Fichte, and to the Declaration of Rights of Man and the Citizen.[80] To this cursory account Dumont has added a crucial corrective note: 'the pedigree of modern individualism is, so to speak, double: an origin or accession of one sort, *and* a slow transformation into another'.[81] Far from being unique to the early Christians, the first traces of such an individualism are thus perceptible both in the Stoics and in the Indian world-renouncers. Dumont sets out from a fundamental distinction between holism, 'where the paramount value lies in society as a whole', and individualism, 'where the individual is a paramount value', and wonders quite how a transition from one societal form to the other might occur.[82] The answer to the riddle is supplied by India, a society characterized by two complementary features, namely, a constraining interdependence and the institution of world-renunciation, which permits full independence. Whereas we know ourselves to be individuals-in-the-world, or 'inworldly' individuals, Indian renouncers, Dumont observes, are individuals-outside-the-world, or 'outworldly' individuals.[83] A holistic society could thus tolerate, as a sort of supplement to itself, the 'outworldly' individual, who might live as a hermit or else in a monastic community. In Christ's teaching too, to be a person was to be an individual-in-relation-to-God, a mode of existence that, outsoaring the polis, rendered personality at once radically particular or, as it were, intimate, and unconstrainedly universal, transcending ethnicity. Much the same might be said of the Cynics, the Epicureans and the Stoics, all of whom remained 'outworldly' to a greater or a lesser degree. Civic duties, even in the case of the Stoics, remained subordinate to a loftier scale of values. This much is still evident in eighteenth-century Stoicism, according to which a proper love of one's fellow citizens was always counterbalanced by a sense of radical estrangement from this world. The last recorded words of the Prairial martyrs, quoted in chapter 1, thus reflect very accurately the outworldly quality of the thought of Seneca or Epictetus.

Perhaps predictably, Dumont's own account of the gradual transformation within Christendom of the outworldly individual into the inworldly individual remains somewhat cursory, for it is never an easy matter to blend ethnographic with historical enquiry. To paraphrase, however, the Church, which had begun in a spirit of uncompromising disparagement of the world, came in time to rule over actual territories (later the Papal States). With the formulation of papal absolutism, and the emergence of the doctrine of the Two Swords, it became possible to transfer to the modern state the essentially ecclesiastical quality of being, not a combination of various functions and orders, but simply an aggregate of myriad individuals.[84] If I find this account helpful, it is because the transition from an age of cities to an age of nations was characterized, in my opinion, by the virtual elimination of outworldliness as an option. One symptom of this transformation of values early in the nineteenth century was the European reappraisal of American liberty, considered at length in chapter 6, and the resulting preoccupation with Christian-Germanic liberty and the legacy of the barbarian invasions. Another symptom of the same great alteration was a general repudiation of suicide, a veritable obsession of Stoic thought and an act construed as the quintessence of liberty. This repudiation was not merely, or not even primarily, a rejection of the supposed pathologies of the Revolution, but is best understood as an admission, in all humility, of inworldliness.[85]

What Dumont does not, however, address is the propensity of the state to concern itself with the salvation not of myriad individuals but of a providentially guaranteed tribe-nation.[86] Yet this is precisely what became possible (thought not, it should be stressed, inevitable), once the transformation of the early nineteenth century reclaimed the outworldly individual from the cycle of cities and at the same time restored the lineages, the peopled earth. In recent years, however, fresh light has been shed upon the classical republican tradition, a casualty of the Restoration, and upon the putative identity of free city with free citizen.

## Negative and positive liberty

In a celebrated lecture, delivered in 1958, Isaiah Berlin isolated two central senses, admitting at the same time that there were others, of the term 'freedom'. According to the first, negative sense, I am free 'to the degree to which no human being interferes with my activity'. This zone of non-interference, under no circumstances to be violated, is protected by the law, which functions to prevent collisions between individuals, to keep them, so to speak, apart. According to the second, positive sense, I am free to the extent to which I participate actively in the government of the polity to which I belong. Whereas freedom in the first sense was 'freedom from', in the second sense it was 'freedom to'. There can, I think, be no doubt that Berlin's distinctions are directly descended from those of Staël and Constant, and there is anyway clear evidence that he had the 1819 lecture to hand when drafting his own. Such debts are not of any intrinsic interest, but a number of deeper parallels are. One might suppose, Berlin continues, that negative and positive liberty were simply two sides of the same coin. For the advocate of the first seems to say, let no one else, in this or this or this, constrain me, while the enthusiast for the second declares, let me, in this and this and this, act with others for the common good. However, although the satisfaction that each seeks is 'an ultimate value which, both historically and morally, has an equal right to be classed among the deepest interests of mankind', they are ultimately 'divergent and irreconcilable attitudes to the ends of life'. This is because – and at this point we hear the leitmotif, not only of this lecture, but of Berlin's entire *oeuvre* – no single formula can be found that establishes harmony between all the diverse ends of humanity.[87]

The lucidity of Berlin's central argument is, however, vitiated by an oddly opaque set of secondary themes, the prominence of which reflects the tensions of the first Cold War.[88] Since his preference, out of two incommensurables, was for negative liberty, he devoted many pages to somewhat imprecise castigations of those who loved, too well, the panacea of positive liberty. In particular, he denounced all those who, in the name of a higher self or of objective reason, had sought to impose their will on the many laggard others. For example, one is left with the distinct impression that J.L. Talmon's thesis is on Berlin's mind, for we are told that Rousseau

[did] not mean by liberty the 'negative' freedom of the individual not to be interfered with within a defined area, but the possession by all, and not merely by some, of the fully qualified members of a society of a share in public power, which is entitled to interfere with every aspect of every citizen's life.[89]

If one were to ask why Talmon's argument, being so palpably false, should have been so widely accepted, one would quickly arrive at the conclusion that it was to no small degree a mirror-image of the Third International's conception of an ostensibly Jacobin, but actually Leninist, Rousseau, whose thought therefore served to justify both a dictatorship of the bourgeoisie and a dictatorship of the proletariat. To shatter so bedazzling an illusion was not an easy task, but the bicentenary celebrations of *The Social Contract* provided an opportunity to rectify the error, and in several of the contributions to the conference at Dijon we therefore find the interpretation of Rousseau as a theorist of negative liberty propounded with conviction. Far from being unconcerned with negative liberty, it was, we are told, his constant preoccupation.[90]

Thus, the fundamental problem to which, Rousseau said, the social contract was a solution, was to identify a form of association that 'will defend the person and goods of each member with the collective force of all, and under which each individual, while uniting himself with the others, obeys no one but himself, and remains as free as before'.[91] Then, famously, in the chapter defining the limits to sovereign power, Rousseau had remarked that 'we have to consider beside the public person those private persons who compose it, and whose life and liberty is naturally independent of it . . . each man alienates only that part of his power, his goods and his liberty which is the concern of the community'.[92] The case of republican Rome, the city admired above all others by Rousseau, was proof of this point. The Romans had, he insisted, 'distinguished themselves above all other peoples on earth by the regard which their government paid to the individual, and by its scrupulous attention to the preservation of the inviolable rights of all the members of the state'.[93] Neither the senate nor the consuls but only the assembled people could condemn an individual citizen, and Rousseau, in recording the fact, presented as exemplary what Fustel and Durkheim would later dismiss as merely archaic. If one wished for still more evidence regarding the importance of negative liberty to the author of *The Social Contract* and the second discourse, one could do worse than reflect upon the importance of the cat in the frontispiece to both works, for, as the cases of *The New Science* and *Customs of the American Indians* prove, the emblems emblazoned on the gate of a book were no small matter to eighteenth-century readers.[94]

The sovereign consisted, in Rousseau's view, of the individuals who composed it.[95] So, where there were ten thousand citizens, each would enjoy one ten-thousandth of the city's sovereignty; where there were one hundred thousand, one hundred-thousandth, and so on in due proportion. As a polis expanded, the increasing disjunction between particular wills and the general will would of necessity bring about a corresponding disjunction between mores and laws; the force invested in government would grow, and there would consequently be a diminution in liberty. The less liberty there was, the more often the sovereign people would have to assemble, if usurpation were to be avoided.[96] One may clearly see from this description that Rousseau set out from an individualism as intransigent as that of Constant, and that, far from being the advocate of a totalitarian state, he held it in particular horror.[97] Meinecke refers at one point to 'the lofty insight that the state is an ideal supra-individual personality', but this was a doctrine altogether alien to Rousseau.[98] It is true that he had stated that each citizen within the *populus Romanus* was a part of the whole, so that harm done to one would damage all the others; the general will, he declared, would no sooner permit one member of the state to wound or destroy another than a man in his right mind would allow his fingers to tear out his eyes.[99] Yet this vision ought not to be confused with the social machine described by Condorcet or by Durkheim, as anyone who reverses Rousseau's dicta will readily allow. For to cry that each citizen is *not* a part of the city, or that harm done to one does *not* damage all the others, is to invite the moral havoc wreaked by a narrowly economic calculus.

Rousseau also had no illusions about the many illustrious examples in the annals of Rome of the sacrifice of an individual to the common good. If virtuous patriots, of their own free will, were to sacrifice themselves, all honour to them. But if the maxim that one should perish for all were taken to mean that a government was entitled 'to sacrifice an innocent man for the good of the multitude', it should be reckoned 'one of the most execrable rules tyranny ever invented, the greatest falsehood that can be advanced, the most dangerous admission that can be made, and a direct contradiction of the most fundamental laws of society'.[100] Staël almost certainly had such passages in mind when she contrasted Brutus's acquiescence in the destruction of what he loved (his treacherous sons) with the Terrorists' hounding of those they hated.[101] Their deeper meaning, however, a meaning at times lost to Staël and Constant, would seem to be that the very possibility of a person freely choosing to sacrifice himself or herself for others serves as a proof that goodness exists, and that the good issues from a displayed, assembled people. In these terms, it would be evil to mistake independence for liberty and therefore to deny the existence of society, and so, in our own day, it has proved.

If, however, to return to the detail of *The Social Contract*, the sovereign consists of the particular individuals of which it is composed, one might at first suppose that an Aristotelian notion of the proper size for a polis had caused Rousseau to despair of modern societies altogether, and to deny, much as Montesquieu had done, that ancient liberty could ever be revived. Although texts to support such an interpretation exist, in the major political writings drafted and published between 1754 and 1762 the example of Rome is used to show that liberty could be sustained on a larger scale, on condition that regular assemblies of the sovereign people were held on specified (and irrevocable) dates. The Roman republic was, Rousseau pointed out, a great state, and Rome a great town; the last census recorded four hundred thousand citizens as entitled to bear arms, and the last computation of the population of the Empire gave a tally of over four million citizens, 'yet few weeks passed without the Roman people being in assembly, and even being so several times'.[102] This key passage, hectoring in tone, defies the Moderns to be true, in spite of complicating circumstance, to the principle of popular sovereignty, and I think it is not fanciful to hear echoes of it in the aftermath of the American Revolution, in the later writings of Diderot.

Having paraphrased Berlin's interpretation of Rousseau, I want now to consider in some detail the debate on the topic of negative and positive liberty that has been held in the years since the lecture was first delivered.[103] One response to the dyad has been to argue that it rests upon a confusion regarding the concept of freedom. If, Gerald C. MacCallum argues, we consider those contexts that are said to be free, we find that 'such freedom is . . . always *of* something (an agent or agents), *from* something, *to* do, not do, become, or not become something'. All liberty may thus be construed as a triadic relation, and when theorists talk of 'freedom from' or 'freedom to', each of which is formulated as a dyadic relation, they are therefore selecting arbitrarily from a more complex circumstance. Although MacCallum claims to be jettisoning the distinction between negative and positive liberty, he is in effect proposing that all liberty is of the former variety. Freedom, he declares, is always and necessarily *from* restraint, and where the advocates of positive freedom speak of persons being made free *by means of* restraint, they are guilty of a contradiction in terms. No one, in short, can be forced to be free.[104]

Another response to Berlin's lecture has been to argue that liberty is best defined as positive, not negative, and that, far from being merely 'a lack of regulation of individual behaviour', it entails both the existence of, and the practice of, a set of agreed or shared virtues. Alasdair MacIntyre, whose thought exemplifies this second, communitarian, position, has claimed that the doctrine of radical incommensurability of values is a counsel of despair, and has argued that the project of reconstructing morality in a disenchanted world should proceed by way of Aristotle, or not at all. In the Aristotelian account, to be properly human is to be a social being or, more accurately, a member of the polis, and to tend towards the good; the virtues are then those qualities that will bring a person nearer to that good. As in the other societies that ethnologists have traditionally studied, so too in the Greek world in which Aristotle lived, such virtues arose out of, and served to reinforce, defined social roles. 'Ought' and 'is' had not been sundered. If moral philosophy flounders in modern times, it is, MacIntyre maintains, because its categories have survived a momentous transformation, so that they are stranded, as it were, after a deluge; to comprehend them, one has painstakingly to reconstruct a vanished context of shared belief. Judging it a hopeless dream 'to reinvent morality on the scale of the whole nation', as the Jacobin Clubs had tried to do, the last best hope for humanity, in MacIntyre's opinion, lies in 'the construction of local forms of community within which the moral life can be sustained through the new dark ages which are already upon us'.[105] A new monasticism, for such it is, seems a poor sort of programme to be offered by an author whose early essays appeared in *The New Reasoner*. It is never clear how anyone might begin to resurrect that lost time when virtues were virtues, and human lives, as if framed by the Scrovegni Chapel, took their measure, deed by deed, from a totalizing narrative.

Quentin Skinner, in his succinct exposition of the central argument of *After Virtue*, observes that Aristotelianism is not the sole alternative to liberalism, and that a third option, the classical republican tradition, permits the supposedly impossible reconciliation of positive with negative liberty. To be more specific, it allows the rehabilitation of two claims that, for Gerald MacCallum, can have no meaning. The first claim, in Quentin Skinner's words, 'connects freedom with self-government, and in consequence links the idea of personal liberty, in a seemingly paradoxical way, with that of public service'. This claim, which rests upon the classical ideal of a participation in government so general as to confound the distinction between ruler and ruled, has conflicted in modern times with the defence of apathy mounted by liberal theorists, from Benjamin Constant to Seymour Lipset. The second, related, claim states that 'we may have to be forced to be free, and thus connects the idea of individual liberty, in an even more blatantly paradoxical fashion, with the concepts of coercion and constraint'. By way of explanation, Skinner adds that this second claim turns upon the assumption that 'we may sometimes fail to remember – or may altogether fail to grasp – that the performance of our public duties is indispensable to the maintenance of our liberty'.[106] If, then, the common good is fragile, and easily destroyed, it is because individuals, left to their own devices, are prey to corruption. The argument thus restores the unity of the ethical and the political, without which the city is lost, but does not require the full list of the Aristotelian virtues. As MacIntyre has himself observed, referring explicitly to the classical republican tradition, virtue is then primary, the virtues secondary.[107]

As in Rousseau's case, so too in that of Machiavelli, all trace of a theory of negative liberty has generally been denied. Yet Skinner's careful scrutiny of the *Discourses* reveals that such a theory does exist.[108] Taking for granted that 'all men are wicked and . . . never do good unless necessity drives them to it', and that their baser appetites are at once ineliminable and insatiable, Machiavelli distinguishes between the 'dispositions' of two opposed categories of people, each of which sets great store by its liberty, but with different ends in mind. The *grandi* desire to dominate, and so to win glory; the *plebe* or *popolo* wish not to be dominated, to lead a quiet life, in secure possession of their property. Both groups seek to be free, that is to say, not to be hindered in the pursuit of their chosen ends. However, their dispositions may cause each to act intemperately, the rich and powerful having, on the one hand, an excessive desire for domination; the populace, on the other, an excessive desire for freedom from interference. In the case of Rome, the tyrannical acts of the once virtuous Quintus Fabius or Manlius Capitolinus were matched by the tumultuous retreat of the insurgent plebs to the Mons Sacer.

Having argued that the given elements in a polity pursue different ends, Machiavelli further insists that only in a free city, where there is a *vivere libero*, can their respective aspirations be met. What criteria must be fulfilled for a city to qualify as free? To begin with, it must be independent of any external master, and therefore driven solely by the general will of its citizens. In this regard, the *Discourses* bear the impress of the claims of the Italian city-state to be *sibi princeps*, or 'a prince unto itself'.[109] Second, a city can only maintain its liberty, and therefore its strength, for so long as citizens value the common good more highly than their own self-interest, and so valuing it, do their duty. So much did virtue here trump the virtues that perfidy and cruelty could be justified, if collective liberty were at risk; here, as I show in chapter 6, the *Discourses* and *The Prince* were equally a scandal to Christendom. An ill-disposed reader might suspect Machiavelli of a readiness to sacrifice negative liberty, to the common good, whereas he merely holds that it is in the best interests of all citizens, high or low, to value the common good. In other, more modern, terms, negative liberty is best guaranteed by positive liberty. As far as external independence was concerned, this tenet found expression in militias, for a city would fall, and its citizens be enslaved, if they failed to fight courageously in its defence. The eighteenth-century critique of classical republicanism rested in large measure upon the claim, later reiterated by Constant, that this was no longer so. Since the rich and the powerful existed everywhere, they might also emerge from within, buy the support of the populace, form factions, subvert the laws and bring about the ruin of the city.

It may be in the best interests of citizens to value the common good more highly than their own, but it is in their nature to fail to grasp, or to forget that this is so, and thereby to seal their own doom. Machiavelli writes of citizens being blinded by 'a false image of the good', so that they either fall into apathy, neglect their public duties and let the city become the prey of factions, or seek to turn law to their own advantage.[110] To maintain liberty, given such countervailing forces, is no easy matter, and although Machiavelli points to the importance of great-souled example, of education and of religion, it is law, above all else, that he celebrates. When, however, Machiavelli advances the oxymoron that law forces us to be free, his interpretation of it ought not to be confused with that of contractarian thinkers, who had generally posited a double, rather than a single contract. John Locke, for example, in the *Two Treatises of Government*, argued that men abandon the state of nature and agree to associate in civil society, in order to guarantee the security of their own persons and property, and then, having entered into such a *pactum societatis*, they make a *pactum subjectionis*, and thereby transfer power to a sovereign. Since individuals bring what they own into civil society, the law can only be said to force them to be free insofar as it guards each from the putative wrongdoing of others. The state, in short, chiefly exists to protect private interests; it seems to draw a circle around individuals possessed of rights, so that the coercion employed to sustain the sovereignty of law is aimed at the miscreant deeds of law-breaking others, and not at the always fragile virtue of the law-abiding self. For all its majestic universality, law in this interpretation functions merely to avert collisions between eternally separated individual wills.[111] By contrast, in the *Discourses*, the law coerces one and all into setting aside their self-interest, and into doing their duty as citizens for, without such rallying of citizens to the common good, the city would dissolve.

The theory of the double contract was endorsed, as we have seen, by the makers of the Constitution of the year III, and by Sieyes and Constant, although a positivist ethnology and jurisprudence had already begun to veil such images of assembly and inaugural decision. In the course of the nineteenth century, the juridical notion of the corporation, first elaborated by Savigny but later embraced by many others, would make it increasingly difficult to present Rousseau's vision of a sovereign, self-governing people in its true colours. For, in *The Social Contract*, the act by which a people submits to its leaders was not a 'contract' but a 'commission', that is, 'a form of employment in which the governors, as simple officers of the sovreign, exercise in its name the power it has placed in their hands'.[112] These radical formulations reflect Rousseau's understanding of the relation between sovereign and government in the ancient city, in which the distinction between the citizenry and the authorities was indeed minimal. In the Athenian democracy, Finley has observed: 'there was no bureaucracy or civil service, save for a few clerks, slaves owned by the state itself, who kept such records as were unavoidable, copies of treaties and laws, lists of defaulting taxpayers and the like'; at Rome, Nicolet has stated, 'despite the imposing spectacle of the magistrates' retinue, the apparatus of government and what may be called the civil service . . . were of a most rudimentary kind'.[113] Furthermore, since citizens were frequently obliged, whether by lot or by election, to serve as magistrates, the distinction between state and civil society was clearly not applicable. In stating that 'the government is in small what the body politic (which includes it) is in large', Rousseau had given aphoristic expression to this fact, whereas Staël, in declaring that representation was not 'a scaled-down representation which gives a picture of the people in miniature', had claimed, for the Moderns, a salutary discontinuity.[114] She further remarked that, in a representative government, it was not the individuals of which a nation was composed, but rather the nation's interests, which were represented.[115] Those who have studied the works of Staël have noted their cosmopolitan temper, and their Enlightenment insistence that *esprit national* was characteristic of ancient, not modern, societies.[116] Nonetheless, I propose to show in later chapters that her writings were from the turn of the century increasingly marked by a rhetoric that, belief in the city-nation being destroyed, derived its hortatory force from the imagined inherence of single persons in a unitary and eternal corporation, the tribe-nation. In short, disillusion with the republican ideals of public service, and of the common good displayed, led her to replace the mourned earthly city with a heavenly city, and so to sacralize the invisible nation as ground of right.

# Noble Savages, Primitive Peoples

## Chateaubriand among the *philosophes*

I wish now to consider the honour in which the New World, and its peoples, was held by educated Europeans in the eighteenth century, and the dishonour that followed hard upon its heels, even as the nineteenth century dawned. The terms of my argument will be carried first by Chateaubriand and then by Volney, for their contrasting philosophies reflect the shifting place of the Americas in the world-view of late Enlightenment France. I have set out in this book to describe the process by which the prestige of the ancient city became tarnished in the aftermath of the French Revolution, and by which the imagined qualities of the noble savage were transferred to the Germanic tribes, the massed origin of the Christian nations. Although a general shift of attention from distant lands to ancestral tombs indubitably occurred, manifest as much in the apparent displacement of the Société des Observateurs de l'Homme by the Académie Celtique as in the recoil from *Les Natchez* to *Les Martyrs*, a clear distinction ought, nonetheless, to be drawn between a Romantic singing of the tribe-nation (Chateaubriand) and an Enlightenment grading of the placed forms of associated life (Volney).

The birthplace of Chateaubriand, the port of Saint-Malo, had long been associated with the New World. His father made his fortune as a ship's outfitter, and had used it to restore the name and honour of his family, in origin a part of the *noblesse de race*. It is a surprise, therefore, to discover that his favourite book was, as his son recalled, the abbé Raynal's *Histoire Philosophique des Deux Indes*, an envenomed and at times bitterly pessimistic balance-sheet of seventeenth- and eighteenth-century colonialism, a sequel of sorts to the Encyclopédie and one of the most radical texts of the closing years of the old regime. It is at any rate possible that the original inspiration for Chateaubriand's *Les Natchez*, his 'epic of the man of nature', was supplied by Raynal's vast, rambling compilation, for the chapter on Louisiana includes a brief account of that famous tribe, together with an account of the three Natchez Wars (1729, 1736, 1741). Had Chateaubriand read Charlevoix's *Histoire de la Nouvelle France* (1744) in his youth, he would have noticed that settlers from Saint-Malo had colonized Louisiana, and even Natchez itself, in the years after 1716. For him, however, satirical traffic between the court of Louis XIV, or the Regency, and forest and savannah, was no abstract matter. If, therefore, his early writings contain denunciations of the follies and cruelties of European settlers, merchants and soldiers, this was not only because he was steeped in Rousseau and Raynal, and caught their tones in the whispering gallery of peoples destroyed. For the quays of Saint-Malo and Combourg were a triumphal arch, framing the general idea of the Americas, much as those of Bordeaux had framed new worlds, and so offered intimations of a new science, for travellers and missionaries (such as Charlevoix and Lafitau) or for essayists and jurisconsults (such as Montaigne and Montesquieu).[1]

Although Chateaubriand's first ambition had been to serve, like his father, in the French navy or, at his mother's prompting, to go with the Jesuits to Canada, an army commission brought him to Paris, at scattered intervals in 1786 and 1787, for longer stretches between 1788 and 1791, and so to the *philosophes*.[2] His years in the capital are sketched in *Les Martyrs*, the hero of which, Eudorus, falls under the spell of the sophists, Voltaireans in Roman dress.[3] In his memoirs, the first volume of which was begun in 1811, the impression is given that his fight against the materialism and atheism of the Enlightenment had begun as early as the 1780s, and that he had always known that an impious age would yield to a revival of Christian belief, yet he had been, as his early writings testify, a *philosophe*, connected by marriage to the illustrious Malesherbes, and numbering among his friends Delisle de Sales, Parny, Fontanes, La Harpe and Ginguené, poets and critics whose primary allegiance at that time was to the tradition of the Encyclopédie. In a number of the lengthy notes to the original edition of his *Essai Historique*, Chateaubriand expressed a yearning for the friendships he had formed in pre-revolutionary Paris, and wished for reconciliation with those whose lives had been driven another way. Only after his sudden conversion (or, more accurately, return) to Roman Catholicism, in July 1798, would his quarrel with such figures as Ginguené or Parny, the author of the scurrilous *Guerre des Dieux*, become too bitter to resolve.

## Volney, Chateaubriand and the French Revolution

During the early years of the Revolution, Chateaubriand spent almost as much time in his native Brittany as in Paris, and it was in fact at Rennes, as he recalled in his memoirs, that his political education began. In the struggles of 1787–89, which brought the magistracy into bitter conflict with king and ministers, and set the Breton aristocracy against the Breton Third Estate, there could never have been any doubt as to Chateaubriand's loyalties: 'I was born a gentleman . . . I have benefited from the accident of my birth and have kept that more resolute love of liberty which characterises the aristocracy, [though] its last hour has struck.'[4] Whereas the *Essai Historique* bears all the marks of the disorientation of Thermidor, and displays at times as bleakly absurdist a view of distinctions of rank as Chamfort had entertained, these lines, written long after their author's return to church and tradition, betray an unmixed pride in his aristocratic descent.[5] The shades of Fénelon, Boulainvilliers and Montesquieu haunt the genealogical proofs, so alien to the sensibility both of Rousseau and of his followers, which are presented, with a stone face, in the memoirs. We learn there that the family name was originally Castrum-Briani, and that Geoffrey, Baron de Chateaubriand, had fought with Saint-Louis in the Holy Land. Moreover, when Louis XIV had enquired, in 1669, into the legitimacy or otherwise of titles of nobility, those of Christophe de Chateaubriand had passed muster. One can readily imagine how, as a sick, near-starving emigré, Chateaubriand might have scrutinized the tombs in Westminster Abbey, in order to discern there the eternal essence of a national tradition and the glowing contrary of a ransacked and desecrated Saint-Denis.[6]

Although the chief resistance to royal or ministerial despotism, as it was known in the 1780s, came from the Parlement of Paris, the provinces also played a crucial role. Brittany, for example, possessed powerful provincial estates, which over the years had clawed back privileges from the central government. The Royal Treasury, in a state of crisis since the end of the American War, had imposed ever more onerous taxes, rejected out of hand by both the provincial estates and the local *parlements*. The latter, adept since the 1750s in the flamboyant use of the terminology of rights and of social contract, were then able to advance their claim, to the distaste of most of the *philosophes*, to be both the champions of the people and the guardians of the fundamental laws of the kingdom.[7] The conflict between the government and the Parlement of Paris came to a head on 5 May 1788, when Loménie de Brienne ordered troops to surround the law courts. Two of the most prominent members of the dissident *noblesse de robe* were arrested, and on 8 May Lamoignon, the Keeper of the Seals, enforced the registration of six edicts by means of a *lit de justice*.

This legislation, if implemented, would have had the most momentous consequences. First of all, the right to register royal edicts was to be withdrawn from the *parlements* and vested in a single 'plenary' court, whose officers would be princes of the blood and appointees of the Crown. To create at a stroke what was in effect a Curia Regis was a significant step on the path to an untrammelled absolutism. Second, the old judicial districts, known as bailiwicks and seneschalsies, were to be abolished. In their place, courts known as upper bailiwicks were to handle the majority of cases both criminal and civil. Lamoignon had hoped by these measures to attract the liberal aristocracy and the advocates and lawyers of the Third Estate to the royal cause, for it was they, not the robe or the sword, who would have filled the new posts, but this attempt to establish a greater degree of absolutism in the kingdom was greeted with the most furious protests. Opposition to the edicts was to be found at every level of the social hierarchy, and in virtually every province in France. Although the remonstrations of the dukes and peers, and of the senior clergy, were of real importance, the most clamorous resistance was provincial. In cities traditionally jealous of their rights and liberties, such as Toulouse, Dijon, Pau, Grenoble, Rouen and Bordeaux, the king's officers were often manhandled, and the populace came close at times to open revolt. In Rennes, the Breton nobility, Chateaubriand among them, assembled to protest at the creation of a plenary court.[8] A declaration of protest was drafted, and twelve 'gentlemen' were chosen to present the document, which was in the name of both the Parlement and the Provincial Estates of Brittany. The twelve were dispatched to the Bastille, as was a second delegation from Rennes. However, as the agitation in the country showed no signs of abating, the king reversed his original decision, granting a third Breton delegation an audience and promising to convene their estates. Finally, on 8 August 1788, he undertook to convoke the States General, on 1 May 1789. Necker was recalled on 25 August, and on 14 September Lamoignon resigned.

There was, however, to be no lull, for the *parlements*, in posing as the people's champion, had unleashed forces that they were no longer able to control. Indeed, no sooner had they declared that the States General would have the same form as in 1614 than their popular support evaporated. Whereas the *parlementaires* insisted that the estates should sit, as they had done before, in three separate orders or houses, each having the same number of deputies and being entitled to only a single vote, so that the first two orders (clergy and nobility) would invariably have the upper hand, the pamphleteers of the Third Estate began to press the case for voting by head, rather than by order, in a single assembly. Although not yet republican, the concept of the nation that the patriot or national party favoured was predicated upon a radical refusal of arguments from historical precedent, dear to both the robe and the sword. Existing constitutions were no better than accidents of history, the fruit of conquests that had installed monarchs, peers and commoners in conquered territories.[9] 'The most respectable title a French noble may possess', wrote Chamfort, on intimate terms with Chateaubriand in the late 1780s, 'is that of being directly descended from some of those thirty thousand helmeted, cuirassed, brassarded and cuissarded men who, on huge, steel-clad horses trampled underfoot eight or nine million unarmed men, the ancestors of the present-day nation.'[10] There is a darker aspect to this Voltairean prose, the piling up of the old French calling to mind the effect achieved by Bresson in *Lancelot du Lac*.

Although it would not do to exaggerate the influence of the Committee of Thirty, which met at the house of Adrien du Port in Paris, and which included Condorcet, La Fayette, Mirabeau, Sieyes and Talleyrand, it is true that the Third Estate pamphlets of the autumn, winter and spring of 1788–89 bear a striking resemblance one to the other.[11] The first priority, evident as much in Volney's *La Sentinelle du Peuple* as in Sieyes's more celebrated *Qu'est-ce que le Tiers Etat?*, was to overturn the rule of the dead which the nobility of the sword, by virtue of Frankish precedent, still defended. Volney, dispatched to Rennes by the Committee of Thirty, remarked upon the overwhelming numerical preponderance of the commoners, and contrasted their industry with the sloth of the aristocracy. Since the commoners enjoyed a monopoly of the useful arts, why should they not brave the disdain of the first two orders by seceding? The Third Estate was, after all, not merely an order, but the nation itself, to which the unproductive nobility and clergy were in fact extraneous.[12] The same arguments were presented still more dramatically in *The Ruins of Empires*, the text that best exemplifies the visionary hopes of 1789–91 and which was to be cherished in Britain by the Chartists. In chapter 15, the diehard nobility declared themselves to be 'the *pure* and *noble race* of conquerors of this empire'. 'Pure race of conquerors!' the people retorted, 'show us your genealogies! Then we shall see what in an individual is *theft* and *rapine* becomes virtue in a nation.'[13] This was the same message that Condorcet had hammered home in 1789, when he had declared that no nation in which there was a legally accredited genealogist could be free.[14]

When Chateaubriand's sisters returned to Paris, late in 1788, he resolved to remain in Brittany, so as to sit with the provincial estates at Rennes. A novelist would be tempted to stage a meeting between the emissary of the Committee of Thirty and the Breton aristocrat, but there is no evidence for it. Chateaubriand later recorded in his memoirs that 'a newspaper, *La Sentinelle du Peuple*, written by a hack from Paris, fomented hatred', but he did not deign to mention the hack's name, nor the fact that he too was a native of Brittany.[15] Several comments are in order here.

To begin with, there is no trace of any sympathy in Chateaubriand's memoirs for the Third Estate, although he does record his own want of enthusiasm, as if to say, with hindsight, that he was neither of one party nor of the other.[16] In January, bitter street fighting broke out between the nobility and the law students of Rennes, supported by a contingent from Nantes, led by Moreau, subsequently a republican general and a potential rival, under the Consulate, to Bonaparte. It was in the summer that Chateaubriand returned to Paris, having missed the opening of the States General, and the Tennis Court Oath. He witnessed the storming of the Bastille, and the killing of the Marquis de Launay, and of Flesselles; he was still more horrified, as I noted in an earlier chapter, by the sight of the heads, paraded on the ends of pikes, of Foulon and Bertier de Sauvigny. Did Chateaubriand really cry out to the rioters, at some personal risk, 'Brigands! . . . is this your understanding of liberty?', or was it with hindsight that he formulated this provocative question? We cannot know, but it is certainly possible that such violence served as a brutal invitation to embark. Morellet had taken his distance from the other members of the Auteuil Circle, Chamfort and Ginguené among them, during the campaign over the composition of the States General, and had recoiled in horror at the murders perpetrated in the summer of 1789; Fontanes and his associates were as appalled as were the *monarchiens* by the events of 5 and 6 October, and would soon be calling for moderation.[17] Chateaubriand may well have felt the same, and Malesherbes, closely linked to the court and preserving a belief in antiquarian and prescriptive justification of rights, could have urged him, as he was again to do in 1792, to quit an increasingly lawless state.

A second consideration needs here to be joined to the first, for Chateaubriand's impulse to flee was very probably fuelled by the separatist aspirations of the Breton nobility. He recalled how, 'weary of being blockaded [in the provincial estates at Rennes] . . . we resolved to sally forth, sword in hand. We made a fine picture. When our president gave the command, we drew our swords, crying "Vive la Bretagne!".'[18] When Brittany had first been united with the kingdom of France, in 1532, an edict had guaranteed its liberties and privileges; once these had been trampled upon, the Breton nobility would clearly not hesitate, as Malesherbes had warned Louis XVI in the summer of 1788, to opt for open rebellion.[19] Indeed, '[they] refused to sit in the States General, because its convocation had breached the fundamental laws of the province's constitution; [they] would later throng to the Princes' Army, be slaughtered with Condée or with Charette in the Vendée'.[20] Throughout his life Chateaubriand would receive help or encouragement from fellow Bretons (Ginguené, the Marquis de la Rouërie, Hingant, Peltier and Boisgelin, Archbishop of Aix), and one biographer has even speculated that his decision to leave London for Suffolk in the autumn of 1793 was prompted not merely by his desperate material circumstances in the capital but also by the wish to avoid volunteering for General Lord Moira's expedition to Brittany to aid the Chouans and the Vendée.[21] This seems a plausible observation, since 340 emigrés enlisted from London alone. For one who had rallied to the Princes, and so marched against his own country, it would have been a redoubled agony to fight for the British in Brittany. There are veiled references to this anguish in the second part of *Les Natchez*, much of which was probably drafted in Suffolk. Given Chateaubriand's Breton origins, it is not in any way surprising to find that his ruminations on French national identity invariably included a reference to the Celtic culture of his own province (and, indeed, to Celtic culture in general). I would, however, contrast his antiquarian researches in this domain, which allow Holy Scripture, ecclesiology and Frankish historical right to obscure the prestige of a 'first people' closely linked to his birthplace, with those of La Revellière-Lépeaux and Volney, who were actively involved, as I show in chapter 9, with the Académie Celtique.

The third, and most obvious, comment to be made upon Chateaubriand's disdainful reference to *La Sentinelle du Peuple* concerns the fact that the memoirs often cut down to size or denigrate figures, for example, Chamfort, Delisle de Sales, Ginguené and Parny, who had featured in the author's early life but who had followed a different path in later years. Memory may by its very nature entail some pruning or cutting back, but a weeding out of the compromised, for vanity's sake, is another matter. There can be few more shameful passages in the whole of French literature than the description of Chamfort, which is belied by the portrait in the *Essai Historique*, and which betrays not a trace of fellow feeling for a friend who, after atrocious suffering, had died by his own hand.[22] At first Volney seems to come under this head, but on closer inspection his proves to be a special case. So many parallels could be drawn between the two lives that Chateaubriand would appear to have taken particular pains to obscure the name, and to scale down the historical importance of his Breton rival. If one bears in mind that *La Génie du Christianisme*, though ostensibly a rebuttal of Parny's *Guerre des Dieux*, was covertly a refutation of the works of Volney, rivalry will not seem too strong a term. For the ruins of Palmyra that Volney's traveller sadly contemplates are in essence the mute witness to despotism and therefore a vindication of a cosmopolitan, universalist rationalism, whereas the traces of human settlement in Chateaubriand's writings announce a return to the sacralized time of Christian-national tradition.[23] The former, in the absence of innate ideas, testify to the primacy of culture as praxis, the latter to the triumph of culture as spirit. So fundamental were the terms of this undeclared contest that Giacomo Leopardi, disregarding the liberal historians (Thierry, Guizot) whom Chateaubriand had inspired, would in the 1820s invoke the example, against the all-pervasive and cloying providentialism of the age, of Volney.

## A journey to America

In the last quarter of the eighteenth century, enthusiasm for America, and for American liberty, became ever more intense in France. The vogue for travel literature showed no sign of abating, and the Jesuits, under attack from reforming regimes everywhere in Europe in the 1750s and 1760s, published many volumes describing their missionary activities in the New World; no account of the formation of the *philosophes* would be complete if it did not refer to their perusal, when young, of the *Lettres Edifiantes*.[24] The incessant wars of the period, though ostensibly dynastic, had invariably sparked off tributary conflagrations at their colonial edge, so much so, indeed, that the ethical and political identity of Europe seemed to lie as much in its settlements abroad and in its trading-posts as in its own land mass. The names of John Law and of Warren Hastings are proof enough of this point.

Rousseau had warned that, once the mores of a people were corrupted, their liberty could never be restored, and many publicists in France in the 1770s and 1780s clearly agreed that the great European monarchies had little future, and that even the republics were hastening to their end.[25] The principle of the ineluctable decline of the earthly city, so central to classical republican thought, did not apply to America, which seemed to be a pristine wall upon which the clear lines of ancient liberty could be drawn, the unmuddied colours of hope be laid. To a greater extent even than Geneva, Philadelphia, a city whose name alone cried redemption, was a standing reproach to Paris or to Versailles.[26]

When the first edition of Raynal's *Histoire Philosophique* appeared, in 1772, the rebellion of the American colonies was still to come. In later editions, however, the war of independence, seen by so many as a reenactment of the heroic struggle of the Swiss cantons or of the United Provinces against the Emperor, was described at length, with the relevant chapters being excerpted as a separate publication in 1781.[27] The fall from power of the *philosophe* minister, Turgot, who was to have ushered in a golden age of enlightened reforms, had caused many to shift their attention wholesale to America, regarding the fate of France with black despair. In the case of Diderot, who had composed some of the most radical passages in the later versions of the *Histoire Philosophique*, a breach with Catherine the Great in 1774 had likewise rendered the liberty on the other side of the Atlantic a more attractive proposition, as his *Essai sur les Règnes de Claude et de Néron*, written between 1778 and 1782, proves. The event that had done the most, however, to promote the colonists' cause in France had been the arrival, late in 1776, of the new ambassador, Benjamin Franklin. *Philosophes* had long been familiar with his researches into the nature of electricity, but his prestige now came to rival that of Voltaire or Rousseau; here, before their very eyes, was a living copy of Cato the Censor, of Fabricius or of Cincinnatus. Modern historians like to poke fun at the enthusiasm, evident as much in court circles as at Auteuil, for the uncouthness of the American ambassador, yet, like the tirades directed at classical republican rhetoric, such jibes betray an anachronistic lack of sympathy for the very political tensions of the times. The point is that the reform that Rousseau had embarked upon, slowly and painfully, in the 1750s, and which had brought to light, perhaps for the first time, the conditions under which an artisan lived and worked, was mirrored in the life story and demeanour of Franklin. This parallel was reinforced by the apparent similarities between the cities of Geneva and Philadelphia, one founded (or, more accurately, reformed) by Calvin, the other by Penn. Although some admirers preferred to emphasize the affinities between Voltaire and Franklin, Chamfort's review of the great scientist's memoirs compared the mores of the artisans of Geneva with those of New England.[28] After the Declaration of Independence, in 1776, the French liberal nobility became enraptured with the American cause. The Marquis de Lafayette set sail, at the age of nineteen, to fight for the rebels, and his exploits made him famous throughout Europe; others in his circle studied the newly drafted American constitutions and, at Franklin's request, translated a number of them. *Philosophes* like Turgot and Condorcet were adamant that New World polities, lacking a hereditary aristocracy, had no need of a mixed constitution. Their preference, therefore, was for the Pennsylvanian solution, which featured just one chamber.[29]

The attention of the French was not only drawn by the colonists' war with the British, or by virtuous communities on the eastern seaboard, for reports were filtering back of the frontier, a honeypot for Utopians of every stripe. In Paris itself, the Sioto Company, founded to promote a colony in the Ohio territories, offered a delightful climate, a river stocked with fish, fine forests with sugar maple trees, abundant game (but no wolves, foxes, lions or tigers) and pasturage. In a land of plenty declared to be free of the most terrible burdens suffered by the peoples of the Old World, particular emphasis was naturally placed upon taxation, the *casus belli* of 1776, and perhaps the most contentious issue in the financially stricken France of the 1780s. 'In the most beautiful canton in the United States', the handbill promised, 'one would be liable neither to tithes nor to a poll-tax, nor to military service nor to garrisoning of soldiers.'[30] Chateaubriand knew of the venture, and of the proposed settlement of Gallipolis; in retrospect he would contrast one emigration with the other, and would bitterly regret his decision to throw in his lot with the Princes' Army at Coblenz rather than with the settlers in the Ohio Territories.[31] Volney, who later visited the colony, as I shall shortly show, was none too impressed by the material shape the dream had taken, and mocked the readers of Brissot and Crèvecoeur for their folly.

Chateaubriand's moral and intellectual preparation for his journey may be seen in terms of the influence upon him of Malesherbes, his mentor in the years between 1787 and 1790, of Rousseau, with whom he identified to the point of idolatry, and of the tradition of Diderot and the Encyclopédie. To separate out these sometimes opposed, sometimes convergent, inheritances is no easy matter, but a start can be made if we recall that Chateaubriand's conversations with Malesherbes returned often to geography, geology, botany and ethnology. Like Rousseau, Malesherbes was a keen amateur botanist, with many specimens from the New World in his collection. One of his nephews, Anne César de La Luzerne, had been appointed Minister Plenipotentiary to Congress in 1779, and was in Philadelphia until 1783, so his ties with America were close. He was on good terms also with all of the American envoys posted to Paris, their talk always of plants and trees; specimens were obtained, for instance from Bartram, the celebrated Quaker naturalist from Philadelphia, but his enthusiasm was more for the agricultural improvements of the *philosophes* than for the wistful botanizing of Rousseau in his last years.[32]

Although Chateaubriand embraced Malesherbes's more strictly scientific enthusiasms and planned in all seriousness to discover the North-West Passage, he had also been swayed by Rousseau's meditations on plant life. The author of *Emile* may long have been a philosopher of solitude, but it is clear that the shock of 1762 worked a change in him, and that botanizing offered consolation for his disappointment in human society, where at times he seemed himself almost a plant among plants, and not a man at all. So many in the late Enlightenment wished to be an Aeolian harp that it is tempting to argue that Hegel's *Phenomenology of Spirit*, to stand as an exhaustive record of the yearnings of a generation, should have included a passage scored for *belle âme* and *bel arbre*.[33]

Chateaubriand set sail for the New World in May 1791, a letter of introduction to General Washington in his pocket. During the crossing he struck up an acquaintance with a seminarist by the name of Tulloch, a recent convert to Roman Catholicism, half-Scottish and with a rare and much-envied talent for declaiming the poems of Ossian in the original Gaelic.[34] When the ship docked at Saint-Pierre, a misty, pine-clad island, the two young men went ashore. Both *Atala* and *Les Natchez* are imbued with the spirit of Ossian, and the landscape of Louisiana has at times an uncanny resemblance, in Chateaubriand's lacquered prose, to the Highlands of Scotland. In the early 1790s we must suppose that Macpherson's inventions were driven by Chateaubriand, as by Constant, against the grain of Holy Scripture, and bore witness to the essentially pagan notion of 'first times' for which the Encyclopedists had campaigned so forcefully. However, in this respect as in so many others, Chateaubriand was a profoundly transitional figure. As a friend of Delisle de Sales, he was already predisposed to resacralize the auroral America of John Locke.[35]

First times required first peoples, and here Chateaubriand drew upon the researches of Lafitau among the Iroquois. In *Customs of the American Indians*, the 'man of nature' was altogether from, and for, God, who 'had inscribed the elementary truths of natural religion in the hearts of all men'. A primordial virtue could in short be glimpsed through a deformed and deforming screen, with pagan religions, idolatrous and magical, being transformations of the pure beliefs of Eden; the gods and goddesses of non-Christian mythology were simply distorted images of Adam and Eve.[36] In the composition of *Les Natchez*, Chateaubriand used not only Lafitau, whose diffusionist hypotheses he accepted, but other Jesuit missionaries also, among them Lafitau's colleague, Charlevoix. Yet *A Discourse on the Origins of Inequality* contained a naturalistic view of the Creation presupposing a far longer time-scale than the Book of Genesis had allowed. As a contributor to the Encyclopédie, Rousseau was familiar with the assault that the *philosophes*, Diderot prominent among them, had made upon Old Testament chronology.[37] Researches into the annals of the ancient historians had cast doubt upon the testimony of Jewish and Christian apologists, and Volney, for example, judged it mistaken to take the chronology of the Jewish people as the yardstick by which all the pagan annals should be measured, and denied outright the dates given for the Creation by Bishop Ussher (4004 BC), by Scaliger (3950 BC) and by Petau (3984 BC).[38] Since many of his strictly scientific arguments were drawn from Buffon's writings, Rousseau was also aware of the threat that recent advances in the earth sciences, even before James Hutton, posed to the account given in Genesis. He knew, for example, of Buffon's claim that the earth was at least seventy-four thousand, and very probably as much as three million, years old.[39]

The *Essai* owed a debt not only to the second discourse but also to Volney's demolition of the traditional chronology of the Old Testament. Thus, in a note, Chateaubriand referred to the calculations of Manetho, an Egyptian priest who wrote in Greek around the middle of the third century BC, the clear implication being that his estimate of five thousand years – obscured in Julius Africanus's account – far exceeded the reckonings of Ussher, Scaliger or Petau.[40] Yet more telling proof of the fact that human history filled but the last page in the earthbook was supplied by 'the movements of nature'. Chateaubriand, instructed by Malesherbes in Buffon's theory of the earth, therefore busied himself, both on the island of Saint-Pierre and elsewhere, collecting fossilized plants and minerals.[41] Recent research into the development of the earth sciences in Europe would seem to have discredited once and for all the notion that the prehistory and history of geology can be ordered in terms of a simple opposition between reason and superstition. As Roy Porter has observed, 'Cosmogony and Scripture formed a matrix of later theories of the Earth, one which . . . proved geologically fruitful.'[42] Yet, in Paris at least, some enquirers indubitably regarded fossilized plants and animals as a threat to the narrative of Creation contained in Genesis. Since Chateaubriand was trying to wrest young Tulloch from the clutches of the holy fathers, and to persuade him to change his plans and travel with him 'among the savages', he probably pitched the theories of Buffon and Boulanger into their swirling conversation. No doubt Tulloch used the Savoyard Vicar as a shield, for he held to his chosen path, proceeding as planned to the seminary in Baltimore, the first to be founded in North America. It is curious to reflect upon this episode in the light of Chateaubriand's later, highly idealized portraits of missions and missionaries. The man who wrestled with the abbé Noyot for the soul of Tulloch was in a matter of years to commit those of Chactas and Atala to the care of the saintly Father Lopez and the forbidding Father Aubry.

*Le Génie du Christianisme* contains covert refutations of both Buffon and Volney, which may, I think, be treated as recantations of youthful error. 'The annals of the Jews', wrote Chateaubriand, 'are the only ones whose chronology is simple, regular and luminous.'[43] Moreover, in a note appended to the 1826 edition of the *Essai Historique*, he repudiated his earlier observations on human and natural history, and drew attention to the many passages in which he had endorsed the authenticity of Holy Scripture. Chinese, Egyptian and Indian antiquities could all, he insisted, be contained within the Mosaic chronology and, he went on, Cuvier's studies in geology and comparative anatomy had undermined the view that our presence on earth went back more than four thousand years.[44] Aligned with the *idéologues*, a founding member of the Société des Observateurs de l'Homme, the author of the *Recherches* is best characterized as an Enlightenment deist.[45] Nonetheless, at a time when, as Porter has noted, counter-revolutionary illiberalism rendered suspect 'all speculative natural philosophy, all science derived from Enlightenment naturalism, all views of Earth history which seemed to assail Christianity', passages in Cuvier's *Discours Préliminaire* offered a trenchant rehabilitation of 'the agreement of the peoples', and, as much in England as in Italy, were widely interpreted as a defence of Genesis.[46] For example, in the preface to the first English translation, the reader is told that the chief significance of Cuvier's work lay in its vindication of the Mosaic version of the Creation and the Deluge.[47] Likewise, in Italy, neo-Guelph publicists such as Cesare Balbo or Antonio Rosmini believed that Cuvier had played a key role, with Chateaubriand and the First Consul, in reversing the impious speculations of the eighteenth century.[48] Under the Restoration, few would admit the fragile place of human culture within annihilatory natural process. Once the late Enlightenment had broken on the reefs of the Terror, and splintered in the racing currents of nascent Romanticism, the general tendency was rather to embrace, through the dialectic, a Christian-Germanic providentialism, and so to pave the way for an age of nations. In this respect, Leopardi's invocation in *La Ginestra* of 'sterminator Vesuvio', and his mocking reference to 'le grande sorti e le progressive', may be construed as a return, against the Christian and Romantic populism of the Restoration, to the levelling truth of ruins. His vulcanism seemed to many archaic, and indeed it was anchored not in the theory of James Hutton, who had denied that there was any 'destructive intention' in nature, but rather in the Enlightenment materialism of Holbach, Helvétius and Volney.[49]

## Philadelphia

Chateaubriand disembarked at Baltimore on 10 July 1791, and took a stagecoach to Philadelphia, at that time the capital of the United States. William Penn, judged by Raynal to be as great a lawgiver as any in classical Antiquity, had taken tolerance for the guiding principle of his Commonwealth, ruling that 'every man who recognised God would have civil rights, and every man who worshipped Him as a Christian would be able to participate politically'.[50] Yet Chateaubriand, though closely connected to circles in Paris that had campaigned long years for toleration, was seemingly little moved by this aspect of the new city. His head still full, he recalled, of Raynal, he had asked to be introduced to a Quaker: 'You can imagine how surprised I was when I was told that, if I wished to be gulled, I merely had to enter a Friend's shop.' Every day,

Chateaubriand went on to observe, another of his chimeras dissolved. Where in fact he does comment upon the highly diverse chapels and churches of Philadelphia in his memoirs, he writes as the author of *Le Génie du Christianisme*, and therefore as an apologist for Roman Catholicism, a religion of priestly authority, of the senses and of the imagination.[51]

If Chateaubriand was disappointed by the Quakers, who made up, according to Raynal, one-third of the city's population, he was still more shocked by the frivolity and luxury he found about him.[52] Being then 'a Cato . . . embarked on a quest for the severity of early Roman mores', he was saddened to discover that fortunes were profoundly unequal, and that banks, gambling saloons, dance-halls and theatres were springing up on every side. What hope was there for liberty if the mores of a nascent society had been eroded? It was as if, at the time of the Second Punic War, Rome and Carthage had been the same. Even General Washington, who should by rights have been behind his plough, was drawn through the city by four prancing horses. 'Cincinnatus in a carriage', wrote Chateaubriand, 'did not a little damage to my image of the Roman Republic in 296 BC'. Disillusioned, then, by the city, and his hopes of winning official support through Washington for his plans to discover the North-West Passage dashed, he turned away in disgust from white settlement in order to inhabit, and then compose an epic of, the 'man of nature'. 'It was not the Americans that I had come to see', Chateaubriand observed in retrospect, 'but something completely different from the men whom I knew.'[53]

## The 'man of nature'

Although the Jesuit missionaries had tended, as we have seen, to represent the aboriginal peoples as morally degraded with respect to the purity of 'first times', they had also made out a flickering light in the dimness of their souls. It is therefore not hard to comprehend why Chateaubriand, failing to find Lycurgus's Sparta or Brutus's Rome in the city of William Penn, should have gone in search of it among the Iroquois or the Natchez. As early as 1609 Lescarbot had compared the native Americans to the Spartans, as had many in the Jesuit Relations of the seventeenth and eighteenth centuries.[54] There are many passages in Lafitau that are Plutarchian in spirit, and which praise the indigenous peoples of the New World for their moral qualities. When raiding the missionary's text, Chateaubriand had merely to set to one side the obligatory references to the degraded condition of the Iroquois, and to gather the elements that recalled a Roman Stoic demeanour. Not only had Lafitau received in Bordeaux an education all but identical to that of Charlevoix or Montesquieu but, in addition, he shared Fénelon's conviction, expressed in *Télémaque*, that epic and ethnography were intrinsically linked. Ulysses, so the argument went, 'seeing himself incessantly kept by Neptune's wrath at a distance from Ithaca, his fatherland, profited by the different errors in navigation to instruct himself about the customs of the nations'.[55] When, therefore, Chateaubriand had admitted in a letter to Malesherbes that the great journey of exploration would have to be postponed, and that he would have to content himself with a preliminary investigation, he was free to revert to what had quite possibly been his original purpose in visiting America, namely, to write 'the epic of the man of nature', following Homer's example and visiting the peoples that he wished to depict.[56]

There is good cause to take Chateaubriand at his word when he avows, in the Preface to *Atala*, that he was young when he first conceived of his epic, for a critic has identified the nucleus of an early draft of *Les Natchez*, which he has called 'the Chactas cycle'.[57] This draft was composed prior to the journey to America, and in it Chactas – named after one of the tribes native to Louisiana – was taken prisoner and abducted to France. There was therefore a symmetry between the predicament of René and that of Chactas, for each had known both civilization and the savage state and, as a consequence, was condemned to drift between the two, without a fatherland. The original cycle, insofar as it is possible to reconstruct it, has all the characteristic features of a *conte philosophique*, in the manner of Lahontan, Montesquieu or Voltaire. Thus, although the wise Indian seems to castigate the pretensions of civilization, in fact he serves to mount a defence, beyond falsity and corruption, of its innermost heart. One is reminded of the ferocious barbs aimed at Ludovican absolutism by Montesquieu, in the *Lettres Persanes*, and it is to a high degree fitting that Fénelon, a key figure in the aristocratic opposition to Louis XIV, should be Chactas's interlocutor in Books 6 and 7 of *Les Natchez*, and in *Atala*.

Upon reaching Albany, Chateaubriand was warned by a fur-trader that a journey to the North-West Coast, and then to Alaska, would be highly perilous – there was in fact endemic warfare between colonists and Indians in the Ohio territories – and that he would do better to live for a time with backwoodsmen or with agents of the Hudson's Bay Company, and study Sioux, Iroquois and Esquimau.[58] In spite of his evident interest in Amerindian languages, reflected in *Voyages en Amérique*, Chateaubriand failed to adopt the systematic approach later recommended by Degérando, Volney and by other members of the Société des Observateurs de l'Homme. Eager to press on, come what might, he hired a Dutch guide, fluent in several dialects, and headed for Niagara. We may the better understand Chateaubriand's intemperate haste if we bear in mind that his overriding concern was less to observe, as an ethnologist might, the aboriginal peoples, than to see and then be that composite and essentially liminal creature, the man of nature. Thus, in the closing chapter of the *Essai*, a celebrated fragment later reworked to fit other contexts but here entitled 'A night spent with the savages of America', Chateaubriand recalled how,

> alone in an ocean of forests, having . . . all of nature at my feet, a strange revolution took place within me. So delirious a state was I in that I followed no road in particular but went from tree to tree, to right or to left regardless, saying to myself, here there are no more paths to follow, no more towns, no more houses, no more presidents or republics, above all no more laws and no more men.[59]

Being less concerned, then, with the plight of the aboriginal peoples than with his own secession, Chateaubriand had been particularly moved by those passages in which Rousseau had contrasted the readiness of the civilized to take to the woods with the reluctance of savages to embrace civilization: 'Nothing can overcome the invincible repugnance they have against adopting our morals and living in our style.' No Hottentot from the Cape of Good Hope had ever been converted to Christianity, yet 'one reads in a thousand places that Frenchmen and other Europeans have voluntarily found refuge among these peoples, spent their whole lives there without being able to leave such a strange way of life'.[60]

In *Atala*, the return of Chactas to the wilds, and Father Lopez's valedictory discourse, call to mind the relationship between the missionary Van der Stel and the Hottentot, as recorded in Rousseau's note. 'Go', Father Lopez declared to Chactas, 'generous child of nature! Reclaim that precious independence of man, that Lopez has no wish to deprive you of'.[61] Another who had recovered his original independence was Philippe Le Cocq, a Frenchman who had lived for many years among the 'savages'. Chateaubriand, already draped in furs purchased from the Iroquois, recorded how

> he had some difficulty in expressing himself: I saw that he struggled to marshal the ideas of civil man which he had formerly known; and I studied the lesson avidly. For example, I had occasion to observe that there were two sorts of relative things which had been entirely effaced from his mind; that of superfluous property, and that of unnecessary harm toward another.

Indeed, his soul was quite free of the strife of passions.[62] By the time Chateaubriand came to publish his *Voyages en Amérique*, he chose to omit the encounter with Philippe Le Cocq, presumably judging it to be absurd and jejune. Everyone in Europe was agreed by the late 1820s that there was no such thing as a state of nature, and no such person as a man of nature. This disenchantment, so manifest in the debate over the Constitution of the year III, seized Chateaubriand only belatedly, but seize him it did. 'Unlike Rousseau', he declared in 1801, 'I am by no means an enthusiast for savages.'[63] It would be an error, however, to tie the notion of a retreat to the woods, which Rousseau had anyway only recommended to those 'to whom the heavenly voice had not made itself heard', too closely to one thinker, for it had been an integral aspect of a pre-nationalist world-view, in which America and, more specifically, America's frontier, had represented an asylum, at once beyond cities and the imagined heart of a new city. By the time this European dream of an untainted place had dissolved, a nationalist vision had taken hold.[64] In the age of cities, however, the frontier had been an enchanted meadow in which a figure like Daniel Boone, already a legend by the time Chateaubriand was travelling through the United States, embodied a culture that, like the aboriginal one, did not destroy nature.

In a second crucial episode, Chateaubriand and his Dutch guide encountered a small band of native Americans beside the Niagara Falls. Since they had already set up camp for the night, Chateaubriand instructed his guide to ask if they might join them. After some Rousseauist play on the theme of huts and palaces, a portrait is painted of the youngest of three warriors in the band:

> The young man alone maintained a stubborn silence; his eyes never left me. In spite of the black, red and blue stripes, the clipped ears, the pearl hanging from his nose . . . one could readily discern the nobility and sensitivity which animated his face. How ill I took it that he did not like me. He seemed to be able to read in his own heart the history of all the ills with which the Europeans have overwhelmed his fatherland.

As his companions lay sleeping, Chateaubriand contemplated them by the light of the fire:

> Europeans, what a lesson for us! These same savages whom we have pursued with fire and sword; to whom our greed would have left not even a spadeful of earth to cover their corpses, formerly their vast inheritance; these same savages, receiving their enemy in their hospitable huts, sharing with them their wretched meals, . . . and sleeping beside them the sleep of the just! Such virtues are as much above our conventional virtues as the soul of these men of nature is above that of the man of society.[65]

This passage very probably reflects the views of its author at the time when he was drafting his second, profoundly Rousseauist version of the epic of the man of nature, *Les Natchez*. If the hospitality of the native Americans, a commonplace of the Jesuit Relations and a point much stressed by Raynal (himself a former Jesuit), is a leitmotif, this is also because Chateaubriand knew, as an emigré, what it was like to be homeless.[66] As well as being incarnations of the spirit of hospitality, and therefore of pity, they are represented as peoples who, lacking the ancestral tombs of the Old World, carry the ashes of their forebears:

> Hapless Indians, whom I have seen wandering in the deserts of the New World with the ashes of your ancestors; you who had offered me hospitality in spite of your own wretchedness! I would not be able to return it today for, like you, I wander at the mercy of men and, being less fortunate in my exile, I have not borne with me the bones of my fathers.[67]

The review of *Atala* in the *Décade Philosophique*, written by Ginguené, contained a jeering reference to this last remark, stinging Chateaubriand into making an anguished reply.[68]

While at the Niagara Falls, Chateaubriand fell and broke an arm. Nursed by some Iroquois for twelve days, very probably his sole period of close observation of aboriginal society, the documentation that we have for the remainder of the journey, which can have lasted no more than a hundred days, is vague in the extreme. He claimed to have joined forces with traders, to have travelled to Pittsburgh, to have navigated the River Ohio, to have passed through the Floridas, to have seen the Mississippi Delta, to have reached Natchez and to have regained European settlements by way of Nashville and Knoxville. However, in the autumn of 1791, a revolt, fomented by the English and the Spanish, made the area west of Fort Washington far too dangerous to traverse, save under armed escort. If, moreover, Chateaubriand had been in this area at all, he would surely have visited Gallipolis, which was close to the ruins described in the memoirs and in *Voyages en Amérique*, but there is no word of the ill-starred settlement. Critics have argued that so arduous a journey could not have been made in so brief a time, that the last stage was purely imaginary and that, for the topography, flora and fauna of the region, Chateaubriand had plundered Imlay and Bartram.[69] In Suffolk he had access to two good private libraries, that of the rector of Eccles, the Reverend Bence Sparrow, and that of the Reverend John Ives at Bungay. The latter had in fact travelled to America in his youth, and it is probable that some of the more celebrated works on the New World were on his shelves. Bence Sparrow had been at Cambridge, around the same time as Wordsworth and Coleridge, and he could have wandered, as they had done, in Bartram's prose. While in Suffolk, Chateaubriand also met two emigrés who had served in the French navy, one of whom had fought in the American War of Independence, and conversations with them could have supplied more material for his manuscripts.[70]

The American journey was brought to an abrupt halt when Chateaubriand read in an English newspaper of the flight of Louis XVI to Varennes and learned at the same time of the Emigration and of the formation of the Princes' Army. Landing in France on 2 January 1792, he was to find the country much altered. Although the liberal nobility had played a prominent role in the deliberations of the Constituent Assembly, to be an aristocrat and a supporter of the monarchy three years after the storming of the Bastille was to run grave risks. On 20 April 1792, the Legislative Assembly had declared war on Francis II, Emperor of Austria and, as Chateaubriand records, hostilities between revolutionary France and the allied powers drove many opponents of the regime into exile. After the armed uprising of 10 August 1792 in Paris, to say a good word for the monarchical principle was to risk one's life. The September Massacres left a blood-filled moat between the revolutionary regime and the courts of Europe. This was the sombre climate in which Chateaubriand conversed for the final time with Malesherbes.

## The Natchez of Louisiana

Missionary and commercial activity flourished in early eighteenth-century Louisiana; by 1713 a trading-post was established, by 1716 a garrison at Fort Rosalie. In 1718 Le Page du Pratz, a historian possessed of genuine sympathy for the Natchez, came to live in the settlement. His history of Louisiana is a key ethnographic source for this people, as is the account of Dumont de Montigny, a planter of a less friendly disposition. The encroachment of Europeans was recorded at some length in Raynal or Charlevoix, and in maps (one I have seen, from 1721, has both Natchez and Fort Rosalie marked), so Chateaubriand had not chosen an altogether lost locale for the staging of his epic of the man of nature.[71]

The first quarter of the century saw three phases of conflict between the Natchez and the settlers, known somewhat grandiosely as the Natchez Wars. Although precipitated by small-scale skirmishes, these hostilities were to culminate in the great conspiracy, and insurrection, of 1729. It was to this same revolt that Chateaubriand had referred in his first preface to *Atala*, in 1801:

Aside from the discovery of America, I can think of no subject more interesting, especially as far as the French are concerned, than the massacre of the Natchez colony in Louisiana, in 1727 [in fact in 1729]. The picture of all the Indian tribes, conspiring after two centuries of oppression, to restore its liberty to the New World, seemed to me to be almost as fascinating as that of the conquest of Mexico.[72]

We are faced, however, with the paradox that the traditional political system of the Natchez was, if Charlevoix's account is trustworthy, despotic in the extreme. We learn there of the absolute powers enjoyed by the Suns, in effect the rulers of the Natchez, and by their wives. Each had only to say of an enemy, 'who will rid me of this dog?', and guards would do away with the poor wretch. 'One is astonished', Raynal remarked, 'to find a nation so poor and so savage being so cruelly enslaved. Yet superstition will account for what reason finds inconceivable. It alone can wrest liberty from peoples who have scarcely anything to lose save liberty.'[73] Every authority noted the extreme respect shown the Suns, the obeisance, the genuflections and the howls. As Charlevoix recorded it, their system was 'entirely despotic', and Le Page du Pratz's description was not markedly different. French observers were especially fascinated by the funeral ceremonies of the Natchez, which were exceptionally sanguinary. When, for example, a female Sun died, her commoner husband was strangled, as were twelve young children and fourteen adult men, all of whom would have been informed years before that they were destined to serve as the dead woman's attendants in the other world. Natchez social and political organization was not only absolutist but was hierarchical also, with distinctions of rank both within the nobility and between nobility and common people (or 'Stinkards', as they were known). Commoners and nobles even spoke, according to some accounts, a different language.[74]

It is a cause for some wonder that Chateaubriand should have chosen this seemingly cruel system to represent the liberties enjoyed by the man of nature. However, bearing in mind Le Page du Pratz's comparison between the Natchez Suns and the Ottoman Emperors, it is clear that, when Chateaubriand was drafting the first version of his epic, the Chactas cycle, no tribe could have been better suited to carrying his satire. Perhaps Le Page du Pratz had himself read Montesquieu's *Lettres Persanes*, published to great acclaim in 1721, just before the third Natchez War, and sensed how a despotism in Louisiana could serve to mirror the Ludovican, and the barbarism and superstition of the one system be shown to be no more execrable than the tyranny and peacock display of the other. At any rate, in book 7 of the published version of *Les Natchez* there is clearly a trace of the original cycle in the horror felt by Chactas, the wise Indian, at the persecution by Louis XIV of the Huguenots.[75]

However, as the Chactas cycle assumed a more Rousseauist shape, Chateaubriand would clearly have wished to paint the Natchez in wholly different colours. How could despots uphold the standard of liberty against colonial oppressors? In order to prove that despotism was not a characteristic feature of the Natchez, Chateaubriand referred to the tribe's council which, as a twentieth-century ethnologist has observed, served to curtail the authority of the Suns.[76] In lending the council of the Natchez some of the gravitas of the early Roman senate, the wonder of Cineas, Chateaubriand was also able to draw upon Lafitau's many comparisons between the Romans and the Iroquois, selecting whatever was lofty, austere and Plutarchian in his description and disregarding the rest.[77] His use of ethnological example to evoke a truly decorous assembly is paralleled in almost every detail by a passage in a text submitted to the Convention by Lanthénas, on 10 May 1793, when the dispute between Montagnards and Girondins was at its fiercest.[78] Yet, to measure up to Machiavelli or Rousseau, the liberties of the Natchez would have to be on still firmer ground. Chateaubriand therefore told of a time in the previous generation when three men (Chactas, Adario and the reigning Sun) had abolished the despotic system traditional among their people. If these three had been a collective Brutus, responsible for chasing out the Tarquins of the New World, Ondouré, the villain of the piece, the suitor of Celuta and the deadly foe of René, was 'a son of Brutus', who dreamed of restoring 'the old tyranny'. We may also suppose that, prior to 1798, Chateaubriand was prepared to justify the cruel actions a citizen might perform for liberty's sake, since he was, I would judge, one of those emigrés whom Burke found a shade too Jacobin in temperament. The readiness of the peoples of Louisiana to kill their own children – condemned in *Atala* and in the redrafted version of *Les Natchez* as a barbarism to be softened by Christian mores – was therefore construed here as Plutarchian virtue. Adario, near the end of the book, strangled his grandson rather than allow him to be sold into slavery.[79]

So as to place these scattered remarks in some kind of perspective, I shall now rehearse the whole of Chateaubriand's narrative, which begins with René's arrival, in 1725, shortly after the third Natchez War. Having travelled by boat from New Orleans, the hero of the book, a deeply troubled figure, catches sight of the principal Indian village, situated 'in a plain dotted with groves of Sassafras trees'. There 'Indian women wandered to and fro, as light-footed as the does that frolicked with them; in their left arms they held baskets hanging from strips of birch bark, and they picked strawberries, the rosy pink of which stained their fingers.'[80] Like the opening pages of *Atala*, the mood and much of the incidental detail of this page from a Book of Hours is drawn from the Quaker naturalist Bartram, although Homer's way with similes is constantly called to mind.[81] The narrative is carried forward by a series of

studied tableaux of native existence, the ethnological minutiae borrowed
from Lafitau, Charlevoix or Le Page du Pratz and painted on quite
delicately.[82] The village is an idyll, in which diurnal routine is in harmony
with natural process. To shatter the illusion, for such it is, Chateaubriand
then introduces Chactas, 'the sage of the woods', the first in a series of
venerable patriarchs to haunt his writings, Demodocus in *Les Martyrs* his
still more Homeric double. Chactas reproaches his people, introducing
at the same time the themes of exile and hospitality: 'Natchez, how could
you have left these Frenchmen for so long on their own? Are you so sure
that you yourselves will never be travellers, far from your native land?'
René, wishing to flee civilization and to take, like Philippe Le Cocq, to
the woods, then asks to be adopted by the Natchez, but Chactas warns
him that 'it is not easy . . . to wander on the paths of the roe-deer' and
that he risks simply exchanging illusions for memories. The advice is lost
on one whose heart is a 'closed book'.[83]

From Raynal and from Charlevoix we know that the revolt against the
settlers was precipitated by the decision of the new commandant of Fort
Rosalie, Sieur Chopart (or Chépart), to establish a plantation of his own
on Natchez land. This petty tyrant demanded that the Indians quit their
fields but, for the harvesting of that year's crop, allowed them a few
months' respite. The Natchez, faced with the threat of the harrow or the
ploughshare being dragged across their ancestral tombs, had no choice
but to rebel. They met several times in council, deciding finally to form a
league to drive out the French. Embassies were therefore sent to a
number of neighbouring tribes.

Chateaubriand refashioned this material to his own purposes, making
out the bullying Chépart to be, as the conventions of epic required, a
'vaillant capitaine'. There is, after all, only one Thersites in Homer. The
conspiracy probably consisted of the Natchez, the Chickasaw and the
Choctaw, but Charlevoix had been adamant that the plan was to 'destroy
the whole colony of Louisiana, so that not a single Frenchman was left',
and this opinion had been reiterated by Raynal.[84] Chateaubriand therefore drummed up massive forces on either side, placing under Chépart's
command as many as fifty companies with fifty captains, each of whom
represents a French city. After this Homeric list, much ridiculed by
reviewers in 1826 and 1827 and handled far more effectively in *Les
Martyrs*, the first book ends.

Book 2 opens with a portrait of Satan, who,

> gliding through the air, above America, cast a despairing glance at this part of
> the earth, where the saviour pursued him, just as the sun, advancing from the
> gates of the east, chases the shadows before it: Chile, Peru, Mexico, Califor-
> nia, already acknowledge the laws of the Gospel; other Christian colonies

cover the Atlantic coastline, and missionaries have taught the true God to the Savages of the Deserts.

Chateaubriand owed much to the second book of *Paradise Lost*, so here too the fallen angel hoped to renew the struggle against God, his plan being 'to arm all the idolatrous nations of the new continent' and 'to unite [them] in a vast plot to exterminate the Christians'.[85] This passage, echoed in book 8 of *Les Martyrs*, would thus seem to conflict with the Rousseauist or Raynalian intention of the work, which had originally been designed to celebrate the conspiracy of all the Indian tribes to restore liberty to the New World. Indeed, the list given of places that had acknowledged the laws of the Gospel follows the order in which the various missions were treated in the Jesuit *Lettres Edifiantes*. It is plain, then, that the published text of *Les Natchez* celebrated the triumphs of missionaries over pagan beliefs rather than the resistance of confederated tribes to colonial oppressors. Chactas, sanctified by his contact with Father Lopez and Father Aubry, is a sage of the Christian, not the Epicurean or Lucretian woods.

In the massacre at Fort Rosalie, Charlevoix records, only twenty-odd out of the six hundred escaped with their lives. This atrocity called down a terrible retribution upon the Natchez, some accounts suggesting that they were annihilated there and then. Raynal, for example, wrote: 'This nation was put to the sword; its living quarters were razed, and nothing but the site was left.'[86] He did, however, admit that some found asylum among the Chickasaw. Others, it would seem, took refuge with the Creeks and the Cherokee. By the time John Swanton was writing his definitive monograph on the tribes of the lower Mississippi, in the first decade of the nineteenth century, only a handful of Natchez could still be traced, and none of them had anything like a thorough knowledge of their own language. It would appear that Chateaubriand had been most moved by the fragmented and degraded state of the ill-starred rebels, and it is possible to discern in the passages on the Iroquois in the *Essai*, as well as in *Les Natchez* and *Atala*, a portrait of small bands of Breton emigrés, poor, hungry and harried from place to place. This parallel was perhaps reinforced by the once impressive nature on both Iroquois and Natchez social organization. The putative relation between the mysterious mound-builders of the lower Mississippi and the Natchez further enhanced this identification, and it seemed as if the latter had fallen, like Chateaubriand himself, from all the pomp of an absolutist system to a wholly nomadic and stateless condition.

The second part of the book, the *Suite des Natchez*, tells of the dénouement of the conspiracy, and of the crushing of the rebellion.

Already, in the most spectacular tableau in the whole work, Chateaubriand had depicted the general assembly of all the American peoples beside Lake Superior, to plot revenge against the whites. I believe that he had originally wished to imitate the cosmopolitan gathering described by Volney in *The Ruins of Empires*. However, by ascribing a Satanic inspiration to the conspiracy, and by shifting the chief responsibility for its instigation to the fiendish Ondouré, Chateaubriand conjured up a savage Jacobinism, with the assembly a caricature of the Convention.[87] In the end the book was so riven by contradictory impulses that it all but fell apart, being abandoned at some point in 1798 or 1799, only to be resumed in the 1820s, when its moment had long since past. How could the French captains be at the same time glorious warriors fit to vie with the Greek heroes in the Iliad and 'a vile heap of men abducted from the corruption of Europe'?[88] *Les Natchez* had in fact become a palimpsest of four overlapping and only partly consistent projects, namely, (1) the Chactas cycle; (2) a Rousseauist or Raynalian tract; (3) a Gothic novel, with the working title *René et Celuta*; and (4) an epic of the man of nature which was increasingly a Christian epic. In later chapters I shall refer in passing to Chateaubriand's shelving of the project and to the moral and political climate which nurtured his celebrated apology for Roman Catholicism, *Le Génie du Christianisme*.

## The observation of the New World

In 1795, shortly after the closure of the Ecole Normale, Volney embarked for America. 'Saddened by the past, apprehensive about the future', he later recalled, 'I went with some mistrust among a *free* people, to see whether a friend of a profaned liberty might find a haven of peace for his old age there, since he could not hope for such a thing in Europe.'[89] I do not propose to retrace the trails that Volney followed, which were often those taken by Chateaubriand five years before, but to reflect upon the sort of scientific traveller, or human geographer, that he was, or aspired to be. If, therefore, we turn again to the lectures delivered in Paris, we find that the most demanding form of history, the analytic or philosophical, ought to concern itself with a people or nation, and to follow it step by step 'for the entire duration of its moral and physical existence'. We further learn that this type of enquiry 'begins by placing in their proper order all the facts pertaining to such an existence, so as to deduce from their interaction the causes and effects of the moral combination known as body politic or government'.[90] What then was the proper order? Like Cabanis and Destutt de Tracy, whose major treatises derived from lectures given at the Institute in 1796, Volney assumed the primacy of physical over moral factors.[91] Thus, in his account of the celebrated journey to Syria and Egypt, he had begun with soil and climate, for they differed so much from the French that, if they were not taken into account, 'a whole host of usages, customs and laws' would remain obscure. Upon this canvas a scientific traveller would then dispose human populations, governments, mores and religious and civil beliefs. By its title alone, the *Tableau du Climat et du Sol des Etats-Unis* may be judged a part of the same project.

Although Volney dreamed of identifying the ecological determinants of moral life, he was quick to pour scorn upon Montesquieu's 'general rule of climate', which was belied by the existence, beneath the same sky, of radically different cultures. Heat, softness and servility were not necessarily linked, any more than cold, energy and liberty were. Such critiques of the human geography of *The Spirit of the Laws* had been commonplace in the early years of the Revolution. Volney, however, took the argument a stage further, by protesting that Montesquieu had borrowed, in oversimplified form, Hippocrates's arguments regarding the impact of earth, water and air upon human constitutions and temperaments.[92] These assertions tally with Cabanis's ninth memoir, entitled 'On the Influence of Climates upon Moral Habits'. For Hippocrates, climate could not be defined simply in terms of the temperature of the air, or in terms of the latitude of the soil, but required that an account be given of the nature of that soil, of its products, and of the rivers and streams that watered it. Hippocrates, Cabanis went on, 'sets out to describe exactly all the . . . distinguishing features of each country . . . Climate is therefore not restricted to the particular circumstances of latitudes, of cold and heat: it embraces, in a wholly general manner, the entirety of physical circumstances operative in each locality.'[93] This ambition could only be realized, as Volney well understood, by the assiduous collection of geological, metereological or botanical data. In America he therefore amassed a quantity of rocks and mineral samples, and kept his barometer and thermometer always to hand.

Volney's inductive method is best exemplified, however, by the earlier journey, to Egypt and to Syria, for there the sections on each country are subdivided into a physical and a political part. The text harps upon the theme of observation, for those who participated in such expeditions wished to make all of human existence susceptible to scientific enquiry, to found, in short, a science of man. As Sergio Moravia has noted, the *idéologues'* methodology of observation, of the gaze, entailed a threefold operation of decomposition, observation and recomposition, the theoretical justification for which had been supplied by Descartes and, crucially, by Locke.[94] Instead of delighting in the outlandish and the bizarre,

scientific travellers should calmly acknowledge the otherness of phenomena received by the senses, taking care not to opt for a premature
picture assembled from fragments drawn from memory and imagination.
Nothing could be more opposed to Volney's method than that of
Chateaubriand in *Les Natchez*, where he had blended reminiscence of his
own encounters with Amerindians with lines from the Iliad or the
Aeneid, the whole, often idyllic tableau being based upon engravings
from Lafitau.[95] A scene or landscape or person should instead be broken
down into their constituent elements by the receptive eye of the traveller;
the single parts should then be observed; finally, they should be recom-
bined, so as to permit the formulation of general laws. In order to
counter the mystificatory procedures of other travellers, so much concerned 'to vaunt the theatre of their voyages', Volney had cultivated a
prose that itself exemplified the analytic method and, more generally, the
Lockean principle that there was nothing in the mind that had not first
been in the senses. The reader, instead of being presented with pre-
formed tableaux, almost always derived from literature, should therefore experience the bedazzling effect of otherness.[96] Historians have
sometimes implied that Volney was something of a cold fish, and as a
consequence his prose has not always been valued. Yet translations of
*The Ruins of Empires* were not disgraced by *Queen Mab*, on Chartist
shelves, and the geographical writings also merit careful scrutiny.

Volney's account of his American journey was to have had the same
basic structure as his treatise on Egypt and Syria; soil and climate were
again to be the canvas, size and distribution of population the under-
drawing, with a blocking-in of occupational patterns and a thick impasto
of mores. Although, for various reasons, the political section of the book
was never published (or, presumably, completed), a number of fragments are extant. Volney had originally intended to write an account of
the struggle for independence from Britain, together with a description
of the various colonies. Nothing survives of the former, but brief essays
on the Floridas, New Hampshire and Vermont were printed as appendices
to the body of the text. Imlay and Bartram were treated with considerable
scorn, and two settlements that Volney had visited in the course of his
travels, that of Gallipolis, on the River Ohio, and that of Poste-Vincennes, on the River Wabash, were anatomized. Both were predomi-
nantly French communities, the former consisting, as we have seen, of
settlers persuaded by the publicity of the Sioto company to delve and spin
in an earthly paradise, the latter comprising colonists of an earlier date,
who had in the past enjoyed amicable relations with the indigenous
peoples. Upon his arrival in Philadelphia, late in 1795, Volney had asked
after the readers of Brissot who had founded Gallipolis; the following
year he visited the settlement, and told a sorry tale of back-breaking

work in an ill-chosen, marshy site, of disappointed hopes and broken dreams. More generally, he remarked upon the success of English and German homesteaders, and upon the failure of the French, contrasting the steady application of the former with the mercurial nature of the latter. Volney was in fact fascinated by the differential effect of national origins upon American mores, and protested at 'the novelistic error of those writers who call a union of the inhabitants of old Europe, Germans, Dutch, and, above all, English of the three kingdoms, a *new, virgin people*'. The settlers were in fact neither the emissaries of humanity nor 'a vile heap of men abducted from the corruption of Europe'.[97] Like Cabanis, Volney wished to banish all such imagined contraries for the sake of a positivist admission of what was in any given locality, be it a whole nation or a river valley or a village, the case.[98] Here his interest in the impact of specific national cultures upon American housing and agriculture seems almost to anticipate studies made by modern geographers of such questions, with particular reference to the frontier.

In the essays on Gallipolis and on Poste-Vincennes, the scales are weighted as much towards the ignoble as towards the noble savage. In either place, the native peoples stand, on a wooded margin, as emblems of cruelty and war. His *Observations Générales sur les Indiens ou Sauvages de l'Amérique du Nord* do not begin, however, with a condemnation but with a simple listing of the tribes who traded with the settlers at Poste-Vincennes, and with a characteristic account of his own first, bemused apprehension of these other beings, their appearance itself 'a new and bizarre spectacle'. His readers were asked to imagine

> virtually naked bodies, bronzed by the sun and the open air, glistening with fat and smoke; their heads uncovered, with long, straight, glossy hair, their faces masked with black, blue and red, divided into round, square and diamond-shaped areas; their nostrils pierced so as to hold large copper or silver rings, with three-tiered pendants descending from their ears on to their shoulders . . . ; with a small square apron to cover the pubis, and with another to cover the coccyx, both being tied by a belt of ribbon or string.[99]

In this detailed, precise description, there is no suggestion that the object of the gaze might stare back, as Chateaubriand's proud companion had done, across the fire. This is in part because Volney, like Cabanis in the domain of medicine, wished to unite the physical and the moral in a psycho-physiological science of man. Any reproachful glances, whereby one soul communicated the essence of a violent history to another, would be out of place in a method founded upon the rigorous control of testimonies.[100]

Volney then sketched in the degraded circumstances of those in the penumbra of Poste-Vincennes, who existed only for alcohol, for brawling and for feuding. He had planned, he says, to go and live among them, but soon learned that they did not recognize the right of hospitality, that they knew 'neither subordination nor government', that the elders, far from being the feared and honoured pillars of a sylvan senate, could not control the young men of the tribe, and that, more generally, 'their social state was one of anarchy and of ferocious and brutal nature, where need and force constituted right and law'.[101] One can discern in this account a residual trace of the ignoble savage of Diderot and Raynal, but Volney was also deliberately drawing the fire curtain of the Terror between his readership and the lantern-shows of Chateaubriand or Bernardin de Saint-Pierre.[102] In this respect, the horrors of the year II had driven not only classical Antiquity but also the man of nature into an alien and objectified, though ever more scrupulously inventoried and surveyed, past. Many of Constant's arguments regarding the war-like disposition of the citizens of the ancient city-states are therefore paralleled by statements in the 'Observations' concerning the cruelty (and the Stoic self-cruelty) of the American Indians.[103]

Because ethnography now requires that the fieldworker suffer a complete moral dispossession, a convincing case can be made for Rousseau as founder of a genuinely scientific ethnology.[104] By contrast, Volney's portrait of the indigenous peoples appears to reduce them to silence, although this had not at all been his intention. He had merely wished to banish ventriloquism; if one voice were thrown, another would go unheard. As early as 1795, in his concluding lecture at the Ecole Normale, he had exhorted scientific travellers to work as historians and to collect living monuments for, aside from ruins, inscriptions, medals and printed texts, there were also 'customs, mores, rites, religions and, above all, *languages*, the construction of which alone *is a complete history of each people*'.[105] This view of the relation between language and culture combined a fervent belief in fraternity with a profound curiosity regarding particular manifestations of diversity. It is thus striking to discover that Volney, in the second edition of *The Ruins of Empires*, appended a footnote in which, having presented a vivid tableau of the general assembly of all the peoples of the earth, he proposed that a gallery of the Louvre be devoted to the impact of climate, custom and diet upon them, and so to comparative physiology.[106] So strong has the reaction against Enlightenment thought been that this characteristic combination of an ethos of confederation with a delight in diversity has been obscured, not merely under the First Empire or during the Restoration, but even in highly influential studies this century by Ernst Cassirer, Benedetto Croce and Friedrich Meinecke.[107] One consequence of the arraignment of the Enlightenment in post-revolutionary Europe has been to deny the *philosophes*, and their heirs, any insights into the phenomenon of cultural difference. An authentically ethnographic sensibility would then be restricted to isolated precursors, such as Vico, or to tendencies outside, and more or less hostile to, the tradition of the Encyclopédie, such as the German lineage of Hamann and Herder. I shall comment upon these historiographical distortions at greater length in later chapters, but suffice it to say here that the *idéologues* resident in Paris, especially those active in the section of the National Institute devoted to 'the analysis of sensations and ideas', had done much to advance Volney's programme, for it was their own, in the closing years of the eighteenth century. The linguistic aspect of ethnology was given particular prominence by the Observateurs, and Joseph-Marie Degérando was adamant that the greatest failure of earlier scientific travellers had been to neglect the languages of the peoples studied. Wilhelm von Humboldt, far from being antagonistic towards this line of argument, was in Paris at the time, in daily contact with several of its leading exponents, and in certain respects was therefore, as Hans Aarsleff has argued, himself an *idéologue*. Volney, in complete agreement with his colleagues in France, had in fact already compiled a lexicon for one of the tribes native to the upper Wabash, the Miami, which is printed at the end of his essay.

Since, however, one of Volney's main aims in composing the 'Observations' had been, as I noted above, to banish from science the ventriloquism of the moralists, from Montaigne to Rousseau, its recognizably modern approach to the study of language is largely subordinated to a more polemical commentary upon the relation between speech and truth. The essay therefore takes the form of a Socratic dialogue between an American, Wels, abducted by 'savages' at the age of thirteen, Michikinakoua, or Little Tortoise, a Miami war chief, and Volney, the observer.

The life story of Little Tortoise is of particular importance, not least because his sagacity is in such striking contrast to the brutalized condition of the American Indians around Poste-Vincennes. There is ventriloquism here too, although the voice cast across the Atlantic, across the centuries, is that of Locke, not Rousseau. Little Tortoise had helped to defeat General Saint-Clair, and had come within a whisker of destroying General Wayne's army. Convinced that further resistance would prove futile, the war chief 'had had the wit to persuade his tribe to surrender on reasonable terms'. So intelligent was Little Tortoise, in fact, that he quickly discerned the benefits to be gained from switching from hunting and gathering to agriculture. With this end in mind, he solicited help from the Quakers, whom Volney accords measured praise, in Philadelphia. The existence of a chief ready and able to lead his people out of a degraded social and economic state served to refute all those who had condemned the Amerindians to an irrevocably animal condition. In this regard, it should be noted that the *idéologues* were wholly committed to the doctrine of the unity of the human species.[108] It is possible to misinterpret the cold eye that they levelled at the object of the ethnographic gaze, and to forget that the apparent blurring of the distinction between humanity and animality was not a consequence of a racism but was, rather, an expression of a resolute refusal to invoke first causes. At the same time, the example of a prudent chief rendered absurd the regret of Rousseau – and, in certain moods, Diderot and Raynal – at the contact between native peoples and Europeans. By raising his defeated people from one socio-economic stage to the next, Little Tortoise was living proof of the principle of perfectibility.[109]

Volney had asked his informant if it were true that many whites preferred the savage life to the one we call civilized. For a genuine transfer of identity to occur, Wels replied, one would have to be very young. He himself, though only thirteen when abducted, 'could not forget the delights of society which he had already tasted'.[110] Many Canadians (that is to say, colonists of French extraction) had opted for a native life, but Wels doubted their motives and their intelligence, and described in harrowing terms the misery of their old age. This story may be seen as a rejoinder to that of the many 'semi-Indians' who haunt the annals of early American history, the Rousseauist Philippe Le Cocq among them.

Nonetheless, Volney remained staunchly opposed to the spiritualist accounts of the origins of language, and therefore of human culture, that were to become so predominant a feature of the age of nations. The very structure of his reports on his major journeys, like that of Cabanis's treatise, militated against any denial of a natural ground to social being. He had stated in 1795 that a language was of itself 'a complete history of each people, and its descent and analogies may serve as an Ariadne's thread in the labyrinth of origins', but his comparative linguistics was predicated upon a genuinely universal history, in which the stories of Greek, Roman or Jew were accorded no special status.[111] I shall elaborate at some length upon these themes in part III, so at this point I want only to note that such principles go some way towards explaining just why those in quest of the founders of scientific ethnology have often paused at the name of Volney. His ethnographic writings belong to the milieu of the Société des Observateurs de l'Homme, and his work in this domain therefore resembles very closely that of Louis-François Jauffret, the founder of the Société, and that of Joseph-Marie Degérando, the author of the crucial *Considerations of the Various Methods to be Followed in the Observation of Savage Peoples*.[112] As far as questions of method are concerned, one should note the care with which his interviews (some nine or ten in number) with Little Tortoise were conducted, and his realization that random remarks, being unguarded, were of value, and should therefore be transcribed with especial care.[113] There is no denying that in these passages Volney describes ways of proceeding that any modern ethnologist would accept as a part of the practice of fieldwork. In addition, as I have already remarked, there is a concern, because of the sheering effects of the gaze, with the particular tribe that is before one's eyes, and beyond that, with those of North America. Grander considerations would fall into the category of spurious universal history – he may have had Bossuet's *Discourse* in mind – and for the same reason speculations regarding the diffusion of culture across the Bering Strait are debarred. Whatever parallels emerged between peoples located at a great distance from each other should be explained in terms of common conditions, material or ecological, or in terms of stated properties of the human mind, rather than as the consequence of some putative, scripturally sanctioned wandering of the peoples.[114] Even where the *idéologues* called for the compilation of an exhaustive inventory of the tribal peoples of the earth, well aware that not a day passed without one such society disappearing forever, their demand had none of the caustic anti-clericalism of Bayle, of Raynal, or even of Rousseau's Savoyard Vicar.[115]

Yet even as some were laying the foundations for the modern science of ethnology, others were replacing the city-nation of the Enlightenment with the tribe- or word-nation, in which immemmorial murmurings assumed an axiological force. For, in the late eighteenth century, the banishment of the noble savage from the garden of ethics was as crucial for the transition from an age of cities to an age of nations as was the dismantling of the ideal of the polis or, again, the challenge posed, in the same period, to the notion of an absolute right of resistance, once vested in an ephorate or in a tribunate.

# The Cities Eclipsed

## Dictators and tribunes

Under the Directory, Staël, Constant and the *idéologues* tacitly agreed to suspend their quarrels over religion, in order to defend the *philosophe* tradition against the increasingly virulent polemics of counter-revolutionaries and neo-Catholics. So dark were the times, however, that republican publicists were obliged to invoke clarity where little was clear, and to champion the rule of law where an unprejudiced observer saw a regime founded upon force and arbitrariness. The Directory's position was so precarious that it lashed out in turn against Jacobins and Royalists. A government that repeatedly acted unconstitutionally, and that owed its actual survival, first on 13 Vendémiaire and then on 18 Fructidor, to the good offices of republican generals, was plainly a travesty. The shadow of Caesar, or of Monck, had fallen across France.

The exaltation of the first years of the Revolution had thus yielded to a grisaille of greed, self-interest and corruption; the deportations to Guyana, the executions and the muzzling of the press could not do otherwise than drive the spirit of enthusiasm still further away.[1] Only military glory, won by the victorious armies of the Grande Nation, could compensate for such domestic degradation.[2] Plutarchian fires, extinguished in the forum, might be rekindled on the battlefield. General Bonaparte, who had twice moved to save the Republic, was known for the simplicity of his life and for the modesty of his demeanour; the astonishing victories of 1796–97 in the Italian peninsula had won him universal acclaim. At a distance from Paris and from the Directory, with room therefore for manoeuvre – military, diplomatic and political – he was honoured as a sincere republican and, as Garat observed upon the occasion of his election to the Institute, 'a philosopher . . . at the head of armies'.[3] Moreover, links between the *idéologues* and the commander of the Army of Italy, forged through his early friendship in Corsica with

Volney and consolidated after the *coup* of 13 Vendémiaire, were further reinforced during the brilliant Egyptian campaign, for which, it should be remembered, the *Voyage en Syrie et en Egypte* served as a guide. By 1799, the Institute was united in its admiration for the *philosophe* general.

We see the taking of power by generals through the gunpowder haze of countless 18 Brumaires, and are barely able to imagine the Roman, indeed, the republican connotations of dictatorship. Yet it had been, as Rousseau had stated, one of a number of exceptional magistracies which, in emergencies, might restore an endangered polity to order and unity.[4] One could, in short, be a fervent republican, invoke the idea of dictatorship, and not be guilty of Augustan hypocrisies, for the force used by a dictator was seen, by a curious paradox, as law's quintessence.[5] Since the frequent rotation of offices blurred the distinction between rulers and ruled, this was also held to be the case, in a well-ordered republic, with the extraordinary appointments. If dictatorship and despotism had remained antonyms for moderates even in the late eighteenth century, it was because Washington in the United States of America had demonstrated that it was possible to hold the highest offices in a republic and, his duty done, to retire, like Cincinnatus, from public life. Volney, so deeply implicated in 18 Brumaire, had himself witnessed Washington hand over the Presidency to John Adams.[6] 'Dictator' was therefore the term adhering to Bonaparte's name in 1800-02, as those with republican sympathies nursed the vain hope that the Citizen First Consul was still of their party, and would do as Cincinnatus had done.[7]

There was, needless to say, no mention of dictators in the constitution of the year VIII, but the French now had, as Chénier observed wrily, 'a senate, a consulate and a tribunate, and . . . even . . . a republic'.[8] Sieyes, a Peter Ramus of constitution-makers, at last had the opportunity to bring one of his schemes to fruition; as an *idéologue*, committed to the principle of analysis, he planned to 'decompose' the political process, much as if it were a person, into distinct faculties, the imaginative (the Tribunate), the ratiocinative (the Legislative Body), the instrumental (the Consulate) and the conservative (the Senate).[9] To this sophisticated but bizarrely abstract arrangement, further refinements were added: the Tribunate could speak, but not vote; the Legislative Body could vote, but not speak. The executive, in Sieyes's scheme, consisted of a Great Elector and two Consuls, each with specific areas of responsibility, domestic or foreign. Bonaparte reckoned that, so long as he enjoyed the lion's share of executive authority, such a system of checks and balances, no matter how intricately arranged, would prove no obstacle. He therefore demanded that the office of Great Elector, a symbolic or even ceremonial function, be replaced by that of First Consul, which was to be vested with virtually autocratic powers; Article 42 of the Constitution stated that the decision of the First Consul was binding, his colleagues having no more than a consultative role. The consuls were responsible for initiating legislation, their draft laws being then discussed by the Tribunate, voted upon by the Legislative Body and checked for constitutional propriety by the Senate. Though ratified by a plebiscite, the new constitution was a sham, a document that was, in Bonaparte's words, 'short and obscure'. Shorn of any Declaration of Rights, of all references to liberty, equality or fraternity, and of any remotely democratic electoral mechanism, it appeared to be but a prologue to despotism.

In spite of the First Consul's quasi-monarchical role, the *idéologues* derived some reassurance from the offices that so many of their number now held. 'The Society of Auteuil', Moravia observes, 'had never seemed so powerful.'[10] Andrieux, Le Breton, Chénier, Constant, Daunou, Ginguené, Laromiguière and J.-B. Say were all tribunes, while Cabanis, Garat, Sieyes, Tracy and Volney were senators. The idyll, for the few brief weeks that it lasted, reminded many of the distant hopes of 1789, and of the Tennis Court Oath. Yet the domination of the assemblies by the *parti philosophique* was an illusion. In the profoundly altered cultural and political climate of 1800, the *idéologues* were bereft of popular support, and it would cost Bonaparte nothing to move against them.

It was the tribunes, not the senators, who spoke out most forcefully against the First Consul's increasingly despotic behaviour, yet the Tribunate of the year VIII bore little relation to the institution that Machiavelli or Rousseau had championed. It was no surprise that this should be so, for Sieyes had endeavoured to erect a wall against the forces of direct, popular, democracy. Since 1794–95, the *idéologues* had in fact constructed a property-owning aristocracy of the talents, a republic of notables in which purchasers of national properties (such as Constant) might rub shoulders with former monarchists. A 'fusion' of this sort was acceptable to Staël and her circle, or to the members of the Institute, whereas the Bonapartist amalgam of regicide Conventionnels and returned emigrés struck them as deeply distasteful.[11] This contrast shows that the *parti philosophique* had burned more bridges to its left than to its right. Thus, a month after the *coup* of 18 Brumaire, Cabanis observed that, in the new constitution, 'everything is done for the people and in the name of the people; nothing is done by it or at its unconsidered prompting'.[12] When, therefore, the tribunes made their protest, they could not advocate anything more radical than the use of petitions as a means to express or take the measure of public opinion. The eloquence of Constant in the Tribunate, celebrated by Staël in a curious chapter from the second half of *De la Littérature*, was therefore a rhetoric of the

Moderns, not of the Ancients.[13] In general, the moderate republicans spoke in the guise of elected representatives in a Parliament, and not as tribunes of the plebs or of the people. Marx and Engels were quite right to observe in 1844 that, when one reads the speeches of the Brumairians, 'one has the impression of coming from the National Convention into a modern Chamber of Deputies', for this was after all how the *idéologues* and their allies saw themselves.[14]

In a justly celebrated passage, Marx described how

> Camille Desmoulins, Danton, Robespierre, Saint-Just, Napoleon, the heroes as well as the parties and the masses of the old French Revolution, [had] performed the task of their time in Roman costume and with Roman phrases . . . The new social formation once established, the antediluvian colossi disappeared and with them resurrected Romanity – the Brutuses, Gracchi, Publicolas, the tribunes, the senators, and Caesar himself. Bourgeois society in its sober reality had begotten its true interpreters and mouthpieces in the Says, Cousins, Royer-Collards, Benjamin Constants and Guizots.[15]

If revolutions by their nature entail the use of borrowed languages, the distinction here is between 'glorifying new struggles' and 'parodying the old', or between 'magnifying the given task in imagination' and 'fleeing from its solution in reality'. There is a case for arguing, however, that the whole of Marx's complex meditation upon the deployment of ancient examples for modern tasks may be interpreted as much in terms of popular sovereignty and the state as in relation to putative sequences of modes of production. Once this is granted, a direct connection may be established between the Rousseauist, the Babouvist and the Marxist vision of the free, self-governing city, raised at once on modern and on ancient foundations.[16] The tribunate was of central importance here, since it was the magistracy that was most directly an expression of popular sovereignty.

The Roman annalists dated the creation of the tribunate of the plebs to 494 BC, some sixteen years after the expulsion of the Tarquins from the city. Although the tyrants had been dethroned, the plebeians were still at the mercy of the patricians, and almost wholly without rights. For the patrician order, organized in its gentes (or clans), filled every magistracy and priestly office, and had a monopoly of the auspices. The plebeians were thus a people apart, belonging to the city but with no access to the consulate or to the senate, deprived of the right of *connubium* (intermarriage) with the patricians, and liable to be thrown into prison, or even executed, for debt. So unjust a distribution of power and authority rested upon extreme economic inequality, depicted with particular vividness by

Vico, with the plebeians working small, increasingly exhausted plots of land while the patricians lived off the Ager Publicus, the public domain.

Matters came to a head after Rome's victories over the Volsci, the Sabines and the Aequi, when Valerius, a dictator with plebeian sympathies, raised the issue of debt in the Senate. Unmoved, the consuls tried to avert civil disorder by calling the people to arms, on the pretext that the Aequi had joined battle again. Whereupon the plebeians, outraged at the slight value accorded to their contribution to the growing might of Rome, withdrew from the city and encamped upon the Mons Sacer, in the celebrated episode known as the First Secession.[17] The unity of the city was in jeopardy. After some negotiation, however, an agreement was struck, with the plebeians being granted two magistrates of their own, whose persons were deemed inviolable (*sacrosanctus*), and in whom were vested the rights of *auxilium* and *intercessio*. By the former right, a tribune could shield an individual plebeian from the imperium of a curule magistrate and, through the *ius provocationis*, make an appeal to the people; by the latter, he could both oppose consuls or Senate and, in addition, block the levy of the army, the imposition of taxes or the holding of elections. Being *sacrosanctus*, anyone who so much as laid a finger on a tribune of the plebs could be slain with impunity.[18]

It is clear, then, to revert to the argument of my fourth chapter, that the Roman constitution, far from being unconcerned with the rights of the individual, was characterized by a pronounced respect for them. As Claude Nicolet has remarked,

> Liberty, associated with the right of *provocatio* and the tribunes of the plebs through which it was exercised, was not only a sentimental or moral climate but a specific right interposed, in a concrete and highly efficacious manner, between the citizen and the shadow of power: an imprescriptible human right on the lines of habeas corpus, which it antedates by eighteen centuries.[19]

No historian of ancient Rome could in all conscience neglect this aspect of the tribunate, for the right of *provocatio*, or appeal to the people, was supposed to date from the founding of the Republic, and was invoked by Saint Paul as late as the first century AD. Niebuhr, Mommsen and Fustel all mention that the tribune's house remained open, day and night, a refuge for imperilled individuals.[20] So stoutly framed a door would clearly have saved many in 1572, or in 1793.

Yet the tribunate was not only a shield protecting the innocent from the imperium of the magistrates; it was also an expression of the right of resistance of the sovereign people. The *intercessio* was in this regard a recapitulation of the moment of secession, which made right, for the classical republican tradition, a matter of willed consent, not consolidated history.[21] This aspect of the tribunate found prominence in the equation current during the French Revolution between secession and strike, which though implicit in much of the rhetoric of the Third Estate in 1788–89 was most strongly emphasized by Gracchus Babeuf.

Convincing parallels have been drawn between Babeuf's formative years on the Plain of Picardy, and Buonarroti's time in Corsica, as if both men had been impelled towards notions of agrarian law, radical egalitarianism and even nascent communism by their direct experience of peasant life, but a contrast should be made between the former's awkward and painful formation in Arras, and the latter's years of study at the University of Pisa. Alessandro Galante Garrone has therefore emphasized the extent of the intellectual debt owed to Buonarroti, and has noted that those issues of *Le Tribun du Peuple* which appeared shortly after Babeuf's release from prison in Plessis reflect theoretical discussions held by the future conspirators in the spring and summer of 1795.[22] A millennarian concern with the advent of universal justice, and with the restoration of primitive equality, had been perceptible in Babeuf's writings since 1791–92, but there was now more extended treatment of the levelling iusnaturalism expounded by the Cercle Social (for example, Nicholas de Bonneville) and embraced by some sansculottes. In addition, republican interpretations of Machiavelli were transmitted to Babeuf by Buonarroti. This, at any rate, is the conclusion I would draw from the notes confiscated at the time of Babeuf's final arrest, which, though little more than transcriptions of chapter headings from Book 1 of the *Discourses*, refer to a cluster of his core preoccupations, namely the Tribunate, the agrarian law and the Dictatorship.[23] Moreover, most of the Roman tribunes listed in the lengthy discussion from the thirty-fifth issue of his newspaper also feature in the *Discourses*. Babeuf was anyway steeped in *Ab Urbe Condita*, the text upon which Machiavelli was commenting, and in Plutarch, the author who had supplied him with vivid portraits of the most celebrated exponents of agrarian law, and his own heroes, the Gracchi.[24]

Babeuf agreed with Machiavelli that the great merits of the Roman constitution had not been arrived at all of a sudden, as had been the case in Sparta, but had been the fruit of unremitting civil strife. *Le Tribun du Peuple* therefore referred constantly to a war between rich and poor, and likened the struggle between the orders to the conflicts of the Revolution. After the Tarquins (the Capets, in Babeuf's narrative) had been expelled, and two consuls had assumed the royal authority, plebeians and patricians had, Machiavelli continued, lived for some years in apparent harmony. If the latter refrained from using their traditional powers and privileges to oppress, it was because they feared that the plebeians might rally to the standard of the exiled kings. Once, however, the Tarquin dynasty was extinguished, nobles and commoners were again at daggers drawn. 'It became necessary', Machiavelli observed, 'to devise some new institution which should produce the same effect as the Tarquins had done in their time.' The tribunes were therefore created, to defend the plebeians, to intercede with the senate, and to curb the arrogance of the nobility.[25] Although the *Discourses* contain passages which may be read as an endorsement of the Polybian mixed constitution, notably in Book 1, Chapter 2, a different emphasis is evident in Book 1, Chapter 5. In answer, therefore, to the question as to 'whether the safeguarding of liberty can be more safely entrusted to the Populace or to the Upper Class', Machiavelli opts in the last analysis for popular liberty, and therefore for Rome (where the plebeians, through the Tribunate, were the guardians of the laws), rather than for Sparta or Venice (where the same task fell to the nobility).[26]

Machiavelli did not try to disguise the essentially revolutionary role of the tribunes, seeming almost to delight in the turbulence of the various acts of secession. The greatness of Rome was in fact inseparable, he concluded, from the animosity between plebeians and patricians.[27] By contrast Montesquieu, in his *Considerations*, agreed with Machiavelli that tumult was the characteristic condition of Rome, but regretted the fact. Admittedly, in his eighth chapter, 'The Dissensions that Always Existed in the City', he had rehearsed the annalists' account of the First Secession, and of the resulting creation of 'a magistracy that could prevent injustices being done to a plebeian' but, firm in his allegiance to the *noblesse de robe*, he deplored the turbulent and aggressive role played by the tribunes.[28] In *The Spirit of the Laws*, he further observed that, if they had saved the liberty of Rome, it was because, as leaders of the populace, they had curbed its riotous energy.[29] Indeed, both books press home the point that the English constitution, being capable of a continual process of self-examination, was superior by far to the Roman, which was always in a ferment, and could not be corrected by its own laws. The importance of the tribunate lay, surely, in its power to return matters to the ultimate source of law and to check government, which tends always to usurpation, yet it was precisely the right of the tribunes to suspend the executive authority that Montesquieu abhorred.[30]

Rousseau's deepest sympathies in this matter were with Machiavelli, not Montesquieu, and he therefore agreed that it had been the First Secession, and the creation of the two tribunes of the plebs, that had brought liberty to Rome. The republic may have been born through the expulsion of the Tarquins but, in leaving the prerogatives of the patriciate, a hereditary aristocracy, intact, it had failed to complete its task:

the form of government, continuously uncertain and wavering, was not fixed (as Machiavelli has proved) until the establishment of the tribunes; only then was there a true government and a true democracy. For indeed the people there was not only sovereign, but also magistrate and judge; and the senate was no more than a subordinate commission to temper and concentrate the government, while the consuls themselves – in spite of their being patricians, chief magistrates and absolute commanders in war – were never more in Rome than the presidents of the people.[31]

Rousseau also echoed Machiavelli's comparison between the Roman, Spartan and Venetian constitutions, observing that in Rome the tribunes had served to protect the sovereign from the government, whereas in Venice the Council of Ten had upheld the cause of the government against the people, and in Sparta the ephors had striven to keep a balance between the two.[32] What he feared most was the usurpation by government of the rights of the sovereign people, exemplified in the case of his native Geneva by the encroachments, across the centuries, of the Petit Conseil upon the Conseil Général. The Venetian Council of Ten was, however, a degraded tribunate, 'a tribunal of blood, which is baneful as much to the patricians as to the people, and which, far from giving supreme protection to the law, serves only, now that the law has been debased, for the striking of stealthy blows that none dare to look upon'.[33] Rousseau might have been expected to look with more favour upon the Venetian *avogadori del commune*, described by Gaspare Contarini as 'tribunes of the law', yet, as Pierangelo Catalano has pointed out, they did not have 'the strictly political function of defending popular or plebeian liberty'.[34] It must constantly be borne in mind that, for Rousseau,

the moment the people is lawfully assembled as a sovereign body all jurisdiction of the government ceases; the executive power is suspended, and the person of the humblest citizen is as sacred and inviolable as that of the highest magistrate, for in the presence of the represented, there is no longer any representation.[35]

It was sentiments of this order that prompted the Genevan Petit Conseil to ban *The Social Contract* for, where Rousseau described the tribunate as the guardian of the laws and of the legislative power, he meant, as Catalano notes, that it was the guardian of the will of each and every citizen.[36]

Since the Roman tribune's *intercessio* was a recapitulation of the dramatic moment of plebeian secession, it could stand as proof that cities could as easily be unmade as made. For Rousseau, certainly, there was a homology between the status of the lawgiver, who had founded the city, and the tribune, who had the awesome power of bringing everything to a halt.[37] If, as one scholar has observed, *The Social Contract* neglects those magistracies that ensured the day-to-day governance of Rome (the consulate, the praetorship, the aedileship and so on), in favour of 'extraordinary' magistracies, it is because the treatise is predicated upon the assumption that government is no more than a matter of commission or imperative mandate and, as such, is wholly answerable to the general will.[38] Tribunes effect a suspension of authority so complete as to permit the pure expression of a right of resistance. Sieyes and Constant, ever mindful of the horrors of the Germinal and Prairial uprisings, repudiated that right, and therefore preferred tribunes who would be responsible, much as the Venetian *avogadori del commune* had been, for guaranteeing that a bill or an edict was constitutional. For, once the notion of returning a city to its first principles had come to seem absurd, the tribunate of Machiavelli, of Althusius or of Rousseau was doomed. In Mommsen's narrative, for example, the revolutionary aspect of this magistracy was altogether obscured, with the tribunician veto being but one instance (and the consul's right of appeal to the tribune being another) of 'the general principle of law that, where two equal authorities differ, the veto prevails over the command'.[39] Marx, however, continued to draw inspiration from Rousseau's vision of a state which, instead of being set over civil society, was a direct and true expression of it.[40]

## The book for republicans

In the Encyclopédie, Diderot had expounded a defiantly republican interpretation of *The Prince*, which was, he said, a satire, designed to show the Florentines what sort of monster they would have among them if they accepted a master.[41] Only in this fashion was it possible to come to terms with the chilling maxims contained in chapters 15–19 of Machiavelli's treatise, which had long been regarded as a breviary of reason of state. Rousseau was on exceptionally close terms with Diderot in the latter half of the 1740s, and may have brought with him to Paris not only the Plutarchian enthusiasms of a child raised in Geneva among radical artisans, jewellers and master watchmakers but also direct knowledge of *The Discourses* and of *The History of Florence*. He anyway agreed that

*The Prince*, far from being a celebration of tyranny, was 'the book for republicans', for 'while pretending to give instruction to kings, [Machiavelli] taught the peoples a great deal more'.[42]

Such interpretations were proposed with increasing vehemence as the century advanced, especially in Tuscany, where Giovanni Maria Lampredi, later Professor of Public Right at the University of Pisa, and in that capacity the teacher of Buonarroti, drafted a life, never to be completed, and compiled an edition of a number of Machiavelli's obscurer writings. In the Preface to the first edition, published in 1760, he wrote that a man so much honoured by his fatherland could hardly have composed a book expressly designed to enslave it, nor could he have intended to raise Lorenzo di Medici to the Principate, since not long before he had been involved in a conspiracy to kill him. Machiavelli was, after all, 'a man who, at the famous gatherings in the Rucellais' garden, always surrounded by great-souled and generous young men, had never studied anything else save the question of knowing how to live in liberty'.[43] The formulation here, as in Diderot and Rousseau, of the 'oblique' interpretation of *The Prince* suggests that it had long been current in republican milieux, and that there is little point in attempting to track down its first occurrence.[44] In Tuscany, the Satanic image of 'the Florentine Secretary' had all but faded away, and even ecclesiastics, albeit of a Jansenist persuasion, sung his praises. A collected works was published in 1782–83, and a monument to Machiavelli's memory commissioned and built, in the church of Santa Croce, Florence. This enlightened policy was due primarily to the Grand-Duke Peter Leopold, son of Maria Theresa and brother of Joseph II, and the most advanced ruler in the Italian peninsula, in effect a *philosophe*, who had granted his protection to the second and third editions of the Encyclopédie (published in Lucca and Leghorn respectively). The death penalty and torture were abolished, physiocratic theories regarding the economy and land tenure were applied and, most remarkable of all, a radical constitution was drafted, through which the Grand-Duke, by his own wish, would have surrendered a part of his sovereignty. The final version of this document, never to be implemented, also dates from 1782, and it is therefore no surprise to discover that Machiavelli's works were promoted by Peter Leopold, a ruler whose desire to increase the participation of his subjects in the res publica exceeded that of even his boldest ministers, and led him to study closely the most radical of the American constitutions, that promulgated by the state of Pennsylvania in 1776.[45] In the Preface to the six-volume edition of Machiavelli's works, the 'oblique' interpretation of *The Prince* was reiterated, and the people were even exhorted to 'be on their guard against tyrants'.[46]

## A new prince for new times

The frankly republican interpretation of Machiavelli's thought was disavowed in the aftermath of the Terror, in the same fashion and, broadly speaking, for the same reasons, as the Liberty of the Ancients had been. When, therefore, moderate republicans reflected upon the Jacobin dictatorship of the year II, a link was often traced between the writings of Rousseau and those of Machiavelli. For example, Giovanni Battista Baldelli – a scholar from Cortona who had lived in revolutionary France but had returned, disillusioned, to Tuscany – delivered a eulogy of Machiavelli in August 1794. He acknowledged the civic virtue of the Florentine but, as Mario Rosa has noted, made a sharp distinction between, on the one hand, the theoretician of popular sovereignty identified by Rousseau and the Jacobins, and, on the other, a publicist who, 'although Europe had no model of such a government in his day, was the first among modern political theorists to regard a mixed government as the only one suited to a corrupt people, as the only one capable of prescribing that dose of liberty compatible with the human passions'.[47] Baldelli thus fashioned a Thermidorian Machiavelli, pausing to denounce both the 'tumultuous' Roman plebs and those 'most skilled in insiduously flattering it', that is, the tribunes.[48] Likewise, the notes attached to the surviving draft of *Des Circonstances Actuelles* suggest that Madame de Staël undertook a critical reading of the *Discourses* in order to refute the advocates of direct democracy, the Babouvists among them.[49] Furthermore, Sismondi, in his manuscript *Recherches*, rejected the view that *The Prince* was a satire, on the grounds that Machiavelli offered, as is in fact the case, equally sanguinary counsel to the leaders of republics in disordered, treacherous times.[50]

The general defeat suffered by the republican cause at the turn of the eighteenth century, sometimes at the hands of peasant armies loyal to throne and altar, and the revulsion felt by many at the depredations inflicted on the vassal states by the Grande Nation had almost immediate consequences, or so it now appears, for the interpretation of Machiavelli. His Florence could no longer turn above earthly cities, as a part of the acropolitical series, but had instead to be anchored more precisely to the historical circumstances in which he had lived. German authors, in particular, maintained that Machiavelli's writings could not be understood unless they were viewed in relation to the calamity of Italy, so readily called to mind by those living in states whose fragmented condition or small scale had occasioned similar sufferings. Thus Hegel, in his unfinished essay, *Ueber die Verfassung Deutschlands*, produced a dazzlingly lucid but caustic account of the weaknesses of the Holy Roman

Empire. Germany's fate was there likened to that of Italy, and a sharp contrast was drawn between their predicament and the development of 'modern' monarchies such as France, England and Spain. Hegel's disillusionment with ancient liberty was clearly exacerbated by his first-hand observation of the Bernese oligarchy, the target of his first published work, and, more generally, by the fate of the other *Kleinstaaten* at the hands of the Directorial Republic's armies.[51] Thus, Venice may have preserved its legendary independence somewhat longer than, say, Pisa, Siena, Arezzo, Ferrara, Milan and hundreds of others had done, 'but it received its coup de grace . . . by a French general, delivered by an aide-de-camp'. Hegel directed a pitiless gaze at the question of *ius gentium*, and concluded, like Foscolo, that in truth it did not exist, for 'the mass of the German states do not constitute a power, [and so] the independence of their individual units can only be respected so long as the advantage of other powers requires'.[52]

In France, Hegel observed, Richelieu had created a unitary national state by crushing the resistance of both the Huguenots and the League, each being 'an armed fanaticism'. The Treaty of Westphalia had been a watershed, after which the great national monarchies increasingly enjoyed religious tolerance, less restricted commerce and equality before the law. In Germany, by contrast, the continued existence of the cumbersome Diet, and the check placed on the right of the majority to compel the minority to adopt its religion, had ensured a degree of toleration but at the same time perpetuated the fragmentation of the Empire into a preposterous number of independent, and often minute, territories. Though willing to accept Montesquieu's claim that modern liberty could be traced back to the Germanic forests, Hegel distinguished between the transmutation of such principles in the national monarchies and the lawlessness (or, more accurately, the plethora of archaic and conflicting rights) of the Holy Roman Empire. The Italian peninsula, being divided into many independent sovereignties, generally either Guelph or Ghibelline in sympathy, had long been prey to invading or marauding armies, and had sunk by the fifteenth century into tyranny and corruption. This, then, was the stage upon which Machiavelli, no Bosola but 'a genuinely political head endowed with an intellect of the highest and noblest kind', had to act: 'profoundly moved by this situation of general distress, hatred, disorder and blindness, a . . . statesman grasped with cool circumspection the necessary idea of the salvation of Italy through its unification in one state'.[53] Hegel therefore quoted at length from chapter 26 of *The Prince*, the famous 'exhortation to liberate Italy from the barbarians', insisting that the whole book be construed as a direct response to Machiavelli's immediate political context. It is now generally agreed, that this *exhortatio* was appended at a later date (1516) to the text, but Federico Chabod, among others, believed that it was always an integral element. My concern is less with the philological intricacies of the dispute than with the historiographical fact that in the eighteenth century this chapter had remained all but invisible to commentators, whereas in the early nineteenth century it gleamed, a mirror for patriots, in the light cast by the camp fires of the Army of Italy.[54]

The Tuscan edition of Machiavelli's works was more complete than any other had thus far been, but nonetheless the selection of materials was dictated by the presupposition that *The Prince* was a 'satire'. While it had long been known that Machiavelli was thrown into prison by the Medicis after the fall of the Florentine republic, in 1512 – Diderot mentions the 'long and cruel persecutions' suffered at their hands – correspondence from the crucial months in which *The Prince* was composed had only recently come to light. The editors of the new edition in fact omitted the majority of letters from the years 1513 to 1515, for their publication would clearly have exploded the theory that Machiavelli's treatise was a satire. No reader of the famous letter of 10 December 1513 to Francesco Vettori, an intimate friend of Machiavelli, could have misinterpreted either its tone or its contents. It would have been still more ill-advised to publish the letter of 31 January 1515, in which the Duke of Valentinois, the infamous Caesar Borghia, was vaunted as the very type of the new prince. No 'honest man' or 'good citizen' could ever in all sincerity have praised the nefarious doings of such a monster.[55] With the publication, then, in 1810, of the letter of 10 December 1513 to Vettori, the perplexing problem of the relation between *The Prince* and the *Discourses* seemed to have been solved. Republics were well and good, in their own time, but the modern world had no place for them; the *Discourses* were an elegy, *The Prince* an exhortation, terrible but historically necessary. As Hans Baron remarked, over thirty years ago:

> In the light of the nineteenth-century ideal of the nation-state, it seemed most natural that Machiavelli, though brought up and sentimentally remaining a Florentine republican, should decide that national independence and monarchical unification of Italy were the goals of the hour. He was thought to have felt – like the Italian republicans of the early nineteenth century who accepted the final triumph of a unified Italian monarchy, or like the Nationalliberalen in Germany who submitted to Bismarck's solution of the German question – that in his own day republican nostalgia had to give way to princely Realpolitik.[56]

The most coherent formulation of this line of argument is contained in an essay by Federico Chabod, published as late as 1925, to which I now turn.

The Florentine Republic of Piero Soderini was overthrown, and the Medici restored to power, in 1512. After a brief spell in prison, Machiavelli withdrew to his villa in the Tuscan countryside. According to Chabod, he spent the early months of 1513 writing Book 1 of the *Discourses*, and perhaps some more besides, but broke off to draft *The Prince*, which was all but completed by December of that same year. For proof of this claim, Chabod (like Pasquale Villari before him) quoted from the second chapter of *The Prince*, where Machiavelli had stated: 'I shall not discuss republics, because I have previously treated them at length.'[57] There is no gainsaying the mood of fervent exaltation in which the first book of the *Discourses* was written, yet it was flecked with iron also, for Rome is celebrated chiefly because it was so consummately what Florence was not. Machiavelli's native city had never truly had a state, and had therefore not earned the right to be called a republic; nor were the other polities in the Italian peninsula in any less parlous a condition.[58] By contrast, republican Rome presented Machiavelli with a boldly carved image of *vivere libero*. Why, if republican Rome were his touchstone, did he abruptly set aside his reconstruction of that city, and embark upon a treatise devoted to the topic of the new prince?

Chabod's answer to this question is simple enough. The *Discourses* constituted a nostalgic withdrawal into the past, albeit one that had opened up a rich seam of exempla, whereas *The Prince* represented a coming to terms with 'the realities of the times'. In this regard, a comparison could be made between Montesquieu's intellectual trajectory and that of Machiavelli, with the early, 'republican' books of *The Spirit of the Laws* being likened to the *Discourses*, and Book 11 to *The Prince*. In either case, a specific itinerary might be said to have precipitated a realization as to where the future lay, namely, in England (for Montesquieu) and in France, England and Spain (for Machiavelli). For either writer, then, if the terms of the argument be accepted, free cities were a thing of the past. In Chabod's account, as in that of Villari, the historical circumstances are used to illustrate the writings, so that the empirical supersession of republic by principate is mirrored in the chronological sequence, from the *Discourses* to *The Prince*.

Thus, in the second chapter of his pioneering essay, Chabod described the inexorable rise to power of the new princes, backed at first by the citizen elite and later by the disenfranchised lower classes of the city and the inhabitants of the *contado* (or rural hinterland). In the course of the fourteenth century, the principates extended their sway over several cities, and in effect over whole regions. This was the case in Lombardy, for example, where the Visconti, the prototypical 'tyrants' of Florentine republican discourse in the early *quattrocento*, became *signori* of Milan, Bergamo and Pavia, yet such regimes were intrinsically fragile, being founded upon little more than corruption, intimidation and the prestige of an individual ruler. Since neither the feudal *gentiluomini* nor the subject cities were ever entirely tamed, a Signoria could dissolve at the death of its prince. Nonetheless, in the sulphurous figure of the new prince, we are led to believe, Machiavelli discerned in crude outline a force – there was no other – that might, in emulation of the national monarchies, found a strong state in the peninsula, perhaps based upon Florence.[59] In 1925, Chabod thus viewed the *Discourses* (largely but not entirely) as a lament for the lost world of the communes, and *The Prince* (largely but not entirely) as an admission that the future lay with nation-states. Machiavelli's republicanism was, he argued, a matter of regret for a lost form of liberty, which could not be reconstituted. Even the divisions of the Florentine territories into *città*, *contado* and *distretto* (that is, Florence itself, its rural hinterland and the subject cities) posed an intractable problem, to which Machiavelli's citizen militias were, in Chabod's view, a thoroughly anachronistic, and therefore Utopian, solution.[60] So turbulent a polity, in which the *contado* was politically and juridically a subject territory, could never vie with ancient Rome, where citizenship was accorded to the inhabitants of *rus* and *urbs* alike.[61]

The terms of Chabod's argument, largely accepted by Antonio Gramsci, would obviously be undermined if it were found that the free city, far from being a residual, merely nostalgic element in Machiavelli's thought, had remained his guiding passion.[62] I shall therefore now consider how a number of scholars have in recent years questioned Chabod's dating of the *Discourses* and *The Prince*, and in consequence have drawn Machiavelli nearer to the republican ideal of politics and, by the same token, away from reason of state.[63]

In 1961, Hans Baron, after a survey (quoted above) of nineteenth- and twentieth-century interpretations of Machiavelli, ventured the opinion that

> [when] we return to a reading of the *Discourses*, we still find ourselves face to face with the undisguised scale of values of a Florentine citizen, who is just as far as eighteenth-century readers had believed him to be from being indifferent to, or merely secondarily interested in, the political and historical role of freedom.[64]

It was after all the case that Machiavelli had declared, in no uncertain terms, that a multitude of citizens, disciplined by good laws, had better judgement than a prince, being able to judge accurately between two speakers and so to choose magistrates. He had also stated unequivocally that the major advances made by nations had occurred when they were republics, as had been the case in Athens and Rome.[65] If the *Discourses* are a republican work, dedicated not to a prince but to two private citizens (Buondelmonti, Rucellai), how had Chabod arrived at the contrary view and phrased it so powerfully that a generation of Italian (and other) scholars were persuaded of its essential accuracy?

Chabod had acknowledged the republican temper of the opening chapters of book 1 of the *Discourses*, but had at the same time remarked upon the faultlines in chapters 16–18, a corridor perhaps to the universe of *The Prince*. It was as if, the argument runs, having wistfully charted the foundation, rise and fall of Rome, Machiavelli had been so reminded of the parlous state of Florence in his own times that, abandoning ideal images of civic virtue, he set to thinking of the extreme means that a new prince might employ in order to restore a disordered city to order. Having drafted chapters 16–18, Chabod claimed, Machiavelli composed *The Prince*. Closer inspection, however, suggests that the putative corridor is blocked. Thus Baron noted that, although in the *Discourses* Machiavelli had admitted that a 'prince' was required for the reform of a 'highly corrupted city', he had baulked at the admission, made with glowing but savage slashes of the palette knife in *The Prince*, that such a ruler should give free expression to the bestial aspect of human nature if and where necessary.[66] In fact we hear only of the instituting of a 'quasi-regal power' in a republic. Gennaro Sasso has argued that the latter concept is a contradiction in terms, masking a problem in the *Discourses* which is solved in *The Prince*, yet neither he nor any other commentator seems to have noticed that, in a chapter containing references to many of the other magistracies of republican Rome, no direct mention is made of the dictatorship, an office which could well be termed 'quasi-regal'.[67] In short, a passage regarded by Chabod and his followers as a bridge between the *Discourses* and *The Prince* may in fact be construed as still, in essence, republican. In the case of Florence, Machiavelli proposed in 1519 or 1520, that is, shortly after the *Discourses* were completed, that Pope Leo X and Cardinal Giulio de' Medici assume an overlordship of the city, but with so many elements of civic participation still intact that, after their deaths, it would once again be a republic.[68] Could they not, in such circumstances, be described as 'quasi-kings' or, in Roman terms, as dictators?

Chabod's case rested, as we have seen, on a sentence in *The Prince* which seemed to have riveted that book securely to the *Discourses*. If the rivet proved, however, to be loose, our perception of the chronological relation between the two works might change. Felix Gilbert had argued in 1953 that the sentence could as well have referred to a lost work on republics as to the *Discourses* themselves, and Hans Baron, rejecting the hypothesis but seizing the occasion, maintained that, although the reference is indeed to the *Discourses*, it was very probably inserted later, in 1516, or even in 1517 or 1518.[69] Might not the *Discourses* have superseded *The Prince*, rather than the other way around?

The greater plausibility of Hans Baron's putative chronology, which hangs on important contributions to Florentine intellectual history by Felix Gilbert, is immediately apparent. To begin with, *The Prince*, rather than being the sudden, one might say unpremeditated, fruit of Machiavelli's enforced retirement in 1513, is shown to be the product of long years of diplomatic experience both across the Alps and in Tuscany and the Papal State. Hans Baron is thus able to present the years in which Machiavelli served the restored republic of Piero Soderini, that is, the period between 1498 and 1512, as 'an uninterrupted exercise in the thought of which *The Prince* was to become an epitome'.[70] It makes sense, after all, that a treatise that, though small, has exerted such a huge influence across the centuries, was many years in the making. Turning the admirably detailed studies of Chabod's school to a different purpose, Baron notes that none of the reports to the Florentine Chancellery were concerned with the workings of the constitution of ancient Rome, but seemed rather to anticipate the 'Machiavellian' precepts of *The Prince*.[71]

The link identified by Baron between Machiavelli's diplomatic and political experience and the drafting of *The Prince* served by the same token to drive a wedge between the years spent in the service of the Florentine Chancellery and the composition of the *Discourses*. How could he have drafted the first book of the *Discourses* so rapidly, between March and August 1513, if its central arguments and its tone differed from all his earlier writings? Furthermore, could he have sustained so fervent a republicanism in his manuscript while at the same time doing his utmost, as the letters to Francesco Vettori attest, to secure a place in the service of the recently restored Medici? To clinch the case, Baron observed that there was no other example in the history of political thought of a writer producing a more complex and more sophisticated treatise before rather than after a simpler, not to say cruder, work.[72]

The missing element in the picture had been supplied by Felix Gilbert, in an essay on the revival in the early sixteenth century of Florentine republicanism, through discussions held in the Oricellari gardens of Bernardo and Cosimino di Cosimo Rucellai.[73] There, from 1514 onwards, Machiavelli was able to deepen his understanding of ancient history, and thereby to rebuild his thought in the light of civic humanism. Thus, as Lampredi had claimed in 1760, it had been through prolonged contact with the Orti Oricellari circle that Machiavelli had learned of the forms of liberty known to free cities, a topic of the utmost importance to several generations of Florentine humanists. Though still concerned, as he had been in *The Prince*, with the desolating fact of power and of its rude application to ever-shifting circumstance, he now saw that the *virtù* of a republic depended, as that of a principate did not, upon the existence of, in Baron's words, 'a social and constitutional fabric that allowed the civic energies and a spirit of political devotion and sacrifice to develop in all classes of a people'.[74] If it is admitted that a *virtù* which gives free rein to the virtues of the community of citizens is much to be preferred to one that is no more than the emanation of a single, uncurbed will, it follows that the move away from *The Prince* was, as Baron asserts, an 'expansion' of Machiavelli's intellectual framework. This, however, poses a serious challenge to all those who, like Chabod, have seen Machiavelli's trajectory in terms of the progressive abandonment of ideal images of Antiquity in favour of representations of the modern world, and have therefore failed to grasp that he is one of those thinkers who have been obliged, in their efforts to prise the earthly city from the grip of an all-seeing providence, to invoke criteria best described as ancient–modern. Machiavelli may in this respect be regarded as the founder of a tradition to which both Rousseau and Marx, to differing degrees, belong. Thus, in the introductory, synthetic chapters of the *Discourses*, Machiavelli, like Leonardo Bruni and Flavio Biondo before him, was concerned to wrest Roman history from all forms of providentialist guarantee, whether Guelph or Ghibelline, in order to summon up a world in which free cities subsist through *virtù* and in spite of *fortuna*. In highlighting the existence, prior to the Roman domination of the peninsula, of a number of different free peoples, he was not repudiating republican Rome but rather insisting that the eternal city was, quite simply, not eternal but one of a potentially infinite series, as vulnerable as any other to the fatal instability of time.[75]

Whereas no one would deny that Machiavelli had recognized and responded to the apparently irresistible rise of the new prince, or that such a recognition and response had coloured all his writings, a growing number of commentators are now, I think, agreed that the *Discourses* and *The Prince* simply cannot be treated as parts of one and the same political philosophy. A distinction may, for example, be advanced between an art of the city, expounded in the *Discourses*, and an art of the state, elaborated in *The Prince*.[76] Where Chabod, and those influenced by him, had cast Machiavelli as the standard-bearer of the nascent nation-state, Skinner and Viroli have shown how deeply indebted his thought was to the world of the communes.[77] At the same time, they have mounted a challenge to the claim, most strikingly formulated by Croce, that Machiavelli had established the 'autonomy' of politics.

What Machiavelli had discovered, in Croce's view, was the independence of politics from ethics. He was, then, a Galileo, and had found that the political sphere had its own laws, which were irreducible to any merely ethical description, and which '[could] not be exorcised or chased out of the world by means of holy water'.[78] At first glance, this line of argument would seem to be incontrovertible, for, where other treatises dispensing advice to princes had exhorted them to cultivate all the Christian virtues, Machiavelli had warned that, to achieve 'great things' and 'to maintain his state', a new prince should trample upon faith, charity, humanity or religion.[79] This is not to say that the new prince is counselled to do evil for evil's sake, but 'not to deviate from right conduct if possible, but be capable of entering upon the path of wrongdoing when this becomes necessary'.[80] All the same, the argument would appear to have destroyed forever the view that politics and ethics are a unity. Once it is allowed that the end justifies the means, all manner of horrors can be inflicted upon human beings in the name of a desired and anticipated good. So it was that 'Machiavellian' arguments were used to justify the massacre of the Huguenots and, in the heyday of reason of state, precepts drawn from Tacitus rendered any reference to civic virtues nugatory.

Machiavelli, acutely aware that the territorial state had supplanted the polis was thus, for Croce, the prophet of force, concerned always to stress that right is born of violence, not consent. As will, I hope, be clear, this account of Machiavelli's thought presupposes the chronology expounded by Chabod and undermined by Baron, and by the same token obscures the survival of republican values in the age of absolutism.[81] Once, however, that chronology is overturned, and the possibility entertained that Machiavelli's real and enduring passion was not for the territorial state but for the city, the claim that he established the autonomy of politics is placed in doubt.

Some gain in clarity is made if we posit the independence of politics, not from ethics, but from theology. John Pocock, for example, has pointed out that the *Discourses*, being 'a drastic experiment in secularisation', were more scandalous than *The Prince*, since in them 'civic ends – including the virtue of citizenship – [were] divorced from the ends of redemption'.[82] Rather than propose the autonomy of politics, it might then be more accurate to stress its primacy, and to note that, for Machiavelli, there was no salvation outside of the city. The unshackling of the polis from celestial scripts, far from sundering politics from ethics, could be said to have united them.

## Monarchies and republics

In order to establish a link between the Florentine tradition of liberty and eighteenth-century Europe, I wish now to consider what kind and degree of prestige republican values were accorded in the years between the publication of *The Social Contract* and the swearing of the Tennis Court Oath. To begin with, it must be understood that, on the margins of the absolutist states, the trading republics of the Italian peninsula, the United Provinces and the Swiss cities and cantons had continued to serve as beacons to those who loved liberty. Rousseau's own vision of the free city, for example, rested upon an unyielding hostility to both strands of absolutism, papal and princely. He therefore celebrated the freedoms won by the cities of the Lombard Plain in the twelfth century, and applauded the success of the Dutch and Swiss federations in casting off both the Habsburg yoke and the tyranny of the Curia.[83] Since much commentary upon Rousseau had emphasized the Utopian quality of his writings, this being sometimes cause for approbation and sometimes for condemnation, it is worth dwelling upon the survival, up until the very end of the eighteenth century, of small European states. Franco Venturi has in fact criticized the 'tendency to regard the survival of the republics into the age of absolutism in the seventeenth and eighteenth centuries as a "myth"'. Indeed, there is much to be gained, he continues, from viewing the rise of the modern state, 'not from the point of view of the victorious monarchies, but from that of the republics surviving with such tenacity'.[84] Notwithstanding the repeated attempts of the absolutist monarchies to destroy them, in the span of time that runs from the Treaty of Westphalia, in 1648, to the Treaty of Aix-La-Chapelle, their position was, by 1748, more or less secure. At times they served as laboratories, with rival *philosophes* squabbling over their respective merits or short-comings, as was the case, to a pronounced degree, with Geneva, in whose political affairs D'Alembert and Voltaire both meddled. At other times, the object of the experiment amazed the wider world by its temerity. For example, Genoa, which had been condemned as unregenerate by Montesquieu, Rousseau and Vico alike, rose in open rebellion in 1746, regaining its independence and, in the process, reshaping its political structure in the most radical fashion. This revolt, which Venturi has called 'the last great blaze of the republican and communal tradition', threatened the privileges of the Genoese oligarchy. While the lesser nobility demanded a greater say in government, armed artisans and peasants developed (or revived) their own democratic forms of representation and mandate. An 'assembly of the people' was constituted, which met 'in the open air, as they do in Poland', electing magistrates, one eye-witness remarked, with tribunitian authority. The thirty-six officers had in fact to give an account of themselves every fortnight to the assembled people. The astonishing deeds of the Senatus Populusque Genuensis were the talk of Europe, presumably because they constituted so pure an expression of popular sovereignty, cast in a mould that Machiavelli, if not Montesquieu, would have endorsed.[85] When Edward Gibbon visited

Genoa, in 1764, the insurrection still seemed to him an exemplary instance of republican liberty.[86]

The particular merit of Venturi's interpretation lies in his grasp of the fact that the Swiss, Italian or German city-states were in many respects cast in the same image as the parliaments, the provincial states general, the urban oligarchies and the municipal privileges that the absolutist states had for two centuries been attempting, within their own frontiers, to tame.[87] So exact was this parallel between cities without and cities within, that it is possible to identify in one and the same thinker a preoccupation with republican virtue abroad and with municipal liberties at home. This is true of, for example, the Marquis D'Argenson, whose significance in the history of political thought has not always been properly recognized, in part because his writings were not published during his own lifetime. Born in 1694, to a father unswervingly loyal to Ludovican absolutism, D'Argenson was profoundly marked by the moral and intellectual ferment of the Regency. A member, like Montesquieu, of the Club D'Entresol, he rejected the constitutional projects of both the sword and the robe, promoting instead a radical combination of the principles of democracy and monarchy. As Secretary of State for Foreign Affairs, D'Argenson had been impressed by the public-spiritedness of the mercantile republics, and he had launched a diplomatic initiative which, if successful, would have resulted in the creation of a federation of small states on the Germanic, Batavian or Swiss model, in the Italian peninsula.[88] Furthermore, in 1746, when the French restored the Genoese oligarchy to power, he observed that the plebs, deprived once again of their own magistrates, might be reluctant in the future to defend their city as vigorously as they had done in the uprising.[89]

D'Argenson abhorred the feudal system, and the usurpations of a conquering aristocracy. His *Considérations sur le Gouvernement Ancien et Présent de la France* were thus, first and foremost, a refutation of the aristocratic constitutionalism of Boulainvilliers, whose Germanist gloss on French history I survey in a later chapter. The same points were reiterated in the discourse that D'Argenson, like Rousseau, submitted to the Academy of Dijon in 1754, in terms that seem to anticipate, or are certainly consistent with, *The Social Contract*: 'public right cannot have its source in the continual abuses recorded in the history of barbarism'.[90] He also remarked that, 'when republics are founded, the common good assembles, and renders equal, all the citizens', but he warned against the inevitable formation of orders, classes and ranks.[91] However corrupted they might become, the free cities nonetheless supplied D'Argenson with a concrete image of assembled equality, of unsullied sovereignty and of magistracies which, being rotated, were not the sinecure of a venal *noblesse de robe*. Popular sovereignty might thus be construed as the attribute of a free city 'protected' by a first magistrate, for whom a precedent might be found in the Flavian and Antonine Emperors.[92] A similar blend of democracy and monarchy proved attractive to Edward Gibbon, to Tuscan reformers in the Grand-Duke Peter Leopold's milieu, some of whom studied the *Considérations*, and again to a Lombard jurisconsult like Gian Domenico Romagnosi, in the aftermath. of the French Revolution.[93]

The mercantile republics had thus retained their power to fascinate, even though their moribund condition was a matter of common knowledge. Venturi, whose researches underlie so much of my argument here, never for a moment seeks to deny the marginal status, as much economic as political, of Genoa, Venice or Lucca, yet he continues to insist upon the capacity of such cities 'to arouse a resolute desire for independence and virtue which . . . the monarchical states were not able to satisfy'.[94] The precise interpretation one gives of *The Spirit of the Laws*, published in 1748, then becomes crucial. Judith Shklar, for example, in a wide-ranging essay on eighteenth-century republicanism, asserts that, for Montesquieu, 'even on purely scholarly historical grounds, . . . the republic was a political form that had no place in the modern age', and was not an object of 'emulation'.[95] His profound disillusionment with the Italian republics, and even with the United Provinces, is well documented, and in no sense controversial. He had weighed the small states of the modern world against the virtue of the ancient world and had found them wanting. Shklar thus allows of only two possible responses to the republican tradition in the latter half of the eighteenth century. Either one could recreate it imaginatively, as Rousseau had done, or one could replace it, as the authors of the *Federalist Papers* would do in 1787–88, with 'a new expansive republicanism to fit the modern political world'.[96] I will not spell out my objections to this eminently plausible description, save to say that I am more drawn to Venturi's interpretation of Montesquieu's great book. For to treat *The Spirit of the Laws* as a mirror of a precariously balanced world of monarchies and republics is both to account for the strikingly diverse views of Montesquieu entertained in revolutionary France, and to highlight a third response to republican tradition, one not directly, or only fleetingly, addressed by Shklar.[97]

By the early 1770s, however, the cause of republicanism appeared to be in full retreat. Even in Rousseau's writings, each passage of fervent exhortation may be matched by a confession of radical disillusion, especially where Geneva was concerned, while *philosophes* such as Diderot, Galiani or Raynal were still more sceptical about the future of the mercantile republics.[98] Although aligned for the most part with the programmes of enlightened absolutism prosecuted in Austria, Prussia,

Russia and Tuscany, they were deeply impressed by the clan-based rebellions on the obscure edge of the European states, which erupted in the late 1760s and early 1770s. If the picture that Venturi has painted in the third volume of his *Settecento Riformatore* of 'the first crisis of the old regime' is accurate, Europe's gazettes were full of references to the rebellion in Corsica, and to the uprisings in Greece and Montenegro. With the expansion of Russian diplomatic and military influence in the Mediterranean, Catherine II, though threatened in her own dominions by the Cossack revolt under Pugachev, was able to foment armed conflict in the Balkans, and thereby to inflict some damage upon the Ottoman Empire. Venturi's account supplies a context for Rousseau's preoccupation in these years with the natural liberty of the Corsicans and thus renders his apparent rejection of city-state liberty less exceptional, and indeed his draft constitutions less Utopian.[99] There was in fact a general fascination in those years with tribal customs and tribal liberties, manifest in the cult of Ossian and in Paul-Henri Mallet's discovery in Copenhagen of the world of the Eddas.[100] Such rebellions certainly heightened the enthusiasm in Europe for the social organization of the clans, whether in Corsica or in the Peloponnese, yet they did not create it from nothing, since the advocates of a stadial theory of society had been reflecting upon the mores of hunting or pastoral peoples since the early 1750s, as I noted in chapter 2. I am equally suspicious of the claim that nationalism was born during this transitional period, no matter how many of the elements of nationalist belief were already on display. For tenacious traditions of city-state liberty and the wider arcs of Enlightenment conviction together inhibited for several decades the formation of the fully-fledged doctrine of the tribe-nation. Venturi thus notes that, by 1784,

> the primitivism that accompanied the first crisis of the old regime and had made one look with new eyes at the Corsicans, at the Danes of the Edda, at the Scots of Ossian, and at the Greeks of Maina had . . . passed . . . The tutelage of the past and of authority was collapsing. It was precisely at this moment that Kant defined *enlightenment* as the departure of humanity from adolescence.

This passage drives a wedge between celebrations of tribal liberties and the advent of the tribe-nation, and thereby provides, so to speak, breathing room for the otherwise endangered notions of city-nation and general city of humankind. Yet Venturi's observation is only valid if the excised sentence is restored: 'At the height of civilisation, at the culmination of the development of sciences and arts, a "new nation" had appeared.'[101] With the Declaration of Independence, in 1776, and the promulgation of the Articles of Confederation, in 1781, the Old World, as much as the New World, was transformed.

Any discussion of the rebellion of the Thirteen Colonies, no matter how cursory, now requires that some reference be made to surviving traditions of republican thought in Augustan Britain. For, notwithstanding the success of the Settlement of 1688 and the remorseless operation of Walpole's machinery of government, radical Whig currents of opinion endured on this side of the Atlantic and later inspired the insurgent colonists. On the basis of a number of pioneering studies from the 1950s and 1960s, Gordon Wood and John Pocock have thus shown how English, neo-Harringtonian versions of civic humanism flourished in America, supplying a theoretical framework for the constitution-making of 1776–81. In France, the *philosophes* had already learned much from the republican ethics of Shaftesbury, from the insurrection in Genoa and from Rousseau's native city, but the thirteen colonies closed the gap between abstract ideals and the reality of modern commercial society in a way that moral exhortation or the aristocratic oligarchies of the Old World could not. More particularly, the Declaration of Independence gave new life to the principle of confederation.

## Liberty and confederation

Pocock has remarked that there is an aporia in classical republican thought respecting the relations between diverse, free, armed and self-governing republics, yet the notion of confederation pervades the history of republicanism, and seems almost to haunt the theory of the modern state.[102] Athens may have stood alone, but the cause of Greek liberty was served in later centuries by leagues or confederations, foremost among them the Achaian League in the Peloponnese.[103] In medieval Europe, the consolidation of the doctrines of Papal and Imperial absolutism was followed, with not so great a delay, by the emergence of the *Eidgenossenschaft*, a league of Swiss cantons forged in 1291 and extended and strengthened in succeeding centuries. In 1579, seven provinces in the Low Countries combined against the Spanish Habsburgs in an equally celebrated federal union, which lasted up until the French Revolution. Machiavelli did not live to see this expression of Batavian liberty, but he was profoundly interested by the principle of confederation. For this reason, I find Pocock's observation to be wide of the mark, and believe it to be a necessary consequence of the architecture of *The Machiavellian Moment*. If an admiring reader of Pocock's vast work sometimes labours in vain to pin it exactly to the historical contexts it surveys, this is, I think, because a phenomenology of city and citizen, of polity and personality, serves to obscure lateral connection.

Machiavelli believed that a people wishing to maintain its *vivere libero* or *vivere civile* had to be wholly independent of domination, internal and external. For the preservation of that independence, three – by implication, four – methods were available. It was possible, first of all, to live in a very small state. Yet in a world in ceaseless flux, vulnerable to the natural rapacity of humankind, a polity had to expand in order to survive. With this end in view, three methods were to hand, as much in the modern as in the ancient world. Of the three, one was rejected as 'quite useless', namely, the policy pursued by Sparta or by Athens in making other, formerly self-governing cities their subjects rather than their allies. Being accustomed to *vivere libero*, the subject cities would have to be ruled by force, and this would overstretch the means of the prince-city. It is, however, of the utmost importance to note that this is not Machiavelli's last word on small states, for a degree of expansion might also be achieved by the league, or confederation.

Machiavelli thus described how Rome, in its rise to power, had encountered leagues of well-armed peoples, who defended their liberty to the last. The Samnites, for example, had resisted for forty-six years, and only Roman virtue could ever have conquered so well-ordered and strong a polity. The Etruscans, too, had been exceptionally powerful, both on sea and on land, founding a colony at Adria and holding the peninsula as far as the Alps by force of arms. Each of the twelve cities in the league enjoyed equal rank and influence, as was the case with the Achaian and Aetolian confederations, and with the Swiss cantons. The Etruscans had failed, admittedly, to expand beyond Italy, or even to control the whole of the peninsula, but they had avoided needless wars and had held whatever territory they took. This crucial chapter does indeed contain a condemnation of the principle of confederation, which 'has always entailed weakness and has produced but small advantages', and is 'wholly useless' if the cities are unarmed. The proper method to adopt, Machiavelli continues, is 'the one the Romans adopted'; from ignorance of it, we, the Italians, 'have become the prey of anybody who has wanted to overrun the land'. Yet he adds that it would be easier by far to imitate the ancient Tuscans than the Romans, whom, after all, no one has ever succeeded in emulating, and this would be particularly true for 'the Tuscans of today'. For their ancestors, though never able to found an Empire like the Roman, 'did succeed in acquiring in Italy such power as this method . . . allowed . . . [which] was for a long time secure, and conjoined with it were the glories of empire and of arms in the highest degree as well as customs and religious observances which are worthy of the highest praise'.[104] These passages evidently constitute something other than outright rejection of the case for confederation. What is anyway not in doubt is the fact that they were so read by many in eighteenth-century Tuscany, and elsewhere.

The notion of confederation, purportedly sustaining free cities in a hostile world, thus featured prominently in eighteenth-century political thought. For example, in *The Spirit of the Laws*, Montesquieu had lauded the federal republic because it provided a solution to the problems of small and large polities alike, the former being vulnerable to foreign armies, the latter to internal corruption. Such a government had 'all the internal advantages of republican government and the external force of monarchy', and was 'an agreement by which many political bodies consent[ed] to become citizens of the larger state'. Sometimes, as in the case of Germany, a confederation might consist of both monarchies (or principalities) and republics, but because the spirit of one was for war and expansion, and of the other, for peace and moderation, the United Provinces and the Swiss cantons, being composed of republics alone, were more worthy to be emulated. Although modern examples feature prominently in book 9, much praise is also accorded the Greek, Italic, Roman and Germanic confederations, the Lycian being singled out as a model.[105] This line of argument, which identifies a third term between the small and the large state, was reiterated by Lampredi, in his *Saggio Sopra la Filosofia degli Antichi Etruschi* [1756], and by Rousseau, in *The Social Contract*, in *Emile*, in his draft constitution for Poland, and in a lost manuscript on small states and their confederation. Lampredi, for example, invoked 'the wise, prudent and excellent civil governance of the ancient Tuscans', and described their federal system, in terms taken directly from Montesquieu, as 'a government that has in its internal ordering all the advantages of the most absolute liberty, and in its external arrangements all the force and authority of a monarchy'.[106]

It is tempting to define Lampredi's interest in Etruscan leagues in terms of a narrowly provincial vision, as, in short, an expression of anti-Roman sentiment by no means unusual in eighteenth-century Italy. Muratori, for example, pitted the bishopric of Milan and the Ambrosian rite against the overweening claims of the Curia. In Tuscany, in particular, antiquarian researches at the Accademia Etrusca in Cortona had fostered a local patriotism. Lampredi was not immune to Etruscomania, but to cry *campanilismo* in such cases is to apply the criteria of an age of nations to an age of cities, and so to court anachronism.[107] The vision of a confederated Italic liberty did, no doubt, serve to enhance the prestige of Leghorn, Pisa and Siena, long subordinate to Medicean Florence, and the municipal magistracies were a target for reformers active under the House of Lorraine, but the Tuscan Enlightenment also promoted administrative and political decentralization, as I have already observed.

In the *Saggio*, Lampredi denied that the Etruscans had ever had a monarchy. Four years later, however, in *Del Governo Civile degli Antichi Toscani e delle Cause della lor Decadenza*, he not only insisted that the Etruscans had been ruled by kings, but also deplored their 'fatal error' in overturning the monarchy and instituting a federal system. For the latter, Lampredi said, was ill-suited to their territory, their religion and their mores, and, to cap it all, could not withstand the nascent Roman state on its borders.[108] Whatever the immediate occasion for this volte-face, both Procacci and Rosa agree that Lampredi had turned book 18 of *The Spirit of the Laws* against book 9. In the *Saggio*, the wealth, diversity and fragmentation of ancient Etruria had not counted against it, but in *Del Governo Civile*, the point was made that federal republics lasted longer, the more forbidding their terrain was, as was proven by the fact that 'almost all [had] been founded in harsh, difficult and infertile places.'[109] This was a direct echo of Montesquieu's determinist geography; liberty, book 18 had stated, thrives in rude mountains and not in smiling plains.[110] When, however, Procacci asserts that this passage from *Del Governo Civile* was also a restatement of Machiavelli's reflections, in book 2, chapter 4 of the *Discourses*, 'perhaps filtered through Montesquieu', I think he goes too far. The version of Machiavelli presented in *Del Governo Civile* had not so much been filtered through *The Spirit of the Laws* as overwhelmed by it.[111]

Because classical political theory is predicated upon the existence of unitary states, confederations elude it. For, as Murray Forsyth has observed, they 'occupy the intermediary ground between the interstate and the state worlds, . . . going beyond the one but . . . not unequivocally reaching the other'.[112] The same author further remarks that our difficulty in arriving at an accurate picture of this transitional form is compounded by the fact that 'retrospective accounts of such bodies are often written with amused scorn by authors viewing them from the high plateau of statehood'.[113] This was especially true of the United States, where historical debate has been dominated, or so it seems, by those entertaining a negative conception of the Confederation, and especially of the 'critical period' which began as the war ended, in 1783. The first point to be made regarding this notoriously complex and controversial topic, the ramifications of which have continued to haunt America down to the present day, is that the initial form adopted by the thirteen states, in November 1777, was never in dispute. John Adams later recalled that no one had even considered 'consolidating this vast Continent under one national Government', and that almost all took it for granted that there would be, 'after the Example of the Greeks, the Dutch and the Swiss . . . a Confederacy of States'.[114] The Continental Congress, the *de facto* authority which had prosecuted the war against the British, had assumed emergency powers but the individual states had soon reclaimed their particular sovereignties.

When, therefore, the Articles of Confederation were drafted, sovereignty was located on the periphery, not in the centre. Article 2 thus stipulated that 'Each state retains its sovereignty, freedom and independence, and every power, jurisdiction, and right, which is not by this confederation expressly delegated to the United States, in Congress assembled.' The Continental Congress could decide upon peace and war; send and receive ambassadors; make treaties and alliances; and regulate coinage, weights, measures and postal services; but the individual states reserved the right to lay taxes and to regulate commerce.[115] It was in fact profound dissatisfaction with commercial policy that precipitated the challenge to the Articles mounted by Madison and Hamilton in the mid-1780s.

The lack of interest in anything remotely resembling an incorporating union may be judged by the fact that, after the Declaration of Independence, far more discussion was given to the constitutions of the individual states than to the powers of the centre.[116] By the early 1780s, Congress had all but collapsed. This circumstance accounts for the fact that in 1783 Filippo Mazzei, much to Benjamin Franklin's displeasure, was conducting separate diplomatic negotiations with his native Tuscany, on behalf of the state of Virginia and therefore in breach of Article 6 of the Confederation.[117] While Congress slept, the state legislatures were caught up in a storm of frenetic activity. As Gordon Wood has shown, an exacerbated mistrust of elected representatives added ever more lustre to the inalienable sovereignty of the people at large. For example, in Pennsylvania, which had a unicameral system, the belief was increasingly held that the people itself, howsoever assembled, constituted the lower chamber. Most of the other states may have had a bicameral legislature, with the senate ostensibly operating as a curb to the passions and as the home of a 'natural' aristocracy, but the drift from the doctrine of virtual representation to direct democracy was manifested in the commonplace practice of holding representatives to an imperative mandate. In the process, the deference shown by the Many to the Few was increasingly set aside.[118] In 1776, John Adams had proclaimed that an assembly 'should be in miniature an exact portrait of the people at large', and that 'it should think, feel, reason and act like them'.[119] A decade later, many American statesmen, Adams among them, were of the opinion that representation should function not so much as a mirror but as a filter. In representative government, Madison argued, one could 'refine and enlarge the public views by passing them through the medium of a chosen body of citizens'.[120] There is an obvious parallel here with the history of revolutionary France, and with the discussions surrounding the Constitution of the year III. As I noted at the end of chapter 4, Staël advanced a similar criticism of representation as mirror, although it is not probable that *The Federalist Papers* were known by that date in Paris.[121]

Nothing remotely comparable to the Terror had occurred under the Confederation, yet many of the states had been in turmoil and everywhere well-to-do persons feared that the principle of property was under threat. If not yet traced out on the ground, agrarian law was certainly in the air. Those who had drafted the state constitutions may have espoused the doctrine of the separation of powers but, in their anxiety to forestall executive (formerly 'Court') interference in the judiciary, had brought it somewhat too close to the legislature.[122] In many states, then, the legislatures acted to overrule legal judgments and to block court actions. The crucial point to be grasped is that the war against Great Britain had been not simply a separation but in addition, and to no small degree, a social and political revolution, in the course of which the position of the colonial elites was challenged. Extensions of the suffrage, where ownership of property in land was rather the rule than the exception, brought new men, often middling or small farmers, into the political arena. In a financially parlous condition after the war, they did not hesitate to pass legislation specifically designed to increase the supply of paper money, to set aside or to redefine contracts retrospectively, or to postpone collection of debts.[123] Quite unforeseen in the heady days of 1774–76, the phenomenon of a tyranny of the majority – Jefferson termed it an 'elected despotism' – was complemented by civil disorder in the wider world, with many county courts being forcibly shut down. Foreign observers such as Mazzei or Condorcet insisted that these troubles had been exaggerated out of all proportion by the British press. Indeed, when an authentic uprising, led by a retired officer by the name of Daniel Shays, broke out in western Massachussetts, the news was greeted almost with relief by the critics of the Confederation, as if they could at last point to a disturbance commensurate with their alarm, and yet, as Condorcet and Mazzei pointed out, the Gordon Riots had been far graver.[124]

Jefferson, in Paris, was less perturbed than, say, Adams or Madison, and continued in effect to believe in the censorship, the tribunate *and* the ameliorative effects of education. His essentially transitional cast of mind more nearly resembles that of Volney or Mazzei, both of whom were on good terms with him, than that of Adam Smith, who had made of the *comitia* a purely inward ethical fact:

> The tumults in America, I expected would have produced in Europe an unfavourable opinion of our political state. But it has not. On the contrary, the small effect of these tumults seems to have given more confidence in the

firmness of our governments. The interposition of the people themselves on the side of government [that is, the volunteers from Boston who quelled the uprising] has had a great effect on the opinion here. I am persuaded myself that the good sense of the people will always be the best army. They may be led astray for a moment, but will soon correct themselves. The people are the only censors of their governors: and even their errors will tend to keep these to the true principle of their institution. To punish these errors too severely would be to suppress the only safeguard of the public liberty. The way to prevent these regular interpositions of the people is to give them full information of their affairs through the channel of the public papers, and to contrive that those papers should penetrate the whole mass of the people.[125]

Contrasting America with Europe, where rulers were to ruled as wolves were to sheep, Jefferson urged Carrington to 'cherish the spirit of our people and keep alive their attention', but two weeks later another correspondent, Abigail Adams, remarked that: 'Instead of that laudable spirit which you approve, which makes a people watchfull over their Liberties and alert in the defence of them, these mobish insurgents are for sapping the foundation, and destroying the whole fabrick at once'. The rebels were, she went on, 'ignorant, wrestless desperadoes', who had called for paper currency, for an equal distribution of property, for the cancellation of debts, for the abolition of the Senate, and for the shutting down of various law courts in Boston. Writing, in fact, from London, where her husband was posted, Abigail Adams had not herself wholly abandoned the idiom of classical republicanism, for she bemoaned the luxury of the post-*bellum* years, which had led to chronic indebtedness and therefore to a fatal loss of independence.[126] Jefferson returned to the theme of Daniel Shays's Rebellion the following day, in a letter to Madison, reiterating his belief in a tribunate of the people, and therefore in the service done the public good by 'turbulence' or 'rebellion'.[127]

Condorcet or Mazzei might echo Jefferson in this regard, but exchange of letters could not compensate for the fact that he was physically removed from the American stage, where events were moving very fast. Madison had requested quantities of books from Paris on politics, history and natural law, and Jefferson duly sent them, little suspecting the use to which such researches would be put. He indubitably shared his friend's disquiet over the failure of the states to respect the separation of powers, and he allowed that it had been an error to deprive Congress of the right to regulate commerce and to impose taxes. He was alarmed, however, by Madison's proposal that Congress have a veto on the state legislatures in all cases whatsoever, and, when a copy of the Constitution finally reached him, he was appalled by the quasi-regal powers vested in the chief magistrate, or President.[128]

For one not well versed in the historiography of the American Revolution, it is no easy matter to weigh up the charges levelled at Federalists and anti-Federalists alike by their respective champions. Jensen, for example, the most prominent advocate of the Confederation in recent years, describes *The Federalist Papers* as a work of propaganda and the Constitution of 1787 as the outcome of a conspiracy to overturn the democratic Revolution of 1776. Others dispute Jensen's social and economic analysis, and argue that his distinction between conservatives and radicals hardly does justice to the precise alignment of forces at the Philadelphia Convention.[129] I will not rehearse these arguments at length, but wish rather to point out that the redefinition of republican liberty in *The Federalist Papers* bears a marked similarity to that of Constant and Staël. If, in Thermidorian or Directorial Paris, one wished to prove a republic in a large country possible, the case would have to rest, implicitly or explicitly, upon the precedent of America. Like Constant and Staël, the authors of *The Federalist Papers* had driven back into the past or, if you will, into the sphere of illusion, the liberty of the single city, and that of the confederations, ancient, medieval or early modern. Madison had thus drawn, from Jefferson's crates of books, arguments to demolish the fame of the much-vaunted Lycian and Achaian Leagues, and Hamilton had written disparagingly of the Amphicthyonic Council, the German Confederation and of the United Provinces.[130] The Constitution of 1789 did not, however, represent the death of confederated liberty. For the United States of America remained in some sense a confederation up until the outbreak of the Civil War in 1861, and the survival of states' rights could be said to justify the use of that term even now.[131] In a commentary upon Gordon Wood's thesis regarding 'the end of classical politics', John Pocock has also argued that, notwithstanding the partial abandonment of classical republicanism in 1787, the vocabulary of virtue and corruption has remained a real and significant force in America culture. Jefferson's agrarian Utopia, for example, rested upon a moral opposition between virtuous small farmers and the 'mobs of great cities', in which one may discern a Roman, Machiavellian, neo-Harringtonian or Rousseauist contrast between the rural tribes and the *turba foriensis*, that is, those who swarmed in the forum.[132] The ineluctable cycle of cities was, however, broken, since

> an infinite supply of land, ready for occupation by an armed and self-directing yeomanry, meant an infinite supply of virtue, and it could even be argued that no agrarian law was necessary; the safety valve was open, and all pressures making for dependence and corruption would right themselves.[133]

Thus, in Pocock's account, the frontier is a saving grace for American political culture.[134]

## Unity and confederation

In revolutionary France a time would come when to express a belief in the principle of confederation was to risk one's life. If one considers, however, the early days of the Revolution, one can discern no conflict, but rather an identity, between the principle of the republic one and indivisible and that of confederation. Thus, the first festivals of federation, staged in 1789 and 1790, often featured solemn alliances between neighbouring municipalities, which were then deemed an apt expression of the citizenry's love of the regenerated fatherland.[135] Since the historical precedent for municipal rebellion was supplied by conjuration, first within the city walls and then between federated cities, these symbolic forms were very much to hand. Note should also be taken of the high degree of decentralization prevailing under the Constituent Assembly. What is, on the other hand, remarkable is the fashion in which, almost by accident, federalism became branded as an essentially counter-revolutionary doctrine, associated ever since with the Girondins. Yet, of the twenty-nine deputies arrested on 2 June 1793, only Buzot and Barbaroux were at all interested in a radical devolution of political authority away from the centre. The accusation had first been made in September 1792, just after the battle of Valmy, and the Robespierrists insinuated from then on that their adversaries were unpatriotic, and that they wished to use their provincial followings to dismantle the republic. As Alan Forrest has observed, 'federalism was less a coherent ideology than a polemical device, the creation of a bitter and concerted campaign of political denigration'. Since the slur had no basis in fact, the surviving 'federalists' were rehabilitated in 1795, many of them rising to position of prominence, both locally and nationally, under the Directory.[136]

Outside France, however, disputes between unitarians and federalists continued unabated under the Directory, remaining urgent in the case of the Italian peninsula up until 1859–60 (or, it could be argued, until the present day). Because the federal structure of the United Provinces had allowed the triumph of the counter-revolution in 1787, patriots in the nascent Batavian Republic favoured unity and indivisibility (and therefore a National Convention), whereas moderates opted for confederation (and therefore a States General). Preservation of the existing system would clearly have perpetuated the powers of the old patriciates and closed oligarchies, and the 'first' Directory was consequently prepared to back the unitarians and to grant them a National Convention.

However, with the unmasking and suppression of the Babouvist plot, centred on France but with fine threads belayed by Buonarroti to the Low Countries and to Italy, the unitarians were abandoned.[137]

Many historians have assumed that federalism in Europe was almost always a thinly veiled expression of oligarchical privilege and of provincial recalcitrance, not least because socialists had at an early stage adopted this view.[138] Jacques Godechot, for example, risks the generalization that in Holland, Italy and Switzerland genuine democrats were for unity, whereas moderates, and those who hoped for only minimal changes, were opposed to it.[139] There is of course no gainsaying the fact that, both before and after the Revolution, those who espoused the cause of local and regional liberties were often ranged against the more progressive and Enlightened tendencies of the age. Thus, in the case of Brittany, the insurgent nobility was determined to resist any encroachments upon their traditional privileges, threatened by the last-ditch absolutism of Loménie de Brienne. Yet when Malesherbes warned Louis XVI that the Bretons, if too much provoked, might well secede from the realm, the precedents that sprang most readily to his mind were the revolt of the United Provinces, and that of the American colonies.[140] Since Brittany was a *pays d'état* rather than a *pays d'élection*, its provincial liberties had survived the earlier attempts at centralization prosecuted from Paris and Versailles. It should be borne in mind also that the Marquis d'Argenson's panacea of a republican monarchy had for its constituent elements the *pays d'état* and the unshackled municipalities.

Since the absolutist states were haunted, as Franco Venturi has shown, first by the old republics shimmering at their edge, and then by a blaze of confederated liberty in the New World, it followed that democratic aspirations in revolutionary Europe could not be the exclusive preserve of the unitarians. In this respect, Godechot's rash generalization is belied by the material that he himself presents on the Italian peninsula where, as he admits, the notion of unity was little better than Utopian in the early months of 1796. Thus, when General Buonaparte, as he then was, announced an essay competition in Milan, the discourses favouring a form of confederation outnumbered those that were avowedly unitarian. Even when unity and indivisibility were invoked, uncertainty as to the Army of Italy's ultimate purpose was reflected in the arguments of the Italian patriots, who sometimes spoke solely of Lombardy, and sometimes ran their thoughts and dreams, with airy gestures, far beyond, to the Po Valley or to the shades of Rome. Venturi, in his fine study of outsiders' perceptions of the peninsula during the Risorgimento, notes how this doubt was reflected in the provincial or municipal scope of the histories written by Italian authors in the aftermath of the Revolution. When *Corinne* and the *History of the Medieval Italian Republics* at last, in

1807, offered patriots an image of the whole land mass and therefore, by implication, of a united Italy, it was from Geneva or Coppet that the muffled exhortation came.[141]

I do not intend to retrace here the story of the Italian campaigns, of the encouragement offered to patriots in 1796, of the founding of the Cisalpine and of the Cispadan Republics, and of the crushing disillusion of 1797, the betrayal of Venice at Campoformio, but rather to show how democratic and republican thought-forms were still built to the scale of assembled and confederated cities, even where unitarian sympathies were manifest. The example I have chosen, Carlo Botta's response in 1796 to the Municipality of Milan's competition, establishes an especially illuminating link between tribunate and confederation.[142]

Botta, a Piedmontese Jacobin, a surgeon in Bonaparte's army and later the author of celebrated histories of Italy and of the United States of America, defined a free government as one in which the people could assemble and express dissent without their tumults being branded as rebellion. In a truly free government, he continued, strife was not only inevitable but was also conducive to the public good. So transparent a reference to the *Discourses* led naturally to a call for a tribune, defined as a magistrate who would voice the complaints of the plebeians and keep a continual watch over their interests. If they trusted the tribune, it was because he was one of their own, indeed, he was 'the people itself gathered up into one person'. Botta thus subscribed to the view that the tribunate was, as Machiavelli and Rousseau had maintained, a direct expression of popular sovereignty, and not merely, as Montesquieu and Sieyes had proposed, a guarantee of the laws. For a free government to survive, it was not sufficient to elect representatives once a year; it had in fact to be democratic at every moment, and the people had to watch over it continuously.[143]

Aware of Montesquieu's tirade against the 'tumultous' tribunes, Botta insisted that undisturbed quiet in a republic was proof not of liberty but of despotism. Turning over in his mind the claim that the Moderns were not as the Ancients had been, he allowed that this might be so but held it to be, if anything, an argument in support of government by the people. For the Romans had been 'proud, fierce by nature, impatient, and so full of martial courage, ever keen to innovate and prone to tumult', whereas present-day Lombards were 'by nature slow, preferring rest to movement', and needed the spur, not the bridle.[144] This is, for a historian, a fascinating inversion of the doctrine of the liberty of the Ancients and of the Moderns.

What is most intriguing, however, about Botta's discourse, is the direct connection posited between the tribunate and the principle of confederation. If the Lombards had no tribune of the people, he went on to say, they would have to have a federal government, for liberty to be sustained. However, book 18 of *The Spirit of the Laws*, which here he preferred to book 9, had reminded him that confederation was suited only to peoples living in deserts or mountainous areas. Lombardy, surrounded by enemies, rich both in manufactures and agriculture, required swift, decisive government, in other words, a unitary, centralized state. Yet the temper of Botta's essay remained essentially federalist, for he warned that a republic one and indivisible was more prone to tyrannical usurpation, as recent events in France had proved, and to coercive action by the centre on the periphery. A confederation therefore had in liberty what a republic one and indivisible had in strength.[145] In my final chapter I shall return to this debate, and to Milan, where its terms were extended in the first half of the nineteenth century.

# PART III

# Word and Tribe

The whole of history was now conceived as necessary development,
and therefore the whole of it implicitly, and to a greater or lesser
degree even explicitly, redeemed . . .

Benedetto Croce, *Teoria e Storia della Storiografia*

# Crossing the Rhine

Had there been no revolution in France, Madame de Staël would doubtless have lived half of her life in Paris and half by Lake Leman, for travelling was at best a 'sad pleasure' for her, as for the imagined Corinne.[1] Her many attempts to win permission, whether from the executive Directors or from Bonaparte, to stay in the city she cherished above all others, suggest that it was not design but unrelenting persecution by the First Consul that drove her to Germany and made of her, in the dramatically altered circumstances of 1813, the figurehead of liberal revolt against tyranny. She certainly did not leave with the express purpose of vindicating Germanic values, for, as she later recalled, 'I entered this Germany whose literary merit I was then barely aware of, with an altogether Parisian fear. I could not consider the rest of the world save in terms of its distance from France.'[2] Indeed, the use of the term 'Gothic' in the journals she kept in 1803–04 almost invariably betrays a judgement, inherited from Petrarch or from Aeneas Sylvius, of the barbaric nature of German mores.[3]

Since the crossing of the Rhine brought Staël close to despair, the cold weather and the dark sky compounding her distress, one may wonder just why she undertook so arduous a journey in the autumn of 1803. First of all, she wished to provide for her son's education by finding him a tutor (August-Wilhelm Schlegel). Second, the praise lavished upon her early writings by Goethe and by Schiller ensured her a welcome in German literary circles, and she plainly hoped that her visit would win her sufficient glory to irk the First Consul. Since the purging of the Tribunate, in January 1802, and the elimination of the class for moral and political sciences from the Institute a year later, few had dared to protest. Rather than languish the required forty kilometres from Paris, Staël chose to remove herself altogether from a silenced stage.

If, in 1803, Staël was not yet preparing to write a *Germania*, and to play Tacitus to Bonaparte's Tiberius, she had certainly offended official taste under the Consulate by celebrating, in *De la Littérature*, the energy and enthusiasm of the peoples of the north. Yet the single chapter she had devoted to German literature was little better than a sketch. To assess what she knew of the subject in 1800, we need to consider what others in her world had known. An ideal place to start such an investigation is with the discourse crowned by the Academy of Berlin in 1784, which supplied answers to the following questions: What is it that has made the French language universal? Why does it deserve this prerogative? May one assume that it will keep it? To understand the importance of the theme, one has to bear in mind that Frederick the Great had himself been aggressively francophone, and had promoted French culture which, in Berlin, revolved around Huguenot exiles and French *philosophes*. Three years earlier, the king had written a treatise on German literature, a work that was to earn Staël's amused contempt in *De l'Allemagne*, but which cannot have seemed at all absurd to Rivarol, the author of 'De l'Universalité de la Langue Française', in 1783.[4] Notwithstanding the protests of Herder or of Klopstock, or of the attempts made by the Duchess Anna Amalia and by Goethe to promote German as the language of the court at Weimar, the majority of thinking persons in Germany would have subscribed to the view that their own language, then lacking a classical literature, was inferior to French.[5] Such attitudes were especially entrenched in Frederician Berlin.

Yet the Academy had made a still grander claim, namely, that the French language was universal. Rivarol, enlarging upon the point, likened the prestige of his native tongue to that of Latin in the past:

> The time would now seem to be ripe to speak of the *French world*, just as formerly one spoke of the *Roman world*; and philosophy, tired of seeing men always divided by the diverse interests of politics, is now delighted to see them, from one end of the earth to another, form themselves into a republic under the domination of a single language.[6]

If French was, as Rivarol insisted, particularly well-suited to the task, why was such an instrument needed? Here he observed, in altogether Baconian guise, that the key events in the birth of the modern world (the Renaissance, the discovery of America, the opening of a sea route to the Indies, the invention of gunpowder and of printing) had so strengthened and unified Europe that it was in truth but 'one immense republic'. As far as the cosmopolitan elites were concerned, such a claim was not controversial. Herder's journal for 1769 reflected the fact, and Vittorio Alfieri likewise recalled that during his travels French was the only language he had heard spoken.[7] This is at first glance a startling observation, if you consider that, between 1770 and 1775, the Piedmontese poet had passed through Lombardy, Tuscany, the Papal States, France, England, Holland, Germany, Denmark, Sweden, Russia, Prussia, Spain and Portugal. To Alfieri, however, a fiercely purist student of *trecento* Italian, of Augustan Latin and of Homeric Greek, a language was not at all what 'the speaking mass', to use Saussure's phrase, incessantly produced. It was, rather, an aulic tongue which an institution such as the Accademia della Crusca or the Académie Française was elected to defend or to refine. Travellers would hear any number of other languages as they passed from region to region, but notwithstanding the cult of Ossian and the auroral lustre it gave to the imperilled culture of mountain peoples, few were as yet prepared to regard them as equal in rank to the, as it were, crowned codes. In France, Rivarol observed, 'the patois are abandoned to the provinces, and they are at the mercy of the lower orders' whim, whereas the national language is out of their reach'.[8] The sole exception he allowed to this unequal relation between centre and periphery, demonstrably present in the case of the great monarchies (England, France, Spain), was ancient Greece, which had managed to 'ennoble' its dialects. This observation concerns not only an empirical fact of classical Greek, namely, the literary dignity of Attic, Doric and Ionian, but also, like the whole of Rivarol's discourse, the question of economic and political organization. Indeed, the prestige of the Greek dialects reflected the miracle of the Amphicthyonic League, an achievement that Italy, to its cost, had failed to emulate.[9]

It is of particular interest in this regard to note that Rivarol, who praised Machiavelli in passing and without qualification, glossed the Florentine's thought as federal rather than unitary-national for, like so many in the Age of Enlightenment, his universalism could accommodate the values of the polis. 'Greece', he wrote, 'gave its laws to the barbarians who surrounded it; and Italy, which failed to follow its example and to constitute itself as a federal republic, was invaded in turn by the Germans, the Spanish and the French.' Although there was in fact some tension between the model of a courtly code elevated to the status of a universal language, and the vision of a multiplicity of confederated poleis, the demons of teleological autochthony had not yet been unleashed. Rivarol might allow that, since the Germanic tribes were a source, the German language was itself a 'mother tongue', but he could not regard it as a serious rival to French, an altogether suaver instrument. At once too rich (as it were, too productive) and too harsh, marred by its guttural pronunciation and its Gothic script, German was not deemed a fit vehicle to serve as an instrument of universal communication between the peoples:

One can therefore establish it as a general rule that, if the man of the north is drawn to the study of the southern languages, long wars would be needed in the Empire to conquer the repugnance of southerners for the northern languages. Humankind is like a river which flows from north to south; nothing can drive it back up to its source.

In the case of Germany, the multiplicity of dialects and capitals was judged a weakness, and there is no trace in Rivarol of the wonder that Charles de Villers or Madame de Staël would later express at the culture of small towns such as Weimar. He took at face value the enthusiasm expressed by so many of the German princes for French culture, and had no reason to suppose that a dramatic reversal of values was imminent. 'Germany', wrote Rivarol,

> will offer for a long time to come the spectacle of an ancient and modest people governed by a host of princes quite captivated by the fashions and the language of an attractive and polished nation. From whence it follows that the extraordinary welcome which these princes and their academies have granted to a foreign language is one more obstacle that they place in the way of their own language.[10]

If reference to another language were needed, few *philosophes* spared a thought for those that had been swept aside by the French of Ludovican Versailles and Paris, deployed with such brilliance by Voltaire and by Montesquieu, by Buffon and by Rousseau. Instead, the arts of speaking and writing were regarded as precious inheritances transmitted from one pinnacle of human endeavour to another, from Chaldea and Egypt to Athens, from Athens to Rome, from Rome to Florence, and from Florence to the Court of Louis XIV. Given such a belief in the *translatio studii*, shared by Turgot and Condorcet to some degree, Rivarol would naturally devote more space to Tuscan, the previous victor in the great race, than to German, English or Spanish. Had not Medicean Florence given Ludovican France its model of an academy entrusted with the task of perfecting the rules of a language? Furthermore, by a remarkable fatality, 'good taste was lost in Italy at the precise moment that it was reviving in France'.[11]

How then had the French language become universal? Rivarol's account traces the process by which, of the two main neo-Latin dialects spoken in France, Picard and Provençal, the former had come to dominate, much as Castilian had triumphed over Catalan in Spain. Had Provençal prevailed, the French language would have had some of the brilliance of Spanish or Italian, 'but the south of France, still without a capital or a king, could not vie with the north, and the influence of the

Picard patois grew with that of the crown. It is therefore the clear and methodical genius of this speech . . . which is today dominant in the French language.' If French prevailed in Europe, it was in fact because the word order of the language faithfully reflected that of thought. Languages that suffered from inversion, such as Latin or Greek, embodied in their construction the propensity of men to frame utterances registering the immediate impact of sensation, naming first of all the object that had struck them first. By contrast, French had the unique privilege of remaining loyal to the direct order, 'as if it were reason through and through'. Rivarol thus shared the opinion of the rationalist proponents of general or universal grammar that his own language, since it obeyed the sequence of subject, verb and object, was the clearest and most logical. Indeed, French was the universal language of which Leibniz had dreamed.[12]

Up until this point in my exposition of Rivarol's argument, I have written as if he were not overmuch concerned with the relation between a language, a culture and a people. If this mistaken impression is so readily given, it is because dominant tendencies within Enlightenment historiography have fostered the view that neither the *philosophes* nor the Jacobins appreciated cultural diversity, and that the latter was the discovery of a German counter-Enlightenment or of Vico, a Neapolitan eagle. The assumption has been that the dream of future confederation, embodied in Anarcharsis von Kloots's much-ridiculed presentation of specimens of humanity to the Constituent Assembly or in Volney's imagined assembly of all the peoples, was incompatible with an interest in specific cultural values. Since the *philosophes* hoped, through the conjoint spread of commerce and *lumières*, to foster *ius gentium*, they were presumed by the same token to wish for the obliteration of the traditions of hunter-gatherers or pastoralists. Yet, in truth, their hopes for the ultimate realization of cosmopolis were matched by an attitude of respect, even piety, towards doomed forms of associated life. This point is borne out, as Hans Aarsleff has intimated, by the debates in the year II regarding the relation between the national language, the minority languages and the patois.[13]

At first glance, however, my claim would seem to be at odds with the tone adopted by Barère and Grégoire in the Convention. For such languages as Breton, Basque, Alsatian, German, Flemish and Corsican Italian, together with the many patois, should, they said, be 'smashed' or 'obliterated'.[14] If the peasantry of the border regions were to be won over to the cause of liberty, they would have to be removed from the influence of priests and feudal nobility.[15] If, moreover, they were to derive full benefit from improvements in agricultural science, knowledge of the national language was crucial.[16]

Language, the precondition of educational reform, would thus have to be 'popularized' or 'revolutionized'. Barère, it has to be admitted, derided the minority languages and the patois, regarding them as relics of feudalism and as obstacles to the propagation of republican values. Where the 'universality' of French was concerned, he echoed Rivarol, emphasizing the subordinate status of Italian, German, Spanish and English. The abbé Grégoire went further, referring directly to the prize essay of 1784, and reiterating the claim of the general grammarians that his own language boasted an especially clear and methodical structure. Whereas Barère's relatively brief speech leaves the reader with the impression that he was not overmuch concerned with the value of the languages and traditions to be extirpated, Grégoire, a resolute adversary of revolutionary vandalism, advised the Convention that 'knowledge of dialects can shed light upon a number of monuments of the Middle Ages'.[17] The caricatural account of Jacobin linguistic policy implies that there must be a contradiction or clash of interests between 'rendering uniform the language of a great nation' and revering the minority languages or the patois, yet the contribution to twentieth-century ethnography of missionaries (such as Maurice Leenhardt) or of colonial administrators (such as H.N. Stevenson) suggests that the predicament of Grégoire or of Volney was not exceptional. Even the Sanskrit studies of Charles Wilkins and William Jones owed much to the political exigencies of the East India Company.

It should further be noted that folklore, far from being a discovery of nascent Romanticism, was a central preoccupation of the *philosophes*.[18] Their enthusiasm is best exemplified by the cult of Ossian, whose Gaelic poems – in fact written, or reworked, by Macpherson – were viewed by Lord Kames and Hugh Blair as characteristic creations of a society of hunters, the first of the four stages through which human communities necessarily passed.[19] Constant, when a student in Edinburgh, became acquainted with these arguments, as did Walter Scott, many of whose novels deploy the stadial theory as a scaffolding or machine of pathos upon which to hang the exotic materials he had gathered on the Borders or in the Highlands.[20] The journeys of Edward Waverley and of Jeanie Deans are as much explorations of historical time as of geographical space. The same theories were current in late Enlightenment Paris, for Turgot and Suard had been responsible for introducing Ossian to a French (and Francophone) readership in 1760–62, while Grimm, Marmontel and La Harpe had all written essays in praise of Gaelic poetry.[21]

In addressing such issues, the historian has no choice but to confront the thorny question of historical periodization, to say, for example, when the Enlightenment ended or Romanticism began, and to assess the usefulness or otherwise of a notion such as pre-Romanticism. Some critics have argued that the Enlightenment closed as the old regime entered its final crisis, and it is true that most of the dominant figures had by then died, and that a number of the surviving *philosophes*, in spite of the irreverent audacity of their writings, were alarmed by the political upheavals of the spring and summer of 1789. Indeed, members of the *côterie Holbachique*, the circle in Paris most famed for its atheism and its materialism, very swiftly drew back from the Revolution, in a mood, its chronicler has said, of 'distrust, contempt and fear'.[22] Such biographical discontinuities have fostered the illusion, then, that the Enlightenment came to an abrupt end in 1789, a periodization that would place *philosophes* on one side of the fence and revolutionaries on the other.[23] The putative link between the outbreak of the French Revolution and the end of the Enlightenment cannot, however, withstand close scrutiny. Thus, Sergio Moravia has demonstrated that the *idéologues*, the immediate heirs of the *philosophes*, continued to champion the cause of the radical wing of the Encyclopédie until at least 1807.

The origins of Romanticism are equally controversial. Michel Löwy and Robert Sayre, for example, have argued that this cultural and political movement, notwithstanding its protean nature, cannot be divorced from the onset of modern capitalism or, more specifically, from the violent upheavals occasioned by primitive accumulation.[24] The phenomenon, they argue, arises first in the years between 1760 and 1770, and will persist, in one form or another, for as long as the cash-nexus wreaks havoc upon customary communities. It should be admitted that this hypothesis is, on the face of it, plausible. One can, for example, trace the cult of Ossian through from 1760 to the first decade of the nineteenth century, noting that very much the same materials were used, and the same colours applied, across a timespan of fifty years. Yet the Ossian of Blair or of Lord Kames, of Turgot or of Suard, is not that of Chateaubriand in 1803–09, when he was avowedly 'singing the nation'. Virtually identical sources (Ossian, Mallet, Tacitus, Saxo Grammaticus) were used in both the *Essai Historique* and *Les Martyrs*, and yet in the latter a new note was sounded, influencing very profoundly the literature and historiography of the age of nations. Where Constant and his circle at Edinburgh had been, in the 1780s, investigating the collectively constructed myths of peoples located at a given stage in a socio-economic sequence, the Christian-national conceptions of the new century restored Scripture as the measure of all human histories.[25] The Anglo-Scottish Enlightenment had embraced, and elaborated upon, Locke's claim that '*Doctrines*, that have been derived from no better original, than the Superstition of a Nurse, or the Authority of an Old Woman; may, by length of time, and consent of Neighbours, *grow up to the dignity of Principles* in Religion or Morality'.[26] In the new century, however, the nation swallowed the prattling nurse by the fireside, and the Homers southern and northern, but divinity subsumed the nation in its turn. Vain and at times vicious primacies were then reinstated, in a historiography markedly narrower than that of, for example, Gibbon or Volney. In the case of Scott, we must resist the temptation to classify him as an Enlightenment novelist, since in *Ivanhoe* the stadial theory is overshadowed by a desire, in Chateaubriand's idiom, to tie 'the cradle of the ancestors' to 'the cradle of the Christian people', and so to vindicate the mission of an elect nation. It is also worth pointing out that Löwy and Sayre's chronology is further vitiated by the fact that a Romantic stance, by their own criteria, may be discerned in the writings of authors living well out of reach of the social and economic disturbances supposedly to blame for the new cultural and political forms. English and Dutch boats were docking in large numbers in the bay of Naples, and some of the more scandalous books from north of the Alps could be found along the Via Biagio dei Librai, but the Italian peninsula could hardly be said to have begun to recover from the economic stagnation of the early seventeenth century by the time Giannone, Gravina and Vico were drafting their very first works, in the 1690s.

The category of pre-Romanticism is a construct of early twentieth-century literary criticism, and is therefore logically of a different order to terms such as Enlightenment or Romanticism, which were used by contemporaries as programmes and battle-cries. Moreover, being designed to reclaim from a purportedly rationalist, Cartesian eighteenth century each and every cultural element that promised to bear fruit in the more congenial circumstances of the nineteenth century, an age of nations, it promotes a false picture of the Enlightenment. For example, Paul van Tieghem, one of the most noted advocates of the theory, started out from the premise that the *philosophes* were committed to an arid concept of reason, and he therefore defined as pre-Romantic all manifestations of sensibility. Yet the passions vaunted by Staël in 1788, and then interrogated in 1796, were the legacy of Diderot and Vauvenargues, as I pointed out in chapter 2. The characteristic attitude of a *philosophe* may more properly be characterized in terms of an enthusiasm, and 'a sensibility illuminated by rational *lumières* and guided by experience'.[27] In seeking to annex so much of the eighteenth century for pre-Romanticism, van Tieghem was in effect still subscribing to counter-revolutionary critiques of the *philosophes*, and thus participating in the trial of the Enlightenment. Since the claim is that the *philosophes* placed no value upon cultural diversity, and did not really understand it, any positive assessments of, say, folklore, had to be judged as, by definition, pre-Romantic. It should also be noted that all such categories are teleological, since they are predicated upon an interminable reading backwards and forwards of the evidence from precursors to heirs. One response to this exasperating proliferation of terms, and of the inevitable raiding parties, has been to dismiss them all. Foucault, for example, barely mentions either the Enlightenment or Romanticism, although *The Order of Things*, a study to which I refer again below, is concerned with '[the] mutation of order into history'. I have preferred to run the risk entailed by another sort of infinite regress, that is to say, a mustering of individuals in the context of the lived categories of Enlightenment and Romanticism.

When, for example, the abbé Grégoire refers in 1794 to 'the genius of a people', there is a temptation to cast the term forward, and to view it as an intimation of *Volksgeist*. Yet one could with greater plausibility invoke Montesquieu or Condillac. If, with the above considerations in mind, we return to Rivarol's celebrated essay, we in fact find that his preoccupation with universal grammar was complemented by an evident fascination with the characteristic features of the full range of spoken languages:

> if one can judge a man by his words, one can also judge a nation by its language. I am not concerned here with the form and substance of the [written] works upon which each person prides himself; one must pass judgement in terms of the character and genius of their language, for almost all writers follow rules and models, but a whole nation speaks according to its genius.[28]

The genius of a particular language, as embodied in its phonology, its prosody and its syntax, was originally, for Rivarol, an expression of climate, with the south imparting a singing and voluptuous quality to speech, the frozen north a rougher, more clipped aspect.[29] When Garat reviewed Rivarol's discourse, in the *Mercure de France*, he was much taken with the claim that thought arises through the act of speaking, and does not pre-exist it. 'If speech is a thought which manifests itself', Rivarol had written, 'thought must be an inner and hidden speech.' The posited identity of thought and speech was a discovery of the first importance, and yet, in Garat's opinion, it was to Condillac that the praise was due.[30] For it was he who had established that language was not a system of labelling, or nomenclature, and that thought and sign arose at one and the same time.

Condillac's equation between language and the character of a people earns him the right to be considered a pioneer in the domain of cultural and linguistic relativity. Indeed, Aarsleff has shown that Herder's celebrated discourse on the origin of language, crowned by the Academy of Berlin in 1772, leans in several important respects upon Condillac.[31] Why then have so many concluded that the *philosophes* were too much committed to the chimerical quest for a universal grammar to appreciate the concrete diversity of actually existing languages? A simple answer to this question would be that their historiography rested, once again, upon an excessive identification with those who, having suffered the domination of French culture, under the old regime and subsequently, had put the Enlightenment on trial. It should be borne in mind that Condillac had advanced a theory of a human, not divine origin of language. This fact, stated very bluntly by Garat at the Ecole Normale in 1795, was cause enough for Bonald and Maistre to misrepresent him after the Restoration.[32]

There are certainly echoes of Restoration polemics in the writings of Benedetto Croce, who posited as polar opposites a spirit of the eighteenth and a spirit of the nineteenth century, with the Enlightenment being cast back and denigrated, and Romanticism drawn forward and applauded.[33] As a consequence, he was less than just in his appraisal of the intellectual legacy of Condillac in Parma, and in Lombardy, as I show in chapter 10. Nonetheless, the sheer scale of the historiographical distortion accurately reflects the violence done to vassal cultures at the gate. For, by the second half of the eighteenth century, the vaunted universality of the French language presupposed the hegemony of French culture also. Thus, Enlightenment critics within the orbit of Paris tended to write in the most disparaging terms of German culture. When, therefore, Henri Meister had urged Staël to come and meet Wieland, one of the inner circle in Goethe's Weimar, she replied: 'One thing you will never see me do is go to Zurich for the sake of a German author. I believe that I already know what is being said in German, and even what will be said for fifty years to come.'[34] Six years later, a letter to Charles de Villers struck a very different note: 'the human mind, which seems to journey from one country to another, is at this moment in Germany. I am studying German assiduously, convinced that only there will I find new thoughts and deep feelings.'[35] There is a temptation, in accounting for so great a change, to list all those in Staël's circle (Constant, Degérando, Jordan, Meister, Stapfer, Villers) who drew away from a notion of *Europe Française*, and embraced the new and flourishing culture of the German states.[36] More generally, one might emphasize the crucial role played by the Emigration in undermining the universalist pretensions of the late eighteenth-century French culture.[37] 'Those who have written histories of the French Revolution', wrote Chateaubriand in 1811 or 1812, 'have forgotten to place a picture of external France beside that of internal France, to paint this huge colony of exiles, whose activities and difficulties reflected the diversity of climates and the difference in the mores of peoples.'[38] Given the scale of the Emigration, it can hardly be disputed that those scattered to the four winds did, to varying degrees, discover new truths regarding the countries that offered them asylum. Yet the phenomenon may be both exaggerated and misinterpreted. Chateaubriand, for example, implies that the emigrés in their suffering made good the *philosophes'* lack of understanding of cultural diversity.

It would be an error, then, to suppose that most emigrés, in their disgust with republicanism in general and with Jacobinism in particular, looked immediately to the Germanic aspects of the cultures in which many of them were immersed; like all political exiles, they were in far too disconsolate and liminal a condition to turn a brightly ethnographic eye on what was all around them. Torn from their world, cast up in another place, they first of all enshrined what they had lost. A ritual consolidation of what was so deeply mourned led also to fierce disputes with fellow exiles, each brandishing their gloss on the catastrophe that had befallen them. The execution of family, friends and king had rendered the funereal aspect of emigré patriotism especially pronounced, but had at first occasioned little alteration in the definitions they offered of a fatherland. It is also true that, as Jacques Godechot has pointed out, the mere presence of so many emigrés in foreign capitals served to transmit, along with French culture, the ideals of the Revolution itself.[39]

Although the moral and intellectual repercussions of the Emigration were, in short, complex, no one would dispute that French culture survived its sudden transplantation. For example, Hamburg, the 'Paris of the North', at one time contained over forty thousand emigrés, with their own theatre, newspaper and cafés.[40] In that city, as in London, displaced publishers produced a steady stream of both books and journals, often with a substantial number of subscribers. In London, one might read Peltier's *Tableau de Paris*, Montlosier's *Courier de Londres* and, after 1798, Mallet du Pan's *Mercure Britannique*, while in Hamburg the *Spectateur du Nord*, edited by Jean-Louis Amable de Baudus, appeared from 1797 to 1802. At least some of these journals were funded, covertly or openly, by the governments of the host countries, and played a part in forming public opinion. Mallet du Pan's famous articles extolling Helvetic liberty were, for example, widely read, and very probably came to the attention of Coleridge, Hazlitt and Walter Savage Landor in 1798.

It is not easy to generalize about the emigré press, yet in the case of the *Spectateur du Nord*, of particular relevance to the issues addressed in the present chapter, we may chart its vicissitudes in some detail. The editor, Baudus, a former magistrate who had rallied to the Revolution in its early stages but who had been unable to countenance the measures taken against non-juring priests in 1791, had joined the Princes' Army. After a couple of ill-starred publishing ventures in Hamburg had failed, he launched – with a publisher, Fauche – the *Spectateur du Nord*, a review of 'politics, literature and ethics' which would promote understanding between peoples and, in particular, between France and the countries of the north: 'Our journal is designed to serve as a meeting-place where they may see each other, study each other and clarify their respective positions and progress.'[41] This liberal ambition appears to prefigure that of the Coppet Circle, and yet the bulk of the readership, formerly aligned with the Princes' Army, was monarchist. Though originally published in both Paris and Hamburg, the journal was banned in France in the wake of Fructidor. In 1798, as the 'second' Directory swung back towards the Jacobins, Baudus even published proclamations by the Count de Provence, the future Louis XVIII. Besides, notwithstanding his avowed wish to learn from the cultures of the north, Baudus admired Rivarol, resident at that time in Hamburg. The author of the discourse on the universality of the French language had opposed the Revolution almost from the start, parading his mordant wit in Peltier's *Actes des Apôtres*, one of the most vicious and scurrilous of the royalist rags. He then enlisted in the Princes' Army, where Chateaubriand, with characteristic immodesty, claimed to have bested him with a swift repartee. Since Rivarol was one of Baudus's most prized contributors, the *Spectateur du Nord* had plainly not cast off the values of *Europe française*. Fontanes and Joubert also had a hand in the journal, its classicism in this regard paving the way for the official culture of the Consulate and of the Empire.[42]

However, the presence in Hamburg or in Lübeck of several key representatives of modern German letters, among them Jacobi, Klopstock and Voss, was also reflected in the pages of the *Spectateur du Nord*. There were reviews, therefore, of books by Wilhelm von Humboldt and by Kant, and translations of odes by Klopstock. This, the German aspect of the journal, was assiduously promoted by Charles de Villers, the contributor who did the most to realize, and ultimately to transcend, Baudus's original conception.[43]

When Bonaparte sent Staël into exile, late in 1803, she set out for Metz, in the company of Constant. There they met up with Villers, whose articles in the *Spectateur du Nord* had been plundered for the chapters on German writers in *De la Littérature*. Born in 1765, Villers was a former artillery officer, his first enthusiasm for the Revolution soured by the turn that events took in 1791. He had joined the Emigration, enlisted in the Princes' Army, studied for a term at Göttingen, and settled there in 1796. He tried upon several occasions to launch a *Revue* or *Bibliothèque Germanique*, a journal that would, with the collaboration of Constant, Jordan, Staël and Stapfer, realize the betrayed ideals of the *Spectateur du Nord*.[44] In 1798 Villers had written of 'the secret providence which watches over the perfecting of our species', and had called upon his fellow emigrés to serve 'as a means of communication between two great peoples'. Did they but know it, they were living through a golden age in Germany. Let them only immerse themselves in the culture of the host country, make it their own, bring it back to France, and French literature would in its turn be reborn.[45]

Baudus was alarmed by such immoderate praise of German literature, and cut the article savagely, but Villers, though at odds with most of his fellow contributors, was the mainstay of the *Spectateur du Nord*, and so could continue for a time to champion the cause of the new thought across the Rhine. His particular concern was with the philosophy of Kant and, despite Baudus's warning that, of the 500 or so subscribers, 450 cared not a jot for metaphysics, he wrote a number of introductory essays on the subject. Benjamin Constant had already responded in passing to one of the philosopher's occasional writings, as we saw in an earlier chapter, but Villers was the first French author to appreciate the importance of the *Critique of Pure Reason*, and to attempt an exposition of the key concepts and arguments. He later wrote a monograph on the philosophy of Kant, and travelled to Paris to make his case.[46]

It had been a commonplace among those who looked with sympathy upon events in Paris to compare the advent of the critical system with the outbreak of the French Revolution. Fichte, for example, had become a philosopher under the combined stress of both events. For Villers, on the other hand, Kantianism was the necessary corrective to the unbridled excesses of the year II. Like so many after Thermidor, he proclaimed a link between the materialism and atheism of the Enyclopédie and the rise of Jacobinism, and deplored philosophies founded upon the senses and the passions. He regarded Kant as a prophet, whose doctrine of the thing-in-itself had put paid, once and for all, to the impious speculations of the materialists and to the moral disquiet of the reluctant sceptics. Thus, in *Lettres Westphaliennes*, he depicted his hero seated upon a rock, facing the 'brilliant imposters' of Paris and pointing to the insurmountable barrier that nature had raised between our weak gazes and 'the country of first causes'.[47] Kant's great achievement had therefore been to restrict knowledge of first causes to God, while at the same time insisting upon the actual existence of a deity, free will and an immortal soul. Where the pugnacious and Promethean Fichte had seen the distinction between the phenomenal and the noumenal, between sensory experience and synthetic a priori judgements as an obstacle to free will, Villers reckoned it a salutary barrier between humanity and the deity, and therefore a conclusive rebuttal of the arguments of the atheists and the deists.[48]

Secure in the conviction that there was no impiety in his monograph, Villers hoped to win Paris over to the Kantian doctrine. Yet the Consulate was moving inexorably towards the restoration of Catholicism, and so towards the reimposition of sacerdotal authority over conscience. In such a climate, Bonaparte's party would not be likely to look with favour upon the work of an author whose declared sympathies were for Germany, for Protestantism and for professorial dignity. Fontanes, despite being altogether ignorant of Kant's writings, duly savaged Villers's book in the pages of the *Mercure de France*.[49] Conversely, the embattled *idéologues*, though willing to pitch the shade of Luther against Napoleon's cynical compromise with the Holy See, regarded the critical philosophy as a spiritualist aberration and an ill-judged challenge to sensationalist gnoseology. The major treatises of the school were just then appearing in the bookshops, and figures such as Cabanis, Daunou and Destutt de Tracy were, and remained, hostile.[50]

Those in France who had long accepted Rousseau's critique, at once ethical and religious, of sensationalism, were more predisposed to welcome Kant's system. This was true, for example, of Staël, who proved more responsive to Wilhelm von Humboldt's exposition of Kantian philosophy than most of the *idéologues* had been.[51] He attended her salon assiduously from the autumn of 1798 and began to teach her German the following year; he also formed close friendships with Constant, Daunou, Garat and Sieyes.[52] Through Jacobi, once a habitué of Madame de Necker's salon, through Humboldt or through the exiled Camille Jordan, Staël learned of the *Spectateur du Nord*, and thereby gained first-hand knowledge of Villers's writings. As a consequence, her account in *De l'Allemagne* of the Kantian philosophy bears a marked resemblance to that outlined by Villers, and may be regarded as a refutation both of the *idéologues'* assault upon the concept of the soul and of Chateaubriand's apology for Roman Catholicism, although her erstwhile allies were dealt the harsher treatment. More generally, *De l'Allemagne* is structured in terms of national cultures, with comparisons of the philosophies of England (or, to be more precise, England and Scotland), France and Germany. Like *Corinne*, which is subtitled *ou l'Italie*, Staël's famous monograph was therefore designed to be a work of comparative anthropology of the sort advocated in the aftermath of Thermidor by Volney and by Wilhelm von Humboldt.[53] The latter had hoped, while in Paris, to compose a study of France, various fragments of which survive, and there is good cause to argue that Staël persevered with a line of enquiry that her friend, after his crucial journey to Spain in 1799–1800, did not so much abandon as transpose to the domain of comparative linguistics. To assess whether *De l'Allemagne* is best described in terms of an Enlightenment understanding of the principle of nationality, as entertained by the *observateurs* in general and by Volney in particular, or in terms of the Romantic account of culture, spirit and the destiny of peoples, of the kind propounded by the Schlegels, I propose to begin by scrutinizing *De la Littérature*. In chapter 9 I shall return to the vexed question of Wilhelm von Humboldt's contribution to this debate.


## The barbarian invasions, the acropolitical series

Posted at the threshold of the new century, *De la Littérature* may be regarded, like *Des Circonstances Actuelles*, as a tribute to Montesquieu. Indubitably a pioneering contribution to what we would now call comparative literature, Staël's book was intended to be a study of 'the influence of religion, mores and laws upon literature, and of literature upon religion, mores and laws'. Observing that perfectly satisfactory treatises on the art of writing and the principles of taste, by Voltaire, Marmontel and La Harpe, already existed in French, she went on to remark that 'the moral, and political causes, which modify the spirit of literature', had not been taken into account.[54] It is thus as clear as day that she wished to emulate Montesquieu, and that her book could as well have been entitled *The Spirit of the Literatures*. Indeed, other members of the Coppet Circle would in later years realize, in more concrete terms, the programme she had outlined in 1799–1800.

A second authority for Staël was Condorcet, and *De la Littérature* ought also to be seen as a tribute to the dead philosopher, and as an impassioned defence of his intellectual, moral and political heritage. The debt owed to the author of the *Esquisse* may be construed in two ways, one relatively abstract and one only too concrete. It was from Condorcet, to begin with, that Staël had drawn one of the leitmotifs of her book, the principle of perfectibility.[55] The reader is constantly reminded of this principle, and Staël's contemporaries were never in any doubt that it was her chief preoccupation. Both Fontanes, in his brutal review in the *Mercure de France*, and Chateaubriand, in his letter to the same journal, saw perfectibility as their prime target. Chateaubriand, for example, referred to it as 'the word around which the whole system turns', and plainly viewed it as the principal obstacle to his own christology.[56] Second, a declaration of loyalty to the shade of Condorcet constituted an alignment with a particular political tendency. For to rally to the banner of perfectibility in 1800, at a time when *philosophes* were the object of ever more vicious attacks, was to stand by the distinction between Enlightenment and Terror. When Chateaubriand, however, challenged Staël to choose between Enlightenment and Christianity, as if the two systems of thought were incompatible, philosophy, revolution and the Montagnard dictatorship had all come to seem part of the same sinister and godless conspiracy. A hostility to Christianity was anyway evident in a number of the key texts of the late Enlightenment in France, among them the *Esquisse*.

Consider, for example, Condorcet's account of the stages in human-kind's progress towards perfection. Early in the *Esquisse*, we read that 'these advances may proceed more or less rapidly, but they will never regress', yet in a later passage we learn of 'the general errors which have more or less retarded or suspended the march of reason, which have often even, as much as political events, caused men to relapse into ignorance'. The chief cause of such errors was, in Condorcet's view, religion and, more particularly, Christianity. Thus, in his description of the sixth epoch, he spells out the disastrous consequences of the triumph of the Christian faith, and of the barbarian invasions. He writes of a precipitous decline, in the course of which the human mind fell from the heights to which it had been raised, and of a time of ignorance, ferocity, corruption and treachery. There was a disdain for the 'human sciences', and the priesthood neglected the knowledge accumulated in the Latin texts which they had in part preserved. Notwithstanding his commitment to the principle of perfectibility, the ancient city still therefore served Condorcet as an ideal, for there citizens had valued praxis above transcendence and, whether Stoics or Epicureans, had agreed that it was 'in the moral constitution of man that one [should] seek for the basis of his ideas, and the origin of his ideas of justice and of virtue'. Christianity was therefore to him a superstition 'more sombre, more dangerous and more hostile to Enlightenment' than the traditional beliefs of the Greeks, and, like most of the other *philosophe* historians, he lauded Julian the Apostate, the emperor who had sought to check the growing influence of the new sect.[57]

Condorcet's distaste for the Christian Middle Ages was balanced by an enthusiasm for the towns, for trade and for municipal structures of self-government. For the feudal system that had emerged in the wake of the barbarian invasions had been, in military terms, too anarchic to effect a wholesale destruction of the cities, which had therefore 'acquired a kind of authority; and were a base of operations for the liberty of the conquered nation'. Moreover, in Italy, 'Latin, which was the sole lan-guage of the people, became corrupted more slowly; ignorance there was not so total, or superstition so stupid as in the rest of the West'. The survival of such traditions then, in Condorcet's opinion, permitted the recovery of communal liberties in the Italian city-republics and the employment of Roman jurisprudence in the Ghibelline cause. The Reformation holds a central place in the *Esquisse*, for Martin Luther is there acclaimed as an instrument of the spirit of liberty and of free examination, which, in the course of the seventh epoch, made progress until, 'seconded by the invention of printing, it was sufficiently powerful to deliver a part of Europe from the yoke of the court of Rome'. Condorcet thus acknowledged the role of printing in the spread of Enlightenment, and understood the importance of the presses for the success of Luther's revolt and for the consolidation of Anglo-Dutch Protestantism. However, he did not regard the use of national languages as evidence that a new kind of providentially guaranteed community was emerging, and he had no objection to the increasingly universal use of French in Europe and beyond. He in fact mentioned the Hanseatic League and the Italian trading republics of Pisa, Florence, Genoa and Venice in the same breath, for he remained convinced of the worth of federations of free cities, and had no suspicion of the shadow soon to be cast by the linguistically defined tribe-nation.[58]

If the national languages were defined in the *Esquisse* as instruments of Enlightenment, rather than as the venerable bearers of a coherent but relatively opaque value firmament, it was because the barbarian tribes were still marked negatively, as the ethnic edge to earthly cities. He shared in this regard the view pioneered by the Renaissance humanists and embraced by Edward Gibbon that, between the Sack of Rome by the Goths in 410 AD and the revival of letters, lay a thousand years of darkness. If I pause here to consider just how the concept of a 'dark age' was forged, it is because, without an understanding of the periodizations of Renaissance and Enlightenment historians, it is impossible to arrive at an accurate assessment of the role played by the barbarian invasions in the historiography of the early nineteenth century.

The overarching schemata of medieval Christendom, through which the all but unbroken lines of popes and emperors ran, had not fostered clear divisions in historical time. 'Affiliation with the empire', as John Pocock has observed,' was affiliation with the timeless.'[59] Late Antiquity was certainly acquainted with sombre images of a time of crisis or decline, for, as night followed day, so might a civilization fall from glory. Both Augustine and Gregory the Great wrote in this fashion of the *eversio Romae*, but the chronicles of the medieval churchmen subordinated every human act to supernatural causes. For the prophecies contained in the Old and New Testaments concerning universal history had been deployed by the Church Fathers, not long after the Sack of Rome, as a framework for interpreting the deeds of all humankind. At the end of both of the divisions of historical time favoured by Holy Scripture, there stood, of course, the Last Judgement. If, therefore, one accepted a division in terms of four world monarchies, the first three being identified as Babylonian-Assyrian, Persian and Greek respectively, the fourth had by definition not yet ended. There was no discontinuity, Augustine and Orosius maintained, between the pagan and the Christian Empire.[60] Neither the Sack of Rome nor the fall of the Empire in the West were reckoned to be terminal, and then the theory of the translation of the Empire to the Franks or to the Germans provided a scaffolding for a universal Christian historiography for centuries to come. Charlemagne's inheritance of the Roman *imperium* in 800 AD, and his coronation that same year at both Aachen and Rome, established the Ghibelline cause upon so secure a foundation that, as late as the sixteenth century, Maximilian I forged policy in its terms. Indeed, the scheme of the four world monarchies, endorsed by Melanchthon, Luther's lieutenant, in 1532, survived in Germany, long after it had been discredited in the Italian peninsula or in France.[61]

Those who, in the early Middle Ages, contemplated the ruins of Rome, did not perceive the world that had been destroyed or lost as a wholly separate entity. As Quentin Skinner has observed,

> A sense of belonging to essentially the same civilization continued to persist, and nowhere more strongly than in Italy, where the legal code of Justinian was still effectively in force, the Latin language was in daily use on all formal as well as learned occasions, and most of the cities continued to inhabit the sites of ancient Roman settlement.[62]

Indeed, the startling thing about the earliest accounts of a dark age, or an age of ignorance, is that its duration was set at little more than a hundred years. Thus, Domenico di Bandino saw the shadows as obscuring the thirteenth century, and a small part of the fourteenth century, his own. In Flavio Biondo's *Decades*, by contrast, the dark age lasted a thousand years. How had this great change occurred?

In spite of the unbroken quality of historical time in medieval Christendom, there was necessarily a chasm between an Antiquity that was pagan, and therefore condemned to darkness and error, and the ascent to truth that Christ's agony on the Cross had made possible. The ineluctable nature of this division is manifest in an especially poignant passage in the *Inferno*, where Virgil explains to Dante that the sole fault of those he sees lying in Limbo was to have been born too soon. Petrarch likewise pitied Cicero because he had been fated to die shortly before 'the end of darkness and the night of error', and before 'the dawn of the true light'. Elsewhere in his writings, however, Petrarch, the author who did most to consolidate (if not to found) the literary and philological movement we know today as humanism, took a different view. At times, indeed, the change in emphasis is tantamount to a reversal of values, with the qualities of light and darkness ceasing to be strictly religious, and acquiring a literary, or even civic connotation. Far from being a dark age, classical Antiquity was now a radiant source, a dawn. A new periodization of history thus emerged, with a dark, middle age dividing Petrarch from the values he wished to restore.[63]

The division of historical time into three distinct stages (ancient, medieval and modern), though adumbrated by Petrarch, was formulated first by Flavio Biondo.[64] There may even be an echo of his assertions regarding the thousand-year span separating the Sack of Rome from the revival of letters in Staël's observation that 'it is fairly generally believed that, for over ten centuries, the human mind retrograded'.[65] If the view that she here contested had been reiterated by Voltaire, in his preface to *Le Siècle de Louis XIV*, by D'Alembert, in his *Discours Préliminaire à l'Encyclopédie*, by La Harpe, in several of his critical writings, by Hume even, in some of his historical writings, and by Condorcet, as we have seen, in the *Esquisse*, it is because all of these authors were still haunted by what I have termed an acropolitical vision of European (and, in fact, human) culture.

According to classical republican doctrine, no city, even if well ordered, could last forever; being the artefact of a single legislator, it fell away in time from its inaugural perfection as the mores of its citizens degenerated. Machiavelli's analysis of the constitution of Rome had, it is true, furnished the exceptional case of a city that grew more perfect as time went on, and flourished, in fact, on internal conflict, and something of that obstreperous life had been transferred by Montesquieu and Ferguson to eighteenth-century England. Yet Rome too, through an excess of military might, had expanded beyond all measure, and so declined. Even in the writings of the *philosophes*, the transience of cities persisted as a motif, albeit one seemingly in contradiction with the cumulative aspect of perfectibility. Thus, in Rivarol's discourse, as in Barère's speech to the Convention on the patois, French might serve as the bearer of perfectibility, yet beneath the blare of trumpets a ground bass, the round dance of the cities, could still be heard. In 1800, however, Madame de Staël observed that:

> The human mind, and above all patriotic emulation, would be wholly discouraged, if it were proven to be a moral necessity that the famous nations are eclipsed from the world after having illuminated it for a time. This succession of dethroned peoples is not an inevitable fatality.[66]

In classical republican thought, the liberty of a city could only be recovered if it were restored to its first principles. Such a restoration required that the people be assembled. In embracing the contrary view, and welcoming the dispersal of good across both space (the national territory) and time (the rising generations), Madame de Staël helped to topple the acropolitical series.

The crowning achievements of human culture – the Age of Pericles, the Age of Augustus, the Age of Pope Leo X or the Age of Louis XIV – had formerly been regarded as beacons shining out across a dark sea of barbarism, and the *philosophe* historians had written as if from a high place, in mournful contemplation of the ruins of once great cities. Consider Gibbon's inaugural vision, on the Capitoline Hill, and the closing references in the *Decline and Fall of the Roman Empire* to Poggio Bracciolini; consider Volney's meditations upon the ruins of Palmyra. Implicit in their station was a dualism, such that reason and superstition ran across the centuries relatively unconnected one with the other. Thus, as Momigliano has observed, it was possible for Volney or Condorcet to divide off the study of the Empire from that of the Church and, prior to the conversion of Constantine, to treat individual emperors as either monsters or paragons of virtue. The great Stoic emperors, Marcus Aurelius and Antoninus Pius, seem therefore to be ghostly figures, who, as embodiments of ideal republican virtues, dwell in the past rather than in the present. Indeed, the Age of the Antonines was usually represented by the *philosophe* historians, in Momigliano's Crocean description, 'almost as if it were a floating island of the blessed, beneath which a current of obscurantism continued to flow'.[67] In this regard there is something undeniably abstract about eighteenth-century philosophic history which, Croce claimed, rarely attended to 'the organic development of the peoples'. The failure of the *philosophes* to interweave the history of the Empire with that of the Church, evident in the division of tasks between Turgot's two orations for 1750, in the structure of Gibbon's great work and in the narrative of Condorcet's *Esquisse*, was a consequence, in Momigliano's view, of the earlier failure of Bossuet and Tillemont to unify sacred and profane events within the one history. Such disjunctures certainly persisted in the writings of Staël, whose Seneca, Epictetus and Marcus Aurelius remain somewhat abstracted and therefore framed by the lost republic rather than by what had in fact surrounded them. Yet her positive assessment of the barbarian invasions and of the impact of Christianity stands in marked contrast to that of Voltaire, Gibbon or Condorcet.

Staël saw that a strong case could be made against the principle of perfectibility if it could be established that for a whole millennium, the span marked out by Flavio Biondo, the European mind had been in retreat. She acknowledged that the barbarian invasions had been a calamity for those who had endured them, but she insisted that they had nonetheless served the cause of Enlightenment. For Christianity, in the aftermath of the invasions, had achieved a salutary exchange of moral qualities between inhabitants of south and north. At this point, Staël confronted the pagan Encyclopédists and their successors directly. 'Several writers have asserted', she wrote, 'that the Christian religion was the cause of the degradation of letters and philosophy . . . .' Whether she had Voltaire or Gibbon or Condorcet as her target here matters little, for she went on to make a strong counter-claim:

> I am convinced that the Christian religion, at the time of its foundation, was vitally necessary to civilization and to the mixture of the spirit of the north with the mores of the south. Furthermore, I believe that the religious meditations of Christianity, no matter what their object, served to develop the mind's faculties for the sciences, metaphysics and ethics.

The great achievement of the new religion had been, in Staël's view, to effect a tie between two profoundly different cultures, the Graeco-Roman and the Germanic.[68]

A vivid picture is painted in *De la Littérature* of the condition of the Roman Empire immediately prior to Constantine's conversion at the Milvian Bridge. Sunk in a universal egoism, corrupted and degraded, knowing nothing of glory, honour or the good, this enervated people had quite lost 'the Roman character, this miracle of national pride and of political institutions'.[69] Day followed day, in pursuit of sensation alone, and where there was still a taste for letters, art or philosophy, it was exercised chiefly on metaphysical subtleties or vain sophistries. To the north, beyond the Rhine, were ranged a wholly different people, fierce warriors, capable of both bravery and cruelty, ignorant and yet not corrupted. The Germanic tribes were a fit material for liberty; they also had imagination, melancholy, a penchant for mysticism and a deep contempt for Enlightenment. There is more than a suspicion of Macpherson or Mallet in this account and, since Montesquieu was Staël's idol, she must have lingered long over books 28 and 30 of *The Spirit of the Laws*. She would of course have had Caesar's *De Bello Gallico* and Tacitus's *Germania* to hand also, but where her use of such sources differed from that of, for example, Edward Gibbon, was in her positive interpretation of the role of Christianity in moulding the mores of both north and south.[70]

The new religion appealed to the northerners' melancholy, to their fondness for sombre images, and to their abiding preoccupation with the memory and ultimate fate of the dead. Furthermore, their rude virtues (their chastity, their loyalty and their courage) were at once preserved and put to new and less barbaric uses. Equity was born of this strange meeting. In the south, on the other hand, superstition, credulity and fanaticism held sway among a people already too dissolute to alter. Monastic institutions proliferated, and a taste for luxury was not so much eradicated as transformed into a penchant for mortification and extreme austerities. Through her opposition between north and south, Staël was promoting, much to the fury of the neo-Catholic party in France, a profoundly Protestant vision of the history of Christianity. Calvin or Luther seemed to stand at the head of the Germanic tribes.[71]

It was once the consensus among literary critics that Staël's historical role had been to blaze a trail for Romanticism. She, along with Chateaubriand, was judged to be the quintessential pre-Romantic.[72] If one were to trace this belief back to its origin, one would no doubt come to the generation of 1830, and to its most influential critic, Sainte-Beuve. Nowadays, however, the tendency is to place *De la Littérature* squarely within the Late Enlightenment, a term that Roland Mortier, I believe rightly, has borrowed from German scholarship to cover the years of transition, from 1780 onwards.[73] Thus, in a pioneering essay, Mortier has described how, 'at the dawn of a new century and of a profound literary transformation', Staël is best regarded as 'the most intelligent and the most faithful heir of the spirit of the Enlightenment'. The view that *De la Littérature* was a manifesto for *lumières*, in a climate of obscurantist reaction, has won widespread acceptance.[74] I maintain, however, that something more needs to be said, and that the barbarian invasions supply the key to the puzzle.

Mortier, for his part, acknowledges the evident divergence between Condorcet and Staël, but propounds the thesis that the crucial chapter in *De la Littérature* on the barbarian invasions derived in large part from passages in Turgot's two orations. In this regard too, then, she remained the unrepentant heir of the *philosophes*, just as her adversaries argued.[75] Lucid and cogent though Mortier's exposition is, he treats the subsequent development of Staël's thought more than somewhat peremptorily, hurrying through her ten years of exile in two brief paragraphs. To arrive at a final judgement on the vexed question of the legacy of the Enlightenment, a more extended treatment of the cultural and political debates of the Consulate and the Empire, the context of *De l'Allemagne* and *Les Martyrs*, is required.[76]

## Arcana imperii

After the purging of the Tribunate, in January 1802, the transition from Consulate to Empire advanced with gathering speed. On 8 May, the First Consul's term of office was extended to ten years, and a plebiscite held shortly afterwards accorded Bonaparte tenure for life. Already Fontanes had written, at his master's bidding, a pamphlet entitled *Un Parallèle entre César, Cromwell, Monk et Bonaparte. Traduit de l'Anglais*, which was widely distributed in the armies and through official channels in France. However, this 'first revelation of his most intimate and cherished thought' proved premature, and Bonaparte therefore hurriedly instructed Fouché, his always compliant henchman, to disown it.[77] As Fauriel observed, 'in times when souls had been tending less precipitately towards servitude, a man of ambition who had given advance notice of such a threat to public liberty would have had little chance of implementing it'.[78] Under the Consulate, however, it was as if moral degradation had reached such depths that the announcement of impending despotism merely brought it closer.

Other signs of an imminent restoration of monarchy soon followed. A draft law proposed that the emblem of the Republic on coins be replaced by a bust of the First Consul. Increasingly, Bonaparte's entourage assumed the demeanour, and revived the etiquette, of a royal court, with its own aristocracy, the Légion d'Honneur. Under the Empire itself, France was nearer to the condition of a police state than at any time in the past: 'What had happened under the Directory occurred again under Bonaparte; with each fresh injustice, with each loss he suffered in public esteem, the police became more worried, more suspicious, more active and more enterprising'.[79] Through the cold, reined-in fury of Fauriel's prose we glimpse a nightmarish world of spies and *agents provocateurs*, in which traps were laid not merely to ensnare those who had already acted but, in addition, to lure others into acting in a fashion that could then be presented in the courts as nefarious.

Fauriel gives an embittered account of the First Consul's foreign policy in 1802, the year in which the island of Elba was seized for France, and Piedmont annexed, with no legitimate title in either case. Although under the Convention, 'the wish of the peoples united with France had been the title by which the Republic had legitimized the extension of its frontiers', Fauriel was too scrupulous an observer to deny that this wish had generally been 'provoked by force or by more or less engineered intrigues'.[80] Lip-service, however, had at least been paid to the principle of popular sovereignty, but in the case of Bonaparte, whose ambition was to construct a patrimonial Empire in a Carolingian image, no justification was offered.

Right was as brazenly a slave to might in the domestic arena, where real or trumped-up conspiracies were crushed in a horrifyingly brutal fashion. Thus, on 15 February 1804, General Moreau was arrested. Under torture, two prisoners had confessed that a prince of the blood, having arrived at an understanding with Moreau, was poised to enter France, and that royalist emigrés were massing at Offenburg. Avowing that the Duc d'Enghien was the prince in question, and learning from his spies that he was then in Ettenheim, on German soil but in striking distance of Strasburg, Bonaparte resolved, in consultation with Fouché and Talleyrand, to have him kidnapped. Arrested, taken to Vincennes at five o'clock in the afternoon on 20 February, and brought before a military commission late that same night, the sacrificial victim was shot at two o'clock in the morning.

The judicial execution of an innocent man, who had been waylaid and taken by force from another country, profoundly shocked public opinion, both at home and abroad. A number of prominent figures distanced themselves from the regime. For example, Chateaubriand, recently appointed ambassador to the Pays de Vaud, declined to take up his post.[81] This refusal, and his subsequent estrangement from Bonaparte, was to bring him closer, closer indeed than one would have supposed possible a few years before, to Madame de Staël. By the summer of 1807, the authors of the Protestant *Delphine* and the Catholic *Génie du Christianisme* had become part of a single unified opposition.

Staël was in Berlin when she read of the arrest and execution of the Duc d'Enghien, both events being reported on the same page of the *Moniteur*. Prince Louis-Ferdinand of Prussia, later to die challenging a French officer in the aftermath of the battle of Jena, brought her the news, outraged that a gazette should refer to the grandson of the Duc de Condé, a celebrated general, as 'le nommé Louis Enghien'.[82] It was the kidnapping from German territory and the judicial murder of the Duc d'Enghien that gave rise to a deep hatred for Bonaparte on the part of Queen Louise of Prussia, who, although she died before the War of Liberation broke out, was to be, with Prince Louis-Ferdinand, imagined as a national martyr. In Staël's retrospective account, special emphasis is placed upon the opposition between force and right and, by the same token, a deep division is implied between the innermost tribunal of conscience and the glaring outwardness of domination.[83] Bonaparte had referred, it would seem, to Corneille, as if to say that the execution of the Duc d'Enghien was a matter of reason of state, and therefore obscure. He wished to deny that there was any passion behind the murder, and to assert, Staël supposed, that it belonged to the realm of pure calculation.[84] He had wished in fact to seal a blood pact with those who had made the Revolution and, more particularly, with those who bore the taint of regicide. Since everyone realized early in 1804 that a restoration of monarchy was imminent, it was vital to show that the hour of the Bourbons had not come, and thus to reassure those Conventionnels who lived in fear of White Terror. 'A bold stroke against the Bourbons', wrote Fauriel, 'could be regarded as just such a guarantee.'[85] In addition, the First Consul wished to demonstrate that he would stop at nothing.[86]

In later years, Garat recalled a conversation between Napoleon and Suard, shortly after the creation of the Empire. The two men, in the presence of the whole court, discussed the merits of Tacitus as a historian. We know that Suard, responsible since its inception for the class of literature and ancient history at the reformed Institute, had been asked to write justificatory articles for the Bonapartist press on the trial of General Moreau, and on the death of the Duc d'Enghien, and that, to his credit, he had refused.[87] It was no small thing, then, to talk of Tacitus, the author whom Napoleon detested more than he did anyone then alive. Indeed, all thinking persons had Tacitus, generally agreed to be the greatest historian of Antiquity and the chronicler of the destruction of the values of republican Rome, constantly in mind and to hand. Thus, on 6 June 1804, that is, shortly before the creation of the Empire and while the trial of Moreau was still in progress, Cabanis wrote to Fauriel confessing that he could not bring himself to pick up his edition of Tacitus, since it brought him too much to Rome.[88] There can be little doubt that Fauriel's own history of the death of the French republic, almost certainly begun in the summer of 1804, was modelled on the example of the great Roman historian, although Sallust may also have been an influence. As the Empire fell silent, to be in opposition and to emulate Tacitus became virtually synonymous. For example, Chateaubriand's article in July 1807 in the *Mercure de France* declared defiantly that Nero might wreak havoc all around him, but the historian Tacitus was already born in the Empire.[89] Furthermore, *Les Martyrs*, begun in 1803 as a pendant to *Le Génie du Christianisme* but published in 1809, featured portraits of Napoleon (as Diocletian) and Fouché (as Hierocles) that owe much to the Annals as well as to Christian chroniclers such as Lactantius. There are comparable portraits in *De l'Allemagne*.

There was, however, another side to Tacitus. For, as the author of the *Germania*, he had furnished Christendom with a striking image of the virtue of barbarian tribes, on the dangerous edge of the Roman world.

# Nations and Tribes

## On the mores of the Germans

It is a curious paradox that Renaissance humanism, inspired as it was by a distaste for Gothic barbarism and by a reverence for classical Antiquity, should have set in train a process whereby, within the space of 150 years, the heroic status of the Ancients was placed in doubt, and another liberty, Germanic and medieval, was established in its stead. In the yawning gap between their own times, when humane studies had been revived, and the decline and fall of the Roman Empire, a new world was revealed to the humanists, the *medium aevum* or middle age, a storehouse of exotic law and custom. For by their philological labours they had shown the Greeks and the Romans to be but two peoples among many, and, in so doing, they had released other peoples from the shadows.

The construction of an imagined ethnic opposition to Rome tended, however, to bring with it a sacralization of the community at odds with the universal city and, in adversity, the destruction of the secular schemes of history expounded with conviction and pride in the Italian Renaissance. In short, the annunciation of the tribe-nation in Europe, in the course of the sixteenth century, obscured the civic and pagan values of Florentine republicanism and thereby served to reinforce what Sergio Bertelli has called a counter-Renaissance.[1] At the same time, the transmission of humanism to north-western Europe, though a lengthy process, was effected during a period in which the Italian peninsula was overrun by French, Spanish and German armies; references to city-state republicanism were therefore scarce in writings north of the Alps.[2] German publicists, in particular, showed little commitment to civic humanist values; their allegiance was to the Empire, and their heroes were Theodoric the Ostrogoth or Frederick I, Barbarossa. Thus, whereas the cities of the Lombard plain, formerly a part of the Regnum

Italicum, had affirmed their newly won liberties in the teeth of Barbaros-sa's Imperial claims, Conrad Celtis took great pride in the discovery three centuries later of the *Ligurinus*, an account of the Emperor's campaigns in northern Italy which exalted him as possessor of 'dominion over the whole world'. The other chroniclers of Barbarossa's exploits, Otto of Friesing and Rahewin, were also much read in Germany at the end of the fifteenth century, as 'a kind of Hohenstaufen nostalgia set in, promoted by men of letters, historians, orators and publicists'.[3]

The flowering of Italian Renaissance historiography had seen the proud demolition of such providentialist guarantees, and the drawing of a clear line between earthly cities and the heavenly city. Machiavelli had proposed this separation in a particularly acute form, as I argued in chapter 6, the scandalous nature of his writings consisting as much in his espousal of a frankly pagan cosmology and ethics as in the terse brutality of his axioms. As several commentators have pointed out, to admit that *fortuna* condemned all cities to transience was, despite Christian eschato-logy, to declare a belief in human liberty.[4] By contrast, the Reformation in Germany was characterized, as we have seen, by the revival of a number of prophetic periodizations of world history, among them the doctrine of the Four Monarchies. In this scheme, Rome was not one of the potentially infinite series of free cities, but the bearer of divine instruction, whose universal task was later assumed, through the *transla-tio*, by the Holy Roman Empire. So completely did the art of the state replace that of the city, to use Maurizio Viroli's terms, that Machiavelli would have found no place in Reformation and Counter-Reformation Europe to speak, save perhaps in Venice. Moreover, by a strange irony, it was his name that stood for two centuries as a symbol of reason of state, against which many pitted the free and ancient tribe.

One Latin text, above all others, has provided a frame for the advocates of tribal-national identity, namely, Tacitus's *De Origine et Situ Germanorum*, commonly known as the *Germania*.[5] This little book has been deployed across the centuries by countless publicists in Europe, of widely varying persuasions. Sometimes it has supplied proof of a link between the open field system and the Germanic Mark, thereby provid-ing communism with ancestral titles far more venerable than those of possessive individualism; at other times it has justified the most perni-cious racism. If we take the long view, and consider the influence of the *Germania* upon European culture from the fifteenth century onwards, the most apt judgement would seem to be that of Alexander von Humboldt, who remarked that the rediscovery of Tacitus was as impor-tant an event as the discovery of America by Columbus.[6] With this observation, Humboldt perhaps said more than he knew, for the shock of an old world was certainly as instrumental as the irruption of the new in determining the fate of the universal schemata of Christendom. For, like those placed in the twentieth circle of the Inferno, publicists possessed by a national belief, whether in the Reformation, in the French Civil Wars of the 1560s and 1570s, or in the resistance to Napoleon in the early nineteenth century, marched towards the future with their heads turned to face a past that, being primitive, aboriginal or even autochthonous, was brought to life through Tacitus.

The cult of primitive Germanic virtue has rested upon two texts in particular, namely, *Annals* books 1–6 and the *Germania*. The former, rediscovered as late as 1509, featured the exploits of Arminius, chieftain of the Cerusci and destroyer of three Roman legions – their numbers, XVII, XVIII and XIX, never to be used again – under the command of Varus. The famous victory, set in the Teutoburger Wald, of a man who was 'without a doubt the liberator of Germany', was to provide Ulrich von Hutten, a militant German humanist, with an almost supernaturally heroic figure. The shade of Arminius, or Hermann, recalled by Hutten in 1518, appeared in many Reformation tracts, and continued to haunt Germany across the centuries. Klopstock, for example, had written a *Hermann*, and in *Lettres Westphaliennes* Charles de Villers described how, on the site of the battle, he had reread the play and heard in his imagination the crude chants of the bards with their harps.[7] There are references to Arminius in both *Les Martyrs* and *De l'Allemagne*, and German publicists and dramatists would celebrate him during the *Befreiungskriege* of 1813–15 and in the aftermath of the Franco-Prussian War. Of still greater importance, however, for the history of European political thought was the *Germania*.

Poggio Bracciolini, a humanist devoted to the quest for the lost works of classical Antiquity, had learned of the existence of a number of minor writings by Tacitus, and had tried to persuade a monk from a monastery in Hersfeld to surrender them to him. Some years later, Enoch of Ascoli was more successful, returning to Italy with the *Agricola*, the *Germania* and the *Dialogus de Oratoribus*. Aeneas Silvius Piccolomini, later Pope Pius II, purchased the manuscript, and it was through him that the Germans first learned of Tacitus's account of their early history.[8]

Few can have been better qualified than Piccolomini to respond to the letter of complaint that Martin Mair, Chancellor to the Archbishop of Mainz, addressed to him in August 1457. First of all, the future Pius II was an accomplished geographer and historian, well versed in early Germanic history. He was familiar with the classical authorities (Caesar, Strabo), and had composed an epitome of an important early medieval source (Jordanes). Now he owned the most crucial text, the *Germania*. Second, as the former secretary of the Emperor Frederick III, Piccolomini had already, in his letter of 1446, treated the question of the 'translation of the Empire to the Germans'. Third, as a former secretary to the Council of Basle, and an author of the history of a part of its deliberations, he was well acquainted with the sorts of complaint that Martin Mair was advancing on behalf of the German 'nation'. Mair, an able statesman committed to both Imperial and ecclesiastical reform, had levelled a string of charges against the Holy See, listing the constant stream of taxes, offerings, fees and annates that flowed from Germany into Rome.[9] Aeneas Silvius, still preoccupied by the Hussite heresy and by the reiteration of the gravamina of the German nation at the Diet of Frankfurt (1456), cast his response to Mair, the tractate-letter *De Ritu, Situ, Moribus et Condicione Germaniae Descriptio* in the form of a series of sharply drawn distinctions between the ancient Germans and those of the fifteenth century. His key source was the *Germania*, and he used its sixteenth and twenty-sixth chapters to prove that, before the Church had brought the Gospel to the pagan tribes, they had endured a bestial existence:

> Among them were no fortified cities nor towns surrounded with a wall. There were no castles built on the high mountains, no temples erected from cut stones were seen. They lacked the delight of gardens and villas; they cultivated no orchards, no farms, no beautiful valleys, no vineyards . . . Silver was rare among them, and gold was even more rare; the use of pearls was unknown. There was no ostentation of gems, no vestments of purple or of silk.[10]

Aeneas Silvius contrasted this desolate picture with the thriving condition of the fifteenth-century cities, singling out for praise the great merchant companies, the Fuggers, the Welsers, the Herwarts, the Imhoffs and the Baumgartners.

However, as resistance to the Papacy grew ever fiercer, German humanists turned the *Germania*'s apparent celebrations of autochthony, purity and rough-hewn vigour into a rallying cry. A pioneer in this respect was Conrad Celtis, whose inaugural oration (1492) at the University of Ingolstadt was a paean to Maximilian, at that time Archduke of Austria and shortly to become Emperor. Embracing the doctrine of *translatio imperii*, which affirmed unbroken continuity between Rome and the Empire of Charlemagne, Celtis regretted the loss of France and of the Regnum Italicum. He exhorted the students to make the 'ancestral virtue' of the ancient Germans their own, and to refute the slanderous aspersions of the Italian publicists. Celtis did not refer directly to Tacitus, but use of proper names such as Marcomanni, Quadi, Bastarnae and Peucini, to mean the Bohemians, the Moravians, the Slovaks and the Silesians, betrayed knowledge on his part of chapters 42 and 46 of the *Germania*. As well as inciting the Germans to heroic deeds, in order to reunite Germany's 'torn and broken territories', Celtis drew a contrast, just as Aeneas Silvius had done, between the rude condition of the ancient Germans and the luxury of Italy. However, where the future Pope had claimed that Germany had been civilized through its contact with Rome and the Papacy, Celtis insisted that it had been corrupted.[11] With the accession of Maximilian I, an unprecedented wave of patriotic feeling swept the Empire, and Tacitus's book became more and more widely known. This was true of chapters 2 and 4 in particular, which expound the origins of the ancient Germans, and which depict them as 'never . . . tainted by intermarriage with other peoples', 'a nation peculiar, pure and unique of its kind', 'autochthonous and extremely little affected by immigration or friendly intercourse with other nations', and which describe a physical type 'everywhere the same . . . wild, blue eyes, reddish hair and huge frames that excel only in violent effort'. Both chapters feature prominently in the writings of Celtis and Hutten and have echoed, to terrible effect, down the centuries. The human mind recoils at the scale of the horror caused by the ill-starred convergence of the Judaeo-Christian notion of an elect people with ethnographic or antiquarian celebrations of an inaugural tribe.

It is, then, a matter of more than merely academic importance to know why Tacitus wrote the *Germania*. The first, and commonest, interpretation, John Anderson informs us, is that Tacitus had fashioned a sort of moral mirror, in which Romans might see, in stark contrast to their own corrupted civilization, the virtues of an uncorrupted, primitive state.[12] The opening twenty-seven chapters do indeed bristle with stated or unstated comparisons between Germany and Rome, a fair number of which are plainly to the advantage of the former. In describing the warrior virtues of the free peoples who, for 210 years, had resisted the armed might of Rome (ch. 37), due tribute was paid to their courage (chs 3, 6, 7, 8, 13 and 14), their physical strength (chs 4 and 30), their loyalty (chs 7, 13, 14 and 21), their hospitality (ch. 21), and their lack of interest in money or precious metals (ch. 5). Tacitus also praised the manner in which the Germans raised their children, respected the institution of marriage and honoured the dead (chs 18, 19, 20 and 27). He likewise admired the *comitatus*, or retinue of young warriors owing allegiance to their *princeps*, or war chief (chs 13 and 14). However, Tacitus also described Rome's most feared adversaries as indolent (chs 4, 14 and 15), prone to licence (chs 11 and 14), to brawling (ch. 21), to drunkenness (chs 22 and 23) and to gambling (ch. 24). Moreover, he plainly disapproved of the unsettled condition of the tribes, and deplored their feckless approach to agriculture (ch 14, 15 and 26). Aeneas Silvius was surely correct to view the observation that 'they plant no orchards, fence off no meadows, water no gardens . . .' as derogatory, and it would, I think, be anachronistic to take Tacitus's detached remarks about communal land tenure as proof of admiration. No Roman of the first century AD would have preferred the *oppida* of the Germans, which were little more than fortified villages or strongholds, to cities with regular streets and adjacent blocks of houses.[13] The landscape and climate of Germany were by no means attractive to those accustomed to the Mediterranean, and if its peoples had not intermarried with others, it was chiefly because, Tacitus remarked, no one would willingly forsake Asia, Africa or Italy for such a desolate spot (ch. 2). Moreover, as Anderson observes, 'if it were merely a moralising homily that Tacitus set out to write, the second part of the treatise (chs 28–46), which contains little of ethical import, would be an irrelevance which could not be imputed to a great literary artist'.[14]

The second interpretation, Anderson continues, has it that the *Germania* was a political pamphlet, written in response to a specific occasion. Trajan, who succeeded to the Principate in 98 AD, the year in which Tacitus's book was written, had been responsible for the provinces of Upper and Lower Germany, on the left bank of the Rhine. Instead of hurrying back to Rome, he stayed for almost a year and a half in the North, reinforcing the army's defences, but not engaging in open battle. Was the *Germania* therefore a tract, written to justify Trajan's decision to linger in Germany, and refrain from further conflict? Although chapter 37, which emphasized that it had taken 210 years to contain the German threat, that 'neither from the Samnites nor from the Carthaginians, neither from Spain nor Gaul nor from the Parthians even, have we had more painful lessons', and that 'the freedom of Germany is a deadlier enemy than the despotism of Arsaces', lends credence to this view, the book as a whole has none of the qualities of a political pamphlet. Indeed, that particular chapter stands out from the rest of the book.

A third possibility, endorsed by Anderson and by almost all other scholars, is that, although due allowance should be made for those passages in which an uncorrupted people serves as a reminder of what Rome has lost, Tacitus's chief purpose in drafting the *Germania* had been to give as exact a picture as possible of the Germanic tribes or, in other words, to compose an ethnographic treatise. The first to write at length of the Ancient Germans had been a Greek (or, strictly speaking, Syrian) historian, Posidonius of Apamea (*c*.135–*c*.51 BC), whose work exerted a profound influence upon Caesar (in *De Bello Gallico*) and Livy (in book 104, now lost, of his history). Both the latter had served as authorities for Tacitus in his turn. In addition, he drew extensively upon the elder Pliny's *Bella Germaniae*, a lost work that, in Anderson's opinion, was 'undoubtedly a storehouse of information about the Germans, their mythology and their customs and institutions, political, social and military'.[15] What Tacitus had gleaned from Pliny was probably checked against the reports of other Roman officers, and Roman merchants also, for much was learned of the northern peoples in the course of the first century AD.[16]

Eduard Norden, in a famous study of the *Germania*, published in 1920 but begun before the outbreak of the First World War, drew attention to the striking parallels between Tacitus's description of the Ancient Germans and earlier portraits by Greek authors, Posidonius among them, of the Persians, Scythians, Thracians, Sarmatians and Celts. In the process, he formulated a pioneering account of the history of ethnology in classical Antiquity. The burden of Norden's case was that ethnography was a well-established genre in the Ancient World, invented by the Ionian Greeks, and that anyone who practised it would have been obliged both to adopt a particular style and to treat a given set of themes (the origins of a people; territory and climate; mores; the individual tribes of which that people was composed) – all of which feature, for example, in Herodotus's celebrated description of the Scythians as well as in the *Germania*. In addition, he identified what he termed ethnographic *Wandermotive*, or 'migratory motifs', which were applied by authors, Greek and Roman, to a range of different peoples. For example, the phrase 'a nation peculiar, pure and unique of its kind' had first been applied to the Egyptians, then to the Scythians, then to the Cimbri (by Posidonius), and finally to the Germans as a whole (by Tacitus).[17] Because reviewers had misrepresented his argument, Norden hastened to add, in the foreword to his second edition, that such motifs had not been borrowed 'mechanically' – or at least not by the best of the ancient ethnographers – but that 'traditional currents' had existed and had exerted an influence upon their writings.[18]

To grasp the wider importance of such seemingly recondite contributions to academic scholarship, it should be borne in mind that the early chapters devoted by Tacitus to the origins of the Germans have long been a focus of racist and nationalist exaltation. German humanists of the pre-Reformation period had themselves been much exercised by the 'autochthony' of the Germanic people, which lent credence to their claims to be *Gottes Volk*, and, in a fateful extension of the terms of the argument, the late eighteenth century witnessed the ascription of the same status to the language. Thus Klopstock, in a celebrated epigram, *Unsere Sprache*, observed that German was still in his own day what the tribes described by Tacitus had been, namely, 'gesondert, ungemischt und nur sich selber gleich'.[19] Likewise, Villers, in the *Spectateur du Nord*, had lavished praise upon the German root system which, being very ancient, 'integral and indigenous', could generate a potentially infinite series of new terms from out of its depths. German was, like Greek, a 'mother tongue', whereas French, Danish, Swedish, Dutch, English, Spanish and Italian were mere 'jargons'. Deeply impressed, as anyone whose first language is, say French or English, must inevitably be, by German's 'capacity to amalgamate', Villers contrasted its productive nature with the static quality of French, which was 'as if deprived of every a priori form, of all constant and uniform means of enriching itself from its own resources'.[20] In this fashion, Kantian categories were equated with the generative depths of an autochthonous language which, though at first construed as German, would be increasingly regarded as Indo-European and, from the latter half of the nineteenth century, as Proto-Indo-European.

A refracted Tacitus was to cast still larger and more sinister shadows during the Franco-Prussian War and the Heligoland Crisis: blood and soil, the land and the dead, and a language that was an undying source of values. In an essay on the uses to which the *Germania* was put under the Bismarckian Reich, and then again under the Third Reich, Lucio Canfora has shown how the racist Houston Stewart Chamberlain exploited one version of the text of chapter 4 in order to justify his pan-Germanist beliefs. Tacitus, in Mattingly's translation, had stated that:

> the peoples of Germany have never been tainted by intermarriage with other peoples, and stood out as a nation peculiar, pure and unique of its kind. Hence the physical type, if one may generalise at all about so vast a population, is everywhere the same – wild, blue eyes, reddish hair and huge frames that excel only in violent effort.

Now the crux here is the phrase 'if one may generalise at all about so vast a population', which leaves room for doubt. Mattingly, like Anderson, has opted for those manuscripts that favour *tamquam* over *quamquam*. For, where *tamquam* gives the above rendering, *quamquam* produces 'although it is so vast a population'. The latter accentuates the supposed physiological uniformity of the Germanic tribes, whereas the former reduces it, so Chamberlain translated the line as follows: 'Die Leibes-bildung ist bei allen diesen Menschen dieselbe.'[21]

Now Norden, as Canfora emphasizes, was one of the first to query *quamquam*, and to propose *tamquam*, in a usage at that time held to be extremely rare, in its stead. Editors had previously tended to opt for *quamquam*, which is the reading that Klopstock, Fichte and Friedrich Schlegel, as well as Chamberlain, would have known. Müllenhoff, a prehistorian and archaeologist with pan-Germanist sympathies and the teacher of Gustav Kossinna, judged in favour of *quamquam*, as did critics writing under the Nazi regime.[22]

In one sense, then, the importance of Norden's literary and philo-logical framing of the *Germania* lay in its subversion of the racist and pan-Germanist interpretations of the book. For, as Canfora points out:

illustrious chapters of Tacitus's book, which lent themselves, as Chapters 2
and 4 had done, to becoming sacred texts of German racism, lost much of their
charisma and their quasi-prophetic character, if they were analysed in terms of
their antiquarian and literary derivation, for they then could be shown to be
the product of a complex stratification, in the course of which ethnic and
cultural elements which originally applied to other peoples had been ascribed
to the Germans.[23]

If, therefore, one considers points of detail, one discovers that the
physical description of the Ancient Germans in Chapter 4 matches that
given by Posidonius for the Celts and Scythians, or even that recorded by
Pliny for the inhabitants of Ceylon.[24] Likewise, the *comitatus* or war
chief's retinue, regarded by Tacitus as a characteristically German
institution and celebrated as such under the Second and Third Reich, was
shown by Norden, using previously little-remarked passages from both
Polybius and Caesar, to bear comparison with the Celtic *ambactus*.[25]

The response of classical scholars in this country to Norden's book has
been to praise it highly, to accept the well-foundedness of its central
theses, but to question the conclusions that have been drawn from them.
Thus, John Anderson admitted that there had indeed been 'transfer-
ences' from one cultural context to another, but denied that this invali-
dated Tacitus's testimony. If the latter had employed commonplaces, it
was, Anderson claimed, because they were tried and tested descriptions
which accorded with the picture given in Tacitus's own sources. Moreover, Anderson continued, Tacitus had tended to retouch whatever he
borrowed, as in his chapter on German hospitality (ch. 21), where,
'above the Homeric colouring applied by Hellenistic ethnographers
there stand out two individual German features, the truth of which is
guaranteed by their survival almost to the present day in some parts of
rural Germany'.[26] Anderson's examples in this case in fact derive from
Norden, but something is smuggled into his treatment that is of more
dubious provenance, as I demonstrate below.[27] E.A. Thompson described Norden's book as 'splendid', but deplored its 'calamitous effect'
upon the study of early Germany.[28]

A reader untrained in the study of early Germanic history is thus
placed in a dilemma, not least because E.A. Thompson's little book
measures the testimonies of Caesar and Tacitus so adroitly against each
other that a highly convincing picture emerges of a society undergoing
rapid and momentous change. If one were to adopt a profoundly
sceptical attitude to Caesar's (first-hand) and to Tacitus's (second-hand)
observations, all of this would be lost.[29] Scholars have also made much of
the remarkable accuracy of the *Germania* regarding matters of objective
fact later confirmed by archaeology. Yet those who, like John Anderson,

have deplored Norden's influence, seem at times to entertain an understanding of the relation between race, culture and language that the doctrine of 'migratory motifs' and of 'traditional currents', precisely because it emphasized transaction between peoples rather than isolation, served to undermine. Do such scholars fully appreciate just how much Norden's book had done to challenge the view that, linguistically, culturally and ethnically, the Ancient Germans had enjoyed a wholly separate, continuous, and therefore privileged existence?

## The speech and wisdom of the Indians

The discovery by the Asiatic Society of Calcutta of affinities both lexical and structural between Sanskrit, Latin and Greek lent a new urgency to European speculations regarding first peoples, not least because Sir William Jones's pioneering statements of 1786 had linked Gothic and Celtic to the same putative family of languages.[30] Within a decade most accounts of the history and prehistory of Europe would contain some references to the theory, although few on the Continent had direct access, as Niebuhr did in 1798–99, to authentic Sanskritic scholarship.[31] The situation was to alter, however, in 1803, when Sir Alexander Hamilton, stranded in Paris after the breach of the Treaty of Amiens, was given permission, upon Volney's recommendation, to teach.[32] A group of orientalists seized upon the opportunity to study Sanskrit, among them Chézy, an eminent scholar of Persian, Fauriel, Friedrich Schlegel and Volney.

Friedrich Schlegel was soon possessed of the notion that Sanskrit, given its great antiquity and startling beauty, might supply the German language, conceived in Tacitian terms as itself ancient and separate and pure, with ancestral titles. Through his studies with Hamilton, he was able to tune the opposition delineated by Villers – one of the few Frenchmen whose company he kept while in Paris – between the profound, generative, organic properties of German and the superficial, stagnant, mechanical qualities of French to a still higher pitch. His journey down the Rhine in the summer of 1802 had already given a more definite shape to the inchoate medievalism of his years at Jena, and now his growing understanding of the linguistic, moral and spiritual unity of the Indo-Germanic caused the barbarian invasions of the fifth century to loom still larger in his mind. A belief in the primacy of the Germans, fuelled by an envenomed hatred of France, was consolidated even as his knowledge of Persian and Sanskrit deepened. Likewise, August-Wilhelm Schlegel, in the Berlin cycle of lectures on literature and art (1801–04), had repudiated the Reformation, calling for a revival in the fortunes of the Papacy, and for a rebuilding of the Holy Roman Empire, so soon to be dissolved. By contrast with Boulainvilliers, Gibbon or Helvétius, he emphasized the Christian destiny of the Germanic tribes, which had, he believed, infused new life into a decadent people. He judged, moreover, that even in modern times a purely Germanic cosmo-politanism, outshining the Grande Nation, might be founded upon the legacy, linguistic and cultural, of the Anglo-Saxons, Goths, Vandals, Burgundians and Franks, and tended as a consequence to play down the significance of any enduring Latin, Celtic or pre-Celtic elements. The Schlegels, whom Constant maliciously used to treat as one person, thus shared a vision of medieval liberty, and called for the restoration of an organic system of estates, or *Stände,* invoking, by way of precedent, the caste system of ancient India.

No more effective underpinning for the primacy of German language and culture could have been imagined than the discovery of affinities between Sanskrit, Greek and Latin, as Friedrich Schlegel's *The Speech and Wisdom of the Indians* proves. In Jena he had still hoped to fashion his country in the image of Greece, but a Tacitian interpretation of the findings of the Asiatic Society of Calcutta placed the Germanic tribes in a direct line from the first and wisest peoples. Where William Jones had supposed Sanskrit, Greek and Latin to be siblings, descended from a common ancestor (later defined by Franz Bopp as *Urindogermanisch,* or Proto-Indo-European), Schlegel's reverence for the wisdom of the Indians was such that he reckoned the language of the Vedas to be the source of the whole family, and a thing of unparalleled beauty and perfection. When Schlegel composed his treatise, the terms 'Indo-Germanic' and 'Indo-European' had not been coined, nor had any laws of sound-change been formulated. The book therefore reflects the relatively crude state of comparative philology early in the nineteenth century, one of its chief preoccupations being with typology. Yet Schle-gel's treatment of the recorded forms relied heavily upon the dichotomy between the organic and the mechanical, terms defined by his brother as follows:

> Form is mechanical when, through external force, it is imparted to any material as an accidental addition without reference to its quality; as, for example, when we give particular shape to a soft mass that it may retain the same shape after its induration. Organic form, again, is innate; it unfolds itself from within, and acquires its determination contemporaneously with the perfect development of the germ.[33]

The Viennese audience of 1808, united in their hostility to Napoleon, knew perfectly well that the enforced imposition of French culture upon an enslaved nation was an instance of mechanical form, just as Racine's classicism had itself been.[34] Friedrich Schlegel deployed this same distinction to heighten the contrast, already formulated in fact by Adelung, between, on the one hand, inflectional languages and, on the other, isolating and agglutinative languages, with the two latter types being vilified and the former praised to the skies. The inflected languages were further subdivided into synthetic and analytic forms. Thus the beauty of Sanskrit, a synthetic language, consisted in its propensity to produce modifications of meaning by inflection alone, without resorting to the use of prepositions, affixes and suffixes. Here the *Ursprache*, Greek, Latin and the Romance languages could be ranked on a descending scale, as the organic perfection of the original language was progressively eroded by 'the merely mechanical process of annexing words or particles to the same lifeless and unproductive root'.[35] Botanical or biological echoes were intended, and suggest debts both to Herder or Schelling and, in Paris, to Cuvier, whose celebrated lectures on comparative anatomy were published between 1800 and 1805, and from whom Schlegel had secured a letter of introduction in the autumn of 1802.[36]

Judging so perfect a language as Sanskrit to be, necessarily, the product of a refined intelligence, Schlegel was at pains to dissociate it from Epicurean or Lucretian notions of feral wandering:

> The structure of language . . . is but one proof added in confirmation of so many others, that the primitive condition of mankind was not one of mere animal instinct, which by slow degrees, and with many a weary effort, at length attained some slight glimmering of reason and intelligence; it rather confirms . . . that . . . the most profound study and the clearest intelligence were early called into operation; for without such labour and reflection it would have been impossible to frame a language like the Indian, which, even in its simplest form, exemplifies the loftiest ideas of the pure world of thought, and displays the entire ground plan of the consciousness, not in figurative symbols, but in direct and immediate clearness and precision.[37]

In fact, Schlegel did not so much repudiate the animal origin of humanity as advance a polygenetic account, which ascribed feral attributes to isolating and to agglutinative languages (and, by implication, to their speakers) and reserved spiritual qualities for tongues (and peoples) descended from the Indian. Thus, where Locke, Leibniz and Vico had all remarked upon the fact that the words designating spiritual entities – such as soul or spirit – tend to have an obvious material (in fact, corporeal) origin, Schlegel denied that this was the case with Sanskrit.[38] As Timpanaro has remarked, this account of the origin of human

language bears a resemblance to that developed in the *New Science* –
which had distinguished between Hebrew, the language of divine Revelation, and the other languages, sprung from the confused phantasy of
the *bestioni* after the Flood – but where Vico's real interests had lain with
the latter, Schlegel condemned the non-inflecting languages as irredee-
mably inferior, and was really concerned only with the divine language,
Sanskrit.[39] That it was indeed a matter of redemption is plain from the
fact that Schlegel deployed the ancient language of India both to supplant
Hebrew in an imaginary genealogy and to found the quality of being
German. A Romantic linguistics of this sort, precisely because it tends to
assume that culture, language and tribe are isomorphic, leads directly to
racism, as several critics have noted.[40] For, underlying Schlegel's putative reconstruction of the history of language there was the assumption
that humankind, in its divinely created form, originated in the mountains
of central Asia. Being the last wave in a long sequence of migrations of
peoples from their ancestral home, the Germanic tribes, closer at once to
the original stock and to the original language, were therefore accorded
by the Romantics a moral and cultural primacy.

Progress in Indo-European linguistics was so marked, and so much
remarked, that nineteenth-century scholars were increasingly of the
opinion that identification of the source of that family of languages was
possible. This conviction was powerfully reinforced by the constant
recourse of comparativists to the family tree model, and by the resulting
analogy with the evolution of species. The claim was that degrees of
resemblance between specified Indo-European or Indo-Germanic languages – more examples of which were found, buried deep or flung far, in
the course of the nineteenth and early twentieth centuries – could be
assumed to reflect moments of separation from a common origin.
Underlying this claim, moreover, was the unproven hypothesis that the
division of each 'branch' from the 'trunk' represented the migration of a
people into a new territory. The shortcomings of this model are mani-
fold.[41] To begin with, it presupposes that a speech community, prior to its
putative splitting, is homogeneous. There is thus in the literature much
talk of the 'undivided' Germans, a phrase that calls to mind the Schlegels, Humboldt or Fichte. It would seem, in fact, more plausible to
cleave to the more empirical argument, notwithstanding the strictly
philosophical difficulties it raises, that 'the language which finally broke
up into a number of independent groups may itself have been formed by
a convergence of elements from different sources'.[42] The second, related
objection to the family tree model is thus that it precludes the possibility
of two (or more) languages passing through a stage of shared development, with their speakers resident in adjacent territories. Sociolinguists
have in recent years offered many detailed descriptions of such processes

of convergence or abrasion, but the crucial point to note here is that, though the tree model seems to rule out the possibility of the exchange of grammatical features across the boundaries between linguistic families – the existence of transferred lexical items is a concession, I suppose, to the brute fact of contiguity of social groups in geographical space – we now know that certain Indo-European languages in northern India were for a long time in just such a relation of symbiosis with other, Dravidian languages.[43] Colin Renfrew, to whose exposition I am much indebted, ascribes the *Stammbaum*, or family tree model, to Augustus Schleicher, whose monograph of 1862 bears the revealing title *Die Darwinische Theorie und die Sprachwissenschaft*. This ascription may be accurate, but the further implication is then that the publication of *The Origin of Species* precipitated the explosion of European racism in the latter half of the nineteenth century. I am not sufficiently well versed in the history of evolutionary theory in Victorian Britain to offer an opinion, but I would nonetheless maintain, on the basis of earlier formulations by, for example, the Schlegels, Humboldt or Niebuhr, that a Cuvierian belief in the fixity of created species could also accommodate racist belief.[44] Where the history of India is concerned, there was thus an insistence upon a radical separation between a Vedic, Indo-European language and culture and an indigenous Dravidian language and culture.[45] I think, therefore, that Bernal's comments upon the family tree model usefully complement those of Renfrew.[46]

With the consolidation of the notion of a Proto-Indo-European language, or *Ursprache*, the hunt was on for a homeland, or *Urheimat*, of the people, or *Urvolk*, who spoke this ancestral tongue. Comparative philologists were convinced that the identification of cognates in a significant number of branches of the Indo-European family, and the consequent extrapolation, following the laws of sound change, of a standard form, could generate a protolexicon. If, then, you could find *birch* in English, *Birke* in German, *berzas* in Lithuanian, *breža* in Old Slavonic, and *bhurja* in Sanskrit, you might plausibly suppose *\*bhergh* in the original language, and such a tree in the habitat first occupied by its speakers. Indeed, you might identify on a map a territory where a specified flora, and only that flora, still was. Much information could also be gleaned, or so it was believed, regarding way of life. The protolexicon thus contained many names of domesticated animals but few denoting grain or vegetables. Given the notion of pastoralism then current, almost all scholars concluded that the people in question were nomadic pastoralists, and in 1890 Otto Schrader declared that their homeland was the South Russian Steppe.[47]

Once an alliance had been forged between comparative philology and archaeology, a discipline whose birthdate cannot seriously be placed much before the 1840s, the quest for a homeland assumed a still greater urgency. Thus, in 1902, Gustav Kossinna argued for a correlation between a particular type of pottery, known as Corded Ware, and the Proto-Indo-European people, whose homeland could, on the basis of finds in grave sites, be identified as north German. By the 1870s, the Romantic equation between an 'Aryan' people and the Germanic tribes had been rendered more concrete through the study of biometric evidence. The Aryans, as they were erroneously termed, were judged to be tall, dolichocephalic and blond, and in this fashion a spurious scientific description reinforced the fateful dicta of Tacitus. Kossinna thus supplied German nationalism and the Nazis with a charter for racism, for *Lebensraum* and, ultimately, for genocide.

To quote Malcolm Todd's (critical) paraphrase: 'the genesis of the Germans was to be sought in the brilliant Nordic Bronze Age culture which covered northern Germany from the Weser to the Oder, Denmark and the west Baltic islands'. This argument, which determined 'the main stream of thought on the subject until the Second World War', rested on the assumption that 'a people and its culture remained in essentials an autochthonous unit over many centuries, now and again absorbing influences from outside, but remaining unaltered at the core', that 'major archaeological culture-provinces could . . . be distinguished by the study of artefacts', and that 'these culture-provinces must be taken to represent distinct peoples or tribal groups'.[48] A reviewer of Anderson's edition of Tacitus had in fact remarked upon his too uncritical acceptance of the theories of Kossinna and his school, an observation that would appear to be well founded.[49]

Kossinna was of course in error in supposing that the presence of a particular culture-complex in the archaeological record could be read as proof of the existence of a particular people, yet this tenet had been accepted by many, as much in Britain as in continental Europe. Gordon Childe, for example, preferred a south Russian to a north German homeland for the Indo-Germanic peoples, but relied very heavily upon Kossinna's theories, and therefore upon the equation between cultures, defined as assemblages of material artefacts, and peoples. The distribution of objects of a given style was presumed to offer an archaeologist clues towards the reconstruction of putative migrations of peoples across land masses, while the protolexicon was a valid index of the *Urheimat*.[50] It is of the utmost importance, then, to bear in mind that, as Claude Lévi-Strauss observed in 1953, 'two cultures developed by men belonging to the same race may differ as much, or more, than two cultures belonging to racially distant groups'.[51] To avoid any confusion regarding this momentous issue, one should perhaps add the rider that the replacement of the term 'race' with that of 'ethnic group' would render still clearer a dangerously confused area for discussion.

With the advent of the age of nations, just such a homology of language, culture and race was generally presupposed. The Germanic tribes, for example, were imagined, across the *limes*, as a unitary, self-subsisting horde, the bearer of fresh values to an exhausted world. In reading Staël or Chateaubriand, Fichte or Schlegel, as I show at greater length in chapter 9, one thus succumbs to the curious illusion that the many individual tribes, differentiated with some care by Tacitus, considered themselves to be Germans, and therefore predestined to promote the universal values of Christendom, even though they did not know themselves by that name at all.[52] A thinker like Vico, being steeped in ancient ethnography, sceptical of its claims and lacking any desire to vaunt a tribe-nation, well understood how traditions were founded upon the transmutation of individual testimonies into billowing myth, but Romanticism produced the consolidation of a Germanist philosophy of history organized around the distinction between the 'historical' and the 'unhistorical' nations. So influential was this latter conception that it left its mark upon Hegel, in most other respects hostile to Romanticism, and upon Engels, one of the founders of historical materialism.[53] In my final chapter, I consider opposition to such conflations of race, language and culture in early nineteenth-century Italy, but here I want to note in passing that the history of modern ethnology is inseparable from that of nationalism, so that insights into the one promote understanding of the other, and vice versa.

For example, Ernest Gellner, a pioneer in the art of interpreting the theories and underlying values of ethnographers in terms of their own cultural context, has shown how discussion of the Polish question can shed light on Bronislaw Malinowski's thought. With Poland condemned to dismemberment and Polish nationalism to defeat, a patriot might respond to the scathing judgement of world history upon an 'unhistorical' nation, or so the argument runs, by formulating a theory of the inner working of societies which at once denied the importance of history and confirmed the worth of organicist community. In this fashion Poles might vindicate their fatherland twice over, albeit at the price of shipping it to the distant Trobriand Islands. Gellner's account of the biographical penumbra of Malinowskian functionalism is declaredly speculative and, for want of the necessary documentation, is no doubt likely to remain so, but it has the virtue of alerting us to that great hall of mirrors in which tribes and nations meet.[54]

Those trained as ethnographers in the inter-war years in Britain, when Malinowski's influence was at its height, were thus encouraged to see a tribe as a single, isolated unit, existing in a quasi-organic equilibrium, outside history. Functionalist anthropologists consequently presented peoples as, to all intents and purposes, autochthonous, as if there had never been constant movement of populations, and therefore exchange of artefacts, beliefs and lexical items, across the land masses they inhabited. So convincing was this mirage that it became genuinely difficult for someone formed in the Malinowskian tradition to describe the concrete interrelation of contemporary and adjacent cultures. The most vivid proof of this is supplied by the experience of Edmund Leach, himself a pupil of Malinowski, who set out for Burma in 1939 with the intention of writing a functionalist study of a single community but, owing to his extensive knowledge of the entire country, acquired during the war, came to see that a strong case could be made for a far more fluid conception of tribal boundaries.[55] His Malinowski Lecture of 1959 may be considered as an especially trenchant expression of his belief that, contrary to the implicit assumptions of some of his colleagues, human societies were not, strictly speaking, reducible to classes, as natural genera and species were. This attack on 'butterfly-collecting' helped to demolish structural-functionalist ethnography, the origins of which lie, I would suggest, in the thought-forms of Napoleonic and Restoration Europe.[56]

In the United States, Franz Boas's innovatory conception of field-work, pitted against the diffusionist anthropogeography in fashion when his scientific career began, also contained a residual Romanticism, inherited in a direct line from Humboldt by way of Steinthal. As a consequence, the illusion of autochthonous value, most evident in the 'strong' version of the Sapir–Whorf hypothesis, was perpetuated by those whom Boas had trained. Thus, Edward Sapir, whose prose is at times lit by a dismay at the ravages inflicted by Europe's tribes within, was driven by outrage at the horror to celebrate the synchronic beauties of tribes without. *Language*, an admirable book, contains a chapter informed by a passionate distaste for the tribe-nations of the European imagination, subverting with calm authority any supposed isomorphisms between language, race and culture, yet its author himself at times entertained the illusion of a perfected, enclosed and self-sufficient tribal unit, patterned against transcience.[57]

While it was possible in the Trobriand Islands or on the North-West Coast of America to forget for a time the murderous primacies of Europe, Durkheim and his pupils were, as staunch Dreyfusards, engaged in an unrelenting struggle to promote lay values and to defeat sacralized notions of the tribe-nation, 'the land and the dead' of Action Française. It is therefore of particular interest to note the approach of the Ecole Sociologique to the prehistory of Europe. For example, in Henri Hubert's lecture course on the ancient Germans we find a warmer reception given to Norden, and a fiercer criticism of Kossinna than in, say, John Anderson's edition of Tacitus. Hubert was also adamant that German, far from being the primordial language of a primordial people, was in reality a creolized form.[58] These same lines of argument were developed by Marcel Mauss in the 1930s and, after the war, by Michel Leiris and Claude Lévi-Strauss, in pamphlets on race and racism sponsored by UNESCO.[59] I should add, however, that the *Annales* historians, themselves influenced by the *Année Sociologique*, have sometimes invoked, as ethnological or archaeological guarantee for the nation, a consoling continuity of settlement from the Neolithic. The much-vaunted diversity of France sits oddly with such impervious homogeneities.[60]

Archaeology has in fact been still more haunted than has ethnology by a mirror relation between tribes and nations, as the case of Kossinna so amply demonstrates. However, one would not at first suppose that anything like the same criticisms would be applied to archaeologists, so often concerned to reconstruct the turbulent movements of peoples across vast distances, as to ethnologists, reproached by Leach for isolating tribal societies in an imaginary condition of self-perpetuating stasis. Autochthony and migration are, after all, antinomies. Yet on close inspection, the gap seems to lessen, since British prehistory in the early part of this century was conceived in terms of a sequence of invasions entailing the wholesale transfer of a population and, in its train, a unitary culture. More recently, however, archaeologists have challenged the view that each and every stylistic innovation could be ascribed to an invasion of peoples from the Continent. The shift in theory away from the migrationist hypothesis may be illustrated by the case of the Bronze Age in Wessex. Anomalies in the evidence had thus caused Stuart Piggott to scale down the extent of the intrusion and, by 1938, to invoke not a whole people but an invading aristocracy, a viewpoint accepted by Gordon Childe in his synoptic account of British prehistory. As a consequence, we read there of 'warlike invaders imbued with domineering habits and an appreciation of metal weapons and ornaments which inspired them to impose sufficient political unity on their new domain for some economic unification to follow'.[61] Indeed, by the late 1950s, pioneers in social archaeology, no doubt influenced to some small degree by parallel developments in social anthropology, were prepared to challenge the view that stylistic change was invariably an index of invasion. Might not the exotic cultural items excavated from sites be 'signs of increasing wealth on the part of native leaders rather than . . . signs of replacement by an invading aristocracy'?[62] Grahame Clark interpreted the collapse of the invasion hypothesis in British archaeology in terms of the end of Empire, but his own references to our 'prehistoric forebears' and to 'an age-long process of organic growth' seem almost to

mirror the sharp turn inwards and, so to speak, landwards, of a war-
locked culture in 1939–45.[63] Be this as it may, the Beaker Folk of Wessex
have fled to the land of chimerae, and their material culture is now
judged to be an expression of indigenous economic and social change.
This radical dissolution of a culture would appear to be a symptom of the
more general demolition of a Romantic metaphysics of invasion, replaced initially perhaps by an equally Romantic metaphysics of ancestral
island stories, but in the longer run by the Enlightenment vision of much
of the new, processual archaeology. No better indication of the transition
from an age of nations to an age of cities could be supplied than the
challenge posed to migrationist hypotheses by the intriguing notion of
'peer polity interaction'.[64]

## Germanic tribes, French nation

While German humanists had used Tacitus to mount a 'national' challenge to the absolutism of a corrupt and nepotistic Papacy, their counter-
parts in sixteenth-century France, though as hostile to all things Roman
or Italian, were more concerned with curbing the powers of the
monarchy, invoking for this purpose Chapters 7 and 11 of the *Germania*.
For Tacitus had both noted that the sovereignty of the German kings was
neither 'unlimited' nor 'free', and had remarked upon the importance of
public assemblies. At a time of intense religious and political strife, a
number of French publicists therefore exhumed 'the ancient constitution', whose defining features could be traced back to the Gauls and the
Franks.[65] Etienne Pasquier, for example, affirmed both the dignity and
the validity of French customary law, remarking upon the inapplicability
of Justinian's Code to barbarian culture. This was the characteristic
position of those who followed the *Mos docendi Gallicus*, pioneered by
Pasquier's teacher, Andrea Alciato, and adopted with particular vigour
by François Hotman. The latter's *Anti-Tribonian* (1567) thus made the
case for a new code, written in French and based upon customary law. If
a man came into a French court, Hotman observed, acquainted only with
the Roman code, though he knew it 'as perfectly . . . as a Cato, a
Scaevola or a Manlius had done', he might as well have been among
American Indians, for he would be able to make neither head nor tail of
the recondite terms descended from the customary law of the Germanic
tribes.[66]

In the *Francogallia*, a tract written shortly after Saint Bartholomew's
Eve, Hotman justified the right of resistance to tyranny in terms of
precedents to be found in the ancient French constitution. In the belief
that the massacre had been planned by Italian advisers in the hire of the

Florentine Catherine de Medici, by then Queen of France, he also contrasted a 'Machiavellian' reason of state with the Germanic liberties of Francogallia. As Quentin Skinner has observed, 'with the presentation of this case, it may be said that the use of historical evidence as a form of political argument . . . suddenly came of age'.[67] A window looking out on to the way things were, although it were of horn and not glass, could serve as a gate to the way things should be. Thus, Hotman began by describing the condition of Gaul before it had become a Roman province, noting that it was divided into many regions, some ruled by kings and some by councils of nobles, but all honouring an obligation to hold 'a public council of the nation' at a fixed time of the year. This assembly, evidently the prototype of the States General, was vested with considerable power, for, following Tacitus, Hotman observed that 'the [elected] kings did not possess an unlimited, free and uncontrolled authority, but were so circumscribed by specific laws that they were no less under the authority and power of the people than the people were under theirs'. A second Germanic people, the Franks, were cast by Hotman as the liberators of the province from Roman oppression. They also had an elective monarchy, the warrior chosen being placed upon a shield and elevated upon the shoulders of those present. The election of Childeric by both Gauls and Franks symbolized the union of the two peoples and the consolidation of a free kingdom: 'the Kings of Francogallia were constituted by the authoritative decision and desire of the people, that is, of the orders, or, as we are now accustomed to say, of the estates, rather than by any hereditary right'. Such kings could also be deposed, as Childeric and Hegidius in fact were.[68]

A century or so after Hotman's death, the triumphant absolutism of Louis XIV prompted a revival in justificatory antiquarianism. Thus, a number of prominent figures in the entourage of the King's grandson, the Duke of Bourgogne, advanced their own descriptions of the primitive constitution of the kingdom. The most celebrated of these accounts, by Henri de Boulainvilliers, covered much the same ground as the *Francogallia*, and therefore referred, as one would expect, to the *Germania*. Once again, the conquest of Gaul by the Franks – a generic term covering, in Boulainvilliers's opinion, all those living between the Rhine and the Weser, or even as far as the Elbe – was held to inaugurate the history of France. Yet, where Hotman had argued that conquered and conquerors had been on more or less equal terms, Boulainvilliers, the chief proponent of the *thèse nobiliaire*, maintained that the Gauls had been subjugated by the Franks. The latter, through the simple fact of conquest, belonged to the nobility, were landowners and were subject to Salic law, while the former were debarred from military service, forfeited much of their property and remained subject to Roman law. Franks, as a warrior caste, could be tried only by their peers, held their fiefs in perpetuity and were exempt from taxation. Two polities, that of the victors and that of the vanquished, thus coexisted on the same territory. Quoting, like so many others, the crucial lines from the seventh chapter of the *Germania*, Boulainvilliers also depicts the Germanic king as no more than a first among equals, simply a civil magistrate appointed by his canton to try disputes between individuals. Kingship was therefore neither absolute nor hereditary, and sovereignty was vested in the assemblies of the armed nobility, the Champs de Mars and the Champs de Mai. The Capetian dynasty, in crushing the *noblesse de race* and elevating commoners to high office, was guilty of usurpation.[69]

In order to refute Boulainvilliers, the abbé Du Bos claimed that the Franks had not in fact entered Gaul as military conquerors, but as allies of the Romans. This argument, reiterated in the 1860s and 1870s by Fustel de Coulanges and endorsed by many modern scholars, meant that the consolidation of the French monarchy could not be regarded as a usurpatory denial of primitive Germanic liberties. Clovis's pre-eminence among the Franks could thus be seen to derive from his status as a Roman general, while Justinian's cession of the crown, around 540 AD, had made the Frankish kings the direct heirs of the Caesars. Where Boulainvilliers had defined the defeated Gallo-Romans as serfs, Du Bos denied the superiority, *de facto* or *de jure*, of the Franks, and laid great stress upon the fusion of the two peoples. He also insisted that the Champs de Mars, which had been claimed by the *noblesse de race* as the original for the States General, and by the *noblesse de robe* as the precursor of the Parlements, had been simply a rallying place for troops for the Spring campaign.[70]

The Romanist viewpoint, which even in the sixteenth century had rested upon the assumption that the fief was derived from Roman, not barbarian law, was thus used to bolster the cause of absolutism. Yet the *thèse royale* also presupposed recognition of the ancient freedom of the municipia, whose senates and magistracies survived in Merovingian Gaul and, in the south, merged centuries later with the institutions of self-government of the renascent communes.[71] As I explained in chapter 6, D'Argenson, like Du Bos, rejected the supposed right of conquest out of hand, observing that the settlement of the Franks in Gaul was more 'an occupation of the chief points of the country' than 'a subjugation of the inhabitants'.[72] He hoped in fact to foster the regeneration of communal liberties in France, believing municipal government in Gaul to constitute a reconciliation of the rights of the Prince with those of his subjects. He therefore proposed that each town, borough or village be given a

'popular' magistrate, chosen by an Intendant from a list.[73] Such republican additions to a fundamentally absolutist framework were to be
proposed by a number of *philosophes*, Condorcet, Mirabeau and Turgot
among them, and help to shed light on the otherwise mysterious leap of
many publicists after 1789 from belief in enlightened despotism to an
endorsement of popular sovereignty as such.[74] Because of the triumph of
doctrines of historical right, in the early nineteenth century, the reputation of D'Argenson was, however, wholly eclipsed by that of Montesquieu. One looks in vain in Thierry's *Considérations* for even a mention
of D'Argenson.

Although *The Spirit of the Laws* was concerned with nothing less than
the full range of human societies, it also contained a lengthy treatment of
the history of France, which, Montesquieu declared, steered between
Boulainvilliers, whose work seemed 'a conspiracy against the third
estate', and Du Bos, whose book appeared to be 'a conspiracy against the
nobility'. In fact he reserved his harshest criticisms for the Romanist
camp, thereby breathing new life into the Germanist interpretation of
French history. Du Bos's book, 'a bad work by a famous author', is given
short shrift; 'my ideas', wrote Montesquieu, 'are perpetually contrary to
his . . . if he has found out the truth, I have not'. Du Bos, as I have
remarked above, all but denied that there had been a conquest at all,
arguing rather that the Franks had formed an alliance with the Romans,
and that their kings had been summoned to Gaul to take the place of the
Emperors. Montesquieu, however, was in no doubt as to the violence
employed in the subjugation of Gaul. He was likewise affronted by Du
Bos's claim that all the Franks had been equal, for this threatened the
time-hallowed status of the royal dynasties of France. Following Caesar
and Tacitus closely, Montesquieu discerned in the 'companions', or
vassals, of the war chiefs, the nobility of the ancient Germans. He also
accepted that the kingship depended, as Tacitus had said, upon public
deliberation but, unlike Boulainvilliers, he never mentioned the Champ
de Mars or the Champ de Mai. Nor did he at any point refer to the States
General, although a tantalizing passage seemed to imply that the very
best form of government ever known had been that of France in the
fourteenth and fifteenth centuries, when all three orders existed in a sort
of balance. Although Du Bos's book earned the rougher treatment,
Boulainvilliers's bluff and blustering apology for a Frankish hegemony
was also handled with some irony. Indeed, Montesquieu rejected out of
hand the view that the Gallo-Romans were in a condition of servitude
under the Franks. Barbarian law being of its nature personal, there could
not be juridical equality between conquerors and conquered, but this did
not mean that the latter were no more than serfs in Merovingian Gaul.[75]

## Rousseau, order and providence

How did Rousseau respond to the tradition of antiquarian research into the history of France? One could, if one so wished, make a case for a Germanist, feudal interpretation of the first discourse, with its somewhat militaristic primitivism, of the second discourse, with its faint echoes of Tacitus, and of *The Social Contract*, with its references to the assemblies of the Franks.[76] Yet the general tenor of his thought is quite different, and his alignments, even prior to the Venetian episode or to his rediscovery of Genevan liberty, were with Romanists such as D'Argenson, rather than with Boulainvilliers. Rousseau in fact shared D'Argenson's scepticism towards philological raids upon storehouses of custom, an acceptance of the transience of earthly cities and a denial of the right of conquest.[77]

No matter how fervently Rousseau affirmed the existence of divine providence, and therefore of justice for all in the life to come, he tended to repudiate teleological interpretations of the course of human history. As a philosopher of liberty, he denied that there was a necessary connection between the workings of providence and the annals of humankind: early societies might well have remained as they were for countless centuries had not a number of purely accidental circumstances arisen.[78] Just as he himself might never have been locked out of the city of Geneva one night, and so never, by chance, impelled towards Piedmont-Savoy, Paris and the hell of literary fame, so might countless small tribes, outside the glare of European history, have continued as they were for millennia, without ever developing an advanced agriculture or metallurgy. Nowhere is the disjunction between salvation and attested history more boldly stated than in the *Profession of Faith of the Savoyard Vicar*. He refers there to the corrosive effect of the biblical scholarship of the second half of the seventeenth century upon religious faith, yet his response to Spinoza or to Bayle was not to ape Richard Simon or the Benedictines of St Maur, who had relinquished some border posts in order to regroup and entrench on higher ground.[79] Instead, he wrenched faith altogether out of history, so that his readers were forced to make a choice between transcribed revelation and the promptings of the human heart: 'Once the peoples were so minded as to make God speak, each made him speak after its own fashion, and made him say what it wished. If one had only listened to what God said to the heart of man, there would never have been more than one religion on earth.'[80] In his caustic rejection of the merely human testimonies upon which revelations rest, Rousseau seems fully to endorse the historical Pyrrhonism, inherited from Bayle and Fontenelle, of Voltaire and his followers. There would, he declared, be no end to the critical scholarship necessary to identify the authentic word of God.

Even when scholars had established a corpus of authenticated texts, their work would not be done, for they would then have to evaluate the vocation of those who had written them:

> one would indeed have to be acquainted with the laws of chance, the probabilities involved, in order to judge what prediction could have been fulfilled without there actually being a miracle; with the genius of the original languages in order to distinguish between what was prediction in these languages and what was merely a rhetorical figure.[81]

This passage is certainly an echo of Spinoza's analysis of the language of the Old Testament, and it restates his claim that much that had been treated as prophecy was in fact enraptured use of metaphor.[82] Spinoza had also argued that it had been rare for God to speak; in virtually every instance, the prophets of Israel saw him in a dream or in a vision. Only Moses and Christ were exceptions to this rule, with the former hearing 'some sort of real voice' and the latter communing with God 'mind to mind'.[83] Likewise, the discussion of miracles in the *Profession of Faith*, and still more in the *Lettres Ecrites de la Montagne*, is indubitably Spinozist in spirit.[84] Both Rousseau and Spinoza deplored the tendency of the vulgar multitude to place their trust in oracles, and both rejected the relation suggested by Scripture or by antiquarian tradition between God, people and territory.

I have already remarked that a land mass never touched by the Corpus Juris Civilis and never lit by Judaeo-Christian revelation had served as a pure contrary to the Old World. Rousseau thus noted that millions of people on the other side of the Atlantic Ocean were no doubt still unaware that missionaries had set foot on their continent, and drew therefore a sharp and mocking contrast between vast, uncharted space and the small area of the Mediterranean chosen by God for the sacrifice of his son. Where Dante could accept, though in sorrow, Virgil's account of the fate of those noble pagan souls who, being born before Christ, were condemned to suffer in purgatory, Rousseau insisted that salvation was for all or for none. It was sufficient that Lycurgus or Numa had the same moral stature as Moses, and that Cato was as virtuous as Christ. As in the second discourse, so too in *Emile*, Rousseau borrowed the voice of the Amerindian, figure of universal humanity, that Montaigne had himself employed to pull the vanity of Europe down:

> You are announcing to me a God who was born and who died two thousand years ago, at the other end of the world, in some small town . . . Why did your

God cause the events which he wished to instruct me by to happen so far from me? Is it a crime to be ignorant of what takes place at the antipodes? Am I supposed to have guessed that in another hemisphere there was a Hebrew people and a town of Jerusalem?

Rousseau then reiterated his philological doubts respecting the transmission of God's word, proceeding, in a passage of Swiftian burlesque, to conjure up a horde of ethnographer-theologians, forever in transit: 'there would no longer be any fixed and stable peoples; the whole earth would be covered with pilgrims travelling at great expense and with great difficulty to check, compare and examine for themselves the various religions which are followed'. In short, neither the ethnographic nor the historical record could ever furnish a secure basis for religious belief.[85]

## Word-nation and tribe-nation

The Americas had, however, been put to a different use by those who took human beings to be mere sensoria, governed by the principle of utility, that is, by self-interest and a calculus of pleasure and pain. This view, derived from Locke, was shared by many of the *philosophes*, and by their intellectual heirs, the *idéologues*.[86] A radical deism posited a God who had absconded, and therefore an unfathomable abyss between creator and creation. Volney, for example, could never bring himself to admit the existence of a Rousseauist 'voice of duty'. More generally, the formation of value both within and against nature was characteristic of much of the anthropological speculation of the Parisian Enlightenment. Helvétius, for example, made much of the 'organization' of the human species, of its flexible hand and fingers, longevity, prematurity of birth, natural weakness, more constant society and plasticity. He all but abolished the barrier between animality and humanity and argued that it was because the human species was both vegetarian and carnivorous that it had attained a more complex social organization, for a greater range of needs gave rise, in the struggle for life, to more inventions.[87]

Such interpretations reflect the challenge that book 5 of *De Rerum Natura* had posed to Genesis, and so declare, or hint, that all specifically human culture was preceded by feral wandering. Where Christian apologists argued that the biblical account of origins was confirmed by *consensus gentium*, the agreement of the peoples, their adversaries, following Locke and Bayle, pointed out that tribes had been found that lacked any belief in a god. Diderot, for example, rejected Christian iusnaturalism, with its belief in the god-given dignity and destiny of humanity, and discerned in the deserts and forests a creature who was 'naked, wandering, without civilization, without laws, reduced to an animal condition'.[88]

However, in Diderot's own circle, a strictly negative assessment of the moral or intellectual worth of religious sentiment had been challenged by Boulanger, who had equated the awe of early human beings at natural process with the first stirrings of Enlightenment, and who had thus granted a dignity to ancient traditions that the *philosophes* had until then generally denied them.[89] Although some Encyclopédists remained intransigently atheist, most gravitated towards a form of deism, or even theism, in the second half of the eighteenth century, their anti-clerical rancour and commitment to dechristianization diminishing as a religion of reason grew more alluring. Because the doctrine and ritual practice of the earliest human societies were widely thought to have been untouched by the priesthood, they supplied the *philosophes* with a model for the religion of the future, given concrete form in the masonic lodges and in the revolutionary cults. Many of those who could no longer countenance Diderot's materialist atheism, with its fierce joy in the, by turns creative and destructive, cycles of nature, therefore embarked in the 1770s and 1780s upon a quest for the original religion of all humankind. Whereas *philosophes* in the past had used the ethnography of the Americas as a weapon against revealed religion, many of their number now hoped to use the venerable traditions of the Old World as the foundation for a new doctrine, for 'regeneration'. Franco Venturi has thus shown that a resacralization of the primitive ground of European culture, far from being peculiar to Germany, was in fact characteristic also of those he terms the epigones of Diderot, namely, Delisle de Sales, Bailly, Court de Gébelin and Rabaut Saint-Etienne.[90]

There was, moreover, a convergence in the second half of the eighteenth century between antiquarian researches into early religion and Germanist readings of French history, the most famed being Mably's *Observations*. His debt to Montesquieu was everywhere apparent, although he gave his sources a more democratic gloss. The seventh chapter of the *Germania* had proved, Mably said, that the government of the ancient Germans had been 'a democracy, tempered by the power of the prince', the latter being simply the first magistrate. A distinction was then made, once again on Tacitus's authority, between the assembly of the Champs de Mars, which could frame laws, and the council of kings and elders, which had the right to execute only the less important or pressing decisions. To sustain his position, Mably was obliged to lean in one particular on Du Bos, whom otherwise he vilified, and to deny that a Frankish nobility had existed at the time of the conquest of Gaul. Two moments were therefore celebrated, an original liberty which barely outlived Clovis, and the introduction by Charlemagne of a system of provincial and national assemblies which returned to the French (or Francogallic) people the right to make their own laws.[91]

Mably's system, though derivative and chimerical, exerted a fascination upon many of those who wished to reform the crisis-ridden monarchy.[92] More generally, Germanist arguments, howsoever inflected, would seem to have swept all before them until late in 1788.[93] Resistance to the attempts of Maupeou, Calonne and Loménie de Brienne to establish a more thoroughgoing absolutism took the form of invocations both of traditional liberties and of reason. *The noblesse de robe*, with the power and prestige of the *parlements* under threat, naturally turned to Montesquieu's defence of the intermediary bodies, and called for a States General.

In chapter 5 I explained how the *parlements*, in insisting that voting at the States General be by orders, as it had been in 1614, rather than by head, forfeited their popular support almost overnight. In outraged response to the overweening presumption of the magistrates, the publicists of the Third Estate, instead of sustaining the delicate balance between tradition and reason characteristic of oppositional arguments since Malesherbes's Remonstrances of 1771, simply repudiated historical precedent altogether:

> The Third Estate has nothing to fear from going back into the past. It will refer back to the year preceding the conquest; and since it is today strong enough not to be conquered, its resistance will no doubt be more effective. Why should it not send back to Franconia all those families that cling to the mad claim that they are descended from the race of conquerors and have inherited their rights? Thus purified, the nation will easily console itself, I believe, for no longer imagining itself composed only of the descendants of Gauls and Romans.[94]

This was not, be it noted, a Romanist statement, nor was it a celebration of ancient Celtic liberties.[95] Sieyes invoked neither Boulainvilliers nor Du Bos, neither Montesquieu nor Mably, but insisted rather that, as Rousseau had shown in *The Social Contract*, conquest could not supply a ground for right. In place of the venerable subordinations of the ancient constitution, he therefore advanced the claims of the city-nation which, being a product of human liberty as such, was not guaranteed in and through historical time. However, as we have seen, the ambiguities intrinsic to the concept of nature in eighteenth-century thought meant that those who had refused all recourse to philologically attested origins, relying instead upon eternal principles, might easily find the two kinds of justification overlapping in the form of the 'man of nature', possessed by definition of such principles. For this reason, the auroral intoxication of

1789, though predicated upon a refusal of all titles, was soon to be reinforced by historical and ethnological enquiries concerning the Celtic origins of France.

Thus, Nicolas de Bonneville, a leading figure in the *Cercle Social*, embraced the democratic Germanism of Mably, but in addition directed attention to those passages in Tacitus which appear to suggest that the Ancient Germans held property in land in common.[96] Since these same lines fuelled a controversy in the nineteenth century over the nature of land tenure in pre-capitalist society, with Engels treating them as proof of the historical existence of a form of communism and with Fustel de Coulanges taking the contrary view, it is of some importance to note Bonneville's preoccupation with such matters. However, I am more concerned here with his magical invocations of a people that, though nominally Celtic, embodied a millennial liberty, equality and fraternity. The ancient Druids therefore merged imperceptibly with Hebrew, Indian, Persian and Egyptian priests in a syncretism of masonic inspiration.[97]

Those *philosophes* who had remained loyal to the atheism and materialism of Boulanger, of Diderot or of Holbach, were careful to insist upon the intellectual and moral distance separating early human societies, however idyllic they might seem in certain lights, from those of modern Europe. Whatever sympathies they might feel for the purity of ancient mythologies or cosmogonies – and here Boulanger's fascination with the essential nature of religious awe seems almost to prefigure the later researches of Constant – they did not wish to make them their own. Yet only the finest of lines divide Volney or Dupuis, who revered all expressions of wonder at natural process and deplored their transmutation into allegory by priests, from Bonneville, who wished quite simply to be Celtic.

As the Revolution fell under the shadow of the Terror, many could no longer sustain a blithe future sense, and looked to a cult of the Ancestors to supply an antidote to the invented belief systems of the day. The sepulchral meditations of Chateaubriand reflect, therefore, a general anxiety at the repercussions for cosmological order of an improper placing of the dead. Thus Jacques Cambry, a former Girondin, dispatched on a mission to Finistère to draft a report on Vandalism, returned early in 1795 with a quite altered sense of the numinous properties of the ancient monuments of Brittany – more particularly of the stone circles of Carnac, reckoned until the 1860s to be Celtic – and of the intrinsic interest of its rituals, folklore and customs.[98] After Thermidor, a significant number of other Breton members of the Third Estate (among them, Amaury Duval, Ginguené, Lanjuinais, La Revellière-Lépeaux, Mangourit and Volney) turned their attention to the lost world of the Celts, some of them discerning in Druidism the principles of a natural religion which might oust Christianity. The antiquarian reconstruction of a national religion resulted, however, in the creation of a religion of the nation, its claim to primacy being constantly reiterated, whether from the point of view of Celts, of Germans, of Etruscans or of Anglo-Saxons. Whereas tribal liberty had been a dying song in a mountain fastness, it was now construed as immanent, ubiquitous and eternal, inhering in lichen-encrusted stones, or in 'monuments' carried in speech across countless generations.

# The Tribe-nation

## Observing Germany

Heinrich Heine once remarked that 'in the din of voices of every sort which cry out from the pages of [De l'Allemagne], the most distinctly audible is always the clear falsetto of Mr. A.W. Schlegel'. He distinguished, however, between those chapters in which Madame de Staël had been true to herself, and to her Protestant and Enlightenment convictions, and those in which 'she obeys suggestions from without . . . [and] does homage to a school whose character is completely alien and incomprehensible to her'.[1] Since her routine, especially at Coppet, was to compose her books in company, and to give a reading in the evening of chapters drafted in the course of the day, it is never an easy matter to pin down influences upon her thought. The difficulty is compounded in the case of De l'Allemagne, the writing of which took almost seven years (from 1803–04 to 1810), and which was retouched between its first printing, in France, and its actual publication by John Murray in 1813. Adam Oehlenschlager, a visitor to Coppet in 1809, was at some pains to deny, twenty years later, that Staël had deferred to Schlegel's judgement, and Jean de Pange, in support of his testimony, would subsequently publish a bulky monograph chronicling relations between the author of De l'Allemagne and her son's tutor.[2]

The burden of Jean de Pange's book, consisting in large part of unpublished letters from the archives at Coppet, is therefore that Staël was by no means as much in thrall to the Schlegels as Heine, among others, had supposed. This apology, coloured by piety towards an ancestor, cannot however be fully understood if its historical context is not taken into consideration, for Jean de Pange's monograph, a doctoral thesis published in Paris in 1938, refers on more than one occasion to the history of twentieth-century Europe and, more specifically, to Hitler.[3] Since Staël's literary reputation had suffered in France in the aftermath of the Franco-Prussian War, with some publicists condemning *De l'Alle-magne* as a treacherous book which had led two generations to view French culture as in its essence Germanic, those concerned to defend her were obliged to distinguish as sharply as they could between her thought and that of the Schlegels. Jean de Pange therefore depicted Staël as a cosmopolitan thinker, the standard-bearer of an ideal Switzerland of the mind and heart, and August-Wilhelm Schlegel as a pan-Germanist, exulting in the larger unity of race and language.[4]

There is no cause to doubt that there were very real divergences between the two central protagonists of Jean de Pange's study.[5] For example, Staël could never bring herself to accept Schlegel's derogatory and Gallophobic comparison between the *Phaedra* of Euripides and the *Phèdre* of Racine, and she was profoundly distressed when, in 1812, a performance in St Petersburg of the latter was brought to a halt by a hostile demonstration.[6] When the German states at last rallied, in 1813, Schlegel's letters became fevered and bellicose, his preoccupation with the purity of the German race sometimes descending into outright anti-Semitism.[7] Meanwhile Staël grew less and less enthusiastic about her study of Germany, which became, almost fortuitously, the literary emblem of the *Befreiungskriege*. If one excepts a number of passages added at the last moment, the book had cast the Germans as contemplative and not disposed to resolute action.[8]

When, in the Preface to *De l'Allemagne*, Staël wrote of '[those] great individuals known as nations', there is a case for arguing that her theoretical perspective even then was consonant with that of Cabanis, Degérando or Volney, and, more generally, with the milieu of the Société des Observateurs de l'Homme.[9] This, at any rate, is the conviction of Sergio Moravia, who has discerned in *De la Littérature* an *idéologue*'s ambition to construct a 'science of man' through 'the objective and experimental analysis of psychological, cultural, ethnological and social structures', and in *Corinne* and *De l'Allemagne* a fulfilment of this ambition.[10] Indeed, *Corinne* contains chapters devoted to the character and mores of the Italians (treated not in general, but as Florentines, Romans, Milanese, Neopolitans, Genoans and Venetians), to popular festivals and to Holy Week, and so extended are some of these observations that the narrative of the novel, which is itself structured as a meditation upon national identity, is often too much interrupted. One can well understand why in 1807 the librarian at the Bibliothèque Nationale in Paris should have hesitated before deciding whether it was a novel or a contribution to the literature of travel. By the same token, *De l'Allemagne* features, as Moravia has argued, 'socio-cultural analyses, which favour concrete observation, . . . the gaze, the search for links between psycho-social features and the material situation'.[11] Staël's evident fascination with cultural diversity thus found expression in accurate descriptions of dances flaring beyond royal courts (for example, the southern Italian tarantella), costumes (for example, that of Siberian shamans) and, necessarily, of folk song.

There is much to recommend this argument, yet a full account of the genesis of *Corinne* and of *De l'Allemagne* would require some reference to the thought of Wilhelm von Humboldt, who was resident in Paris in 1797–99, and who frequented Staël's salon at the Rue du Bac. For the founder of comparative linguistics had earlier hoped to create a comparative anthropology, which he was still refining in 1798.[12] This ambitious project never came to much, largely because the terms of the argument were transposed to the domain of language and, in the process, rendered more precise, yet two linked essays from 1795–97 have survived.[13] Since Humboldt devoted much of his time in Paris to the accumulation of materials reflecting the character and mores of the French, including a meditation upon the collection of statuary and sepulchral monuments at the Musée des Petits-Augustins, it seems plausible to argue that Staël set out to emulate in Germany what he had aspired to do in France.[14] The parallel is reinforced by the fact that both authors were at the same time anatomizing national cultures and putting the eighteenth century, matrix of the Revolution and the Terror, on trial.[15] In order to assess Staël's intellectual debt to Humboldt, we need, however, to understand the nature of his chosen task, and the degree to which it either conflicted with or complemented the human science of the *idéologues*.

Humboldt had in fact conceived of the idea of writing a biography of a nation as early as 1793, since he firmly believed that the diversity of national cultures fostered the diversity of persons, and thereby promoted what was, from his (Leibnizian) perspective, God's ultimate purpose, namely, the proliferation of individuality. It is easy to discern an affinity between Constant's church of one and a Humboldtian conception of the person which yields, by implication, a strictly modern conception of literature or art. Moreover, there was by 1795 no diminution in the cosmopolitan emphasis to his thought:

> . . . it is only jointly that humankind can reach its highest peaks, and it needs union not so much in order to produce greater and more lasting works through the mere increase of strength, but in order, rather, to show, through the greater diversity of talents, its nature in its true richness and in its full range. A man is only ever made for one form, for one character, and so it is likewise for a class of men. The ideal of humanity, however, exhibits as many, diverse forms as may coexist peaceably with one another. It cannot therefore appear otherwise than in the totality of individuals.[16]

In short, if national diversity is a good, it is because it guarantees the diversity of myriad individuals. It is significant, then, that Humboldt, notwithstanding his description of the Swiss as a 'branch' of the Germanic 'trunk', esteems the cantons precisely because, being so close to nature, they differ from the German states. There is not a hint of pan-Germanism in this passage; the tribe-nation is nowhere to be seen.[17] For this reason, Meinecke emphasized what was to him Humboldt's shortcomings, since, as 'a son of the individualistic and cosmopolitan eighteenth century', he had 'a consciousness of the national' but not yet (in the 1790s) 'a national consciousness'.[18]

While in Paris, Humboldt made the acquaintance of Cuvier and Bougainville, and was on good terms with Constant, Degérando, Garat, Ginguené and Sieyes. As we have seen, this milieu resisted the lure of the critical philosophy. Thus, Humboldt recalled that his exposition of Kant's system to, among others, Sieyes, Tracy, Laromiguière and Le Breton, left the lecturer and his audience 'in different worlds'.[19] There has been a tendency among historians to take such testimony at face value, and consequently both to overstate Humboldt's debt to Hamann and Herder and to underestimate the importance of his years in Paris, notwithstanding the fact that they immediately preceded his crucial journey to Spain, which inaugurated his life's work on the comparative study of language. In order to rectify this historiographical bias, I shall attempt a paraphrase of Hans Aarsleff's authoritative treatment of the emergence of Humboldtian linguistics.

Although passages in Croce or in Meinecke would have served Aarsleff's purposes just as well, he takes *The Philosophy of Symbolic Forms* as his preferred target. To begin with, the French *philosophes* had, in Cassirer's opinion, treated language as a strictly cognitive, never creative or imaginative instrument, originating in need and agreement and serving solely for the purposes of communication. Second, they had tended to interpret the workings of ordinary language in terms of some perfect philosophical language. Third, they had assumed that a language was in essence a system of nomenclature, with words becoming attached to percepts through ostensive definition. Fourth, their notion of linguistic diversity was at best superficial, since they constantly invoked the rationalist principles of universal grammar. Conversely, Cassirer held that all of the above tenets were overturned by Hamann and Herder's deployment of the genius of languages, since it restored to human cultures both their creativity and their diversity.[20] If, however, one consults Condillac's *Essai* one finds that it contains, as I noted in chapter 7, an extended discussion of 'the genius of languages'. Moreover, debate at the Berlin Academy for a full twenty years, culminating in Herder's celebrated text of 1772, drew its inspiration from the *Essai*.[21] There was even an extended reference to Condillac's doctrine in Rivarol's discourse, as Garat reminded readers of the *Mercure de France* in 1785.

If Aarsleff's arguments hold good, the caricature of eighteenth-century thought discernible in Cassirer, Croce and Meinecke may be traced back to the trial of the Enlightenment, opened in the aftermath of Thermidor. Early witnesses for the prosecution, such as La Harpe, denounced the Encyclopédists for having preached 'atheism, irreligion, impiety, hatred of all legitimate authority, contempt for all moral truths and the destruction of all social ties'.[22] La Harpe's crude and immoderate assault upon the dying century was roundly criticized by many, yet it became something of a fashion to wander among the ruins of the old order, accusing one *philosophe* but sparing another. The debate in its original form lasted in France until 1807, when the Emperor silenced all the contending parties, but in reality it dragged on for many decades, bequeathing posterity a severely distorted image of the Enlightenment. As Roland Mortier has observed, we still have not taken the measure of the envenomed and vengeful treatment accorded to the thought of the *philosophes* under the Restoration, which more nearly resembled a court martial than trial by jury.[23] No matter how loudly François Furet protests that the French Revolution has ended, in this respect at least, it plainly has not. To take one small example, the Crocean interpretation of Vico, predicated upon the sorts of misrepresentation of the *philosophes* described above, still colours our understanding of the Enlightenment.[24]

In the early nineteenth century, with all the furies let loose, the criticized and compromised would sometimes don the masks handed to them by their critics, and even carve a still more grotesque expression upon them. It is thus no easy matter to interpret the trajectories of those who, in response to the trial of the eighteenth century, put their own thought on trial, although we can perhaps go some way towards understanding the difficulty if we reflect upon the fashion in which socialists in our own day, under the neo-liberal onslaught, have retreated from previously secure theoretical principles, sometimes so fast and so far that they seem almost to have merged with those driving them back.

In Staël's case, a distinction ought then to be made between her notion of 'first times', and that of Cabanis or Constant, Fauriel or Sismondi. For, while most would accept the accuracy of Moravia's account of *Corinne* and of *De l'Allemagne*, the ethnographic facets of which shine now more brightly, 'the mores and character of the Italians' in the former lack the numinous value accorded 'the mores of the Germans' in the latter. As Heine noted, *De l'Allemagne* was designed to be in part an accusation, in the image of Tacitus's *Germania*, against both the First Empire and the *philosophes*. There is therefore a shade more pan-Germanism in the book than Jean de Pange was prepared to admit, especially in its third part, which is devoted to the critical philosophy, and which very probably dates back to the period, commencing with the first German journey of 1803-04, at which Staël was most open to the influence of the Schlegels.

Even the chapters devoted to philosophy were phrased in terms of nationality, for Staël wished to contrast an English or a German with a French cast of mind. Notwithstanding her protestations of love for France, its philosophers were charged with having put the thought of John Locke to scandalous uses. The author of the *Essay on Human Understanding* had, she said, been both 'moral and religious' in character, and had therefore not entertained any of the 'corrupting arguments which necessarily follow from his metaphysics'. He may well have set out to prove that there were no innate ideas in the soul, but this was having first defined an 'idea' as 'a development acquired through experience'. Sentiments, dispositions and faculties, on the other hand, were not brought into being by external objects.[25]

Staël perceived how crucial to Locke's case were the examples he had marshalled of countries in which crimes (such as murder, adultery or patricide) were held in honour, and countered his relativism by insisting that, although the just and the unjust might be defined in a different fashion in different places, there was no people on earth that denied the existence of duties (or of a god of some description). The savage who killed his father when he was old, believed he was rendering him a service, and his action was therefore an expression of the spontaneous (and immutable) altruism of the human soul. This argument, which owed as much to Rousseau's critique of Helvétius's utilitarian ethics as to Kant's (related) account of practical reason, banished forever the caustic ethnography of the *philosophes*, and paved the way for a scientific ethnology. The religious sentiment was common to all cultures.[26]

Fauriel, in his generally favourable review of *De la Littérature*, had concluded that 'there are as many distinct literatures as there are peoples with different mores, that is to say, a different climate and government', and this judgement made of Staël's book an *idéologue*'s treatise through and through. Yet he had also found the distinction between a literature of the north and a literature of the south crude and schematic and, like Cabanis, had challenged the view that the barbarian invasions and the advent of Christianity had constituted an advance in Enlightenment for Europe.[27] In forever harping on the two strings of north and south, Staël was proposing an opposition between philosophies that located motives within ourselves, thus making us 'the sons of heaven', and those that placed them on the outside, thus condemning us to be 'the slaves of earth'.[28] In her opinion, Leibniz had proved that there existed operations of the intelligence that were irreducible to sensation.[29] By the same token, the *Critique of Pure Reason* had shown that space, time and the categories were properties of our minds and not of objects external to them.[30] Like Villers, Staël lauded Kant for his clear discrimination between the phenomenal and the noumenal spheres, which appeared to secure both religion and liberty.[31] Yet the price to be paid for establishing a dichotomy between the earthly city and the heavenly city, between sensual fatality and moral liberty, was the invocation of a providential first people, as human link between God and the word- or tribe-nation. Following the Schlegels, Staël cast the Indians as bearers of the ideal, and the Greeks and Romans as the bearers of the material:

> The religious systems of India are very melancholic and very spiritualist, whereas the peoples of the south of Europe have always had a penchant for a somewhat material paganism. Those English scholars who have travelled in India have made profound researches into Asia; and Germans who, unlike the princes of the sea, have had no such opportunities to learn such things with their own eyes, have by dint of study alone made some very interesting discoveries regarding the religion, the language and the literature of the Asiatic nations; they have been led to believe . . . that supernatural *lumières* formerly illuminated those countries, and that ineradicable traces of them remain.[32]

She then remarked upon the peculiar affinity of the German idealists with ancient Indian thought, and praised *The Speech and Wisdom of the Indians*. For there, we read, Friedrich Schlegel had posited a primordial people, 'the tutor of the human race', formed by an original revelation. Nor had it escaped Staël that Schlegel rejected out of hand the Enlightenment account of the gradual and natural origin of human language.[33] Whereas Cabanis and Constant remained wholly unimpressed by the notion of a primordial Indo-Germanic revelation, Chateaubriand's thought drifted away from the New World and towards the tribe-nation in the years between 1803 and 1809.[34] There were many parallels, therefore, between *Les Martyrs* and *De l'Allemagne*.

## Singing the Franks

*Les Martyrs* is set in the Roman Empire at the time of Diocletian, when 'Christianity was not yet the dominant religion of the Roman Empire, but its altars were raised alongside the altars of the idols'. Since there are other moments as well-suited to the staging of a Christian – or, indeed, a Christian-national – epic, one cannot help but wonder why the period of the tetrarchy was chosen.[35] Why did Chateaubriand not opt, like other

French writers of epic in the early nineteenth century, for Clovis or for Charlemagne, or, like Voltaire, for Henry IV?

Chateaubriand wanted, first of all, to paint the Roman provinces in their entirety, it being his view that epic by its nature required a broad ethnographic and geographic purview. Thus, although he had begun work in 1802, and had certainly completed a first draft by 1806, he thought it necessary in that same year to embark upon a long journey from Paris to Jerusalem and back, in order to track down images for his poem. Since he accepted the then commonly held view that the barbarian invasions of the fifth and sixth centuries had been colossal inundations of an apocalyptic kind, it had been necessary to choose a historical moment when the administrative apparatus and infrastructure of the Empire were in sufficiently good repair to permit a peregrination. His choice of period had allowed him to treat both profane and sacred Antiquity, to paint the various provinces of the Empire, to take the reader amongst the Franks and the Gauls, 'to the cradle of our ancestors', and at the same time to depict Greece, Italy, Judaea, Egypt, Sparta, Athens, Naples, Jerusalem and much else besides.[36]

Second, with the collapse of the tetrarchy and the triumph of Constantine, the focus of the Empire shifted to the Emperor's newly founded city in the East. *Les Martyrs* ends, in fact, with the martyrdom of the hero and heroine of the work, the terrible death of the last and most vicious of the tetrarchs, Galerius, and the entrance of Constantine's army into Rome. It could therefore be argued that the period of the Great Persecution (303–313 AD) was the last moment at which Chateaubriand could have employed Rome as a backdrop for his book.

A third reason for choosing the Rome of the tetrarchs lay in the commonplace identification between the sufferings of the early Christians and the Terror. Thus, in 1810 Chateaubriand had observed that his readers had been anticipating 'a kind of Book of Martyrs, a historical narrative of the persecutions suffered by the Church from Nero to Robespierre'.[37] This was to equate Terror with dechristianization, and in a letter to the young François Guizot, whose father had died on the scaffold at Nîmes in 1794, Chateaubriand drew a direct comparison between the martyrs of the Great Persecution and those of the Revolution, and expressed the fervent hope that the prayers of the latter in heaven might win expiation for the guilt of the French.[38]

Fourth, Boulainvilliers had been especially concerned with the period of Diocletian and the tetrarchs, and had claimed that Constantius Chlorus, father of Constantine, had been responsible for settling a number of Franks, known as *laeti*, on the left bank of the Rhine. Since Eudorus, the hero of *Les Martyrs*, joins Constantius's army at the end of book 5, and fights the Franks in book 6, one cannot help but be struck by the following passage in Boulainvilliers:

> Constantius Chlorus . . . made [a major incursion into] Germany, in the course of which, having subjugated many different peoples, he judged that it would be useful to the Empire . . . to transfer some into Gaul. He in fact effected this transfer of persons, with the permission of the Emperors Diocletian and Maximian, in around 302 AD.[39]

Since Constantius Chlorus was the tetrarch most reluctant to persecute the Christians, it was peculiarly fitting that Eudorus should have enlisted in his army. It is also curious to note that the historical Eumenius – the rhetoric teacher of Eudorus, Constantine, Jerome and Augustine in the early books of *Les Martyrs* – should also have been the author of the Latin panegyrics to Constantius telling of the settlement of the *laeti*. The Franks had been altogether unknown to Tacitus, and so, for the composition of a truly national epic, embracing Celts (Armoricans), Romano-Gauls and Franks, Chateaubriand could have chosen no earlier period than that of the tetrarchy.

Chateaubriand's ambition in *Les Martyrs* was to connect 'the cradle of the ancestors' to 'the cradle of the Christian religion', or, in more concrete terms, to link the peoples of France both to Jerusalem and to Rome. In order to illustrate the arguments expounded in *Le Génie du Christianisme*, he displaced the Rome of Fabricius and of Curius Dentatus, and celebrated in its stead Judaea and the birth of the Catholic Church in the Catacombs. Like the Schlegels and Staël, Chateaubriand contrasted barbarian religion, a pure polytheism which saw God in everything, with the paganism of Antiquity, corrupted by false imaginings:

> crude though these Franks are, they have a huge advantage over the Greeks and the Romans: they open their hearts more easily to Jesus Christ. If they are so docile, it is because they have virtually no old errors to uproot. They have not, like the pagan peoples, divinised their passions in order to worship them.[40]

In short, savages in their forests, whether in the Americas or on the other side of the fortified line of the Roman Empire, were less corrupted than pagans, and therefore better able to appreciate the Gospel.

The martyrs of the title are Eudorus and Cymodocea, and their encounter – and subsequent love for each other – allowed Chateaubriand to stage a contest between Homeric and Judaeo-Christian values. For Cymodocea was the daughter of Demodocus, a priest and descendant of

the Homerides, who lived formerly on the island of Chios and traced
their descent from Homer. Eudorus, although also Greek, was a convert
to Christianity. As Chateaubriand observed in 1810:

> Through the fiction of this family of Homer, I was able to trace mores back to
> the heroic centuries without offending probability overmuch. One may read-
> ily suppose that an old priest of Homer, the last descendant of this poet, and a
> poet himself, should have preserved, so to speak, the mores of his family. In
> the highlands of Scotland one may see clans or tribes which for centuries have
> kept the language, dress and customs of their forefathers.[41]

Reviewers of *Les Martyrs* plainly found the presence of pristine Homeric
values in the third century AD a little incongruous, but Chateaubriand
justified his decision in terms of the need to provide nascent Christianity
with a worthy adversary.[42] Had he not presented a thriving Homeric
culture, he would then have been rebuked, he said, 'for having contrasted Christian mores in all their youth and beauty with pagan mores in
their decadence'.[43] Just as Rousseau had demanded uncorrupted mores
for the founding of a free polis, so too for the creation of Christian-
national community in the post-revolutionary period one had to summon
forth tribal values from the wild edge of history. If the nation is at once
very young (uncorrupted) and as old as time (autochthonous), it is
because it lies outside the annals of decadence.

The 'great literary trial' of Antiquity begins with Cymodocea's discovery of the young Christian, Eudorus, asleep in a wood. 'Je suis fille
d'Homère', Cymodocea announces, 'aux chants immortels'; to which the
stranger replies, 'Je connais un plus beau livre que le sien'.[44] In the
second book, the two meet again. Cymodocea chants, to the accompani-
ment of her lyre, legends of the Greek gods and passages from the
Odyssey; Eudorus takes down a Hebrew cinnor from a willow tree, and
sings a canticle incorporating motifs from both the Old and the New
Testament. The 'systematic' comparison between paganism and Christianity is then interrupted by book 3, which contains a much-criticized
account of Heaven, of the saints and angels and of the Holy Trinity. In his
defence, Chateaubriand invoked the Christian epics of Dante, Tasso and
Milton, all poems that were not well known in France at this date.

Fauriel aside, there were, for example, almost no serious students of
the Divine Comedy in Paris. It is also true, however, that Chateaubriand's Christian 'marvellous' is no more successful here than it had
been in *Les Natchez*. The function of book 3 was quite simply to apply
the gold of providence to the wooden frame: Eudorus was fated to be a
martyr who would, through his death, bring Christianity to Rome and
therefore to the whole world. Contemporary critics were offended by the

fact that Eudorus was not a historical figure, nor, indeed, a character taken from an earlier epic (as Demodocus, for instance, was). Yet Chateaubriand, in planning a specifically Christian epic, had been mindful of the thousands of martyrs who had died, as Milton had written, 'unsung', and he aimed therefore to celebrate the many for whom Eudorus stood. Refusing the values of paganism, humility was of more weight than a proud name:

> This victim who would overcome Hell by virtue of the sufferings and merits of the blood of Jesus-Christ; this victim who would march at the head of a thousand other victims, was not chosen from the ranks of princes and kings. Born of an obscure condition the better to imitate the Saviour of the world . . . through him, a martyr forgotten by history, those poor whom the world disregards, and who will suffer for their faith, find honour.[45]

When, therefore, Chateaubriand defended his choice of unknown martyr, he contrasted the humble Eudorus with 'these great men Plutarch has transmitted to us'. He then observed that

> God often chooses in the most humble of circumstances the man whose trials will draw down the blessings of heaven upon the nations . . . Eudorus will thus be the representative of the heroes of two religions; those who are disregarded by the world but crowned with glory in heaven; and those others who are illustrious while on earth but deprived of divine glory.[46]

The reader also learns that Eudorus will sin, and therefore offend the Church; that the Angel of the Lord will take him by the hand and lead him among the nations of the earth, so that he may see the Gospel being established on every side; that he will marry Cymodocea, a fellow martyr, and that Constantine will make the Empire Christian.

With the fourth book of *Les Martyrs*, Eudorus's narrative begins. Travelling from Brindisi along the Appian Way to Rome, he is overwhelmed by the splendour of the Forum, the Capitol, the Campus Martius and the Pantheon. Yet there are no echoes here of the pronouncements of Montesquieu and Rousseau on the course of Roman history. There are no references, indeed, to the fatal expansion of the city after the Second Punic War, and to the subsequent corruption of mores and loss of republican liberty. The free, armed republic of Machiavelli's *Discourses* is replaced by an opposition, deeply Augustinian in tone, between pagan idolatry and Christianity. It is therefore peculiarly fitting that Augustine himself should appear, anachronism notwithstanding, in books 3 and 4.

However, three, not two, systems of values are on display. For between barbarian, polytheistic mores and Christianity there lie the perniciously negative doctrines of the sophists, who are evidently followers of Voltaire in Roman dress. Eudorus's experience of Imperial Rome is modelled upon Chateaubriand's own time in old regime Paris: 'The three years of a dissolute youth spent in Rome were enough to cause me almost entirely to forget my religion. I almost attained that state of indifference which is so hard to cure, and which leaves one with fewer resources than crime does.'[47] Having all but forgotten 'the humble church of the Christians', Eudorus takes up the study of rhetoric, much as Chateaubriand himself had become a *philosophe* in Paris. While studying under Eumenius, Eudorus forms a friendship with Augustine, with Jerome and with Constantine, the future Emperor and saviour of the Church. The passages featuring Augustine and Jerome are among the most delightful in *Les Martyrs*, and book 5, set in an altogether Greek Naples, has a particular charm. Glancing references to the *Aeneid* and to the *Civitas Dei* serve at the same time to reinforce Chateaubriand's systematic comparison between the values of paganism and those of Christianity.

To understand why the representation of the Imperial Court altered in Chateaubriand's drafts of his book, between 1802 and 1809, we require a thumbnail account of his relations with Napoleon in those years. He had returned to France in 1800, thanks to the restoration of order which the First Consul had effected, and the fame he had won with *Atala* was redoubled through Fontanes's careful handling of *Le Génie du Christianisme*, the publication of which was timed to coincide with the Concordat. Yet the execution of the Duc D'Enghien had shocked him deeply, placing him at odds with the nascent First Empire. A series of increasingly critical articles in the *Mercure de France* culminated in a savage attack upon Napoleon, in which Chateaubriand had cast himself as a Tacitus who would write a *Germania*:

> The Muse has often had to narrate crimes. But there is something so lofty in the diction of the poet that even sin seems to be rendered less heinous by it. The historian alone refuses to diminish its horror. When in the silence of abasement nothing is left but the chains of slavery and the voice of the traitor, and it is as dangerous to incur his favour as to earn his displeasure – then the historian appears as the avenger of nations. In vain does Nero count upon his luck. Tacitus was born in his kingdom, unknown he grew up near the ashes of Germanicus; and Providence had already delivered the reputation of the world's master into the hands of an obscure child.[48]

This passage, which Guizot learned by heart, and recited to Staël shortly after its publication, precipitated the shutting down of the *Mercure*, at the end of July 1807.[49] So it was that Chateaubriand and Staël, in opposed camps under the Consulate, formed a common front which, by the very nature of their predicament, helped to breathe new life into the Germanist interpretation of liberty in general, and of the history of France in particular. In the process, the Tacitus to whom the *idéologues* such as Cabanis and Fauriel had referred during the last days of the Consulate, the unrivalled chronicler of tyrannies, was superseded by the author of the *Germania*. The German Wars of Liberation further reinforced the image of tribal liberties beyond the fortified line of the Roman Empire and, as a consequence, French national identity after 1815 remained a curiously hybrid affair. There was, on the one hand, the Grande Nation, perpetuated, in parodic form, in Napoleon III's military adventures, and, on the other hand, a culture whose essence was thought to be Germanic or Celtic. Guizot and Thierry might strive to preserve a balance between Roman and Germanic elements in French history, but the triumphant Indo-Europeanism of the mid nineteenth century favoured rather the aristocratic, militarist and Germanist positions adopted by Ernest Renan in *La Réforme Intellectuelle et Morale*, although not in his now better-known lecture on the nation.

Harsh as Chateaubriand's veiled judgement of Napoleon was, the passages on the 'sophists', a catch-all term designed to refer to the Encyclopédists, the Conventionnels and the *idéologues*, far exceed it in ferocity. There had been some admiration for the Jacobins, in the *Essai Historique*, but this had now evaporated. Hierocles, the principal villain in *Les Martyrs*,

> endlessly spouts such phrases as liberty, virtue, science, the progress of Enlightenment, the happiness of mankind; but this Brutus is a vile courtier, this Cato is prey to shameful passions, this apostle of tolerance is the most intolerant of mortals, and this worshipper of humanity is a blood-thirsty persecutor.[50]

The historical Hierocles was responsible, according to the shrill and obsessive testimony of Lactantius, for 'instigating' and 'recommending' the persecutions of the Christians, and Chateaubriand therefore took care to blame this sophist, along with Maximinus Galerius, rather than Diocletian himself.[51] In book 16 of *Les Martyrs* there is a debate on the nature of religion between Hierocles, Symmachus, high priest of Jupiter and in fact the author of a famous apology of pagan beliefs, and Eudorus, and in book 18 the persecutions suffered by the early Christians are likened to those of the Terror. 'In depicting the sorrows of the Romans', wrote Chateaubriand, 'I seek to depict the sorrows of the French . . . we too, we have seen you on the scaffold and in the catacombs.'[52] Even the administrative apparatus of the Terror is described, and the mass drownings at Nantes mentioned.[53]

Excommunicated by Marcellinus, Bishop of Rome, Eudorus made his way, in the company of Augustine and Jerome, to Naples. Chateaubriand takes his habitual delight in landscape, depicting Posilippo, the sun rising above Vesuvius, and the chain of volcanic islands in the bay. Noting that Parthenope was built upon a siren's tomb, he sees the city as so many others on the Grand Tour had seen it, as the site of luxury and indolence, home of the *lazzaroni*. The reader observes Augustine, his *Aeneid* in his hand, wandering beside Lake Avernus and, at Virgil's tomb, reading the story of Dido. There follows a scene at the tomb of Scipio Africanus, in the course of which Jerome and Augustine declare their respective vocations, the one bound for Carthage, the other for Gaul. Back in Rome, Eudorus hears rumours of marauding armies of Goths and Franks in the northern marches. Exiled and disgraced, he enlists in Constantius's army, based in Agrippina (Köln).

In books 6, 7, 8, 9 and 10 of *Les Martyrs*, Chateaubriand addressed the task of, in his own words, 'singing the nation'. The Greek hero of the epic, whose martyrdom in book 24 would precipitate the final adoption of Christianity by the Roman Empire, here encountered the Gauls and Franks in battle array. We may gather something of the impact of Chateaubriand's account upon his audience by considering Augustin Thierry's famous reminiscence of his first reading of *Les Martyrs*, while at college, in 1810:

> At first I had a sense of a vague charm, and something akin to a bedazzlement of the imagination; but when I came to Eudorus's narrative, this living history of the Empire at the time of its decline, an indefinable but more active and more reflective interest tied me to the picture of the eternal city, of the court of the Roman Emperor, of the march of a Roman army into the swamps of Batavia, and of its encounter with an army of Franks.

Although he had read the standard textbooks on Clovis and on early Frankish history, he had not expected the Franks to be so 'terrible', clad as they were 'in the hides of bears, seals, urochs and wild-boars', nor had he had any inkling of 'this fortified camp . . . with chariots harnessed to huge oxen, of this army disposed in a wedge formation in which one could make out only a forest of javelins, animal hides and half-naked bodies'. Thierry had been struck by the dramatic contrast between 'the savage warrior' and 'the civilised soldier', and the war chant of the Franks had made a truly electric impression upon him. He paced up and down, repeating at the top of his voice:

Pharamond! Pharamond! We have fought with the sword.
We have hurled the double-bladed franchisc;
The sweat dripped from the warriors' brows
And streamed down their arms.
The eagles and the yellow-footed birds uttered cries of joy;
The crow swam in the blood of the dead; the whole ocean
Was but a single wound.
The virgins have wept for a long time . . .

As far as Thierry and Guizot were concerned, the beauty of this passage, which closes with a stirring evocation of the *barditus* described in the third chapter of the *Germania*, lay in the ethnographic colouring, which marked out Chateaubriand's prose from that of Boulainvilliers, Du Bos or Mably.[54] Under the Restoration, however, as I explain in chapter 10, the liberal historians would heighten the exotic qualities of the Merovingian Franks still more, in order to found the substance of the nation upon the less flamboyant continuities of the Gallo-Roman cities.

## Observing the Celts

Even as Chateaubriand was transferring the attributes of tribal liberty from the New World to the Old, members of the Société pour les Observateurs de l'Homme, disbanded in 1804, were flocking to the Académie Celtique, whose inaugural meeting was held at the Petits-Augustins on 30 March 1805.[55] Yet the *idéologues* were so much out of favour under the First Empire that this aspect of the new organization's researches was initially somewhat masked. Indeed, the inaugural discourses were all more or less chauvinist in tone. Thus Joseph Lavallée, mindful of Napoleon's present enemies, charged the Celtic Academy founded under Charles II with usurpation, on the grounds that Britain's original peoples had come from Armorica (Brittany), which therefore had right of precedence. Lavallée followed up his preliminary drum-rolls with invocations of the primordial nature of the Celtic language, culture and religion. The Celts, he declared, were the first people, who had colonized Europe and much of Asia, and whose language had left its mark upon every other. The followers of Pythagoras, Orpheus and Zoroaster, Lavallée continued, had inherited the religion of the Druids, as had the Chinese and the Indians. Monotheism, the doctrines of the immortality of the soul, of the punishment of the wicked and of the redemption of the good were all, in Lavallée's view, Celtic inventions.[56]

In the second inaugural discourse, delivered by the philologist Eloi Johanneau, we learn that 'almost all the peoples of Europe are the descendants of Celts, almost all are the children of Celtic: reunited they form even today a single large family'.[57] Pan-Celtism was here a syrup to sweeten the concept, often canvassed early in the First Empire, of a universal, patrimonial monarchy, and other contributors who had reached an accommodation with the regime would also pour it where necessary. Yet the Académie Celtique's brief was less narrow than one might at first suppose. The *Mémoires* were subtitled 'Researches into Celtic, Gallic and French Antiquities', and took the whole of the early history of the country as their field of enquiry. Thus Alexandre Lenoir, in charge of the Musée des Antiquités Françaises since 1791, wrote at length on the French cathedrals, while Dulaure's comments upon the municipal senates of Roman Gaul seem almost to prefigure the studies published after 1820 by Thierry and by Guizot. Furthermore, where the questionnaires drawn up by Volney and by Degérando for the use of scientific travellers have rightly been recognized as pioneering documents in the history of modern ethnology, similar claims have been made, with as much justification, for the contribution of the Académie Celtique to the study of folklore.[58] This is particularly true of the list of questions drawn up by Dulaure and Mangourit and dispatched to Prefects, so that every single inhabitant of each department might be quizzed as to their language, beliefs and customs.[59] The first series of questions concerned festivals relating to solstices and equinoxes; the second, customs relating to birth, marriage and death; and the third, ancient monuments (that is to say, megalithic monuments at that time reckoned to be of Celtic provenance). Finally, a fourth category of questions touched upon general beliefs and superstitions, and would have provided a researcher in the field with a compellingly interesting programme of study. When Arnold Van Gennep, generally held to be the founder of modern French folklore studies, drew up his own questionnaire for use in the Savoy, in the 1930s, he in fact adopted as his own the first, second and fourth categories, merely replacing questions regarding ancient monuments with enquiries into 'material ethnography' (houses, gardens and furniture).[60]

Just as Van Gennep's monograph on rites of passage and Durkheim's study of the elementary forms of the religious life still bore, even in the early twentieth century, the scorch-marks of the year II, so too in the volumes published by the Académie Celtique we may discern, because the fire had only recently been put out, many signs of the Revolution's investigations into the essential nature of ritual. Thus, as one reads Dulaure and Mangourit's famous questionnaire one is constantly reminded of Marie-Joseph Chénier, Rabaut Saint-Etienne and Romme's work on the calendar, or of the meditations of La Revellière-Lépeaux (himself an active member of the Académie Celtique) on rites of passage, or of the reflections concerning tombs and monuments under the Directory.[61] A history of ethnology, to be altogether accurate, would have to provide some account of the impact of the French Revolution upon enquiries into the origins of social forms.

So diverse are the theoretical allegiances of those who contributed to the Académie Celtique that it is difficult to supply a generalization that will cover every case. Some were Romantic Druidists, and, like Jacques Le Brigant or Nicholas de Bonneville, saw Celtic culture everywhere, and in everything. By contrast, Volney ridiculed the notion that Celtic might be the first, antediluvian language, and Mangourit and Johanneau agreed with him.[62] Besides, if the Celts had really preceded all other peoples, as was claimed, what then could the relation between the Celtic language and Sanskrit be? We know that Volney, who had acquired a smattering of both Persian and Sanskrit from Alexander Hamilton, had wished to model the Académie Celtique upon the Asiatic Society of Calcutta. Yet in Sir William Jones's pioneering statement, the chief emphasis had been upon the affinities between Sanskrit, Greek and Latin, with the case for Gothic and Celtic being considered somewhat weaker. Friedrich Schlegel had responded to French claims of primacy by elevating Sanskrit to the status of an *Ursprache*, while treating German as eldest son and heir and strenuously denying any kinship between the latter and Celtic.[63] Even though the advocates of primacy did not cry so shrilly in France as in Germany, the evidence from the Académie Celtique suggests that historians have been in error in ascribing the invention of cultural nationalism to the Germans alone.[64] For there was a general replacement in Europe of the city-nation by the tribe-nation, vested at the same time with a universal mission and a particular, earthed origin. Through this momentous transformation, the agora fell silent just as stones began to speak, in a remarkable development not entirely explicable in terms of the birth of the science of archaeology.

## Addressing the nation

In response to the special claims made, during and after the First World War, for the German nation's universal mission, a number of French philosophers saw it as their duty to refute the arguments, derived from Fichte, upon which such claims rested. Thus Emile Boutroux, a Kantian who had collaborated with Durkheim, denounced the entire legacy of German idealist philosophy, and the pernicious influence of the *Addresses to the German Nation* in particular. After the battle of Jena, so the argument goes, Fichte had come to distinguish between the purity of a German essence and the impurity of other peoples, and had as a consequence treated the German race as God's representative on earth. Proof of this mission was supplied by 'the essentially spontaneous, primitive and living character of the German language as opposed to the Latin language'.[65] This 'spiritual' Germanism, finding its fullest expression in the Wars of Liberation of 1813–15, was later to become a 'material' Germanism, and Fichte's lofty pedagogic vision an alibi for the use of brute force.[66] Boutroux recalled his visit to the University of Heidelberg in January 1869, and lamented the fact that, although Germany was for him the land of metaphysics, music and poetry, outside the lecture halls the talk was not of Kant, Beethoven or Goethe, but of seizing Alsace and Lorraine. Heinrich von Treitschke's lectures were, he said, 'inflammatory harangues against the French, incitements to hatred and war'.[67] Where German liberals had contested Prussian hegemony, nationalists such as Treitschke had argued that liberty would be realized through the creation, by force, of unity.

No publicist writing of such issues in 1915 could do otherwise than recall the Franco-Prussian War, and the disputed title to Alsace-Lorraine. If, then, I linger over the more than somewhat shabby propaganda skirmishes of 1870–71, it is because for many decades it provided scholars and pamphleteers from France, Germany, Italy and England with a benchmark by which to measure their various positions on the principle of nationality.

Theodor Mommsen, the celebrated historian of ancient Rome, sent a number of open letters, later republished as a pamphlet, to the Italian press, in order to establish a link between the two most prominent national causes of the day, that of Italy and that of Germany. In the second of his letters, dated 20 August 1870, he justified his country's claims to Alsace and Lorraine or, rather, Alsatz and Lothringen, on the grounds of race, language and historical precedent, his arguments then being contested point for point by Fustel de Coulanges, the author of *La Cité Ancienne*. In the most general terms, Mommsen asserted that Alsace and Lorraine were German territory, and that the war fought in response to French aggression was not one of conquest, but one of restoration. If the disputed territories were essentially German, it was because their populations were of the German race; for want of biometric evidence, Mommsen then had recourse to linguistics. For in Alsace, 917 communes spoke German, whereas a mere 20 spoke French; in Lorraine, of 46,508 people resident in the 76 communes of the Meurthe, a mere 6,870 could speak French.[68]

In reply, Fustel distinguished between two principles of nationality, that espoused by Germany and by the German pamphleteers, and that

defended by the rest of Europe. Where Germany professed itself justified in seizing a province by force, so long as it could claim that the same
race – defined, in terms identical to those employed later by Kossinna, as
Aryan, dolichocephalous and blond – occupied both territories, the rest
of Europe maintained that the principle of nationality simply entitled a
province to withhold obedience from a foreign ruler. In order to drive
apart, for the purposes of his polemic, the cases of Italy and of Germany,
Fustel noted that this principle would not entitle Piedmont to conquer
Milan and Venice, but would justify the Milanese and the Venetians in
throwing off the Austrian yoke and joining up, of their own free will,
with the Piedmontese. For, he continued, 'the distinguishing feature of a
nation is neither race nor language. Men feel in their hearts that they are
one and the same people when they have a community of ideas, interests,
affections, memories and hopes. This is what makes a fatherland.'[69] The
importance of the dispute over the principle of nationality at the time of
the Franco-Prussian War lies not only in the fact that it coloured some of
Nietzsche's early writings, *The Birth of Tragedy* among them, and
Renan's lecture, delivered in 1882. For, in addition, it defined the terms
in which the problem has until very recently been posed, in, for example,
Federico Chabod's lectures on *L'Idea di Nazione*, given in the winter of
1943–44 in Milan, or in Thomas Mann's *Doktor Faustus*.

For Boutroux, then, the 'War of Unification' of 1864–71 had been a
critical exacerbation of lines of argument laid down during the 'Wars of
Liberation' of 1813–15, and it had found its logical conclusion in the 'War
for World Domination' which had broken out in 1914.[70] The central
charge levelled against Fichte by Boutroux, and subsequently repeated
by many others, had been that, though a cosmopolitan thinker up until
1806, the shock of the Battle of Jena had transformed him into a
nationalist and a pan-Germanist. What truth is there in such accusations?

To begin with, no one would dispute the impact of the defeat of the
Prussian army upon Fichte's thought. Everyone in Europe was aware of
the scale of the catastrophe, and there is no reason that Fichte should
have been less appalled than, say, Hegel, or Niebuhr, by an event that
led to the wholesale subjugation of the German states to Napoleon. We
know also, from the testimony of his son, that Fichte was in the habit of
reading aloud the passages in Tacitus that featured Arminius even as he
was composing the *Addresses*, and that he finished his own translation of
*Annals*, book 1, chapters 55–72 shortly after he had completed the
crucial fourth address, on 'the chief difference between the Germans and
other peoples of Teutonic Descent'.[71] When Fichte gave the *Addresses*,
Berlin was under French occupation, yet the first three can hardly be
mistaken for an incitement to insurrection, since references to an 'alien
power' are both rare and discreet, and serve merely to introduce the

topic in hand, that of defining, in Kantian (and, of course, Fichtean) terms, an authentically national education. With the fourth discourse, however, reminders of the *Germania* occur at every turn; the Germans, it was asserted, were particularly suited to this radically new pedagogy. Epithets such as 'special' and 'peculiar' seem to derive from chapters 2 and 4 of Tacitus's treatise, as does the claim that the Germans, if the recent catastrophe be bracketed out, had always been as they then were.[72]

What, then, were the Germans? In Fichte's view they belonged, like the Scandinavians, to a branch of the Teutonic race which had remained true to its origins. For they had both 'remained in the original dwelling places of the ancestral stock' and retained their original language, which 'has been alive ever since it first issued from the force of nature', whereas the other branches of the Teutonic race 'speak a language which has movement on the surface only but is dead at the root'.[73] Boutroux, reflecting upon the claims made by Fichte for the 'first people' and the 'first language', believed that the *Addresses* advocated the ultimate obliteration of foreigner by *Urvolk*. Just as the Absolute Ego in Fichte's system was supposed to overwhelm and annihilate the Non-Ego, so the Germans, being purely and absolutely a people (even *the* people), would obliterate other, non-Germanic peoples. Furthermore, his apparent admission that *ius gentium* did not exist was interpreted as an expression of *Realpolitik* as brutal as that espoused by Treitschke. However, Boutroux's contemporary, Xavier Léon, aghast at the militarist call to 'send Fichte into the trenches', set about the task of rehabilitating his philosophical hero. In order to press home the point that the chauvinisms of world war had not altered his views, Léon published the first volume of his monograph in precisely the form in which, in 1913, it had been delivered to the printers. For Fichte's system had enjoyed considerable prestige in pre-war France, for example among the Durkheimians, and Léon himself had believed it to be true for all time. If, nonetheless, he embarked upon the writing of a study designed to establish the exact relation between Fichte's writings and the dominant intellectual and philosophical currents of the age, it was in order to establish the essential continuity of his thought.[74] The gist of Léon's case was that Fichte, in a climate dominated by an increasingly aggressive Romanticism, had simply adapted his doctrines to those of his adversaries in order, surreptitiously, to overturn them. He had remained at heart a revolutionary and a Jacobin, with a visceral dislike of Caesarism and of pan-Germanism.

In his monumental study, Léon thus showed in exhaustive detail how Fichte had repeatedly echoed the mystical, neo-Catholic positions of the Schlegels and Schelling, the better to refute them. In particular, he had denied that the stages of world history were direct expressions of divine providence.[75] Indeed, in both the *Grundzüge des gegenwärtigen Zeit-alters* and in the *Addresses*, the Romantics were blamed for the decadence of the historical epoch, one of 'mere material self-seeking', which had ended with the battle of Jena. Léon's case hangs upon the close correspondence that may be discerned between chapters 4 and 7 of the *Addresses*, and lectures given by August-Wilhelm Schlegel in Berlin, in 1803–04 (recast for a Viennese audience in 1808). There Schlegel, in epistolary contact with his brother in Paris, sang the praises of medieval Christendom, and celebrated the legacy of the barbarian invasions. If modern peoples were viewed as, first and foremost, the descendants of Franks, Burgundians, Goths, Lombards or Vandals, then all were of Germanic stock.[76] The Schlegels' nationalism thus combined an emphasis upon cultural diversity or specificity with a cosmopolitanism, to be carried politically and religiously by Holy Roman Emperor and Roman Catholic Church and culturally by the German language. To restore the unity of Christendom, even a Crusade would be justified.

Although Fichte echoed what the Schlegels had to say on German history, language and culture, his intention had been, in Léon's opinion, to appropriate the central theses of Romanticism in order to correct or to combat them.[77] His philosophical system had arisen in step with the French Revolution, and represented to a large extent a transposition of its founding principles. For example, he regarded the Absolute Ego's struggle to eradicate the thing-in-itself (defended by many in Germany, as we have seen, for theological motives), as analogous to the insurrection of the sovereign people of France against feudal residues. So loyal was Fichte to the principles of the French Revolution that he had twice, in 1795 and in 1799, thought of offering his services as militant philosopher and orator to the First Republic. Far from being disillusioned, he believed that, after 1806, Germany might assume the mantle that France had let fall. Nor should Fichte's Jacobin conception of a revolutionary nation be confused with the Schlegels' rapturous paeans to the Holy Roman Empire, which are explicitly criticized in the thirteenth address.

On closer inspection, the charge of pan-Germanism proved to have been wide of the mark also. For although Fichte had his singing robes on, he was especially concerned, as Martial Guéroult rightly emphasized, with exchange between cultures.[78] The vocations of both Germans and neo-Latins were honoured:

each part must recognise . . . its own vocation and that of the other, and in accordance therewith each part must make use of the other. It is especially necessary for each part to consent to assist the other, and to leave its characteristic quality untouched, if good progress is to be made in the general and complete culture of the whole.[79]

Guéroult further remarked that Boutroux had been wrong to wrench the Fichtean term *Anstoss* (absolute limitation by clash) from its proper context, which concerned the annihilation of the thing-in-itself by the Absolute Ego. Where relations between different egos, whether individuals or individual nationalities were involved, the terms used were *Einwirkung* (influence), *Zusammenwirkung* (cooperation) and *Wechselwirkung* (reciprocal action).[80] Thus, in the fifth address, Fichte noted that those peoples who had separated off from the Mother Nation had, through the Renaissance, acquired a much closer relation to classical Antiquity, so that 'when these images of the ancient World in their new form reach that part of the original stock which, by its retention of the language, has remained in the stream of the original culture, they will arouse the attention of the people and stimulate them to activity on their own part'.[81] In the sixth address, Fichte then paid tribute to the Italian Renaissance for the *Anregung* (stimulation) it had offered to Luther, to Descartes and to Leibniz.[82] That he believed revolutionary France, through the Declaration of Rights of Man and the Citizen, to have supplied as great an inspiration to the world is plain from all his writings.

The *Addresses* also at points sever the connection between the quality of being German, or a free, reasonable being, from either race or language.[83] There is no denying the philological accuracy of the defences of Fichte mounted by Léon and Guéroult, not least because they are to some extent reinforced by Meinecke's more critical account, and yet, for the purposes of my own argument, something more remains to be said. It is true, first of all, that many in the Napoleonic period were driven too much on to hostile ground, mined by categories closely associated with Romanticism. Much as in our own times one might be forced, no matter how reluctantly, to use the term 'postmodern', a catch-all hanging like a cloud over only too real and momentous changes, so Hegel, for example, employed the category *Volksgeist*, which, though derived from Montesquieu, had an irrationalist flavour by 1806. In Fichte's case, the difficulty is compounded by the fact that his own ethical system, having exerted a profound influence upon the Schlegels and Schelling at Jena, where he too had resided between 1795 and 1799, had been much derided in the new century. Off balance and battered, he appears to have given too many hostages to Romanticism. Secondly, and at a deeper level, Fichte's transcendental idealism bears all the characteristic marks of the transition between an age of cities and an age of nations. Like many whose thought was forged in the fire of 1789, he set little store by Rousseau's wistful retreat to the haven offered by small cities or sheltered tribes, preferring to stride open-eyed on causeways, in the belief that a freely acting will could, as Kelly observed, 'correlate right with the teleological "plan" of history'.[84] Instead of deriving solace from a completed nature,

Fichte took it to be the duty of humankind to subdue it altogether, and so to eradicate the wilderness between cities. Volcanoes, earthquakes, even death itself, are tamed in his breathless vision of redeemed time. The acropolitical series of golden ages is explicitly repudiated in the *Addresses*, the 'round dance' deplored.[85]

Yet a price was paid for dissolving the cities of transience into the mirage of the eternal nation. For, as Kelly again noted, while nature for a Jacobin bespoke equality, 'the teleological perspective of idealism, which abases "nature" and sets the liberation of spirit as its goal, introduces a qualitative disparity between those more and those less able to achieve this.'[86] The damaging exclusions produced through Friedrich Schlegel's reading of the distinction between inflected and agglutinative languages are matched, albeit in another form, in Fichte's seventh address:

> whoever believes in spirituality and in the freedom of this spirituality, and who wills the eternal development of this spirituality by freedom, wherever he may have been born and whatever language he speaks is of our blood; he is one of us, and will come over to our side. Whoever believes in stagnation, retrogression, and the round dance of which we spoke, or who sets a dead nature at the helm of the world's government, wherever he may have been born and whatever language he speaks, is non-German and a stranger to us, and it is to be wished that he would separate himself from us completely, and the sooner the better.[87]

It is true that the 'German' is defined here as one who, irrespective of their place of birth or language, practises the true philosophy, that is, transcendental idealism. Yet Fichte incontestably leaves the reader with the impression that transcendental idealists are produced within or through the German language, and not otherwise. The only solution to the paradox would seem to be that, while at one level he may be differentiated from the Romantics, whom he resolutely opposed upon so many occasions, at another, more inclusive level, he was swept downstream with them. A somewhat similar story must be told of Niebuhr, who recast the ancient city in terms of the tribe-nation.

## Recasting the city

Georg Barthold Niebuhr, the author of the *Roman History*, was born in Copenhagen in 1776. His father, Carsten Niebuhr, was a celebrated explorer who, from 1761 to 1767, had led an expedition across Egypt, Arabia, India and Persia.[88] The son inherited a passion for languages and, more specifically, an ambition to link classical Antiquity to cultures beyond the Mediterranean.[89] His time was divided between service of the state, first in Denmark and then in Prussia, and pure scholarship, but to say that he was torn between contrary vocations would not be accurate. For he claimed in later years that no one without first-hand knowledge of the political process could really understand the history of ancient Rome.

Because Niebuhr's hostility to the French Revolution grew deeper with the passing of the years, the events of 1820 and of 1830 leaving their mark upon the second edition of the *Roman History*, it is by no means a simple matter to arrive at a precise account of his response to that epochal event. One could perhaps begin by noting, first of all, that he did not altogether turn a deaf ear to the demands of 1789; second, that his paramount aim as a scholar and historian was to reclaim ancient Rome from the Jacobins; and third, that the image of the city that he bequeathed to his readers was, in several crucial respects, Germanic or, in Staël's terms, of the north and not of the south. As a child, Niebuhr was quite simply a prodigy, astonishingly erudite and possessed of a remarkable historical imagination. Precisely because he had been impressed, like so many of his contemporaries, by the Stoic virtue of the heroes of republican Rome, the Terror shocked him, although it did not occasion a complete disillusion with revolutionary Paris. Indeed, in the winter of 1794, he contemplated enrolment at the Ecole Normale.[90] Had he persevered with this plan, he would of course have heard Volney's lectures on historical method.

Niebuhr's own distinctions between true and distorted accounts of the ancient city turned upon a hostility towards the concept of social contract and an esteem for tradition. Several passages in the first edition of the *Roman History*, originally lectures at the University of Berlin in 1810–11 but published in 1811–12, thus distinguish between the systematic disdain shown in revolutionary France for time-honoured values and the respect of Roman republicans for their 'rich inheritance of laws and reminiscences'.[91] Tribute is therefore paid to Servius Tullius, in terms that remind us irresistibly of Edmund Burke, because his census was 'no arbitrary system, but the application of a form, transmitted by ancient usage'.[92] Niebuhr's first, rapturous audience included the founder of the historical school of law, but one should be wary of presuming a complete harmony between the arguments expounded in the *Roman History* and the essentially conservative doctrine of Karl von Savigny. In many passages, it is true, 'abstract' and 'geometric' destruction are reviled, but *Volksgeist* is not everywhere the presumed subject of history, as it was in the writings of Savigny and his circle.[93] A careful reading of the *Roman History* reveals, rather, a moderate reformist position akin to that of

Benjamin Constant in *Des Réactions Politiques*, or to that of Vincenzo Cuoco in his *Saggio Storico*. Notwithstanding Niebuhr's criticism in 1810–11 of all those who had written on Roman history politically rather than philologically, namely, Machiavelli, Montesquieu and, by implication, Rousseau, his own knowledge of the social structures of Schleswig-Holstein (then a duchy attached to Denmark), Prussia, England, Scotland and Ireland had taught him that contemporary disputes between the estates could be illuminated by reference to the struggle between the orders in republican Rome, and vice versa.[94]

Reference to plebeians and to patricians was a commonplace of revolutionary discourse, and Niebuhr could well have set eyes on the most intransigent formulations, by Babeuf, of the central conflict of Roman history.[95] To this pure case, however, Niebuhr brought his own knowledge, painfully won in 1796–97 and in 1800–06, of the domination of the political process in Schleswig-Holstein by a restricted number of German aristocratic families. Perceiving that the path of the Danish to high office was blocked, he transposed the haughty demeanour of the German oligarchs to the Roman patricians, in his *Geschichte der Römischen Staatsländerein*, drafted in 1803–06, and in both editions of the *Roman History*. When composing the *Geschichte*, a study of land tenure in Rome but really a trial run for his larger project, Niebuhr observed in a letter that 'no nobleman and landed proprietor will like it, at least if he is consistent'.[96] This would seem to be a wholly accurate observation, and it is worth adding that his sympathies for the excluded class were extended, in the case of Ireland, to cover the Irish Catholics and, in the canton of Berne, the Vaudois 'subjects'. Niebuhr therefore advocated reform, just so long as it were not violent or overly radical. He was no Ultra, then, and certainly the picture he gave of the history of Rome would serve to reinforce rather than to contradict the claims of Marx and Engels in 1848 regarding the all-pervasive fact of class struggle in human existence. 'Had the plebeians and their tribunes, which are called riotous', he noted in the *Geschichte*, 'not on the contrary displayed an indescribable patience, civil war must surely have broken out.' For the Patriciate, he warned, 'had become the victim of its own unjustified obstinacy and arrogance'.[97] Neither version of the *Roman History* undermined this central thesis, or wholly obscured the 'Machiavellian' or Rousseauist tribunate.[98]

The power of the patricians in ancient Rome derived, in Niebuhr's view, from the brute fact of conquest, which had established a caste system. Influenced by his father, by the intellectual traditions of the University of Göttingen and by the Schlegels, Niebuhr took the emphasis upon caste very seriously indeed, and so dissolved the history of Rome back into the prehistory of Europe, of the Near East and of Asia. He therefore noted the importance of the Lex Canuleia, which had accorded plebeians the right of *connubium*, or intermarriage, with patricians.[99] Yet the real achievement of Rome had been, in Niebuhr's opinion, to temper the power of the patrician gentes by ascribing a real (though not wholly symmetrical) entitlement to the plebeians. Thus, alongside a warrior nobility and its troops of armed vassals (the *clientela*), Servius Tullius raised up ' a class of free not noble land-owners'.[100] Had the king – although Niebuhr, as I show below, doubted his historical existence – not achieved so brilliant a compromise between the opposed parties, Rome would have suffered the fate of Etruria or of Sparta, polities that had failed to reform their constitutions, and therefore their armies. It was after all the Roman infantry, organized in the centuries, that had ensured the city's military triumphs, whereas the Etruscan and Spartan tactics depended upon 'nothing more than hasty incursions of cavalry and a half-armed mob of plunderers'.[101] Niebuhr's caustic criticisms here of the shortcomings in war of oligarchies undoubtedly reflect the case for the reform of the Prussian army made in the aftermath of the Battle of Jena, while his Whiggish insistence on the need for a creeping extension of the governing class, and his undisguised admiration for the Settlement of 1688, also matched the preoccupations of Chancellor von Stein.[102] For the defeat of Prussia in 1806 had shown that a conscript army of peasants commanded by a haughty, privileged aristocracy was no match for the battle-hardened French troops and an officer class open to the talents. Niebuhr had come to the notice of the Chancellor, and so set foot in Berlin, on 5 October 1806, a matter of days before Jena. Between 1806 and 1810, he was one of Stein's closest collaborators; privy, therefore, to the abolition of serfdom, and to far-reaching reforms of municipal administration, of the guilds and of taxation. At the same time, his plans for a history of Rome were taking shape. Once Stein had left office, Niebuhr tendered his own resignation and, as official state historiographer, delivered his celebrated lectures.[103]

The crucial step taken by Niebuhr, as by all advocates of the tribe-nation, was of course to deny the fact of transience, the eternity of a people then being guaranteed by the continuity of a lineage. In this respect his debt to Savigny, and to the historical school's deployment of the opposition in Roman jurisprudence between *societas* and *universitas*, between partnership and corporation, was certainly very great.[104] For what Niebuhr revered in the traditional social structure of Ditmarsh was its possession of the attributes of a corporation, namely, collective moral responsibility (as in the blood-feud) and organic cohesion.[105] This residual structure was paradoxically both on the edge of Germany's history and its essence, so that the nation was in truth a tribe-nation. Friedrich Meinecke objected in 1907 that Fichte's celebration, a hundred years before, of what was 'truly primal' or supra-historical in the German character reflected his inability, because of his residual cosmopolitanism, to arrive at a truly positive picture of the history of his nation. Yet if Fichte 'always aspired toward the eternal in the temporal', as Meinecke maintained, this was altogether the characteristic attitude, at once theological and political, of a prophet of the tribe-nation. At the point of transition between an age of cities and an age of nations, primacy was a necessary attribute of the promised community, imagined as at once outside the annals of decadence and the quintessence of the historical process. Notwithstanding Meinecke's acute insight into the ideological forms assumed by that epochal transformation, he stood so firmly within the age of nations, and subscribed so completely to the view that the state had all the attributes of a 'supra-individual' personality, that he was not able to apprehend the religious aspect of the principle of nationality.[106]

The *Roman History* is perhaps best known for the claim that, in addition to the annals composed by the pontiffs and tilted towards the patrician cause, there had existed *carmina*, or banquet songs, recording the travails and triumphs of the plebeians. Indeed, the entire history of the kings of Rome, which had supplied the scaffolding for the narratives of Machiavelli, Montesquieu and Rousseau, was but a prose version, Niebuhr maintained, of a sequence of lays.[107] As anyone who has read Macaulay's *Lays* will recall, the *carmina* have an aura of heroism, in part because Niebuhr in 1810 and 1811 was plainly attempting to substitute a Prussian or a German for a French Rome. He stood in his imagination with Fabricius or with Cato the Censor, casting the Greek mores which had so offended them in a Parisian mould. This reworking of Livy's providentialism was in a sense traditional, since it echoed the *translatio imperii*.[108]

Niebuhr advanced two seemingly contradictory claims regarding the relation between peoples. On the one hand, he declared that conquest, because it produced racial mixing, was almost invariably damaging to the conquered people which, in the long term, would lose its peculiar language, culture and laws.[109] The Ditmarshers, like the Samnites, stand in the *Roman History* as the paradigm of a free, original people. On the other hand, Niebuhr admitted that the Romans had never been an 'original' people, but from the start a coalition. Yet they had made a massive contribution to European civilization through the very existence of their vast empire.[110] Rome had founded or revived countless cities, and classical literature, Greek as well as Roman, had remained accessible, owing to the existence of the Romance languages. Roman law, likewise, had formed the nations within the *limes*, and would have as great a contribution to make to the culture of the Germans, who had lost touch with the mores of their ancestors.[111] Like Fichte, Niebuhr was thus

at pains to acknowledge the part played by the Romans in the formation
of European culture. The Germanism of the Napoleonic period did not
require a dogmatic denial of the intrinsic worth of the cultural inheritance of Rome. Savigny, for example, might as a historicist mock the
sublime legislators invoked by Machiavelli or by Rousseau, but his
research into the survival of the Roman municipalities, in the aftermath
of the barbarian invasions, later inspired Thierry, Guizot, Fauriel and
Cattaneo. Nonetheless, there was the clear implication in the writings of
a wide range of publicists that, just as there had once been a *translatio
imperii*, through the Merovingian and Carolingian dynasties, so too
would there be, in place of the godless universality of the French
Enlightenment, a characteristic expression of abstract, anatomizing reason (*Verstand*), a deeper universality established in the new century, a
*Vernunft* at once Christian and Germanic. In the exaltation of the
struggle against Napoleon, a pan-Germanism was increasingly evident in
the work of many publicists, Niebuhr among them. The German nation,
in his view, comprised those races that had not 'forsaken their home',
together with those that, having invaded the provinces of the Roman
Empire, 'did not drop their character', and so 'preserved the noble
peculiarities for which nothing can compensate'.[112] As a consequence, he
would in later years insist that the German-speaking areas of Switzerland
were by rights a part of a greater Germany.[113] I would give much to know
upon what general lines the talk ran when, as Prussian envoy to the Holy
See, he conversed with the young Giacomo Leopardi, the proponent of a
very different view of relations between north and south, and of the
overall impact of the barbarian invasions.

# PART IV

# City and Nation

The communes are the nation; they are the nation in the innermost asylum of its liberty.

Carlo Cattaneo, 'Sulla Legge Comunale e Provinciale'

# A Postscript from Milan

The Congress of Vienna sealed the triumph of legitimacy over popular sovereignty. At the mercy of the Holy Alliance, behind the bulwark raised by Metternich and Tsar Alexander I against the spread of liberalism, Europe lay chained in thought and frozen in an imagined Christian Middle Ages. The Habsburg dynasty once again ruled not merely Austria but also large areas of present-day Poland, the Czech lands, Slovakia, Croatia and Italy. In Lombardy and the Veneto, many patriots had turned against Napoleon in his last years, but the return of Austrian troops was to prove no less of a disillusionment. For with the army came a Viceroy, a swollen bureaucracy, a meddling and obtuse censorship and a feared secret service. Ludovico di Breme, one of the most prominent of the Lombard Romantics, observed in May 1816: 'Things are quiet here, very quiet: degradation, the extinction of all national energy and the evaporation of all thought proceed with barely a sound; nothingness itself is not more silent; it is the peace of the grave. I fear that the next generation may well find us all asleep.'[1] Stendhal described his beloved Milan in very much the same terms in 1817, but since he knew and admired Ludovico di Breme, the model in some respects for Fabrizio del Dongo, this is no cause for surprise. The fact, however, that the young Giacomo Leopardi, born in Recanati, an obscure corner of the Papal States, the son of a man wholly aligned with the Restoration and with the Maistrian arraignment of the Enlightenment, should adopt a similar lexicon, suggests that all those at odds with the settlement of 1815 contrasted the tedium of a suppressed life with the Titanic deeds of the previous generation.

There was nonetheless some comfort to be derived from the fact that Milan was not, and would not again be, as somnolent as Savoyard Turin or as the Curia.[2] Patriots from every corner of the peninsula had flocked to a city that, as the capital first of the Cisalpine Republic, then of the Kingdom of Italy, had been a flourishing cultural centre. 'Even at this late hour', Stendhal recorded in 1816, 'in the streets of Milan you may meet three or four hundred *enlightened* individuals, the intellectual cream of all the lands of Italy, recruited by Napoleon . . . to hold high office in his Italian kingdom.'[3] If the author of *Scarlet and Black* felt so much at home in Milan, and not only at La Scala, it was because the moral and political culture of the city was altogether to his taste. Steeped in the thought of Cabanis and Destutt de Tracy, Stendhal recognized that figures such as Vincenzo Cuoco, Melchiorre Gioia and Gian Domenico Romagnosi were *idéologues* in all but name.[4]

The Austrian government in Lombardy, judging the effects of twenty years of French rule to be ineradicable, tried to convince a sceptical and wounded public opinion that the tradition of Josephine reformism might be revived.[5] Since so many Italians had been persuaded after 1799 that Napoleon's regime in Italy was itself a sort of enlightened despotism, serving to heal the catastrophic divisions between intellectual elite, on the one hand, and the plebeians and peasantry on the other, it was not unreasonable to suppose that those who had been functionaries under the Kingdom of Italy might switch their allegiance to Vienna.[6] Ugo Foscolo was offered the editorship of the official journal of the regime, the *Biblioteca Italiana* and, although he turned the offer down, other patriots, Pietro Giordani among them, were willing at first to cooperate. Yet the Austrian authorities could not afford to yield too much ground to those who had recognized that the future lay with territorial and political unity, and that free trade, and its precondition, intellectual liberty, could not be long denied. The Viceroys therefore compromised with the liberals to some extent in the early years of the Restoration, permitting the publication of the *Conciliatore*, but unleashed the most fearful repression after the events of 1820–21, committing Count Confalonieri and Silvio Pellico, both of whom were on intimate terms with di Breme and Stendhal, to long years in the fortress of the Spielberg. Such then, was the context in which the first shot in the dispute between Romantics and Classicists, Staël's famous article on translation, was fired.

## Romantics and Classicists

The nations, Staël had declared in *De l'Allemagne*, should derive mutual enlightenment from their respective qualities.[7] In the first issue of the *Biblioteca Italiana*, she likewise argued that, since invention was rare, the literatures of the modern world should benefit as much as was possible from the transfer of works from one language to another. Renaissance scholars and poets had written in Latin, a dead language but a lingua franca, and there had been no call for translation. If, however, the humanists of that time lay unread, it was 'because nature works in such a way that the language that is a companion and enduring part of our life precedes the language which is learned from books, and is only to be found in books'.[8]

Staël had from her youth championed direct experience of nature, often in Rousseauist accents, and had decried mimesis. On the slopes of Vesuvius, she had thus confided to her journal that 'the memory of the poets, of Milton and of Virgil, is the only thing that diminishes the impression of this spectacle. If only one could see it in its wild state, without having read a thing.'[9] Her delight in the primitive, the original, was not suffused here with a sense of confining Revelation; in Homer, cast for over a century as the elemental contrary to the rule-bound artifices of French classicism, she discerned the 'ancient simplicity' of the dawn of human culture. Like Cabanis, she saw in the traditions and customs of the Homeric age 'something primitive which is a source of inexhaustible delight . . . there is a beginning of humankind, a youth of the centuries which, as we read Homer, repeats to our souls, the affection that remembrance of our own childhood at times occasions in us'.[10] If, then, one were to strip the *Iliad* and the *Odyssey* of their vernal simplicities, as Alexander Pope in his versions had done, one would be taking from them the very qualities that had made them most remarkable. As translator, Voss had come nearer the mark, but Staël's most fulsome praise was reserved for Vincenzo Monti, a poet whom she had known and admired in 1804–05, and whose views she was in part echoing here. There is indeed more than a hint in her essay of the purist argument that, of all known languages, Italian was best suited to the rendering of Homeric Greek.[11]

There is in fact surprisingly little space allotted in Staël's brief essay to her essentially Romantic conviction that, just as the barbarian invasions had instilled a new, Christian vigour into a decadent Empire, so too should Italy's culture draw fresh inspiration from England and Germany. Homeric mores were not as clearly transcended as they had been in *Les Martyrs*. Nonetheless, Staël urged the Italians to follow the example of the rest of Europe, set aside pagan mythology and look north, across the Alps. In spite of her admiration for Monti, she would not have agreed when, in the presence of Ludovico di Breme, Byron and Stendhal, he had claimed that, since the originality of the Ancients (foremost among them, Homer) could never be equalled, modern writers ought simply to copy the old models.[12] Knowledge of English and German literature would, she said, add 'new colours' and 'alien beauties' to a sterile, impoverished tradition, in which Italians spent their time raking over ashes in search of a grain of gold.

Many Italian publicists were wounded by such assertions, and rallied to the defence of their academies, their theatres and their literary

culture. Notwithstanding evidence to the contrary in *Corinne*, they felt
that Staël was hostile towards their country, and contemptuous of its
great literature; they believed that she was exhorting them to adopt an
alien mythology, be it Gaelic, Scandinavian or Germanic, as their own.[13]
However, Giordani, a purist of Enlightenment provenance and the
mentor of the young Leopardi, denied that Staël had meant to give
offence. Her arguments should, he said, be treated on their merits. For
example, she had urged the Italians to devote themselves to study, the
only course still open to them after the Restoration, and this was advice
they could in good faith accept. If, however, other paths might be
followed, they should tread them. The criticisms that Staël had offered of
the Italian theatre were, Giordani reckoned, largely justified. Much of
what was staged was frivolous, and Italian playwrights should therefore
prepare 'worthy and useful' materials, but drawn from their own cultural
tradition, not from that of the North. For all the outrage expressed at the
call for the abandonment of the myths of pagan Antiquity, Giordani
admitted that, in the hands of mediocre versifiers, such practices were
the height of tedium. Only a truly learned and discriminating poet would
be able to decide what use could be made of classical myth in modern
times, since it 'was . . . no longer a popular religion and a universal
belief, as it had been in past centuries'.[14] Giordani deplored the sheer
quantity of bad verse produced in Italy, noting that, although every city,
town or hamlet had an academy, its labours would be devoted not to the
serious study of classical literature, natural science or 'civil' history, or to
research into improvements in the sphere of agriculture or manufacture,
but to the composition and recitation of odes, madrigals, elegies and
sonnets. In this regard, as Timpanaro has noted, Giordani was in full
agreement with Staël and the Milanese Romantics in their concern with
the spread of Enlightenment. Since it was rare for a person to be destined
by nature to be a poet, he generally discouraged those who submitted
their manuscripts to his judgement, urging them to pursue a course of
study more useful to their country, and advising even Leopardi – who
read his articles in the *Biblioteca Italiana* with rapt attention – to begin
with the reading and writing of prose.[15]

This much granted to Staël, Giordani ventured some criticism of her
essay. First of all, he could not countenance her low estimate of classical
studies. He therefore lauded the discoveries made in the first fifteen
years of the century by Italian antiquarians and philologists, of lost texts
– not a single grain of gold but a veritable mine. One of the three scholars
mentioned by name, Angelo Mai, had recovered from the Vatican
archives some of the correspondence of Fronto, a rhetorician of the
second century, with the Emperor Marcus Aurelius, a discovery that had
so enraptured the young Leopardi that he had rendered the fragments in

verse. The more important discovery, in 1820, of some lost books from Cicero's *De Republica*, a valuable source for the second edition of Niebuhr's history, would later inspire the canzone 'Ad Angelo Mai'. Second, Giordani denied that 'northern phantasies', as he termed them, would really serve to enrich Italian literature. Turning to his own purpose Staël's admission that in the arts one could not go beyond Homer, he noted that, although progress in the sciences was cumulative, in the arts it was finite: 'once the beautiful was achieved and found, and expressed, one could rest content'.[16] If one were to chase after German or English models, merely for the sake of novelty, one risked producing centaurs, creatures that were neither one thing nor the other. It would do no harm to know northern literature, Giordani continued, but to imitate it would be disastrous, as the influence of Cesarotti's versions of Ossian had proved. Italians would do better, then, to cultivate their 'paternal store', and to study their own classics, Latin and Greek, for Italian was a branch from the same trunk, and fresh grafts could be made, whereas 'the other [languages] have a wholly different root'.[17] Giordani was evidently unacquainted with the notion of an Indo-European family of languages, which was little known in Italy before the 1830s and 1840s. Like many hostile to northern Romanticism, he conceived of Italian culture as the quintessence of Etruscan, Greek and Latin values, and therefore as the unrivalled ground of humane civilization. It would be disingenuous, therefore, to pretend that Giordani was wholly free of that mania for primacy which then afflicted antiquarians, both in France itself and in the nations ranged against it in the Napoleonic Wars, and which has haunted nationalism to the present day. Yet advocates of a classicist, Enlightenment theory of culture tended rather, as I shall shortly show, to dissolve the spurious eternity of the tribe-nation.

The first of the Lombard Romantics to rally to the defence of Staël was Ludovico di Breme, a fervent believer in the principle of perfectibility and later one of the leading lights behind the Milanese *Conciliatore*. He began, much as Giordani had done, by denying that Staël had made scornful and unjust aspersions regarding Italy, and by noting that she had urged Italians not to copy the literatures of the north but to know them. Again like Giordani, di Breme castigated the sonneteers for their pedantic antiquarianism, mocked their gilded academies and contrasted their useless productions with the momentous achievements of the Enlightenment. From the list given of *philosophes* and *idéologues* to be emulated, one could readily conclude that Lombard Romanticism represented a continuation, not a repudiation, of the tradition of *Il Caffè*.[18] Staël, Ludovico di Breme avowed, had merely called upon Italians to 'enter with all the civil nations into a daily exchange of ideas and Enlightenment'.[19]

Leopardi's contribution to this same debate took the form of two letters to the *Biblioteca Italiana*, which were never published, and a lengthier riposte to Ludovico di Breme. Like Giordani, Leopardi could agree with much of what Staël had said. The academic study of the authors of the past could not compensate a poet for the lack of the divine spark. For Homer, the greatest of all poets, had had no models, and could trust, like Dante after him, to his *bella negligenza*.[20] If the Moderns were unable to equal the achievement of the Ancients, it was because 'when they wished to describe the sky, the sea or a landscape, they simply undertook to observe it, whereas we pick up the work of a poet, and when they wished to depict a passion, they imagined themselves to be feeling it, while we embark upon the reading of a tragedy'.[21] The Ancients, and the Greeks, in particular, had been able to do without models, whereas almost all the writings of the Moderns were no more than copies of copies. It would be a grave error, however, for Italians to imitate northern poets. Directly echoing Giordani, Leopardi insisted that the grafting of Ossian on to Homer, Virgil or Tasso would produce monsters more absurd than the Satyrs and more obscure than the Harpies. For in the northern poets we tend to find 'exaggerations and gigantic images, and fairly rarely the true, most chaste, most lovely nature'. Italians should therefore cultivate their own literature, which was, Leopardi insisted, closer than any other to Greek and Latin, that is, to 'the only true literature, because the only natural literature, and one that is altogether without affectation'.[22]

Leopardi then disputed the claim of the Romantics to have gone beyond the sensationalism of Locke or Condillac. Poetry, Leopardi proclaimed, ought not to stray too far from the senses; it had been an error to produce it by means of the intellect alone, 'to drag it from the visible to the invisible, from things to ideas, and to alter it from being material and fantastic and corporeal, as it had been, to being metaphysical and reasonable and spiritual'. His conception of the proper condition of poetry thus rested upon a vision of the first times, known to us through the Old Testament, Homer and other ancient authors, when the first peoples had been so immersed in nature that their senses were in harmony with earth, sea and sky. In so enchanted a world, they knew the magical operation of objects upon them, and imagined 'countless supernatural forces, dreams and spectres'. Yet reason, science and industry had brought disenchantment, the hold of the fables had been broken and intellect held sway. Both nature and the human heart had been scrutinized with such ferocity that innocent delight in objects, the particular concern of ancient poets, was all but lost.[23]

Ludovico di Breme had insisted that modern poetry had to measure up to such changes, and therefore to be a thing of intellect. In Leopardi's view, however, the Romantic project was riven with contradictions. First, the Romantics had mocked the veneration of the Classicists for the heritage of Greece, Rome and *trecento* or *cinquecento* Florence, but had themselves quarried Turkish, Arabic, Persian, Indian, Scandinavian and Celtic folklore. Second, they had failed to honour their own conviction that knowledge of causes had banished all illusions and, wishing to make their art popular, had ransacked the folklore of the unlettered populace for raw materials for their literature. Third, they had celebrated expressions of emotion that were 'sentimental' or 'pathetic'. Yet the Moderns did not have a deeper knowledge of the human heart; it was rather that, in Leopardi's judgement, their souls had aged.[24]

Instead of imitating the diverse and transient mores of men, the task of the poet was to cleave to nature, which was eternal. The immutability of nature rendered poetry immutable also, and Homer therefore as true as ever he was. As Moderns, we could do no better than imagine ourselves 'in the primitive condition of our ancestors'.[25] There is again a temptation to brand Leopardi a Romantic here, just as one might wish to attach the same epithet to Constant, Cabanis and Fauriel after 1804–05. While one can allow that a reverence for objects, creatures and persons unmarked by civilization was manifestly not characteristic of the early Enlightenment challenge to superstition mounted by Bayle and Fontenelle, it must also be acknowledged that neither Leopardi nor Constant confused the auroral candour of the primitive with the primacy of a barbarian people. It may seem pedantic, where the tradition of the Encyclopédie was under attack from all sides, to insist upon fine discriminations between related attitudes. Yet, as Timpanaro has observed, if one conceives of Romanticism as a cultural movement characterized by a sensibility so all-pervasive as to leave no thinker or publicist untouched, one risks confusing

> a sensationalist anti-rationalism (based on a reassessment of enthusiasm and passion as natural primitivity, as a transformable but not annullable link with the 'feral' origins of humanity) with a religious irrationalism (based on the attribution of a cognitive power superior to that of the intellect to 'sentiment', hence the affirmation of the primacy of mystical experience).[26]

There are still sufficient traces of the former position in Cabanis, Constant and Fauriel, for it to be appropriate to deny them the status of Romantics. This is still truer of Leopardi, although it lies beyond the scope of my argument to gloss in any detail the gradual alteration of his thought, as his early Rousseauism and civic purism yielded at first to a historical pessimism and then, in a term that reads awkwardly in English but must be used for want of an alternative, to a cosmic pessimism. Here

I aim only to establish that even in 1818 Leopardi refused to view the barbarian invasions, and the advent of Christianity, as a historical moment at which a new tribe-nation was founded, for at the same time Gian Domenico Romagnosi was expounding a parallel line of argument in the pages of the *Conciliatore*.

## The native and the dative

A freemason, active in the most advanced circles of late eighteenth-century Parma, Romagnosi rallied to the French Revolution, welcomed the Declaration of Rights of Man and the Citizen, writing moderate tracts in defence of its guiding principles in the early 1790s, and subsequently adopting positions in harmony with those of the French *idéologues*. Rousseauist celebrations of the noble savage were therefore not to his taste, his concern being always with the manner in which the capacity of humankind for perfection found concrete realization in the process of *incivilmento*.[27] He revered the enduring impact of labour upon nature, whereby a transformed territory bore a mark, or memory, of a social relation. The paramount instance of such a fruitful transformation, mightier by far than any armed conquest, was the intricate system of canals and locks by which the Lombard Plain had been irrigated across the centuries, and his most important treatise was therefore devoted to the legal implications of this seemingly recondite topic.[28] Yet because natural forces were not altogether subsumed by spirit, he viewed culture as more 'dative' than 'native'. In distinguishing between 'first culture', that of early human society, and 'second culture', Romagnosi envisaged the process of *incivilmento* in terms of proliferating transactions between ethnic groups, whereby the world would by definition become less 'national' and more cosmopolitan. He therefore heaped praises upon those he termed *themisphoroi*, the lawbearers, who brought isolated 'first' cultures into the domain of *ius gentium*. In this sense, and in this sense alone, he acknowledged the existence of the wilderness between cities, a space of free and universal mind increasingly repudiated in the age of nations.

Stendhal's account of the eminent functionaries who, formerly employed by the Napoleonic regime, could still be seen in 1816 on the streets of Milan, calls to mind the career of Romagnosi. For in 1806 he had been summoned to the Lombard capital to supervise the drafting of a penal code which should not, he insisted, be a pale imitation of the French model, but should reflect the particular features of Italian history. Echoes of the arguments of Vincenzo Cuoco, a prominent figure at that time in the Kingdom of Italy, are reinforced by a shared concern with the workings of Etruscan confederation, which, when all due allowance is made for wounded Italic pride, reflected Romagnosi's conviction that the concrete specificity of a given form of associated life, be it a city or a region, not be subsumed with undue haste into a higher unity. Although such convictions were shared by Constant and, initially, by Thierry, a particular preoccupation with the obdurate fact of specific polities within their shaped terrain informed the Lombard challenge to formulaic centralization, whether Jacobin or Napoleonic, and made it possible to establish the principle of confederation upon a secure philosophical basis. Romagnosi had thus defined the Etruscan League in terms of the spread of culture, through a network of ramifying transactions, from one city to the next, and affirmed that this was the most progressive form possible. He then ascribed the resurgence of the *comuni* in the ninth, tenth and eleventh centuries to the survival of the Roman *municipia*.[29]

If such sentiments caused some offence in French Milan, the Austrian authorities were still more suspicious of the eminent jurisconsult, not least because in 1815 he had published a tract in favour of constitutional monarchy. In 1817, the law schools where Romagnosi, like Beccaria and the Verri brothers before him, had taught, were shut down, and he was forced to hold his classes at home. At the same time, a disillusionment with the *Biblioteca Italiana* had led the Milanese intelligentsia to plan the launch of a new journal, the *Conciliatore*, which would serve, as its name promised, to reconcile 'not the loyal with the false, but all those who sincerely love truth'.[30] Romagnosi was, however, unable to mask his doubts regarding the more vaporous aspects of Romantic doctrine and, ever fond of coining new and generally rebarbative terms from the Greek, Romagnosi called for the abandonment of both titles, 'Romantic' and 'Classical', and their replacement by the epithet 'ilichiastic', or 'adjusted to suit the times'.[31] Confusion had arisen, he said, because such titles had been used indiscriminately to refer both to historical periods and to the defining characteristics of literatures produced at various times. It had been an error to imply a historical periodization, for in fact three periods (ancient, medieval, modern) were involved, not two, and an accurate account ought therefore to be given of the specific features of each. Romagnosi himself favoured Vico's distinctions between theocratic, heroic and civil societies, noting that this sequence applied both to 'first' culture, existing prior to the fall of the Roman Empire and the 'Nordic' invasions, and to 'second' culture, established with the rise of communal civilization. The terms 'Classical' and 'Romantic' could not be said to have a strictly literary reference either, for the latter invariably implied a historical link between a particular poetry and 'barbarian times', as the following passage from *De l'Allemagne* made clear:

The name 'Romantic' has recently been introduced in Germany in order to designate the poetry inaugurated by the songs of the Troubadours, and born of chivalry and Christianity . . .

   The word 'Classical' is sometimes taken to be a synonym for perfection. I employ it here in another fashion, regarding classical poetry as that of the ancients, and romantic poetry as *that which pertains in some fashion to chivalric traditions*. This division also relates to two eras in world history, namely, that preceding the establishment of Christianity, and that which followed it.[32]

When challenged to identify himself as a Classicist or as a Romantic, Romagnosi therefore denied that he was unequivocally either. Like Giordani and Leopardi he denounced both the reactionary and pedantic Classicism of certain ultra-purist milieux and the replacement, in some versions of Romanticism, of 'our own origin' and 'the inheritance of our ancestors' with 'new, specifically Germanic remembrances'. Germanic peoples could justifiably nourish their national pride, and illustrate the origins of their modern civilization with 'gloomy and silent woods, with turreted and pinnacled castles, with crowns of acorns, with chivalric customs, and with a magical marvellous', but so too might the glories of human culture be exemplified by 'temples, altars and Latin squares, by political customs and by the mythological marvellous'.[33]

   If Romagnosi called for a literary diplomacy, based upon the principles of parity and reciprocity, and if he noted the particular need for it in the treatment of epics, it was because he was well aware that, in the age of nations, the 'boria dei dotti', the vanity of the learned, was fuelled by the imagined precedence of a people's story. Writing almost as a historical geographer or as an ecologist, he denied cultural traditions any sort of primacy, defining them merely as sets of values that subsist in any given place at any given time. As in Leopardi's case, the tradition of eigh- teenth-century sensism remained so powerful an influence that the spirit of a nation was subordinated to the constraining force of nature. The characteristics of a literature would thus be determined 'by time and place, that is to say, by the national genius driven and modified by the prevailing circumstances, the whole of which forms part of that supreme economy, with which nature governs the nations of the earth'.[34] Catta- neo's early studies of Lodi and Cremona, and his great essays on Lombardy, and on the city as an ideal principle in Italian history, were thus formed in a mould cast by Cabanis, by Volney and by Romagnosi.

   It was plain from the outraged response of Giovanni Berchet to Romagnosi's essay that behind these literary skirmishes there lurked the vexed question of the relation between Christianity and Enlightenment or, more specifically, the legacy of Edward Gibbon. Thus Berchet, a member of the editorial board, pressed for the addition of a corrective note, in which he objected that, 'after the mixing of the peoples of the North with the degenerate sons of the Romans, there arose a new generation of Italians, from whom we are directly descended, and who could not be considered as, strictly speaking, a nation of Latin origin'.[35] In his rejoinder, Romagnosi confessed his ignorance as to whether, in the aftermath of the barbarian invasions, the population consisted of a majority of Latins or of a majority of Northerners.[36] Insisting that 'races naturalise themselves in the countries where they have migrated, and really cease to be foreigners', an assertion shortly to be challenged by Manzoni, Romagnosi argued, more generally, that a distinction ought to be established between 'the physical derivation of present-day Italians' and 'the origins of modern civilization'. I would suggest that Chateaubriand, Staël, the Schlegels and some, at least, of the Lombard Romantics, had sometimes disregarded this distinction. Romagnosi continued as follows:

Distinguish then if you will a first from a second barbarism, a first from a second culture. You will invariably find that this second culture derived chiefly from the influence of Latin things, with the sole difference that in the first was operative the force of government, while in the second customs, habits, language, traditions and opinion were at work; and in the latter I also include free and civil laws, the Roman pontifical regime and a hundred other residues that survived the barbarian destruction. Since the second civilization was revived upon the basis of such things, it is clear that we should look for the true origin of it in the prior state of the Latin things to which I have referred.[37]

An accurate exegesis of this crucial passage requires some understanding both of the doctrine of *corsi* and *ricorsi*, and of the 'fortune' of Vico in early nineteenth-century Milan, so it is to these linked issues that I will now turn.

The conventional wisdom, founded upon Manzoni's memories and upon Croce's influential writings, has long been that it was exiles from the doomed Parthenopean Republic, foremost among them Cuoco, who brought the *New Science* to Milan. According to this eminently symbolic fable, a philosophy that was so out of place in its own time could not at first be recognized by enlightened Lombards, *philosophes* in all but name, but had to be expounded by an emissary from southern Italy, the heir to a different, more historicist, tradition. However, as Sergio Moravia has shown, there is a strong element of caricature in this account. To begin with, thinkers of the late Enlightenment in Lombardy knew more of the *New Science* than has often been supposed. Second,

Cuoco's own appraisal of Vico involved repeated reference to eighteenth-century texts by, for example, Blair, Boulanger and Dupuis. Third, Cuoco's own hostility towards the Enlightenment has been much exaggerated for, notwithstanding the Burkean coloration of some of the key passages in the *Saggio Storico*, he may quite reasonably be bracketed with the *idéologues*. Each of these distortions may be accounted for, of course, in terms of the trial of the Enlightenment.[38]

Since the dominant tendency of post-revolutionary historiography had entailed a positive estimate of the contribution of the barbarian invasions, which, according to Staël and Sismondi, brought the liberty of the Moderns to a decadent Europe, readers of Vico would naturally tend to view his account of the great *ricorso* of the Christian Middle Ages in somewhat similar terms. The opening of book 5 does, after all, contain some of the most unequivocal statements to be found in the whole of the *New Science* regarding the trumping of ordinary by extraordinary providence:

> When, working in superhuman ways, God had revealed and confirmed the truth of the Christian religion by opposing the virtue of the martyrs to the power of Rome, and the teaching of the Fathers, together with the miracles, to the vain wisdom of Greece, and when armed nations were about to arise on every hand destined to combat the true divinity of its Founder, he permitted a new order of humanity to be born among the nations in order that [the true religion] might be firmly established according to the natural course of human institutions themselves.[39]

Yet the ideal, eternal history, as Vico termed it, in no way required such Bossuetian guarantees. For example, the Amerindians would still have known the same sequence of theocratic, heroic and civil society, even if they had never been discovered by the Europeans.[40] This observation serves to remind us both that Vico's concept of providence is essentially immanent and that the theory of *corsi* and *ricorsi* could be reconciled, much as Romagnosi and Cattaneo intended, with 'the times and the places' or, if you like, with the stubborn contingencies of human history.

What Romagnosi had hoped to achieve in the above passage was thus to combine the theory of *corsi* and *ricorsi* with the Condorcetian or Constantian principle of perfectibility. In a world already marked and fashioned by the *certezze* of 'first' culture, second barbarism could not, self-evidently, have the same effect as the first. Likewise, second culture, that of the *comuni*, drew sustenance from the obscured, even buried but never annihilated values of the first. Indeed, notwithstanding the turbulent character of second barbarism, 'the mind [was] impelled and as if obliged to run along traces left by the prior culture', so that 'the Latin intellectual element shed its light upon the German intellectual element, and impressed its movement upon it'.[41] In an essay devoted to the influence of Gibbon's great work upon nineteenth-century Italian scholarship, Momigliano has argued that the most ferociously anti-Christian chapters were generally passed over in silence, and that attention was focused instead upon his treatment of the Italian Middle Ages. There, for obvious reasons, Gibbon's sources had been in the main Italian, and had cast the history of the early Church in a kinder light. Although *Decline and Fall* had been on the Index, chiefly on account of chapters 15 and 16, its reputation in moderate, neo-Guelph circles had so much altered that it could be shelved without embarrassment alongside Vico and Sismondi.[42] These observations echo Momigliano's oft-repeated charge that down the centuries historians of Rome have failed to produce a serious analytic account of the history of the early Church.[43] The charge is no doubt justified, and yet some of Momigliano's laconic descriptions of Vico and Cattaneo strike me as being wide of the mark, chiefly because they neglect the emphasis perceptible in either writer upon the persisting element of Roman law evident in the practice of the bishops in 'iron times'.[44] Likewise, Romagnosi, by celebrating the enduring city, was able to separate tribe or, in his idiom, 'first' culture, from nation.

Although, as Timpanaro has noted, such challenges to Romantic doctrine indubitably had some effect upon the *Conciliatore*, later issues of which contained serious, one might say Stendhalian, criticisms of a merely sentimental medievalism, Romagnosi contributed little. However, in *Dell'Indole dei Fattori dell'Incivilmento*, an elaboration of themes already treated in a review of a book on the barbarian invasions, Romagnosi discussed those passages in *Decline and Fall* that celebrate the flourishing condition of the Empire under 'the five good emperors', in the second century AD. Much credit went to the Flavians (Nerva, Trajan and Hadrian), but the highest praise was lavished upon the two Antonines, Titus Antoninus Pius and Marcus Aurelius Antoninus. The years between 138 and 180 AD, Gibbon declared, constituted 'possibly the only period of history in which the happiness of a great people was the sole object of government'. Rome had thus survived the iron age of 'the dark unrelenting Tiberius, the furious Caligula, the stupid Claudius, the profligate and cruel Nero, the beastly Vitellius, and the timid, inhuman Domitian', and, after breathing again under the Flavians, enjoyed unparalleled peace and prosperity.[45]

It was for good cause that Voltaire, Hume, Gibbon and Condorcet had depicted the Antonines as virtuous, honourable and wise, as in fact philosopher kings of the first water, yet their writings seem to turn upon a paradox, namely, that liberty in the second century both was and was not dead.

The first proposition is stated quite unequivocally in Gibbon's third chapter, where he surveyed the different kinds of monarchy, a tempered form being counterposed to a despotic. To forestall despotism, 'intrepid and vigilant guardians' were needed, for example, 'a martial nobility and stubborn commons possessed of arms, tenacious of property, and collected into constitutional assemblies'.[46] Although a glancing reference to the English constitution, in Montesquieu's rendering, may well be intended here, the listed elements fit still more exactly with republican Rome. As in *Considerations*, so too in the *Decline and Fall*, the republic is viewed as a victim of its own military success. For, by unrelenting conquest, the city fell out of all due proportion, and war, instead of remaining a patriotic duty, became first an art and then a trade, prosecuted by corrupted mercenaries. After the Civil Wars, Augustus was able 'artfully to collect in his own person all the scattered rays of civil jurisdiction'.[47] Censor, consul, tribune and supreme pontiff at home, proconsul and imperator on campaign, he managed at once to restore and to tame the senate. The Principate was therefore 'an absolute monarchy disguised by the forms of a commonwealth', for Augustus was careful to honour the proprieties by continuing with the annual election of consuls, praetors and tribunes. That Gibbon wished his readers to judge the Principate a hollow charade is evident from his choice of terms. We hear, for example, of 'the mask of hypocrisy', of a 'comedy' and of 'surround[ing] the throne with darkness'. How then could such a travesty serve as a backdrop both to Marcus Aurelius and to Nero? As Momigliano once observed, the philosophic historians had tended to treat the Imperial system as a given, concerning themselves with the qualities of individual rulers, degraded or exalted as the case might be. The age of the Antonines, in particular, was represented almost as if it were a 'floating island of the blessed, beneath which the current of obscurantism continued to flow'.[48] The miraculous accession to the Principate of an enlightened despot did not make it any the less a despotism, in which a philosopher like Marcus Aurelius could be followed by a monster like Commodus.

The contrary proposition may also be identified, however, in the *Decline and Fall*:

The gentle, but powerful influence of laws and manners had gradually cemented the union of the provinces. Their peaceful inhabitants enjoyed and abused the advantages of wealth and luxury. The image of a free constitution was preserved with decent reverence. The Roman senate appeared to possess the sovereign authority, and devolved on the emperors all the executive powers of government. During a happy period of more than fourscore years, the public administration was conducted by the virtues and abilities of Nerva, Trajan, Hadrian and the two Antonines.[49]

In the light of my earlier observations, use of such terms as 'image' and 'appearance' implies a damning with faint praise of the Augustan charade. Yet Gibbon described the senate under the Antonines as a civil and criminal court with extensive powers and prerogatives, and as 'a last refuge of the spirit of ancient eloquence'. Even the emperors 'gloried in the name of senators' and 'sat, voted and divided with their equals'.[50] Gibbon thus celebrated not only the extension of civil liberties to both slaves and aliens under the Flavians and Antonines, but also the unimpeded advance of production and trade.[51]

We may begin to resolve this paradox by considering the treatment of the theme of liberty in the political writings of David Hume, a friend in fact of Gibbon. In the most detailed and nuanced discussion as yet presented of Hume's political thought, Duncan Forbes has elaborated upon his own distinction between a scientific or sceptical Whig position and a vulgar Whiggism. The latter rested, we are told, upon uncritical justifications of the Revolution of 1688, upon the contrast between English liberty and French 'slavery', upon eulogies of the ancient (Saxon) constitution by the seventeenth-century common lawyers, and upon denunciations of the wickedness of the Stuart kings. Far from being the preserve of Whigs, these tenets could be espoused as much by Tories and Jacobites as by commonwealthmen. Hume, a Scottish philosopher, was of course deeply cosmopolitan and, as a committed francophile, contested the view that there was anything especially ancient or matchless about the English constitution. To accept one historically contingent form as supreme would be, in his view, to vitiate any comparative science of politics. Hume was more especially concerned to vindicate the 'civilized' monarchies, France foremost among them, and he therefore challenged the vulgar Whig belief, endorsed by Locke, that there was a qualitative, rather than a merely quantitative, distinction between 'free' and 'absolute' governments. He judged that 'civilized monarchies' attained to the fundamental object of all governments, namely, that of placing the liberty and security of the individual under the rule of law. It was no doubt true that in France the monarch was absolute, and that such a regime was therefore not, in vulgar Whig parlance, a republic, since in the latter laws alone, and not men, are held to rule. Yet the commonplace equation between Oriental and French despotism obscured the fact that in Turkey individuals were at the mercy of each and every magistrate, whereas in France ministers obeyed general laws governing the whole of society.[52]

Gibbon was evidently a sceptical Whig also, or at least to some degree. Yet, as Duncan Forbes allows, even Hume reverted to vulgar Whiggism upon occasion.[53] John Pocock has likewise argued that the Anglo-Scottish historians of civil society were in general given to the use of the language of virtue and corruption when elaborating upon the moral risks to personality occasioned by the advance of commercial society.[54] The above-mentioned paradox therefore derives, in his view, from Machiavelli, who had bequeathed to the West an ineluctably cyclical view of the city and its virtue, since 'the forces that built up human personality were identical with the forces that undermined it'. The advance of commerce and the division of labour promoted human felicity, and yet in so doing subverted the relation of citizen to city upon which such felicity rested.[55] In this respect, Gibbon's account of the censitary system in 'the purer ages of the commonwealth', a topic that had captured his imagination at least as early as 1764, tallies in every respect with that of Machiavelli, Rousseau and Montesquieu.[56] Progress, then, was a lure and a deception. Yet primitivism was not an option for the Anglo-Scottish Enlightenment either, since the earliest stage of human society revealed, as Pocock has put it, 'a warrior so devoid of the reflective capacity which only the progress of the arts, the circulation of goods, and the division of labour could bring, as to be altogether incapable of citizenship'.[57] Unable fully to embrace the doctrine of indefinite perfectibility, Gibbon continued to subscribe to a deeply pessimistic view of culture as *anakuklōsis*.

Pocock thus observes that 'neither Montesquieu nor Hume, Smith nor Jefferson was fully able to overcome the proto-Rousseauan vision of a future in which commerce, progress and specialization corrupted civilization even as they advanced it', and Gibbon, whom he places between Machiavelli and Hume, 'was no exception to this rule'.[58] Such historical pessimism might, however, be obviated by the perception, referred to in chapter 6, that republican values, crystallized as laws, could be perpetuated within the 'civilized monarchies'. Rousseau doubtless had his back to the future, and his face to the dying light of the *Kleinstaat*, and yet his remarks in *Emile* regarding the 'the simulacra of the laws' suggest that the essence of the city might subsist even in great states. Still more was this the case with Hume, Smith or Gibbon.

While Gibbon's 'image of a free constitution preserved with decent reverence' could therefore be read as pejorative, Romagnosi, being himself fully committed to the view that the process of *incivilmento* was cumulative and unbroken, plainly did not think so. Noting the persisting influence of the senate, the existence, therefore, of senatorial and equestrian aristocracies and, more generally, the survival of a moderating public opinion, he insisted that the Principate, up until the constitutional changes implemented by Diocletian and Constantine, had been a tempered monarchy under which Roman civil law had known continuous improvement. As a jurisconsult, he paid particular attention to the many eminent pupils of Papinian, Ulpian among them, who had flourished at the time of the Emperor Alexander Severus. How, he asked, could a violent and despotic regime have ever produced 'the laws, doctrines and the majority of princes, ministers and councillors that do honour to this first period of the Roman Empire'?[59] The Flavians and Antonines had curtailed strife between the classes, promoted respect for persons, property and commercial contract. Romagnosi agreed with Sieyes and Constant that the civil order was an absolute, primitive, immediate good, and the force of government a relative, secondary good, and took care to credit the jurisprudence of the Empire, not the forests of Germany, with the invention of the state of right. It was from Destutt de Tracy that he took his Montesquieu, and not from Staël, whose sympathy for the principle of hereditary aristocracy he deplored.

Chateaubriand had drawn a stark contrast between the rule of the baneful Tetrarchate and that of Constantine, but Romagnosi held the latter equally to blame for introducing an oriental autocracy which inflicted lasting damage upon both civil right and the *municipia*.The new religion did not so much invent, but rather transmit the principle of equity, and its priesthood, '[il] clero depositario', deserved the praise of a historian chiefly because a precious culture had been in its safekeeping.[60] It was not Rome that had served Christianity, but Christianity that had served Rome.

Romagnosi therefore took the view, pioneered by Machiavelli and embraced in the early eighteenth century by jurisdictionalists like Giannone and Muratori, that it would have been better for Italy if the Lombards had conquered the whole territory, subject in the south and the east to Greek (Byzantine) and Saracen domination. For Pope Hadrian I's plea to Charlemagne to crush the Lombards had introduced a fateful division into the peninsula, split from then on between the Regnum Italicum, the Papal States and the Kingdom of the Two Sicilies, and ravaged in later centuries by conflict between the Ghibelline and Guelph factions. Romagnosi maintained, on the basis of earlier discussions by Muratori and Giannone, that the Lombards had been 'generous' enough to permit the defeated population to live under Roman law. A Lombard judge was appointed to give judgments, but in collaboration with a college of eminent lawyers, both ecclesiastical and lay, who would be Italian when the litigants were themselves Italian, and mixed (that is, both Lombard and Italian) when conqueror and conquered were in dispute.[61] At the same time, the barbarians, belonging to a ruder civilization, were neither competent in, nor unduly concerned with, the economic administration of the *municipia*, structures that, having preserved some of the arts, trades, weights and measures of Roman Italy, would later supply a framework for the resurgent *comuni*.[62] Moreover,

on the basis of Muratori's commentary upon a law promulgated by
Lothar, the grandson of Charlemagne, Romagnosi concluded that municipal offices with a modicum of authority, elected by the people, had
survived the barbarian invasions and were still fully operative within the
Regnum Italicum.[63]

In order to grasp the full implications of the debate in Milan on the
historiography of the early Middle Ages, I propose now to turn to the
parallel dispute in Restoration Paris. Lest this change of scene seem
artificial, I hasten to add that there were many links between the
Milanese publicists and the Parisian. Romagnosi, for example, had been
profoundly marked by the experience of the Jacobin *triennio*, and of
Napoleonic Milan; Manzoni was on intimate terms with those who
gathered at the Maisonette under the First Empire, Fauriel being a
particularly close friend; and Cattaneo married Anna Woodstock, who
had known Thierry in Paris.[64]

The entire legacy of the Revolution was threatened by the return to
France, in 1814, of the most intransigent of the emigrés, those who had
left in 1789, and by the coronation of Louis XVIII, the executed king's
brother. In that same year, the Count of Montlosier, an associate of
Chateaubriand in emigré London and at that time a *monarchien*, published a history in four volumes of the French monarchy which, though
originally commissioned by the Emperor, constituted an embittered
restatement of the *thèse nobiliaire*. A readiness to criticize Boulainvilliers
and Montesquieu, and a reliance, at times, upon the testimony of Du
Bos, could leave a casual reader with the impression that Montlosier's
bizarre treatise was not an apology for aristocracy. Yet a tendency to play
down the importance of the barbarian invasions, chiefly because he was
not wholly aligned with the *noblesse de race*, was offset by a Germanism
as uncompromising as that of Boulainvilliers. To simplify a complex
narrative, one could put it that Montlosier believed that the Capetian
kings had destroyed a social order built up under the Merovingians and
Carolingians. The first five centuries of the monarchy had thus witnessed,
he maintained, a gradually consolidated opposition between the free,
whether of Roman, Gallic or Frankish origin, and a commonality
consisting of former serfs or slaves. Feudalism had not been introduced
wholesale by the Franks, Montlosier insisted, but was simply a crystallization of patron–client relations common to all three peoples.[65]

The various invasions of transalpine Gaul had been characterized less
by devastation, Montlosier claimed, than by toleration. The Romans, for
example, had treated the defeated Gauls as their allies, and had allowed
the towns to keep their senates, their curies and their militias. The
Franks, too, had respected Gallo-Roman institutions. There had in fact
been a divided social order, with the Franks dominating the countryside

and living according to Salic law, while the Gallo-Romans resided in the cities and followed Roman law. This 'state of separation' did not last long, however, for the Gallo-Roman aristocracies soon deserted the cities for the châteaux. By the time of Charles the Bald, all the free were known as Franks, although they might well be Gallo-Roman by origin.[66]

In Montlosier's history, completed by 1807, we thus discern a stable, ordered hierarchy, accommodating itself to changes as they took place. It was this essentially Germanic world which, after the enfranchisement of the communes and the liberation of the serfs, went to its destruction:

> We will see arise, in the midst of the old state, a new state; in the midst of the old people, a new people; in the midst of the old mores, old institutions and old laws, new mores, new institutions and new laws. We shall see a double state, a double people, a double social order, proceeding for a long time in parallel, then attacking each other.[67]

In the dire circumstances of 1815–16, Thierry acknowledged the 'terrible and sombre truth' that France was not one nation but two, haunted by wholly different memories and implacably opposed one to the other, but rejected Montlosier's disdainful account of the origins of the Third Estate.[68]

Thierry first applied the two-race theory to England, for him the *locus classicus* of liberal values, and, most tellingly, to the centuries after the Norman Conquest, the history of which he would later write. His interest had been stirred by Sharon Turner's researches into the history of the Anglo-Saxons, and by *Ivanhoe*, a novel set four generations after the battle of Hastings which depicted the masses rather than heroic individuals, and 'interests, wholly separate existences, two peoples, a double language, mutually opposed and conflicting mores'.[69] He then transposed his sympathetic identification with those who, in Scott's novel, had languished for so long under the Norman yoke, to French soil, upon which two 'races' had also, he claimed, long existed. A reading of Sismondi's history of the medieval Italian republics, at the prompting of either Saint-Simon or Fauriel, therefore inspired Thierry to investigate that of the French communes, and to publish a number of essays on the subject, first in the *Censeur Européen* and then in the *Courrier Français*. 'Born a plebeian', as he later recalled, 'I wished the common people to have their share of glory in our annals, that the memory of plebeian honour, of the energy and liberty of citizens, should be preserved.'[70] He noted that, although the standard view – in fact enshrined in the Charte of 1814 – was that Louis VI had granted a municipal system to the towns of Laon, Amiens, Noyon and Saint-Quentin, the truth was that, prior to the granting of such freedoms, the larger cities of Provence, Languedoc and Burgundy (namely, Narbonne, Béziers, Lyons, Marseilles and Arles) had been municipal cities with laws of their own and freely elected magistrates. Louis VI's grants had therefore been in imitation of freedoms already won in the south, and had been made in response to the militant demands of citizens.[71]

The Gallo-Roman cities, islands of trade and manufacture in a sea of barbarism and sloth, had thus clawed back their independence from the feudal aristocracy and from the Capetian monarchs. Citizens proudly rebuilt the walls from the debris of ancient monuments and declared themselves free:

> Externally they were fortresses; internally, fraternities; they were, in the language of the period, spots of friendship, independence and peace. The energy of these authentic names suffices to convey an idea of the equal association of all, consented to by all, which formed the political condition of these men of liberty, thus separated from the world of illegality and violence.[72]

To those who were aligned with the liberal cause in 1820 it was clear that, in a country beset by the dangers of counter-revolution, Thierry wished to match celebrations of the ancestral settlement of the *laeti* (Boulainvilliers), or of an ancient aristocracy of Roman, Gallic and Frankish origin (Montlosier), with the still more venerable titles of the *municipia*. Indeed, Guizot objected, in a letter to Fauriel, that Thierry had been so intent upon doing for the commons what Boulainvilliers and Montlosier had done for the nobility that he had overstated his case, and in the process had underplayed the role of the monarchy in the freeing of the communes.[73]

In 1834, Fauriel published a *Histoire de la Gaule sous la Domination des Conquérants Allemands*, a study in which he too emphasized the enduring division between invaders and invaded, and in which he noted the limited contribution of the former to the magnificent flowering of Provençal culture. This book, no more than the central panel of a hugely ambitious project, was to have surveyed changes in the region from prehistoric times up until the end of the thirteenth century. From surviving sketches we know that the third panel of the triptych contained detailed discussion of commercial and political relations between southern France and Italy; of the survival of Gallo-Roman municipal institutions through to the tenth and eleventh centuries; of the transformation of city self-government in Italy, with the emergence (or reemergence) of consulates in Genoa, Brescia and Milan at the very beginning of the twelfth century; and of the duplication of that same pattern a few years later in the cities of Provence and Languedoc.[74]

Alessandro Manzoni was largely resident in Paris between 1805 and 1810, on intimate terms with Cabanis, Sophie de Condorcet and Fauriel, and fully informed of the progress of the latter's researches. This would have been still more the case in 1819–20, when he returned to France, renewing his friendships with the surviving *idéologues* and making the acquaintance of Cousin and Thierry. We know that a draft of Fauriel's history of southern Gaul was already in existence by 1824, when Thierry first set eyes on it, if not some years earlier. At any rate, Manzoni was in Paris when the *Lettres sur l'Histoire de France* were appearing in the *Courrier Français*, and in daily contact with Fauriel, who was, as all his contemporaries recognized, a pioneer in the field of historical enquiry. Once back in Milan, he wrote to Fauriel, informing him that he was already at work on a tragedy concerning the fall of the Lombard Kingdom in the eighth century.[75] So seriously did Manzoni study the extant documentation regarding the barbarian settlements that, in Sainte-Beuve's opinion, he was competent, had he so wished, to compose the sort of history of the Lombards that Thierry or Fauriel might themselves have written.[76] Although the fruit of his labours was a tragedy, *Adelchi*, he appended to it a historical study which, in passing, challenged Romagnosi's conclusions concerning the mores of the Frankish and Lombard conquerors and the fate of the *municipia*. So as not to complicate my exposition unduly, I shall not at first distinguish between the various versions of the text, although at a later stage I show how tendencies present in embryonic form in the drafts of 1820–21 and of 1822 had assumed a more definite shape by 1845. Lest even such minimal clarification should seem otiose, I should add that particular assistance was given to Manzoni upon his return to Milan by Carlo Cattaneo, who was able through his uncle, Gaetano Cattaneo, to exploit the resources of the Brera library to the full.[77] So complete was the divergence of Manzoni from Cattaneo in later years, as I explain below, that it is illuminating to reflect upon what was, in some but not in all respects, a common point of departure.

Romagnosi had argued, as the reader will perhaps recall, that the Lombards had been at once generous and merciful towards the defeated people of Cisalpine Gaul, allowing them to maintain some of the legal and political structures of the *municipia*. Yet, Manzoni objected, generosity and mercy were not the sort of qualities to be found in a barbarian camp. Having in mind Vico's brilliantly painted distinctions between the suavities of late Imperial civilization and the rudeness of the *bestioni*, the 'giants', who had existed under both original and returned barbarism, Manzoni judged it a failure of the historical imagination to credit the Lombards with an urbane clemency. The error consisted in applying to the origins of humanity, of necessity 'small, rude and highly obscure', criteria derived from 'enlightened, cultivated and magnificent times'.[78] Yet Montesquieu had demonstrated for fifth- and sixth-century Europe, and Scott for twelfth-century England, that barbarian invasions invariably left 'two peoples living in the same country, but with different names, language, dress, concerns and in part laws'.[79] In Lombardy, Manzoni pointed out, some of the Roman law had fallen into disuse, and whatever remained was not immune from the interference of the conquerors, the 'popolo padrone', who would hardly have allowed the native people free use of their own judges. As with every other early nineteenth-century meditation upon the moral, cultural and political repercussions of conquest, French domination of Europe was a thinly veiled preoccupation here.

Although Manzoni was as moved as Thierry had been by the sufferings of the humble and defeated, 'an immense multitude of men, a series of generations that pass across the earth, across their own earth, unobserved, without leaving a trace', he did not so much glorify their struggles as pity their condition.[80] Notwithstanding the fame of *I Promessi Sposi*, its author's attitude of resignation was already the object of harsh criticism in the 1830s and 1840s, and again this century by Croce and by Gramsci. Manzoni did not in fact deny the fact of struggle, or avert his gaze from the brute violence of the world, for in his great novel Renzo and Lucia are adrift in terrible scenes of war, plague and riot. The point is, rather, that the struggle had no issue; the comedy was divine, not human. When Croce therefore claimed that Manzoni, in spite of his altogether modern interest (fostered, after all, by Fauriel) in the laws, customs and opinions of the masses, did not have an authentically historical intelligence, what he meant was that in *I Promessi Sposi* there was no appreciation of 'whatever is new and positive that emerges even in historical periods that seem decadent and chaotic'.[81] Not being altogether of the new century, Manzoni's apprehension of the past was marred by an abstract moralism, as if he could peer into the heart of his characters, strip them of the relative values of their time, and summon them before a tribunal acknowledging only eternal values. This was the gist of Croce's argument, to which Manzoni would have countered that the Christian Revelation had a monopoly on truth; history, the domain of fallen beings, could not be wholly vindicated.

Convinced, then, that earthly existence was but a prelude to Eternity, Manzoni's paramount concern was neither for communal liberties nor for the Christian-national providentialism of Chateaubriand or, later, of the neo-Guelph party in Italy. Where Romagnosi had maintained that the assembled people in eighth-century Lombard cities had preserved the right, even under the Franks, to elect their own officers, Manzoni denied it. He was sceptical about the formal continuity between *municipia* and *comuni*, an article of faith for Fauriel, Guizot and Thierry. The survival of Roman values in the Middle Ages had therefore less to do with politics than with ethics and law, and the concept of *populus*, being utterly changed by the Gospel, referred not to the city nor to ethnicity but to suffering humanity.[82] In France, liberals had responded to the Montagnard assault upon local, municipal and provincial liberties by calling for their reinstatement and, in so doing, had revived memories of the reform programme of D'Argenson, Turgot, Condorcet or Mirabeau, yet Manzoni remarked that a hundred or even a thousand *municipia* did not amount to a state, an admission that neither Romagnosi nor Cattaneo would have accepted.[83] If we take 1848–49 to be the turning-point of the Italian Risorgimento, the regrouping of patriots in the 1850s would find Manzoni firmly aligned with the Piedmontese moderates, and therefore with a unitary-national solution which, in Cattaneo's eyes, was no better then a royal conquest.

Manzoni's neglect of communal liberties, and disdain for the principle of confederation, reflected the fact that, since 1809–10, his thoughts about earthly cities had been increasingly subordinated to the logic of the heavenly city. When addressing the matter of right and wrong in history, he acknowledged no other yardstick save that of the Gospel. The evidence from the *Osservazioni sulla Morale Cattolica* suggests that in 1818 he was still closer to the liberals than to the Ultras, yet as the years passed he came to disavow even the events of May and June 1789. There had been no legal justification, Manzoni stated, for the Third Estate to constitute itself as sovereign. The achievements of the first national assembly, so much vaunted by Cabanis, Constant or Staël, were latterly seen by Manzoni as the unjustified attempts of mortal beings to seize the helm of state. In revolutions, he observed in 1845, a search is made for the principle of power 'where it does not lie, that is to say, in a created, contingent, relative entity, such as man, in an entity which, not being its own principle, cannot contain the principle of anything whatsoever'.[84] In earthly cities, inhabited by fallen beings, virtues were not, as they had been for Cabanis, the apanage of a free and elevated soul, but the gift of God; Roman Stoicism drained as inexorably from his world as it had from that of Staël. Yet from Manzoni's Jansenist sympathies, or from his debt to Augustine, one should not draw too hasty a conclusion. For in the matter of theories of divine providence revived and reinforced in the aftermath of the French Revolution there are some crucial distinctions to be made.

Manzoni thus could not subscribe to Joseph de Maistre's cruel vision of marionettes in the grip of a coldly destroying hand, finding Constant's formulations more congenial. In *De la Religion*, the latter had reworked

Bossuet's distinction between 'certains coups extraordinaires', through which God manifested himself to an awestruck humanity, and the general run of secondary causes. So ordinary providence would prevail until the, in itself inexplicable, leap from polytheism to monotheism required the miraculous agency of Moses.[85] Under the First Empire, Manzoni may well have been familiar, through Cabanis or Fauriel, with an earlier version of Constant's theories, but after his reconciliation with the Catholic Church he took his distance from liberal Protestantism. While fervently embracing the truth of the Christian Revelation, as embodied in the seemingly more than human heroism of the first martyrs and therefore in the authority of the universal apostolic church, he was unable to believe that such values found cumulative expression in degraded, earthly time. He wrote of 'the marvellous immutability of the Church in its perpetually Evangelic morality', fulfilled in the midst of mutability, as if human souls, being already redeemed by Christ, were not timebound.[86] There was no place in such a scheme for the doctrine of Accommodationism, hence Croce's charge that Manzoni lacked an authentically historical intelligence, since that doctrine could be construed as a theological precursor of cultural or historical relativism. The Rule of Faith, that is, the hallowed oral tradition of the early Church, was likewise regarded by Manzoni as more nearly a time-stopping fact of ecclesiastical authority than a long-whispered and world-inhabiting song. In the case of Rome, the *carmina*, or lays, which Niebuhr had attributed to the plebeians, could not, in Manzoni's opinion, have been handed down by so oppressed a multitude (originally the vagabond rabble of Vico's first asylums), but were in reality the work of the patricians. Right was not the creation, then, of a submerged but emergent collectivity, but of a 'popolo padrone', whether in early republican Rome or in eighth-century Lombardy.[87] It is easy to see why Gramsci should have found this vision lamentably paternalist.[88]

As Massimiliano Pavan has noted, Manzoni could not conceive of a common measure between human history, which was relative, and universal principles, which were God-given.[89] Whereas Constant believed that in the longest run the equality promised by the Gospel, and latterly by 1789, would be realized on earth, Manzoni did not. A polity might be governed by someone who was 'human' or, to use Vico's phrase, 'most human', yet it would still not see absolute justice. Where Manzoni was closer, however, to Constant than to the neo-Guelphs was in his rejection of Bossuet's concept of 'the people of God', and therefore of that of peoples distant from, or extraneous to, God.

The *Discorso Storico* inaugurated the tradition of neo-Guelph historiography, inspiring a cohort of young historians in the 1830s and 1840s to emulate Manzoni and, in the process, to blaze a trail for that most immoderate expression of nationalist providentialism, the *Primato* of Vincenzo Gioberti. For this reason, Manzoni has often been reckoned a neo-Guelph or at least, as in Croce's account, a lapsed member of the school. Yet he did not actually believe in the temporal power of the Papacy, or in the religious and political mission of Italy. He was not in fact, most scholars now concur, a neo-Guelph at all.[90]

If Manzoni has been assimilated to a historiographic and political current to which, properly speaking, he did not belong, it is because he shared with Cesare Balbo, Carlo Troyat, Vincenzo Gioberti and others a common set of enemies. For the argument of the *Discorso Storico* was designed to refute Machiavelli, who had blamed the Papacy for the perennial weakness and division of Italy, charging it with having repeatedly invited barbarians across the Alps, and had judged Pope Hadrian I's invitation to Charlemagne especially damaging in this regard, not least because the Lombards, after 232 years 'strangers only in name' and holding ' a sort of kingship over the whole of Italy', might have united the peninsula. With the defeat and capture of King Desiderius (father of the eponymous Adelchi), however, the Papacy had been secured against Lombard attack, and Italy was from then on condemned to territorial division and therefore to the invasions of foreign armies.[91] In order to undermine this version of the peninsula's calamitous history, reiterated in the early eighteenth century, in a jurisdictionalist spirit, by Giannone and Muratori, Manzoni applied the two-race theory of the French liberal historians to his own country. Just as the Gallo-Romans had remained separate from the Franks, and the Anglo-Saxons from the Normans, so too had the inhabitants of northern Italy remained distinct from the conquering Lombards. Because the latter had occupied Italy for so long a period of time, because they held no other territories, because they had converted from Arianism to Roman Catholicism, and because they had intermarried with the Romans, Muratori and Giannone had reckoned that they were no longer a separate people.

Manzoni devoted a whole chapter to the refutation of the above claims. Yet he did not actually believe in the ·temporal rights of the Papacy, or in the religious and political mission of Italy. When, therefore, we turn to the vexed question of Pope Hadrian I's invitation to the Franks to overthrow the Lombards' kingdom, we find that Manzoni was not centrally concerned with the future of the Papacy, but rather with the quantum of justice available to the suffering masses. The brute fact of conquest could not be denied, yet in the decrees of Charlemagne, Pepin or Louis the Pious, all references to race were rigorously excluded, 'and this more general, more human and, so to speak, less *ethnic* intention is one of the characteristics that distinguish the Lombard Laws of the Frankish kings or emperors from their [Lombard] predecessors'.[92] This refusal to attribute an ethnic content to such concepts as 'people of God' or 'Christian people' is of particular significance in the context of a discussion of the eighth century, which ended with the *translatio imperii*, or transfer of the Empire to the Franks. Bossuet's *Discours sur l'Histoire Universelle*, written to instruct the Dauphin, closed of course with Charlemagne, Holy Roman Emperor, King of the Franks and therefore bearer of divine providence. Manzoni, however, was more attracted to the doctrines of Massillon and Nicole than to those of Bossuet, and believed that salvation never concerned a whole people but always separate individuals.[93] Nothing followed from the mere fact of belonging to one people rather than another, for the true faith was not inherent in, say, the Jews, the Franks or the Italians.[94]

There is evident in the spiritualist philosophies of the Restoration, in part because of their abhorrence for sensism and materialism, in part because of their rejection of Baconian induction, a disturbing propensity towards a narrowing of ethnographic purview, as tribes within acquired qualities formerly ascribed to tribes without. Vico's lofty vision of the *corsi* and *ricorsi* of the nations had been predicated upon an outright refusal of national primacies, and therefore upon a repudiation of his *De Antiquissima Sapientia*. If, by contrast, one considers the thought, or the art, of the age of nations, there is sometimes a sense of almost suffocating enclosure. Giovita Scalvini, an early reviewer of *I Promessi Sposi*, thus noted that there was an excessively uniform and insistent quality to Manzoni's novel, that readers were not granted 'freedom to roam at will amidst the great variety of the moral world', and that they were placed 'not under the great vault of the firmament', which covers 'all the multiform existence [of the world]', but beneath that of the 'temple which covers the faithful and the altar'.[95] These remarks call to mind Heine's criticisms of 'the dog-like humility and . . . angelic patience' vaunted by spiritualist Romanticism, of his insistence that 'material things also have their good side and are not totally evil', and of his vindication of 'the pleasures of the earth, of this beautiful garden of God, our inalienable heritage'.[96] Given the airless, confined nature of so much Christian-national thought, one can readily understand the attractions of Feuerbach's materialism, notwithstanding its crude and undialectical nature, for Heine or for the young Marx.

Where Restoration Milan is concerned, there is a temptation to draw a line between opposed camps, with Rosmini and Manzoni on one side, and Romagnosi and Cattaneo on the other. More subtle distinctions need, however, to be made. One cannot, for example, assume that all thinkers committed to the rejection of the Epicurean or Lucretian hypothesis of feral wandering invariably invoked a providential destiny for a people of God, or a Christian people. This correlation may, in many cases, hold, but Manzoni was plainly something of an exception.[97] Though aligned with Rosmini, the scourge of Romagnosi and the opponent of Cattaneo, and deeply committed to the revision of Enlightenment accounts of the origin of language and culture, Manzoni consistently refused the characteristic teleologies of the tribe-nation.[98] Consider, for example, his outrage at the idea of a national religion.[99] With these considerations in mind, we may the better understand Cattaneo's unwavering respect for the author of *I Promessi Sposi*, notwithstanding their very real differences, which grew greater with the passing years.

Both Romagnosi and Cattaneo wished to breach the high walls of idealist historiography. Thus, the former noted in 1832 that the sequence elaborated in *The Philosophy of Right*, whereby liberty had ascended a ladder with Oriental, Greek, Roman and Germanic rungs, had rested on a 'massive historical mutilation'. Where in Hegel's series, he objected, was America?[100] There can be no disputing the fact that Romagnosi had only a second-hand knowledge of Hegel, and was therefore in no position to mount a serious critique of his writings.[101] Rather than labour this point, however, I would stress that Romagnosi hoped to create a genuinely universal history, by means of which cultures scattered across all the continents might be ordered in terms of a single chronology, and that in this regard he shared the *idéologues*' ambition to place Julius Caesar's campaigns and events in China, the exploits of Napoleon and contemporaneous occurrences along the Zambezi, within the one narrative, that of all the peoples.[102] Cattaneo likewise rejected the Hegelian notion of the 'unhistorical' nations, and protested at Heinrich Leo's decision to omit China from his universal history and to introduce the Hebrews only very belatedly.[103] It was perhaps his deepest preoccupation, as his essays on Mexico, India and China testify, to meditate upon all of human culture, and so to construct an inductive science of social life. If, therefore, he abhorred idealist philosophy, it was chiefly because its a priori deductions concerning 'the shadows of the I, and the abysses of the entity and of the infinite' obscured 'the times and the places'. There is a striking contrast between his lucid apprehension of non-European cultures and Gioberti's specious subordination of all of human time to the exhaustive prefigurations of Scripture.[104] Locke's exemplary achievement, in Cattaneo's opinion, had been to banish innate ideas, and so to lay the groundwork for a genuine 'science of man', yet neither he nor the *idéologues* had got the measure of the 'collective intelligence of the nations'.[105] This Vico had done, studying

> not only one or other segment of things here below, but . . . as if from a lofty place in the heavens, the universal course of humankind, which *under specific laws and with a specific sequence of developments* gradually draws, from the

childlike ferocity of the savage and the native squalor of the globe, peoples, cities, arts, sciences and customs.

As deeply moved by the observed particularity of culture as he was by that of geological form, Cattaneo believed that the gap between a cannibal on one side of the globe and a European philosopher on the other could not be bridged by 'the weak and doubtful light of metaphysics'; Plato and Aristotle, Descartes and Kant, had attributed the same categories to both, and had as a result failed to describe 'the whole, inexhaustible sequence of national varieties and historical transformations' which separated them. It was simply not possible to deduce a priori the full variety of fables, musical forms or political systems, for they were displayed only in the observed lives of others, that is, in history (or, to be more exact, in histories), and not in the nebulous depths of the self. The human spirit should in short be studied in as many different contexts as possible; only by contemplating the countless faces of 'the ideological polyhedron' could one hope to advance the science of 'social ideology'.[106]

Though the honoured founder of such a science, Vico had rendered it too coherent and too uniform. His 'ideal, eternal history' had been modelled upon classical Antiquity and, more particularly, upon the exhaustively documented changes across the centuries in Roman law.[107] Given such limited sources, he had been free to suppose that the moral chasm between the *bestioni*, the giants, of heroic times and the suavities of late Imperial jurisprudence had everywhere been closed by a sequence inaugurated by gangs of armed patricians, who had held a monopoly of sacred and profane authority, and who had created an asylum to which vagabonds, later their clients, might flee. Yet, as Romagnosi had already objected, the residual (buried but not extirpated) grip of Greek, Roman and Judaic categories meant that the returned barbarism of the Christian Middle Ages was in no wise to be mistaken for the original form.[108] Nor could the resurgent *municipia* be deemed identical to the first cities.[109]

Croce, in his brilliant and influential account of developments in nineteenth-century Italian historiography, scaled down the intellectual debt owed by Cattaneo to Romagnosi.[110] Entertaining, as we have seen, an almost parodic notion of eighteenth-century thought as abstract and anti-historical, he described in the latter's sometimes ponderous treatises a *philosophe*'s attitude, method and criteria, and chose to damn him with faint praise.[111] The glory went all to the new century, for blowing a weather-worn wreck past the reefs of iusnaturalism: 'even he, though formed in the previous century, did not wholly escape the stimulus of new needs, and was a historian and philosopher of history and of what he termed the civilizing process [*incivilmento*]'. The new historiography, however, at once historicist and Vichian, had been founded upon the concept of 'the organic development of the peoples', whereas Romagnosi believed *incivilmento* to be an art that was 'wholly special, wholly traditional and wholly industrial'. In according overmuch importance to the 'dative', to the detriment of the 'native', he had, in Croce's opinion, succumbed to all of the most preposterous fallacies of the Encyclopédists, for whom *incivilmento* was

> a discovery that had appeared at one point on the earth, and which is sometimes operative and sometimes not, and which is introduced among primitive, natural men by means of authority, and above all by credulity, after the method employed by the Jesuits in Paraguay; in short, something that was caused *from outside*, as this process was understood in the eighteenth century, through the actions of a wise legislator, or (what amounts to the same thing) of a single inventive and masterly people.[112]

It is true that Romagnosi had conceived of the civilizing process in terms of the lateral diffusion of techniques, sciences and law codes between peoples, yet so too had Cattaneo (even to the extent of reinstating the Greek provenance of the Twelve Tables, denied so clamorously by Vico). Croce praised Cattaneo for having given a merely empirical value to the terms 'native' and 'dative', where his teacher had posited a 'popolo inventore e incivilitore del genere umano', yet in practice Romagnosi had been of much the same opinion; indeed, he had expressly warned against speculations regarding origins.[113] Croce's taunts regarding the putative origin of the process of *incivilmento*, namely, Oceania, implied that Romagnosi's conception of a maritime chain of brilliance was as absurd or as pernicious as the delusional claims to primacy made for Italy by a neo-Guelph philosopher like Gioberti.[114] There was an element of *boria nazionale*, certainly, in his preoccupation with the Etruscans and with early Italic wisdom, just as there had been in Cuoco's *Platone in Italia*, yet he aimed rather to ward off than to foster a confusion between divine providence and civil philosophy.[115]

The attempt to drive a wedge between the supposedly eighteenth-century, Enlightenment Romagnosi and a historicist, Romantic Cattaneo was always doomed to fail, for the latter time and time again reiterated his teacher's central thesis regarding the native and the dative. In tracing back the new historiography to the rediscovery of Vico, Croce had at once painted out the Enlightenment elements in the thought of Cuoco, the most prominent advocate of the *New Science* in Napoleonic Milan, and obscured the already flourishing tradition of Lombard Vichianism.[116] He contended that Cattaneo, being convinced that there was such a thing as the organic development of the peoples, had captured the genuine spirit of the *New Science*, whereas Romagnosi had not. Yet the notion of a spontaneous, contained and self-sufficient unfolding of national cultures was the very thing that Cattaneo could not countenance. To identify an 'inner impulse', that is to say, the *vis veri*, driving persons from the woods to the fields, from the fields to the cities, from the cities to the nation, and from the nation to humanity, as Vico had done, was in Cattaneo's view to disregard 'the times and the places'.[117] In spite of a declared break with Descartes, the new science had not been truly founded upon erudition, for empirical materials had been moulded to fit the central doctrine of *corsi* and *ricorsi*.[118] What history in fact taught was that no nation had ever arisen by itself; 'it confirmed rather Romagnosi's opinion that one and the same flame of civilization lit through the clash of unknown events in Asia, was then borne from people to people'.[119] Yet Cattaneo, while embracing and extending his teacher's concept of the dative, also used the study of language to shed new light upon the native. Sustaining a balance between the aboriginal and the themisphoric, he at the same time honoured the telling obduracy of human culture across generations and refused the mirage of the eternal tribe-nation. The French and Austrian armies of occupation had sounded the bugle-calls for Cattaneo's thought, but Milanese dialect had been the nightingale. To hear these Mahlerian motifs aright, we have to consider his very first meditations upon the history of language in the context of the barbarian invasions.

## The bugle and the nightingale

Carlo Cattaneo was familiar almost from the start with the dispute raging in Milan between Classicists and Romantics. Between 1820 and 1824, private study with Romagnosi and frequent debate with Manzoni helped to consolidate his abiding interest in moments of historical transition.[120] Intimations of the central themes of his mature writings are thus evident in a synopsis, drafted in 1824. Although the manuscript has affinities with *Ivanhoe* (note, in particular, the opposition between lexicons of war and the hunt and lexicons of agriculture and trade), with Thierry's early essays on the history of France and with Manzoni's discourse of 1822 (note, for example, the emphasis upon the asperities of 'returned' barbarism), closer scrutiny reveals a number of original features.

It would, for example, have covered 'the state of the Latin language *before* the immigration', its opening chapters being listed as: (1) of the origin and of the confused descent of all the European peoples, and of the languages; (2) the first Italics were of various stocks, and of various tongues, all of which were mixed; (3) the first commercial or social Italic language was Etruscan; and (4) dissolution of the Etruscan federation.[121] There is here a characteristic concern with 'confusion' and 'mixture'; the historical record, in Cattaneo's opinion, bore witness to unceasing trans- actions between diverse peoples, and it was out of this complex process of negotiation and translation that the light of law unified the scattered and isolated tribes of the globe. Where the conquest of England was concerned, it had been an error to suppose that it had resulted in the simple juxtaposi- tion of two peoples, conquerors (Normans) and conquered (Angles, Saxons and Danes). For the Angles and Saxons had themselves conquered the island at an earlier date, defeating and displacing Celtic peoples in the process. The Norman Conquest, like the campaigns of Charlemagne, the territorial expansion east of the Elbe by the Teutonic Knights, or the Crusades, was thus not a conflict between nations, a notion wholly alien to Latin Christendom, but 'the continual growth of a religious and patrician confraternity, that was gradually woven from the intermingled fragments of Roman, Celtic, Germanic and Slav peoples'. It was a grievous error, therefore, 'to go about distributing with a haughty or humble hand the constant and absolute name of conquerors and of conquered; since there were both in every race and in every language'.[122] Like Romagnosi, Cattaneo believed that conquest or invasion in Europe had generally involved not vast inundations of peoples, but marauding aristocracies. What were a few thousand Vandals or Goths as against millions of Celts, Iberians and Africans?[123]

It was in fact in the context of a critique of the neo-Guelph histori- ography of Cesare Balbo, predicated upon the special mission of Italy, that Cattaneo countered the spurious salvation of organic belonging with the obdurate fact of dialect, a song not trodden down. He noted that the settlement patterns of the pre-Roman tribes had left their mark upon the dialects (Venetian, Friulian, Lombard, Ligurian, Tuscan) of the penin- sula, at once imparting a particular phonological colouring to Latin (or proto-Romance) and pruning its 'flourishing wood of neuters, passives, middles, optatives [and] duals'.[124] To celebrate the survival across so many centuries of traces of Etruscan, Celtic or even Pelasgic languages was obviously to risk meeting up with the advocates of primacy by another way, as Timpanaro has noted.[125] Cattaneo certainly had an ear for words not born for death, yet the cast of his mind, being austerely philological, resisted the consolation of an eternity bodied forth by the arresting categories of the tribe-nation.

With the arrival in Milan of Bernardino Biondelli, a scientist from Verona versed in Indo-European linguistics and an active collaborator on the recently launched *Politecnico*, Cattaneo was inspired to apply his hard-won insights into the history of the Romance languages to still larger questions regarding a previous sequence of invasions.[126] If the incursions of the fourth and fifth centuries AD had been on a smaller scale than had once been supposed, might not the same be true of the earlier *Völkerwanderung*? Other authors, Friedrich Schlegel among them, had conjured up a picture of vast migratory hordes flowing from the valley of the Indus, reckoned to be 'the cradle of the human race', through Persia, along both shores of the Caspian Sea and across the Caucasus or the Urals to the north-west.[127] The implication was that Europe had been a wooded silence, and that the overflowing population of India had driven others to the most westerly point of the land mass. Yet, Cattaneo objected, Europe had been inhabited by many different peoples at the time of the 'invasions', labouring masses which, though ostensibly subjugated by the military castes, had survived across the centuries. Conquest, being a matter of enforced sovereignty, generally entailed the transfer of the name of an invading aristocracy to the peoples it had subdued, hence the illusion of vast migratory hordes.[128] In the case of Italy, the original 'nationalities', pre-Celtic or Celtic, still whispered in the phonology and lexis of regional dialects, long after Rome had tamed the peninsula or the Germanic tribes had overrun it.[129] If, moreover, one weighed with care the testimonies of Caesar and Tacitus, the tribe-nation of nineteenth-century pan-Germanism also proved to be chimerical. Not only did the *Germania* itself contain references to the presence and consolidated settlement of pre-Germanic peoples (Slavs, Finns and Estonians, Swedes), but in addition the supposedly primordial language had been shown by Heinrich Leo to be a *Michsprache*.[130]

This emphasis upon the stability of placed groups allowed Croce, as we have seen, to counterpose the example of Cattaneo, who had grasped the principle of 'the organic development of the peoples', with Romagnosi, a benighted victim of eighteenth-century thought, who had not. Yet the celebration of ethnic diversity served in all of Cattaneo's writings to add a frayed hem to the providential unity of the Romantic tribe-nation. Rome itself, being from the start a confederation of three peoples, had been, up until Diocletian's reforms, the instrument of *ius gentium*, founding *municipia* on every littoral.[131] The defended, concave beauty of the city walls was complemented by jetty, quay and harbour, where transactions spread truths in creolized garb. If even the Empire is depicted here in terms that call Etruria to mind, it is chiefly because the Etruscans were pioneers in the art of confederation.[132] Although Cattaneo therefore appears at times to be, like Gioberti, celebrating an Italic primacy, this is by no means the case. It was as *themisphoroi*, not as incarnations of the tribe-nation, that the Etruscans earned his praise.[133] In the consolidated bond between city and *contado*, often obscured but never obliterated, lay the ideal principle of Italian history, which was otherwise a sombre labyrinth of Guelph and Ghibelline strife, in which the mind strayed, quite at a loss.[134]

The enduring presence and prestige of the city in Cattaneo's historiography stands in marked contrast to its gradual elimination, notwithstanding appearances to the contrary, in the writings of Augustin Thierry. In his early text on nations, mentioned in passing in chapter 4, the emphasis is all upon confederation. A nation, Thierry observed, was a league, which lasted only as long as its object subsisted, and then dissolved.[135] The Lombard League and the United Provinces were, given the above definition, prime instances of the principle of nationality. In spite of Rousseau's claims regarding the deleterious effects of the sciences and the arts upon valour, the merchants of the allied cities of Lombardy had stood firm against the knights of Frederick Barbarossa's armies. The battle of Legnano had proved that souls could be fashioned as much by a passion for a peaceful independence as by a passion for a war-like independence.[136]

There is thus nothing in Thierry's text of 1817 to suggest that the city would shortly be submerged in the *longue durée* of nationality. Indeed, it seems rather to be a vindication of those persons reviled by Montlosier in 1814. Where the latter, however, had deplored the admission of the labouring classes to civil and political rights, Thierry welcomed the inclusion of those who, in Antiquity, had been excluded. He applauded, in fact, the growing tendency in twelfth-century Europe to turn inwards what had long been cast outside.[137] By the same token, one could claim that, in many of the letters on the history of France, the nation is equated with the cities of which it is composed.[138] Yet the balance of inwardness and outwardness had indubitably shifted. In 1817 one could still hear in Thierry's writings, as in those of Constant, the Rousseauist cry that peoples are not herds at the mercy of princes but are possessed of their own inalienable sovereignty.[139] By 1820, however, there had been a subtle change of emphasis.

Consider the following passage from the letters on the history of France:

> The obstinacy of historians never to attribute any spontaneity, any conception to bodies of men, is a very singular thing. If a whole nation emigrates and seeks a new dwelling for itself, it is in the opinion of annalists and poets, some hero who to illustrate his name chooses to found an empire; if new customs are established, it is some legislator who imagines and imposes them; if a city is organized, it is some prince who gives it life: the people and the citizens are materials for the thought of one man. Do you wish to know precisely who created an institution, who conceived a social enterprise? Look who were those who really wanted it; to them must belong the first idea, the will to act, and at least the largest share in the execution.[140]

Marx, like Cattaneo, would stand by the contrast drawn here between annalists or poets, who sing the praises of the hero, the lawgiver, the prince, and historians, who celebrate the people, the citizens.[141] Yet the refusal of influence from without can generate a purely inward and therefore solipsistic, truth. A genealogical guarantee through migration is then replaced by a myth of autochthony. As Lionel Gossman has observed, Thierry

> insists on unity even where his own historicising gaze constantly discovered division. This inconsistency points to an essential aspect of [his] work as a historian. The conquest theory transformed the logical priority of unity over division into an historical anteriority, and thereby defined division as a stage or a phase, as something that had happened to an original unity, and not as an essential condition.[142]

Once such an original unity is posited, peoples may be ranked in terms of their supposed distance from it, as we saw in the case of the Schlegels, Humboldt or Fichte. In this regard, the principle of nationality has always and everywhere threatened, once the saving grace of good governance in the city is occluded, to topple over into racism. For the gaze of the elect, the undivided, sweeps past the peoples defined by Bossuet as 'distant from God'.

If, with these considerations in mind, we turn again to Croce's critique of Romagnosi, we find that, in his formulations of the distinction between the inward and the outward, the native and the dative, he speaks in accents that Thierry would have recognized. Indeed, his concept of the organic development of peoples stands in a direct line of descent from the letter on the history of France quoted above, and is inextricably linked to the principle of nationality. Gramsci once observed that Croce tended to take the Restoration, not the French Revolution, as the starting-point for his historical narratives, and to this illuminating observation I would add the rider that Enlightenment thought was thereby viewed from the perspective of the Counter-Revolution, and the precise nature of the relation between Romantic and philosophic history obscured.[143] Furthermore, an inveterate hostility towards any form of humanitarian cosmopolitanism led Croce, in blatant disregard of the evidence, to dig a trench between eighteenth-century iusnaturalism and Constantian liberalism. As Norberto Bobbio has shown, the essay on Constant and Jellinek, reviewed in chapter 4, is irremediably skewed, for the simple reason that liberalism was not a repudiation of the Declaration of Rights of Man and the Citizen but, in certain key respects, a defence of it.[144] In Constant's own thought,

individual liberty preserved, notwithstanding the world-inhabiting implications of accommodationist theology, a world-renouncing force. The
work of Amnesty International turns upon just such an equivalence
between imprisoned souls and a universal liberty, as recent debates in the
United Nations, ostensibly on the question of cultural difference and
human rights, at once demonstrate and place under threat. Croce, by
contrast, condemned as abstract moralism any elevation of value above
the organic development of the peoples, and it is this that accounts for his
judgements upon Manzoni and for the more troubling moments in his
long career, notably the rapprochement in Giolittian Italy with the
Florentine reviews, and the sometimes dubious articles of 1924, a chilling
year.

# Abbreviations

Abbreviations that appear in the references as *italic* (e.g. *TNS*) refer to specific titles, given in full at the first instance.

## Collections

| | |
|---|---|
| AMW | *Aesthetic and Miscellaneous Works* |
| CC | *Correspondence Complète* |
| CG | *Correspondence Générale* |
| CP | *Collected Papers* |
| CW | *Collected Works* |
| ELH | *Essais Littéraires et Historiques* |
| GS | *Gesammelte Schriften* |
| MLP | *Mélanges de Littérature et de Politique* |
| OC | *Oeuvres Complètes* |
| OP | *Oeuvres Philosophiques* |
| ORV | *Oeuvres Romanesques et Voyages* |
| OS | *Opere Scelte* |
| SF | *Scritti Filosofici* |
| SL | *Scritti Letterari* |
| SP | *Scritti Politici* |
| SV | *Scritti Vari* |
| SW | *Selected Works* |
| TO | *Tutte le Opere* |

## Journals

| | |
|---|---|
| A | *Antiquity* |
| AA | *American Anthropologist* |
| AC | *Antiquité Classique* |

AESC      *Annales: Economie, Société, Civilization*
AHRF      *Annales Historiques de la Révolution Française*
AJJR      *Annales Jean-Jacques Rousseau*
AJP       *American Journal of Philology*
AP        *Archives Parlementaires*
ASRSP     *Archivio Storico Romano di Storia Patria*
CJ        *The Cambridge Journal*
DHS       *Dix-Huitième Siècle*
E         *Ethics*
EG        *Etudes Germaniques*
EHR       *English Historical Review*
FI        *Forum Italicum*
GSLI      *Giornale Storico della Letteratura Italiana*
HT        *History and Theory*
JWCI      *Journal of the Warburg and Courtauld Institutes*
LP        *La Pensée*
LRB       *London Review of Books*
MAC       *Mémoires de l'Académie Celtique*
MF        *Mercure de France*
NASMI     *Newsletter of the Association for the Study of Modern Italy*
PBA       *Proceedings of the British Academy*
PP        *Past and Present*
PPS       *Proceedings of the Prehistoric Society*
PR        *Philosophical Review*
PS        *Political Studies*
PSQ       *Political Science Quarterly*
PRIA      *Proceedings of the Royal Irish Academy*
RCFI      *Rivista Critica della Filosofia Italiana*
RDM       *Revue des Deux Mondes*
RESS      *Revue Européenne des Sciences Sociales*
RH        *Revue Historique*
RLC       *Revue de Littérature Comparée*
RLMC      *Rivista di Letterature Moderne Comparate*
RSF       *Revue de Sociologie Française*
RSI       *Rivista Storica Italiana*
SN        *Spectateur du Nord*
SS        *Studi Storici*
SVEC      *Studies on Voltaire and on the Eighteenth Century*
WMQ       *The William and Mary Quarterly*
YFS       *Yale French Studies*

For the sake of brevity, the subtitles of some books have been omitted.

# Notes

## Introduction

1. H. Maine, *Village Communities in the East and West*, London 1871.
2. H. Beyle (Stendhal), *Rome, Naples et Florence en 1817* [1817], in V. Del Letto, ed., *Voyages en Italie*, Paris 1973, p. 155. François Picavet's study, *Les Idéologues*, Paris 1891, has been largely superceded by S. Moravia, *Il Tramonto dell'Illuminismo: Filosofia e Politica nella Società Francese (1770–1810)*, Bari 1968, to be read in conjunction with three other works by the same author: see chapter 5, nn. 94, 106; chapter 10, n. 4. The literature on the Coppet Circle is vast yet fragmented, and there is, to my knowledge, no synoptic study of the group.
3. C.-A. de Sainte-Beuve, *Chateaubriand et son Groupe Littéraire sous l'Empire* [1848–49], Paris 1948, vol. 1, pp. 38–42. It was self-evident to contemporaries that Staël, for example, wished to emulate Montesquieu; see Beyle, *Rome, Naples et Florence* [1826], in *Voyages*, p. 326.
4. A.L.G. de Staël, letter of 22 October 1794 to A. de Ribbing, in S. Balayé, ed., *Staël, Lettres à Ribbing*, Paris 1960, p. 181. There are succinct sketches of Constant in B. Fontana, *Benjamin Constant and the Post-Revolutionary Mind*, New Haven and London 1991, ch. 1, and G.A. Kelly, *The Humane Comedy*, Cambridge 1992, pp. 6–17. Simone Balayé has written *Madame de Staël: Lumières et Liberté*, Paris 1969.
5. J.N.A Thierry, 'Première Lettre sur l'Histoire de France' [13 July 1820], in *Dix Ans d'Etudes Historiques*, OC, vol. 3, Paris 1884, p. 559.
6. J. Armstrong, *Nations before Nationalism*, Chapel Hill, North Carolina 1982; A.D. Smith, *The Ethnic Origins of Nations*, Oxford 1986.
7. P. Gay, *The Enlightenment: An Interpretation*, vol. 1: *The Rise of Modern Paganism*, New York 1966.
8. G. Vico, *The Third New Science*, translated by T.G. Bergin and M.H. Fisch, Ithaca and London 1984, pp. 98, 103, 122.
9. E. Troeltsch, *The Social Teaching of the Christian Churches* [1911], translated by O. Wyon, London and New York 1931, vol. 1, p. 67.
10. Thierry, 'Première Lettre', in *Dix Ans*, p. 560.
11. J. Michelet, *Introduction à l'Histoire Universelle* [1831], in P. Viallaneix, ed., J. Michelet, OC, Paris 1971, vol. 2, pp. 251–7.
12. P. Anderson, 'Fernand Braudel', in *A Zone of Engagement*, London 1992, pp. 251–6.
13. F. Meinecke, *Cosmopolitanism and the National State* [1907], translated by F.B. Kimber, Princeton 1970.

# Chapter 1 Passion, Pity and the Last of the Romans

1. *Moniteur*, reprinted edn, Paris 1854, 26 Brumaire year II, vol. 18, p. 541.

2. A. de Lezay-Marnésia, *Des Causes de la Révolution et de ses Résultats*, Paris, April 1797, pp. 33–4; M. Regard, ed., R.-F. de Chateaubriand, *Essai Historique, Politique et Morale sur les Révolutions Anciens et Modernes*, [1797] Paris 1978, p. 85.

3. J. Chaumié, 'Les Girondins', in A. Soboul, ed., *Actes du Colloque Girondins et Montagnards*, Paris 1980, p. 26; and see A. Galante Garrone, *Buonarroti e Babeuf*, Turin 1948, pp. 10–11, 17, 41.

4. T. Carlyle, *The French Revolution: A History*, London 1891, p. 602.

5. E. Hobsbawm, *Echoes of the Marseillaise: Two Centuries Look Back on the French Revolution*, London 1990, pp. 27, 29–31; and S. Mellon, *The Political Uses of History: A Study of Historians in the French Revolution*, Stanford, California 1958, ch. 2, especially pp. 28–9.

6. J.N.A. Thierry, *Dix Ans d'Etudes Historiques*, OC, vol. 3, Paris 1884, pp. 156–66; J.C.L. Simonde de Sismondi, *Histoire des Français* [1821], Brussels 1847, vol. 3, pp. 6–7.

7. Although much of his *Nations and Nationalism since 1780*, Cambridge 1990, especially the final chapter, seems to invite such a treatment. Mellon likewise dates to the Restoration lines of argument that, in my opinion, may be traced back to the Directory.

8. B. Constant, *De la Force du Gouvernement Actuel de la France et de la Necessité de s'y Rallier*, Paris 1796, pp. 32–3.

9. Hobsbawm, *Echoes*, p. 92.

10. F.-A. Boissy d'Anglas, 5 Messidor year III, *Moniteur*, vol. 25, p. 81.

11. A.L.G. de Staël, *De l'Influence des Passions sur le Bonheur des Individus et des Nations*, OC, Paris 1871, vol. 1, p. 146; and C. Lehec and J. Cazeneuve, eds., P.J.G. Cabanis, Preface, *Rapports du Physique et du Moral*, OP, Paris 1956, vol. 1, p. 117.

12. R. Mortier, 'Le Traité "Du Sentiment" de P.-S. Ballanche', in *Approches de Lumières: Mélanges Offertes à Jean Fabre*, Paris 1974, pp. 319–31.

13. Boissy d'Anglas mentioned this episode three times in as many pages, in his crucial speech to the Convention, 21 Ventôse year III, *Moniteur*, vol. 23, pp. 662–4. For testimony from the trial, see B. Baczko, *Comment Sortir de la Terreur: Thermidor et la Révolution*, Paris 1989, p. 212.

14. Constant, *De la Force du Gouvernement*, pp. 32–3; see also Henri Meister's objections to this passage, quoted in B. Jasinski, ed., Staël, CG, vol. 4, pt 1, p. 225n6.

15. Lezay-Marnésia, *Des Causes de la Révolution*, pp. 33–4.

16. B. Constant, *Des Effets de la Terreur* [May 1797], a supplement to the second edn of *Des Réactions Politiques*, now in O. Pozzo di Burgo, ed., *Benjamin Constant: Ecrits et Discours Politiques*, Paris 1964, vol. 1, pp. 93–112.

17. M.-J. Chénier, 6 Messidor year III, *Moniteur*, vol. 25, pp. 70–1. For his remarks on 3 December 1792 to the same effect, see AP, vol. 54, pp. 144–5.

18. Staël, *De l'Influence des Passions*, p. 142; and see M. Ozouf, 'Thermidor ou le Travail de l'Oubli', in *L'Ecole de la France*, Paris 1984, pp. 91–109.

19. Quoted by Georges Lefebvre in *The Coming of the French Revolution*, translated by R.R. Palmer, Princeton 1967, p. 119.

20. G. Romme, letter of 23 July 1789 to G. Dupreuil, in A. Galante Garrone, *Gilbert Romme: Storia di un Rivoluzionario*, Turin 1959, p. 214.

21. Romme, letter of 27/28 July 1789 to Dupreuil, in Galante Garrone, *Gilbert Romme*, pp. 214–15.

22. E. Biré, ed., Chateaubriand, *Mémoires d'Outre-Tombe*, Paris 1880, vol. 1, pp. 275–6; compare the eye-witness account of his friend, Chamfort, in P.R. Auguis, ed., OC [1824–25], Geneva 1968, pp. 341–50.

23. J.C.A.N. de Caritat, Marquis de Condorcet, 'Le Véritable et le Faux Ami du Peuple' [1790–91], in M.F. Arago and A. Condorcet O'Connor, eds., OC, Paris 1847–49, vol. 1, pp. 530–2.

24. F.A. Mignet, *History of the French Revolution from 1789 to 1814* [1824], London 1906, p. 168.

25. A.C. Thibaudeau, *Mémoires sur la Convention et le Directoire*, Paris 1824, vol. 1, p. 36.

26. M. Dorigny, 'Violence et Révolution: Les Girondins et les Massacres du Septembre', in *Actes du Colloque Girondins et Montagnards*, pp. 103–20. For a less harsh assessment, see M.J. Sydenham, *The Girondins*, London 1961, pp. 117–20, yet Burke was acquainted with the basic facts as early as 1793, and Carlyle reiterated them in his history. On Brissot's preoccupation, prior to the Revolution, with penal reform, and on his championing of Beccaria's theories, see F. Venturi, *The End of the Old Regime in Europe, 1776–1789*, vol. 1: *The Great States of the West*, translated by R. Burr Lichfield, Princeton 1991, pp. 426–38.

27. Dorigny, 'Violence et Révolution', pp. 111–12. Compare T. Jefferson, letter of 30 January 1787 to J. Madison, in J.P. Boyd, ed., *The Papers of Thomas Jefferson*, Princeton 1955, vol. 11, p. 93.

28. N. Machiavelli, *The Prince*, translated by R. Price, Cambridge 1988, p. 61. For a discussion of the 'fortunes' of Machiavelli, see chapter 6 of this volume.

29. Galante Garrone, *Buonarroti e Babeuf*, pp. 203–14.

30. A. Manzoni, *La Rivoluzione Francese del 1789 e la Rivoluzione Italiana del 1859: Osservazioni Comparative*, in A. Chiari and F. Ghisalberti, eds., Manzoni, TO, Milan 1963, vol. 4, pp. 309–10.

31. Constant, *De la Force du Gouvernement*, p. 48.

32. Thibaudeau, *Mémoires*, vol. 1, pp. 43–4.

33. Sydenham, *The Girondins*, pp. 202–3.

34. For the whole debate, see AP, vol. 63, pp. 107–16.

35. J.-J. Rousseau, *A Discourse on the Origins of Inequality*, translated by M. Cranston, Harmondsworth 1984, p. 57; B. Gagnebin and M. Raymond, eds., Rousseau, OC, vol. 3, Paris 1964, pp. 111–12.

36. See, however, A. Soboul, 'Jean-Jacques Rousseau et le Jacobinisme', in *Etudes sur le Contrat Social de Jean-Jacques Rousseau*, Paris 1964, pp. 405–24.

37. F. Lanthénas, 'Bases Fondamentales de l'Instruction Publique et de Toute Constitution Libre', AP, vol. 64, p. 485, published 10 May 1793 but probably written in March. See also A.L.L. Saint-Just, *Fragments sur les Institutions Républicaines*, OC, Paris 1908, vol. 2, pp. 530–2.

38. C. Brinton, *The Jacobins: An Essay in the New History* [1930], New York 1961, p. 181; J. Godechot, *La Grande Nation*, Paris 1956, vol. 2, pp. 420, 437–9. Mention should also be made of the Pennsylvania Council of Censors, set up in 1776.

39. M. Robespierre, 10 May 1793, AP, vol. 64, p. 197.

40. For example, Saint-Just, *Fragments*, OC, vol. 2, p. 507.

41. L. Legendre, 5 Fructidor year III, *Moniteur*, vol. 25, p. 524.

42. R. Andrews, 'Le Néo-Stoicisme et le Législateur Montagnard', in *Gilbert Romme et son Temps (1750–1795)*, Paris 1966, p. 197.

43. H.T. Parker, *The Cult of Antiquity and the French Revolution*, Chicago 1937.

44. A. Keaveney, 'The Three Gracchi: Tiberius, Caius and Babeuf', in *La Storia della Storiografia Europea sulla Rivoluzione Francese*, published by the Istituto Storico Italiano per l'Età Moderna e Contemporanea, Rome 1990, pp. 417–32.

45. A. MacIntyre, *After Virtue*, London 1981, p. 238.

46. MacIntyre, *After Virtue*, pp. 181–7, 239–43.

47. Gilbert Ryle, in 'Jane Austen and the Moralists', CP, London 1971, vol. 2, pp. 276–91, gave to *Emma* the subtitle 'Influence and Interference'.

48. R.R. Palmer, *The Age of the Democratic Revolution: A Political History of Europe and America 1760–1800*, Princeton 1964–65, vol. 2, pp. 124–5; also G. Wood, *The Creation of the American Republic 1776–1787*, Chapel Hill, North Carolina 1969, pp. 569–71.

49. Wood, *The Creation of the American Republic*, pp. 571–2, 610–13; I. Kramnick, Introduction, in J. Madison, A. Hamilton and J. Jay, *The Federalist Papers*, Harmondsworth 1987, p. 54.

50. R. Cobb and G. Rudé, 'Le Dernier Mouvement Populaire de la Révolution à Paris: les Journées de Germinal et de Prairial An III', RH, vol. 214, pp. 250–81; Galante Garrone, *Gilbert Romme*, pp. 467–8.

51. A. Soboul, 'Présentation de Gilbert Romme', in *Gilbert Romme et son Temps*, p. 19. There are many damning references to the *Messager du Soir* in *Le Tribun du Peuple*.

52. G. Lefebvre, *La Révolution Française*, Paris 1963, p. 441; a view shared by George Rudé and by Denis Woronoff.

53. D.J. Garat, in *Mémoires Historiques sur la Vie de Suard, sur ses Ecrits, et sur le XVIIIe Siècle*, Paris 1820, vol. 2, pp. 337–8, runs together, in a strangely confused paragraph, the murder of Féraud, Boissy d'Anglas's salute and the suicides of the martyrs of Prairial, as if they were all part of the same monstrous and unparalleled disorder; see also A. Lezay-Marnésia, *Les Ruines, ou Voyages en France, pour Servir de Suite à Celle de Grèce*, Paris 1795, p. vin2, an inferior pastiche of Volney's famous book.

54. We do know, however, that the martyrs of Prairial swiftly became exemplary figures for the Babouvists; see G. Babeuf, *Le Tribun du Peuple*, republished in Milan 1966, nos. 36, 37, 38.

55. M. Eude, 'Le "Suicide heroïque" d'un Montagnard en Prairial An III, Jacques-Philippe Rühl (1737–1795)', in *Gilbert Romme et son Temps*, p. 184.

56. J. Dautry, 'Réflexions sur les Martyrs de Prairial, Sacrifice Héroïque et Mentalité Révolutionnaire', in *Gilbert Romme et son Temps*, p. 204.

57. B. Constant, letter of 10 Prairial year III to A. de Nassau, in D. Mélégari, ed., *Journal Intime de Benjamin Constant et Lettres à sa Famille et à ses Amis*, Paris 1895, p. 234.

58. B. Constant, reminiscences of 1828, in Pozzo di Burgo, ed., *Benjamin Constant*, vol. 1, p. 7; R. Cobb, 'Notes sur la Répression contre le Personnel Sans-Culotte de 1795 à 1801', AHRF, vol. 26, 1954, pp. 31–2.

59. Françoise Brunel, in 'Les Derniers Montagnards et l'Unité Révolutionnaire', AHRF, vol. 49, 1977, p. 385, gives the impression that this title was first accorded to Romme and the others by M.A. Baudot, a Montagnard and an associate of Babeuf, in memoirs published posthumously in 1893. Yet Carlyle had also applied it to the last of the Montagnards, in 1837. I would imagine that, being a familiar usage in Roman history, occurring in, for example, Edward Gibbon, it was frequently applied to the Prairial martyrs.

60. C.E. Vaughan, ed., *Political Writings of Jean-Jacques Rousseau*, Cambridge 1915, vol. 1, p. 320.

61. A. Soboul, 'Robespierre and the Popular Movement', PP, 5, 1954, pp. 57–60.

62. Soboul, 'Robespierre', pp. 65–6. Robespierrists such as Le Bon and the Baudots had been convinced that the decrees were to be implemented immediately throughout France; see Galante Garrone, *Buonarroti e Babeuf*, p. 89.

63. Brunel, 'Les Derniers Montagnards', p. 400, and note G. Williams, *Artisans and Sans-Culottes: Popular Movements in France and Britain during the French Revolution*, London 1989, 2nd edn, p. 91.

64. Galante Garrone, *Gilbert Romme*, pp. 374, 421, 433, 441n and 488n2; Lefebvre, *La Révolution Française*, p. 372.

65. Galante Garrone, *Gilbert Romme*, p. 479.

66. Andrews, 'Le Néo-Stoicisme et le Législateur Montagnard', p. 199.

67. Galante Garrone, *Gilbert Romme*, p. 478.

68. By this time Constant had declared himself 'altogether Tallienist', see letter of 14 October 1794 to l. de Charrière, in D. Candaux, C.P. Courtney, P.H. Dubois, S. Dubois-de Bruyn, P. Thompson, J. Vercruysse, D.M. Wood, eds, l. de Charrière, OC, Amsterdam and Geneva 1979–84, vol. 4, p. 605.

69. Galante Garrone, *Gilbert Romme*, pp. 321–3.

70. Galante Garrone, *Gilbert Romme*, pp. 339, 397.

71. Dautry, 'Réflexions', in *Gilbert Romme et son Temps*, p. 204.

72. Dautry, 'Réflexions', in *Gilbert Romme et son Temps*, p. 204.

73. R. Legrand, *Babeuf et ses Compagnons de Route*, Paris 1981, p. 162.

74. Andrews, 'Le Néo-Stoicisme et le Législateur Montagnard', p. 199.

75. Saint-Just, *Fragments*, OC, vol. 2, p. 494.

# Chapter 2 Word and City

1. Boissy d'Anglas, 21 Ventôse year III, *Moniteur*, vol. 23, pp. 660–1. The three men arrested were Barère, Billaud-Varenne and Collot d'Herbois.

2. B. Muntéano, *Madame de Staël et la Constitution de l'An III*, Paris 1931.

3. On the Pennsylvanian constitution, see F. Mazzei, *Recherches Historiques et Politiques sur les Etat-Unis de l'Amérique Septentrionale*, Paris 1788, vol. 1, pp. 193–202.

4. A. Deleyre, 30 Messidor year III, *Moniteur*, vol. 25, p. 276; for an earlier formulation, see Condorcet, 'Lettres d'un Bourgeois de New-Haven à un Citoyen de Virginie', OC, vol. 9, pp. 474–84, originally a part of Mazzei's *Recherches*.

5. Boissy d'Anglas, 5 Messidor year III, *Moniteur*, vol. 25, pp. 98–9.

6. Boissy d'Anglas, 5 Messidor year III, *Moniteur*, vol. 25, p. 91.

7. Boissy d'Anglas, 21 Ventôse year III, *Moniteur*, vol. 23, p. 661.

8. C.-F. de Volney, *Les Ruines*, in A. Bossange, ed., Volney, OC, Paris 1847, p. 32; *Leçons d'Histoire*, OC, p. 576; also A.L.G. de Staël, *Réflexions sur la Paix Intérieure*, a text written even as the Constitution of the year III was being drafted, OC, Paris 1871, vol. 1, pp. 57–8. Such sentiments were denounced by Babeuf in *Le Tribun du Peuple*, Milan 1966, no. 34, pp. 12, 52.

9. G. Lefebvre, *La Révolution Française*, Paris 1963, pp. 457–8; D. Woronoff, *The Thermidorean Regime and the Directory 1794–1799*, translated by J. Jackson, Cambridge 1984, pp. 29–30.

10. Robespierre, 24 April 1793, AP, vol. 63, p. 197.

11. Robespierre, 24 April 1793, AP, vol. 63, p. 198.

12. J. Mailhe, 26 Thermidor year III, *Moniteur*, vol. 25, p. 497.

13. G. Wood, *The Creation of the American Republic 1776–1787*, Chapel Hill, North Carolina, 1969, p. 285.

14. On the natural law tradition, and accounts in Locke, Grotius and Pufendorf regarding the relation between private property and common ownership of the earth, see R.L. Meek, *Social Science and the Ignoble Savage*, Cambridge 1976, ch. 1, and I. Hont and M. Ignatieff, 'Needs and Justice in the Wealth of Nations', in I. Hont and M. Ignatieff, eds., *Wealth and Virtue*, Cambridge 1983, pp. 1–31.

15. T.W. Tate, 'The Social Contract in America, 1774–1787: Revolutionary Theory as a Conservative Instrument', WMQ, 3rd series, 22, 1965, pp. 375–91.

16. L. Colletti, 'Rousseau as Critic of Civil Society', in *From Rousseau to Lenin*, translated by L. Merrington and J. White, London 1972, pp. 143–93.

17. J.G.A. Pocock, *The Machiavellian Moment: Florentine Political Thought and the Atlantic Republican Tradition*, Princeton 1975, p. 545.

18. M. Forsyth, *Unions of States: The Theory and Practice of Confederation*, New York [Leicester University Press] 1981, a study to which I owe much.

19. Forsyth, *Unions*, p. 139.

20. See, however, F. Brunel, 'Mélanges sur l'Historiographie de la Réaction Thermidorienne: pour une Analyse Politique de l'Echec de la Voie Jacobine', AHRF, vol. 51, 1979, pp. 455-74. For the revival of Jacobinism, see I. Woloch, *Jacobin Legacy: The Democratic Movement under the Directory*, Princeton 1970.

21. La Harpe, *De la Guerre Déclarée par nos Derniers Tyrants à la Raison, à la Morale, aux Lettres et aux Arts*, reprinted in *Cours de Littérature Ancienne et Moderne*, Paris 1851, vol. 2, pp. 78, 79, 81.

22. La Harpe, *De la Guerre*, p. 91; 'Nouveaux Eclaircissements sur l'Eloquence Ancienne', in *Cours*, vol. 2, pp. 295–310.

23. La Harpe, *De la Guerre*, p. 81.

24. La Harpe, *Cours*, vol. 2, p. 213; compare Condorcet, 'Vie de Voltaire' [1789], OC, vol. 4, pp. 20–24.

25. B. Constant, *Des Réactions Politiques*, in O. Pozzo di Burgo, ed., *Benjamin Constant: Ecrits et Discours Politiques*, Paris 1964, vol. 1, p. 57.

26. S. Moravia, *Il Tramonto dell'Illuminismo: Filosofia e Politica nella Società Francese (1770-1810)*, Bari 1968, p. 271n.

27. J.-J. Rousseau, *The Social Contract*, translated by M. Cranston, Harmondsworth 1968, p. 82; B. Gagnebin and M. Raymond, eds., Rousseau, OC, vol. 3, Paris 1964, pp. 379–80; see A.L.G. de Staël, *Lettres sur Rousseau*, Geneva 1979, pp. 77–8.

28. See M. Rosa, *Dispotismo e Libertà nel Settecento: Interpretazioni 'Repubblicane' di Machiavelli*, Bari 1964, ch. 2.

29. La Harpe, *De la Guerre*, pp. 85–6n.

30. A.J. Bingham, *Marie-Joseph Chénier: Early Political Life and Ideas, 1789–94*, New York 1939, pp. 56–60, 117–25.

31. For example, B.G. Niebuhr, letter of 18/19 May 1794 to his parents, in S. Rytkönen, *Barthold Georg Niebuhr als Politiker und Historiker*, Helsinki 1958, p. 34.

32. La Harpe, *Cours*, vol. 2, p. 271.

33. La Harpe, *Du Fanatisme dans le Langage Révolutionnaire ou de la Persécution Suscitée par les Barbares du Dix-Huitième Siècle, Contre la Religion Chrétienne et ses Ministres*, Paris 1797, pp. 6, 34; 'Nouveaux Eclaircissements', p. 301.

34. J. Rancière, *Les Mots de l'Histoire*, Paris 1992, pp. 184–5.

35. C. Springer, *Ruins and Representation in Italian Romanticism, 1775–1850*, Cambridge 1987, p. 64.

36. B. Constant, *Des Effets de la Terreur*, in O. Pozzo di Burgo, ed., *Benjamin Constant: Ecrits et Discours Politiques*, Paris 1964, vol. 1, p. 108, 111n.

37. V.E. Giuntella, 'La Giacobina Repubblica Romana (1798–1799)', ASRSP, vol. 73, 1950, pp. 8–12.

38. J. Godechot, ed., A.L.G. de Staël, *Considérations sur la Révolution Française*, Paris 1983, p. 348.

39. J.B. Galley, *Claude Fauriel: Membre de l'Institut 1772–1843*, Saint-Etienne 1909, pp. 43–5, and, more generally, R.R. Palmer, *The Improvement of Humanity: Education and the French Revolution*, Princeton 1985, pp. 208–18.

40. Volney, *Leçons d'Histoire*, OC, pp. 570–1; Locke, *An Essay*, pp. 44–7.

41. Volney, *Les Ruines*, OC, pp. 70–1. *La Loi Naturelle*, published in 1793 as *Catéchisme du Citoyen Français*, is a pendant to *Les Ruines*.

42. Volney, *Leçons d'Histoire*, OC, pp. 580–1, 593.

43. P. Bénichou, *Le Temps des Prophètes*, Paris 1977.

44. Volney, *Les Ruines*, OC, p. 50.

45. Compare P.J.G. Cabanis, 'Lettre à M. F[auriel] sur les Causes Premières' [1806–07], OP, vol. 2, p. 261.

46. A. Galante Garrone, *Gilbert Romme: Storia di un Rivoluzionario*, Turin 1959, p. 405n1.

47. Volney was at odds with many of his allies on the Comité d'Instruction Publique, which had staged the Pantheonization of Rousseau on 19 Vendémiaire; see J. Roussel, *Jean-Jacques Rousseau en France après la Révolution, 1795–1830*, Paris 1972, pp. 11–20. The mood of the festival might fairly be compared with that of the audience for Bernardin de Saint-Pierre's lectures at the Ecole Normale.

48. Volney, *Leçons d'Histoire*, OC, p. 573n2, p. 581.

49. Volney, *Leçons d'Histoire*, OC, pp. 568, 569.

50. Volney, *Voyage en Syrie et en Egypte* [1787], OC, p. 47.

51. See also D.-J. Garat, *Mémoires Historiques sur la Vie de Suard, sur ses Ecrits, et sur le XVIIIe Siècle*, Paris 1820, vol. 1, p. 145.

52. Rousseau, *A Discourse on the Sciences and the Arts*, translated by G.D.H. Cole, in Rousseau, *The Social Contract and Discourses*, London 1913, p. 119; OC, vol. 3, p. 5.

53. Staël, *Lettres*, p. iii, pp. 5, 10, 12, 22, 32, 43, 62, 64, 70, 71, 82, 84, 85, 104, 109, 127.

54. Rousseau, *Emile, ou de l'Education*, OC, vol. 4, p. 547.

55. Roussel, *Jean-Jacques Rousseau*, pp. 321–5.

56. Mme Necker de Saussure, 'Notice sur le Caractère et les Ecrits', in Staël, OC, Paris 1871, vol. 3, p. 7.

57. I. de Charrière, 'Eloge de Rousseau' [1790], OC, vol. 10, pp. 202–3.

58. Staël, *Lettres*, p. 12.

59. Rousseau, *A Discourse on the Sciences and the Arts*, Cole, pp. 128, 138; OC, vol. 3, pp. 14, 25.

60. Staël, *Lettres*, pp. 81–2.

61. For example, D. Mornet, *Les Origines Intellectuelles de la Révolution Française*, Paris 1933.

62. R. Barny, 'Jean-Jacques Rousseau dans la Révolution Française (1787–1791)', AHRF, vol. 51, 1978, p. 113.

63. D. Hume, 'Of Eloquence', in T.H. Green and T.H. Grose, eds., *Essays Moral, Political and Literary*, London 1898, vol. 1, pp. 166, 170–1. Even those who present Hume as a staunch advocate of modern, not ancient liberty, tend to add some fine shading to their thesis. See, for example, J.W. Burrow, *A Liberal Descent: Victorian Historians and the English Past*, Cambridge 1981, pp. 25–8, and the crucial admission, touching upon the thought of Adam Smith also, on pp. 22–3.

64. I. Kant, 'On the Common Saying: "This May Be True in Theory but it does not Apply in Practice" ', in H. Reiss, ed., *Kant: Political Writings*, Cambridge 1991, p. 79.

65. M. Viroli, *Jean-Jacques Rousseau and the 'Well-Ordered Society'*, translated by D. Hanson, Cambridge 1988, pp. 10–11. In other respects, I owe much to Viroli's exposition.

66. Rousseau, *Emile*, OC, vol. 4, p. 858.

67. Reiss, Introduction, *Kant: Political Writings*, p. 28.

68. See, in particular, Staël's account of her visit to Rousseau's tomb at Ermenonville, *Lettres*, pp. 124–5, which contrasts, as Roussel has rightly observed, with the use to which the same episode is put in *Des Circonstances Actuelles*.

69. R. Mauzi, *L'Idée du Bonheur dans la Littérature et la Pensée Française au XVIIIe Siècle*, Paris 1960, p. 14n1.

70. Staël, *Lettres*, pp. 84–5.

71. Barny, 'Rousseau dans la Révolution', p. 20.

72. J.W. von Goethe, letter of 5 December 1796 to J.C.F. von Schiller, in *Correspondence between Goethe and Schiller, from 1794 to 1805*, translated by L.D Schmitz, London 1877, vol. 1, p. 266.

73. Beyle (Stendhal), 8 August 1805, Journal, *Oeuvres Intimes*, Paris 1961; for harsher judgements, *Rome, Naples et Florence en 1817*, in V. Del Letto, ed., *Voyages en Italie*, Paris 1973, pp. 233–4.

74. A.L.G. de Staël, *De l'Influence des Passions sur le Bonheur des Individus et des Nations*, OC, Paris 1871, vol. 1, p. 136; on her dialogue with Diderot and Vauvenargues, see Mauzi, *L'Idée du Bonheur*, ch. 11, and R. Mortier, 'Madame de Staël et l'Héritage des "Lumières" ', *Clarté et Ombres du Siècle des Lumières*, Geneva 1969, p. 127.

75. C. Rosso, 'Mme de Staël e il Trattato "De l'Influence des Passions sur le Bonheur" ', RLMC, vol. 20, Sept.–Dec. 1967, p. 190.

76. Staël, *De l'Influence des Passions*, p. 109.

77. Montesquieu, *The Spirit of the Laws*, translated by A.M. Cohler, B.C. Miller and H.S. Stone, Cambridge 1989, p. 21.

78. Staël, *De l'Influence des Passions*, p. 110n.

79. H. Grange, ed., Constant, *Fragments d'un Ouvrage Abandonné*, Geneva 1991.

80. Staël, *De l'Influence des Passions*, pp. 108–9.

81. For further discussion of this point, see chapter 6 of this volume.

82. Staël, *De l'Influence des Passions*, p. 172.

83. Compare P. Déguise, *Benjamin Constant Méconnu*, Geneva 1966, ch. 2.

84. Mauzi, *L'Idée du Bonheur*, p. 455.

85. L. de Clapiers, Marquis de Vauvenargues, *Introduction à la Connaissance de l'Esprit* [1746], in H. Bonnier, ed., *Oeuvres Complètes de Vauvenargues*, Paris 1968, vol. 1, p. 239.

86. D. Diderot, *Pensées Philosophiques* [1746], OC, Paris 1875, vol. 1, p. 127.

87. J. Chouillet, *Diderot: Poète de l'Energie*, Paris 1984, ch. 1.

88. F. Venturi, *Utopia and Reform in the Enlightenment*, Cambridge 1971, pp. 71–73.

89. M. Delon, 'La Théorie de l'Energie à Coppet', in E. Hofmann, ed., *Benjamin Constant, Madame de Staël et le Groupe de Coppet*, Oxford and Lausanne 1982, pp. 443–5.

90. G. Ryle, 'Jane Austen and the Moralists', CP, London 1971, vol. 2, pp. 276–91.

91. Staël, *Essai sur les Fictions*, OC, Paris 1871, vol. 1, p. 70; see Mauzi, *L'Idée du Bonheur*, pp. 30–6, 455–7.

92. Staël, *Lettres*, p. 1v; letter of 30 May 1800 to J.A. Martin-Gourgas, CG, vol. 4, pt 1, p. 279.

93. Rousseau, *Emile*, OC, vol. 4, p. 596.

94. K. Mueller-Vollmer, 'Politique et Esthétique: l'Idéalisme Concret de Benjamin Constant, Guillaume de Humboldt et Madame de Staël', in Hofmann, ed., *Benjamin Constant*, pp. 453–73.

95. M.L. S. de Grouchy, Marquise de Condorcet, *Lettres sur la Sympathie*, appended to Smith, *Théorie des Sentiments Moraux*, Paris 1798, vol. 2, p. 356.

96. A. Smith, *The Theory of Moral Sentiments*, ed. D.D. Raphael and A.L. Macfie, Oxford 1976, p. 23.

97. Preface to Condorcet, *Esquisse d'un Tableau Historique des Progrès de l'Esprit Humain*, in M.F. Arago and A. Condorcet O'Connor, eds., OC, Paris 1847–49, vol. 6, p. 7.

98. I rely here on D.D. Raphael, 'The Impartial Spectator', in A.S. Skinner and T. Wilson, eds., *Essays on Adam Smith*, Oxford 1975, pp. 83–99.

99. Raphael, 'The Impartial Spectator', p. 93.

100. Raphael, 'The Impartial Spectator', p. 91.

101. Raphael, 'The Impartial Spectator', p. 92.

102. Staël, *De l'Influence des Passions*, p. 290.

103. Grouchy, *Lettres sur la Sympathie*, pp. 370–1.

104. The most controversial text within the *idéologue* tradition, from this point of view, is Cabanis, 'Lettre à M. F[auriel]'.

105. Meek, *Social Science and the Ignoble Savage*, ch. 2.

106. See, for example, D.-J. Garat, *Mémoires Historiques sur la Vie de Suard, sur ses Ecrits, et sur le XVIIIe Siècle*, Paris 1820, vol. 1, pp. 133–50.

107. N. Phillipson, 'Adam Smith as Civic Moralist', in Hont and Ignatieff, *Wealth and Virtue*, pp. 179–202.

108. Grouchy, *Lettres sur la Sympathie*, p. 426.

109. For example, Cabanis, 'Lettre à M. F[auriel]', pp. 295–7.

110. A. MacIntyre, *After Virtue*, London 1981, p. 236.

111. The *Lettres sur la Sympathie* contain several passages (pp. 362, 366, 369, 374–6, 408) infused with an intensely egalitarian tone, strangely at odds with the spirit of, for example, Cabanis's pronouncements in 1798–99, to which I refer in chapter 6.

## Chapter 3 Rousseau's Rome

1. J.-J. Rousseau, CC, ed. R.A. Leigh, Geneva and Madison, Wisconsin 1969, vol. 10, p. 26.

2. J.-J. Rousseau, *A Discourse on the Sciences and the Arts*, (henceforth *DSA*) translated by G.D.H. Cole, in Rousseau, *The Social Contract and Discourses*, London 1913, p. 123; OC, vol. 3, p. 9.

3. There were many more or less barbed retellings of the story, among them C.-F. de Volney, 'Observations Générales sur les Indiens ou Savages de l'Amérique du Nord', in A. Bossange, ed., OC, Paris 1847, p. 718n.

4. J.-J. Rousseau, *Lettre à C. de Beaumont*, OC, vol. 4, p. 928, and *Troisième Dialogue*, OC, vol. 1, p. 930; also, R. Hubert, *Rousseau et l'Encyclopédie*, Paris 1928, and P. Burgelin, 'Le Social et la Politique chez Rousseau', in *Etudes sur le Contrat Social* (henceforth *ECS*), Paris 1964, p. 165. For discussion of the writings on Corsica and Poland, see J. Fabre, 'Realité et Utopie dans la Pensée Politique de Rousseau', AJJR, 1962, vol. 35, pp. 181–216, and on the relation between the plainly delusional dialogues and the earlier writings, see J. Proust, 'Le Premier des Pauvres', *Europe*, vol. 391–2, November and December 1961, pp. 13–21. This said, my intention in this book has always been to discover faultlines in the thought of particular individuals. In this regard, I owe much to Timpanaro's account of Herder, Rousseau and Vico, and to Venturi's comments on Montesquieu.

5. J.-J. Rousseau, *The Confessions*, translated by J.M. Cohen, Harmondsworth 1953, p. 327; OC, vol. 1, p. 351.

6. Rousseau, *The Confessions*, Cohen, p. 328; OC, vol. 1, p. 351.

7. Rousseau, *The Confessions*, Cohen, p. 361; OC, vol. 1, p. 388; see also Rousseau, *The Confessions*, Cohen, p. 379; OC, vol. 1, p. 407.

8. Rousseau, *DSA*, Cole, p. 128; OC, vol. 3, 14–15.

9. J. Starobinski, 'La Prosopopée de Fabricius', RSF, vol. 16, 1976, pp. 85–6.

10. Duncan Forbes, in the Introduction to A. Ferguson, *An Essay on the History of Civil Society*, Edinburgh 1966, p. xxiv, observed that: 'The Legislator myth flourished in the eighteenth century, for a number of reasons, and its destruction was perhaps the most original and daring *coup* of the social science of the Scottish Enlightenment.' Yet the myth persisted to some extent in the writings of, for example, David Hume and Adam Smith; see Duncan Forbes, *Hume's Philosophical Politics*, Cambridge 1976, pp. 316–19, and D. Winch, *Adam Smith's Politics*, Cambridge 1978, pp. 159–60.

11. For example, A.L.G. de Staël, *Lettres sur Rousseau*, Geneva 1979, pp. 84–5.

12. M. Gauchet, 'Les Lettres sur l'Histoire de France d'Augustin Thierry', in P. Nora, ed., *Les Lieux de la Mémoire*, vol. 2: *La Nation*, Paris 1986, p. 264.

13. L. Gossman, 'Augustin Thierry and Liberal Historiography', in *History and Theory: Studies in the Philosophy of History*, vol. 15, no. 4, 1976, p. 22.

14. Gauchet, 'Les Lettres', p. 256; and see chapter 10 of this volume.

15. J.-J. Rousseau, *Deuxième Dialogue*, OC, vol. 1, pp. 828–9.

16. Rousseau, *DSA*, Cole, pp. 123–5, OC, vol. 3, pp. 10–12.

17. Rousseau, *Troisième Dialogue*, OC, vol. 1, p. 935.

18. J.-J. Rousseau, *The Social Contract*, (henceforth *SC*) translated by M. Cranston, Harmondsworth 1968, p. 89; OC, vol. 3, p. 385.

19. J.-J. Rousseau, *A Discourse on the Origins of Inequality*, (henceforth *DOI*) translated by M. Cranston, Harmondsworth 1984, p. 58; OC, vol. 3, p. 113; and *Jugement sur la Polysynodie*, OC, vol. 3, pp. 637–8.

20. R. Barny, *L'Eclatement Révolutionnaire du Rousseauisme*, Paris 1988.

21. B. de Jouvenel, 'Rousseau the Pessimistic Evolutionist', YFS, vol. 28, 1961–62, pp. 83–96.

22. See G.A. Kelly, *Idealism, Politics and History: Sources of Hegelian Thought*, Cambridge 1969, chs 1 and 2.

23. J.-J. Rousseau, *Les Rêveries*, OC, vol. 1, p. 995.

24. Rousseau, *Confessions*, Cohen, p. 155; OC, vol. 1, p. 159; letter of 4 October 1737 to J.A. Carbonnel, CC, vol. 1, p. 61.

25. Starobinski, Introduction, Rousseau, OC, vol. 3, pp. xliv–xlviii.

26. B. Baczko, 'Rousseau et l'Aliénation Sociale', AJJR, vol. 35, 1962, pp. 223–31.

27. J.-J. Rousseau, Preface, *Narcisse*, OC, vol. 2, p. 968; *DOI*, Cranston, p. 147; OC, vol. 3, p. 202.

28. K. Marx, *Capital: A Critique of Political Economy*, translated by B. Fowkes, London 1976, vol. 1, p. 876. But note Rousseau, *DOI*, Cranston, p. 152; OC, vol. 3, p. 206.

29. I owe a debt, again, to L. Colletti, 'Rousseau as Critic of Civil Society', in *From Rousseau to Lenin*, translated by L. Merrington and J. White, London 1972, pp. 143–93.

30. Rousseau, *DOI*, Cranston, pp. 114–15, 118–19; OC, vol. 3, pp. 169–70, 174–5.

31. L. Gossman, 'Time and History in Rousseau', SVEC, vol. 30, 1964, pp. 311–49.

32. Fabre, 'Realité et Utopie', p. 213, but contrast Franco Venturi's line of argument, paraphrased in chapter 6 of this volume.

33. J.-J. Rousseau, *Lettres Ecrites de la Montagne* (henceforth *LEM*), OC, vol. 3, p. 810.

34. M. Launay, *Jean-Jacques Rousseau: Ecrivain Politique*, Cannes and Grenoble 1972, chs 2 and 3.

35. Rousseau, *DSA*, Cole, p. 123; OC, vol. 3, p. 9.

36. Rousseau, *LEM*, p. 820. J. Cousin, 'J.-J. Rousseau Interprète des Institutions Romains dans le Contrat Social', *ECS*, pp. 13–34, is therefore misleading. Compare P. Andrivet, 'Jean-Jacques Rousseau: Quelques Aperçus de son Discours Politique sur l'Antiquité Romaine', SVEC, vol. 151, 1976, pp. 131–49, a more sensitive appraisal.

37. Rousseau, *SC*, Cranston, p. 61n; OC, vol. 3, pp. 361–2.

38. T. Livy, *Ab Urbe Condita*, 1, 7, Loeb, vol. 1, p. 6.

39. J.-J. Rousseau, *Dernière Réponse*, OC, vol. 3, pp. 88–9.

40. Rousseau, *Dernière Réponse*, pp. 86–7.

41. Plutarch, *Les Vies des Hommes Illustres*, Amyot's version, Paris 1951, vol. 1, p. 754.

42. Dionysius of Halicarnassus, *Roman Antiquities*, 20.13.1, Loeb, vol. 7, pp. 422–3.

43. Cicero, *De Republica; De Legibus*, 2.58, Loeb, pp. 442–4.

44. Livy, *Ab Urbe Condita*, 9.16.19, Loeb, vol. 4, pp. 224–5.

45. G.B. Niebuhr, *History of Rome* (henceforth *HR*), 2nd edn, translated by J.C. Hare and C. Thirlwall, London 1837, vol. 1, p. 502.

46. J.-J. Rousseau, *A Discourse on Political Economy* (henceforth *DPE*), Cole, pp. 246–7; OC, vol. 3, p. 255.

47. Rousseau, *DOI*, Cranston, p. 63; OC, vol. 3, p. 118.

48. Plutarch, *Les Vies des Hommes Illustres*, vol. 1, pp. 890–2.

49. C.L. de Secondat, Baron de Montesquieu, *Considerations on the Causes of the Greatness of the Romans and their Decline*, translated by D. Lowenthal, London and New York, 1965, ch. 10.

50. Rousseau, *DSA*, Cole, p. 127; OC, vol. 3, p. 14.

51. D. Strong, *Roman Art*, Harmondsworth 1976, p. 275.

52. Plutarch, *Les Vies des Hommes Illustres*, vol. 1, pp. 754–5; a fact mentioned by Bacon and, in the nineteenth century, by both Constant and Niebuhr.

53. Plutarch, *Les Vies des Hommes Illustres*, vol. 1, p. 785.

54. Rousseau, *Dernière Réponse*, p. 76.

55. C.E. Vaughan, ed., *Political Writings of Jean-Jacques Rousseau*, Cambridge 1915, vol. 1, p. 320; R. Derathé, editorial comment in J.-J. Rousseau, OC, vol. 3, pp. 1494–5. R.A. Leigh, 'Jean-Jacques Rousseau and the Myth of Antiquity in the 18th Century', in R.R. Bolgar, ed., *Classical Influences on Western Thought 1650–1870*, Cambridge 1979, p. 165, remarks upon the 'oddly protracted study of Roman institutions and voting methods', and Cousin, 'J.-J. Rousseau', is frankly hostile. This hostility is common to many who read Rousseau through the Jacobins, and whose anti-Jacobin sentiment is often informed by a barely disguised distaste for socialist ideas and values. For a defence, see P. Catalano, *Populus Romanus Quirites*, Turin 1974, and Viroli, *Jean-Jacques Rousseau*.

56. Rousseau, *SC*, Cranston, p. 157n; OC, vol. 3, p. 444n.

57. L. de Beaufort, *Dissertation sur l'Incertitude des Cinq Premiers Siècles de l'Histoire Romaine*, Paris 1738, a work later dismissed out of hand by Niebuhr, and rightly, as merely negative in scope and intent.

58. Rousseau, *SC*, Cranston, p. 85; OC, vol. 3, p. 382.

59. Rousseau, *SC*, Cranston, p. 85; OC, vol. 3, p. 382; B. Gagnebin, 'Le Rôle du Législateur dans les Conceptions Politiques de Rousseau', *ECS*, pp. 278–80.

60. G. Vico, *The Third New Science* (henceforth *TNS*), translated by T.G. Bergin and M.H. Fisch, Ithaca and London 1984, p. 168.

61. Vico, *TNS*, pp. 253–4.

62. Rousseau, *SC*, Cranston, p. 84; OC, vol. 3, p. 381.

63. Rousseau, *SC*, Cranston, p. 84; OC, vol. 3, p. 381, quoting Montesquieu.

64. Rousseau, *SC*, Cranston, p. 59; OC, vol. 3, p. 359.

65. Rousseau, *SC*, Cranston, pp. 136–7; OC, vol. 3, p. 426.

66. Rousseau, *DOI*, Cranston, pp. 120–1; OC, vol. 3, pp. 176–7; *SC*, Cranston, pp. 59–62; OC, vol. 3, pp. 360–2.

67. Rousseau, *DOI*, Cranston, pp. 121–2; OC, vol. 3, pp. 176–7, and see OC, vol. 3, pp. 273, 288, 475.

68. Aristotle, *The Politics*, translated by S. Everson, Cambridge 1988, p. 4 [1253a].

69. J.-J. Rousseau, 'Histoire de Lacédémone', OC, vol. 3, p. 546; Montesquieu, *Considerations*, Lowenthal, p. 23.

70. J.-J. Rousseau, *Considérations sur le Gouvernement de Pologne*, OC, vol. 3, p. 958.

71. N. Machiavelli, *The Discourses* (henceforth *D*), translated by L.J. Walker, London 1950, vol. 1, pp. 233–4.

72. N. Machiavelli, *The Prince*, translated by R. Price, Cambridge 1988, p. 21.

73. Livy, *Ab Urbe Condita*, 1.8.1–2, Loeb, vol. 1, pp. 30–1.

74. Rousseau, *DOI*, Cranston, pp. 77, 137; OC, vol. 3, pp. 131, 194.

75. Rousseau, *SC*, Cranston, p. 115; OC, vol. 3, p. 406.

76. F. de Martino, *Storia della Costituzione Romana*, Naples 1951, vol. 1, pp. 28–32.

77. Rousseau, *SC*, Cranston, p. 164; OC, vol. 3, p. 450.

78. *The Twelve Tables*, in E.H. Warmington, ed., *Remains of Old Latin*, London and Cambridge, Mass. 1967, pp. 490–1.

79. Vico, *TNS*, pp. 11, 53, 66, 186, 200.

80. Niebuhr, *HR*, 1st edn, translated by F.A Walter, London 1827, vol. 1, pp. 251–2; T. Mommsen, *The History of Rome* (henceforth *HR*), translated by W.F. Dickson, London 1911, vol. 1, pp. 61–2; N.-D. Fustel de Coulanges, *La Cité Antique*, Paris 1910, 21st edn, pp. 307–8.

81. Niebuhr, *HR*, 2nd edn, vol. 1, p. 326; K. Marx, *Grundrisse*, translated by M. Nicolaus, Harmondsworth 1973, pp. 471–9.

82. Plutarch, *Les Vies des Hommes Illustres*, vol. 1, pp. 52–3.

83. Cousin, 'Jean-Jacques Rousseau', p. 18; contrast Launay, *Jean-Jacques Rousseau*, pp. 448–9.

84. Rousseau, *Emile*, OC, vol. 4, p. 858.

85. Rousseau, *SC*, Cranston, p. 89; OC, vol. 3, p. 385.

86. Montesquieu, *Considerations*, Lowenthal, pp. 27, 39.

87. Rousseau, *Constitution pour la Corse*, OC, vol. 3, pp. 929–30; *DPE*, Cole, 264–6; OC, vol. 3, pp. 273–5.

88. Plutarch, *Les Vies des Hommes Illustres*, vol. 1, pp. 153–4.

89. Rousseau, *DOI*, Cranston, p. 118; OC, vol. 3, p. 174.

90. Montesquieu, *The Spirit of the Laws* (henceforth *SL*), translated by A.M. Cohler, B.C. Miller and H.S Stone, Cambridge 1989, pp. 44–7.

91. Montesquieu, *SL*, bk 27; Rousseau, *DPE*, Cole pp. 254–5; OC, vol. 3, pp. 263–4; *Constitution pour la Corse*, OC, vol. 3, p. 942.

92. Rousseau, *DPE*, Cole, p. 250; OC, vol. 3, p. 258.

93. Rousseau, *SC*, Cranston, p. 73; OC, vol. 3, p. 372.

94. Machiavelli, *D*, Walker, vol. 1, p. 164; Rousseau, *DOI*, Cranston, p. 131; OC, vol. 3, p. 187.

95. Machiavelli, in Rousseau, *SC*, Cranston, p. 73n; OC, vol. 3, p. 372n.

96. Machiavelli, *History of Florence*, London and New York 1960, p. 310.

97. Livy, *Ab Urbe Condita*, 1.42.4, Loeb, vol. 1, pp. 148–9; Machiavelli, *D*, Walker, vol. 1, p. 240.

98. Machiavelli, *D*, Walker, vol. 1, pp. 240–1, translation modified.

99. Rousseau, *SC*, (Geneva ms), OC, vol. 3, p. 292.

100. Rousseau, *SC*, bk 1, ch. 1.

101. Rousseau, *Constitution pour la Corse*, OC, vol. 3, p. 943; and see T.W. Tate, 'The Social Contract in America, 1774–1787: Revolutionary Theory as a Conservative Instrument', WMQ, 3rd series, 22, 1965, p. 386.

102. Rousseau, *DPE*, Cole, p. 241, translation modified; OC, vol. 3, p. 249.

103. Rousseau, *Considérations sur le Gouvernement de Pologne*, OC, vol. 3, pp. 957–8.

104. Rousseau, *SC*, Cranston, p. 158; OC, vol. 3, p. 445.

105. Vico, *TNS*, pp. 11–12.

106. Rousseau, *SC*, Cranston, p. 158; OC, vol. 3, p. 445.

107. Rousseau, *SC*, Cranston, p. 158; OC, vol. 3, p. 445, and see Livy, *Ab Urbe Condita*, 1.43.13, Loeb, vol. 1, pp. 152–4.

108. Rousseau, *SC*, Cranston, p. 158; OC, vol. 3, p. 445.

109. Rousseau, *SC*, Cranston, p. 61; OC, vol. 3, p. 361.

110. Livy, *Ab Urbe Condita*, 9.46.15, Loeb, vol. 4, pp. 352–3.

111. Rousseau, *SC*, Cranston, p. 159; OC, vol. 3, p. 445.

112. Rousseau, *SC*, Cranston, p. 160; OC, vol. 3, p. 446.

113. Livy, *Ab Urbe Condita*, 1.43.1–9, Loeb, vol. 1, pp. 148–53; Dion. Hal., *Roman Antiquities*, 4.19, Loeb, vol. 2, pp. 328–31.

114. Rousseau, *SC*, Cranston, p. 161, OC, vol. 3, p. 447.

115. Rousseau, *SC*, Cranston, p. 82, OC, vol. 3, p. 379.

116. Rousseau, *SC*, Cranston, p. 61n, OC, vol. 3, p. 361–2n.

117. Niebuhr, *HR*, 2nd edn, vol. 1, p. 434, and pp. 238–40, 283, 442; *HR*, 1st edn, vol. 1, p. 295.

118. Niebuhr, *HR*, 2nd edn, vol. 1, p. 435.

119. Niebuhr, *HR*, 2st edn, vol. 2, p. 60.

120. G. Sasso, *Niccolò Machiavelli e il suo Tempo*, Naples 1958, pp. 111–14.

121. C. Nicolet, *The World of the Citizen in Republican Rome*, London 1980, translated by P.S. Falla, pp. 54–5.

122. Rousseau, *DOI*, Cranston, p. 132; OC, vol. 2, p. 189.

123. Rousseau, *DOI*, Cranston, pp. 171–2; OC, vol. 3, pp. 222-3.

124. Aristotle, *The Politics*, 130lb, Everson, p. 111.

125. Dion. Hal., *Roman Antiquities*, 4.19.3, Loeb, vol. 2, pp. 328–31; Nicolet, *The World of the Citizen*, p. 92.

126. Niebuhr, *HR*, 2nd edn, vol. 1, pp. 448–9; *HR* 1st edn, vol. 1, pp. 283–4.

127. Aristotle, *The Politics*, 1318a, Everson, p. 146.

128. Niebuhr, *HR*, 2nd edn, vol. 1, p. 448.

129. For example, Fustel de Coulanges, *La Cité Antique*, bk 4, ch 7.

130. K. Marx, *Grundrisse*, translated by M. Nicolaus, Harmondsworth 1973, p. 485.

131. Niebuhr, *HR*, 2nd edn, vol. 1, pp. 446–7.

132. Livy, *Ab Urbe Condita*, 1.43.10, Loeb, vol. 1, pp. 152–3.

133. Dion. Hal., *Roman Antiquities*, 4.21.1., Loeb, vol. 2, pp. 334–7, and 4.20.1, Loeb, vol. 2, pp. 330–1.

134. Montesquieu, *Considerations*, Lowenthal, pp. 86–7; *SL*, pp. 12–13; 'Remarques sur Certaines Objections que m'a Faites un Homme qui m'a Traduit mes Romains en Angleterre', OC, vol. 2, p. 1211; Vico, *TNS*, p. 392.

135. Rousseau, *SC*, Cranston, p. 158; OC, vol. 3, p. 447.

136. Montesquieu, *Considerations*, Lowenthal, p. 95n1.

137. Sallust, *De Bello Jugurthae*, 36.2–4, Loeb, pp. 322-3.

138. Montesquieu, *SL*, p. 203; Rousseau, *SC*, Cranston, p. 162; OC, vol. 3, p. 448; and see Nicolet, *The World of the Citizen*, pp. 92–3.

139. Rousseau, *SC*, Cranston, p. 158; OC, vol. 3, p. 445; L.H. Morgan, *Ancient Society*, Chicago 1877, pp. 343–4, 349–52, 561–2.

140. Colletti, 'Rousseau', pp. 185–7.

141. K. Marx, excerpts from Morgan's *Ancient Society*, in L. Krader, ed., *The Ethnological Notebooks of Karl Marx*, Assen 1974, 2nd edn, pp. 218, 224, 231–3; F. Engels, *The Origin of the Family, Private Property and the State* [1884], in Marx and Engels, SW, London 1968, pp. 552–4, a book explicitly defined by its author as an elaboration of Marx's ethnological notebooks.

142. Rousseau, *SC*, Cranston, p. 80; OC, vol. 3, p. 378.

143. For example, M. Löwy and R. Sayre, *La Révolte Mélancolique: Le Romantisme à Contre-Courant de la Modernité*, Paris 1991.

144. Marx's resolutely anti-teleological approach served, in general, as a barrier against the tribe-nation. See, for example, letter of 16 January 1861 to F. Lassalle, CW, vol. 41, 246–7. Particular passages in his writings and, to a still greater degree, in those of Engels, do nonetheless reflect the Germanism of the age. Note, for instance, *The Origin of the Family*, pp. 544–5, 576, and his linked essay on *The Mark* [1882], CW, vol. 24, pp. 441–56.

# Chapter 4 The Liberty of the Ancients and the Liberty of the Moderns

1. E. Hofmann, ed., B. Constant, *Les 'Principes de Politique'* (henceforth *PP*), Geneva 1980, vol. 2, p. 419; and see Condorcet, 'De l'Influence de la Révolution d'Amérique sur l'Europe' [1786], OC, vol. 8, pp. 4–5, 11–12, first published in F. Mazzei, *Recherches*

*Historiques et Politiques sur les Etats-Unis de l'Amérique Septentrionale*, Paris 1788, vol. 1, and see pp. 166, 173, 192.

2. Condorcet, *Esquisse d'un Tableau Historique des Progrès de l'Esprit Humain*, OC, vol. 6, pp. 96–7.

3. C. Desmoulins, *Le Vieux Cordelier*, Nos. 3 and 4, Frimaire year II, reprinted Paris 1825, pp. 62–6, 69, 72–3.

4. J. Debry, 27 Messidor year III, *Moniteur*, vol. 25, p. 259.

5. J. Viénot, Introduction, Staël, *Des Circonstances Actuelles qui Peuvent Terminer la Révolution en France* (henceforth *DCA*), Paris 1906.

6. L. Omacini, Introduction, Staël, *DCA*, Geneva 1979.

7. B. Jasinski, in Staël, CG, vol. 4, pt 1, Paris 1976, p. 167.

8. Staël, *DCA*, pp. 107–10.

9. There are direct references, though, to Montesquieu, *The Spirit of the Laws* (henceforth *SL*), translated by A.M. Cohler, B.C. Miller and H.S. Stone, Cambridge 1989, p. 603, and echoes, perhaps, of D. Hume, 'Of the Populousness of Ancient Nations', in T.H. Green and T.H. Grose, eds., *Essays Moral, Political and Literary*, London 1898, vol. 1, pp. 381–443.

10. P. van Tieghem, ed., A.L.G. de Staël, *De la Littérature Considérée dans ses Rapports avec les Institutions Sociales* [1800], Geneva and Paris 1959, vol. 1, p. 37.

11. E. Kedourie, *Nationalism*, London 1960, chs 2 and 3, but note the conflicting admission on pp. 52–3.

12. Dion. Hal., *Roman Antiquities*, 20.13.2, Loeb, vol. 7, pp. 422–5; C. Nicolet, *The World of the Citizen in Republican Rome*, translated by P.S. Falla, London 1980, p. 78.

13. Consider in this regard G. Bonnot de Mably, *Observations sur le Gouvernement et les Loix des Etats-Unis d'Amerique*, Amsterdam 1784, who called for the powers of the Pennsylvanian Council of Censors to be extended so that it might be 'attentif aux symptomes qui annonceroit quelque vice nouveau, et de venir au secours de quelque coutume honnête, de quelque usage louable et de quelque vertu qui paroitroit s'altérer et affoiblir', p. 93. Constant later deplored Mably's influence upon those who made the Revolution in France.

14. Nicolet, *The World of the Citizen*, p. 74.

15. Staël, *DCA*, pp. 111–12.

16. I. Kant, 'Idea for a Universal History with a Cosmopolitan Purpose' [1784], in H. Reiss, ed., *Kant: Political Writings*, translated by H.B. Nisbet, 2nd edn, Cambridge 1991, p. 44.

17. L. Sozzi, 'Le Groupe de Coppet et les Sociétés Primitives', in E. Hofmann, ed., *Benjamin Constant, Madame de Staël et le Groupe de Coppet*, Oxford and Lausanne 1982, pp. 535–46.

18. B. Constant, *De La Force du Gouvernement* (henceforth *DFG*), Paris 1796, pp. 95–6.

19. Constant, *DFG*, pp. 95–6; 'De la Perfectibilité', in *Mélanges de Littérature et de Politique* (henceforth *MLP*), Paris 1829, pp. 404–7.

20. Constant, *DFG*, pp. 96–7n.

21. Constant, *DFG*, p. 15; 'De M. Fox et de M. Pitt', *MLP*, pp. 322–31.

22. B. Constant, *Des Réactions Politiques* (henceforth *DRP*), in O. Pozzo di Burgo, ed., *Benjamin Constant: Ecrits et Discours Politiques*, Paris 1964, vol. 1, p. 65; Staël, *DCA*, p. 13.

23. Constant, letter of 13 June 1797 to S. de Constant, in E. Hofmann, ed., *PP*, vol. 1, p. 140n.

24. Constant, *DRP*, p. 67.

25. Constant, *DRP*, pp. 68–9.

26. C. Violi, *Benjamin Constant: per una Storia della Riscoperta; Politica e Religione*, Rome 1985.

27. R. de Constant, letter of 7 October 1806 to C. de Constant, in Hofmann, ed., *PP*, vol. 1, p. 335.

28. Constant, *DFG*, p. 30.

29. E. Sieyes, *Opinion*, in *Oeuvres de Sieyes*, Paris 1989, vol. 2, pp. 6–7.

30. Not Constant's coinage but a commonplace usage under the Directory.

31. Hofmann, ed., *PP*, vol. 2, p. 23.

32. Hofmann, ed., *PP*, vol. 2, pp. 25–7, 50.

33. Hofmann, ed., *PP*, vol. 2, p. 49; M. Minerbi, ed., J.C.L. Simonde de Sismondi, *Recherches sur les Constitutions des Peuples Libres*, Geneva 1965, pp. 111–12.

34. Hofmann, ed., *PP*, vol. 2, p. 419.

35. Hofmann, ed., *PP*, vol. 2, p. 135.

36. Hofmann, ed., *PP*, vol. 2, p. 432.

37. Constant, 'Aperçus sur la Marche et les Révolutions de la Philosophie à Rome', *MLP*, pp. 1–27.

38. J. Starobinski, 'Benjamin Constant et l'Eloquence', in Hofmann, ed., *Constant*, pp. 320–1.

39. Hofmann, ed., *PP*, vol. 2, p. 421; C.-F. de Volney, 'Observations Générales sur les Indiens ou Sauvages de l'Amérique du Nord', OC, p. 722.

40. Note Hume, 'Of the Populousness of Ancient Nations', p. 400.

41. Aristotle, *The Politics*, translated by S. Everson, Cambridge 1988, p. 178 [1333b40].

42. Hofmann, ed., *PP*, vol. 2, p. 430.

43. N.-D. Fustel de Coulanges, *La Cité Antique*, Paris 1910, 21st edn, pp. 348–52.

44. Also J.N.A. Thierry, *Politique des Nations et de Leurs Rapports Mutuels* [1817], in *Oeuvres de Saint-Simon et d'Enfantin*, Paris 1868, vol. 18, pp. 19–127.

45. Quoted by G. Jellinek, *Allgemeine Staatslehre* [1900], Berlin 1905, p. 289n.

46. Jellinek, *Allgemeine Staatslehre*, pp. 289–90.

47. Fustel de Coulanges, *La Cité Antique*, pp. 1–3.

48. By, for example, Edward Evans-Pritchard, Meyer Fortes and by too many to list within the Durkheimian school.

49. Fustel de Coulanges, *La Cité Antique*, pp. 166, 265.

50. Fustel de Coulanges, *La Cité Antique*, p. 265; Condorcet, *Esquisse*, OC, vol. 6, pp. 69–70, 75; *Sur l'Instruction Publique*, OC, vol. 7, p. 201.

51. He was not, strictly speaking, the very first author to challenge Constant's thesis, as P. Catalano demonstrates, *Populus Romanus Quirites*, Turin 1974, pp. 50–1, 64–70. It is, however, true that theoreticians of liberalism such as Croce and Bobbio have formulated their own positions in relation to the viewpoints of Constant and Jellinek.

52. Jellinek, *Allgemeine Staatslehre*, pp. 290–1.

53. G.W.F. Hegel, *The Philosophy of Right* [1821], translated by T.M. Knox, Oxford 1967, pp. 107–9.

54. Jellinek, *Allgemeine Staatslehre*, p. 290.

55. R. de Mattei, 'La Libertà presso i Greci e presso i Moderni', RCFI, 1948, pp. 155–69.

56. Aristotle, *The Politics*, 1310a, Everson, p. 129.

57. A. Zanfarino, *La Libertà dei Moderni nel Costituzionalismo di Benjamin Constant*, Milan 1961, pp. 112–13.

58. B. Croce, 'Constant e Jellinek: Intorno alla Differenza tra la Libertà degli Antichi e quella dei Moderni' [1930], in *Etica e Politica*, Bari 1945, pp. 294–301.

59. Constant, 'Du Développement Progressif des Idées Religieuses', *MLP*, pp. 125–6.

60. Constant, 'Du Développement Progressif', pp. 95–6; A.L.G. de Staël, *Considérations sur la Révolution Française*, Paris 1983, p. 64.

61. G.W.F. Hegel, *Lectures on the Philosophy of World History*, translated by H.B. Nisbet, Cambridge 1975, pp. 54–5, and *The Philosophy of Right*, pp. 219–23.

62. For a valuable commentary on Croce's odd misconstrual of Constantian liberalism, see N. Bobbio, 'Benedetto Croce e il Liberalismo', in *La Politica e la Cultura*, Bari 1955, pp. 244-50.

63. L. Colletti, 'Idea della Società "Cristiano-Borghese" ', in *Il Marxismo e Hegel*, Bari 1976, vol. 2, pp. 403–34.

64. Aristotle, *The Politics*, 1253a, Everson, p. 4.

65. Aristotle, *The Politics*, 1264b, Everson, p. 29.

66. E. Durkheim, *The Division of Labour in Society*, translated by W.D. Halls, London 1984, pp. 36, 61; and *Montesquieu and Rousseau*, translated by R. Mannheim, Ann Arbor, Michigan 1960, pp. 26–8.

67. Durkheim, *The Division of Labour*, pp. 88–90.

68. Durkheim, *The Elementary Forms of the Religious Life*, translated by J.R. Swain, New York 1965, p. 488.

69. S. Lukes, *Emile Durkheim, His Life and Work: A Historical and Critical Study*, Harmondsworth 1973, p. 339n71.

70. Durkheim, 'Individualism and the Intellectuals' [1898], PS, vol. 17, no. 1, 1969, pp. 14–30; B. Lacroix, 'La Vocation Originelle d'Emile Durkheim', RSF, vol. 17, April–June 1976, pp. 213–47.

71. S. Collins, 'Categories, Concepts or Predicaments? Remarks on Mauss's Use of Philosophical Terminology', in M. Carrithers, S. Collins and S. Lukes, eds., *The Category of the Person: Anthropology, Philosophy, History*, Cambridge 1985, p. 63.

72. Durkheim, *The Division of Labour*, p. 122.

73. Radcliffe-Brown's lecture notes betray the extent of his debt; G.W. Stocking, 'Dr. Durkheim and Mr. Brown: Comparative Sociology at Cambridge in 1910', in G.W. Stocking, ed., *Functionalism Historicized: Essays on British Anthropology*, Madison, Wisconsin 1984, pp. 106–30.

74. A. MacIntyre, 'Is Understanding Religion Compatible with Believing?' [1964], and E. Gellner, 'Concepts and Society' [1958], reprinted in B.R. Wilson, ed., *Rationality*, Oxford 1970, pp. 62–77 and pp. 18–49 respectively. See the discussion of Edmund Leach, in chapter 8 of this volume.

75. M. Mauss, 'A Category of the Human Mind: The Notion of Person; the Notion of "Self" ', *Sociology and Psychology*, translated by B. Brewster, London 1979, pp. 61–2.

76. G. Glotz, *The Greek City and its Institutions*, London 1929, pp. 3–5.

77. Mauss, 'A Category of the Human Mind', p. 85.

78. A. Momigliano, 'Marcel Mauss e il Problema della Persona nella Biografia Greca', RSI, vol. 97, 1985, pp. 284–5.

79. Momigliano, 'Marcel Mauss', p. 261.

80. Mauss, 'A Category of the Human Mind', pp. 87–9.

81. L. Dumont, 'A Modified View of our Origins: The Christian Beginnings of Modern Individualism', in *The Category of the Person*, p. 94.

82. Dumont, 'Origins', p. 94.

83. Dumont, 'Origins', p. 95.

84. Dumont, 'Origins', pp. 101–19.

85. For example, A.L.G. de Staël, 'Réflexions sur le Suicide' [1812], a codicil to *De l'Influence des Passions*, OC, Paris 1871, vol. 1, pp. 176–92. On this question, D. Outram, *The Body and the French Revolution*, New Haven and London 1989, is less illuminating than M. Launay, 'Contribution à l'Etude du Suicide Vertueux selon Rousseau', in *Gilbert Romme et son Temps (1750–1795)*, Paris 1966, pp. 175–82.

86. Compare, however, L. Dumont, *Essays on Individualism*, Chicago 1986, chs 4–6.

87. I. Berlin, *Two Concepts of Liberty*, Oxford 1958, pp. 6–11, 52, 54.

88. C. Taylor, 'What's Wrong with Negative Liberty?', in A. Ryan, ed., *The Idea of Freedom*, Oxford 1979, pp. 175–9; P. Anderson, 'The Pluralism of Isaiah Berlin', *A Zone of Engagement*, London 1992, pp. 234–5.

89. Berlin, *Two Concepts of Liberty*, p. 48.

90. J. de Soto, 'La Liberté et ses Garanties', in *Etudes sur le Contrat Social*, Paris 1964, pp. 227–30.

91. J.-J. Rousseau, *The Social Contract* (henceforth *SC*), translated by M. Cranston, Harmondsworth 1968, p. 60; OC, vol. 3, p. 360.

92. Rousseau, *SC*, Cranston, p. 74; OC, vol. 3, p. 373.

93. J.-J. Rousseau, *A Discourse on Political Economy* (henceforth *DPE*), translated by G.D.H. Cole, in Rousseau, *The Social Contract and the Discourses*, London 1913, p. 249; OC, vol. 3, p. 257. Also OC, vol. 3, pp. 86–9, 538–43, 809.

94. M. Viroli, *Jean-Jacques Rousseau and the 'Well-Ordered Society'*, translated by D. Hanson, Cambridge 1988, p. 149.

95. Rousseau, *SC*, Cranston, p. 63; OC, vol. 3, p. 363.

96. Rousseau, *SC*, Cranston, p. 103; OC, vol. 3, p. 397.

97. J.L. Talmon, *The Origins of Totalitarian Democracy*, London 1952, ch. 3; for a defence, see R.A. Leigh, 'Jean-Jacques Rousseau and the Myth of Antiquity in the 18th Century', in R.R. Bolgar, ed., *Classical Influences on Western Thought 1650–1870*, Cambridge 1979, pp. 166–7.

98. F. Meinecke, *Cosmopolitanism and the National State*, translated by F.B. Kimber, Princeton 1970, p. 15.

99. Rousseau, *DPE*, Cole, p. 247; OC, vol. 3, p. 256; also *SC*, Cranston, p. 63; OC, vol. 3, p. 363.

100. Rousseau, *DPE*, Cole, p. 248; OC, vol. 3, p. 257.

101. A.L.G. de Staël, *De l'Influence des Passions*, Paris 1871, OC, vol. 1, pp. 146–7.

102. Rousseau, *SC*, Cranston, p. 136; OC, vol. 3, pp. 425–6.

103. I owe a particular debt here to three essays, listed below, by Quentin Skinner.

104. G.C. MacCallum, 'Negative and Positive Freedom', PR, vol. 76, 1967, pp. 312–34.

105. A. MacIntyre, *After Virtue*, London 1981, pp. 238, 263.

106. Q. Skinner, 'The Republican Ideal of Political Liberty', in G. Bock, Q. Skinner and M. Viroli, eds., *Machiavelli and Republicanism*, Cambridge 1990, pp. 294–5.

107. MacIntyre, *After Virtue*, p. 237.

108. Q. Skinner, 'The Idea of Negative Liberty', in R. Rorty, J.B. Schneewind and Q. Skinner, eds., *Philosophy in History*, Cambridge 1984, pp. 193–221, especially pp. 204–6; Q. Skinner, 'Machiavelli on the Maintenance of Liberty', *Politics*, vol. 18, 1983, pp. 3–15.

109. Q. Skinner, *The Foundations of Modern Political Thought*, vol. 1: *The Renaissance*, Cambridge 1978, pp. 63–5.

110. N. Machiavelli, *The Discourses*, translated by L.J. Walker, London 1950, vol. 1, pp. 543–4.

111. See G. Vlachos, 'L'Influence de Rousseau sur la Conception du Contrat Social chez Kant et Fichte', *Etudes sur le Contrat Social*, Paris 1964, pp. 470–2.

112. Rousseau, *SC*, Cranston, p. 102; OC, vol. 3, p. 396; *Considérations sur le Gouvernement de Pologne*, OC, vol. 3, p. 979.

113. M.I. Finley, *Democracy Ancient and Modern*, London 1973, p. 18; Nicolet, *The World of the Citizen*, p. 324.

114. Rousseau, *SC*, Cranston, p. 105; OC, vol. 3, p. 398.

115. Staël, *DCA*, p. 17.

116. T. Zemek, 'Mme de Staël et l'Esprit National', DHS, vol. 14, 1982, pp. 89–103.


# Chapter 5 Noble Savages, Primitive Peoples

1. E. Biré, ed., R.-F. de Chateaubriand, *Mémoires d'Outre-Tombe* (henceforth *M*), Paris 1880, vol. 1, p. 19, p. 192.

2. Chateaubriand, *Voyages en Amérique* (henceforth *VA*), ORV, Paris 1969, ed. M. Regard, vol. 1, p. 666.

3. Chateaubriand, *Les Martyrs*, ORV, vol. 2, p. 168.

4. Chateaubriand, *M*, vol. 1, p. 4.

5. J. Roussel, *Jean-Jacques Rousseau en France après la Révolution, 1795–1830*, Paris 1972, pp. 164–8.

6. Chateaubriand, *M*, vol. 2, pp. 116–18.

7. J. Egret, 'Les Origines de la Révolution en Bretagne (1788–1789)', RH, 1955, pp. 189–215.

8. Chateaubriand, *M*, vol. 1, pp. 249–50.

9. Condorcet, 'Lettres d'un Bourgeois de New-Haven', OC, vol. 9, p. 83.

10. S.R.N. Chamfort, *Maximes et Pensées*, (more properly entitled *Produits de la Civilisation Perfectionnée*), in P.R. Auguis, ed., *Oeuvres Complètes de Chamfort*, Paris 1824–25, vol. 1, p. 436; see M. Forsyth, *Reason and Revolution: The Political Thought of the Abbé Sieyes*, New York 1987, p. 71.

11. G. Lefebvre, *The Coming of the French Revolution*, translated by R.R. Palmer, Princeton 1967, pp. 53–4.

12. C.-F. de Volney, *La Sentinelle du Peuple*, appendix to L. Séché, *Volney*, Paris 1899, p. 113.

13. C.-F. de Volney, *Les Ruines*, OC, p. 33; and see Chamfort, OC, vol. 3, pp. 359–78 for a review.

14. Condorcet, 'Idées sur le Despotisme', OC, vol. 9, pp. 153–4.

15. Chateaubriand, *M*, vol. 1, p. 206.

16. Chateaubriand, *M*, vol. 1, pp. 205–6.

17. S. Moravia, *Il Tramonto dell'Illuminismo*, Bari 1968, pp. 116–18.

18. Chateaubriand, *M*, vol. 1, p. 263.

19. P. Grosclaude, *Malesherbes, Témoin et Interprète de son Temps*, Paris 1961, pp. 652–3.

20. Chateaubriand, *M*, vol. 1, p. 263.

21. P. Christophorov, *Sur les Pas de Chateaubriand en Exil*, Paris 1961, pp. 106–9.

22. Chateaubriand, *M*, vol. 1, pp. 227–8.

23. See R. Mortier, *La Poétique des Ruines en France*, Geneva 1974, pp. 136–42, 170–93.

24. M. Duchet, *Anthropologie et Histoire au Siècle des Lumières*, Paris 1978, pp. 76–7.

25. For example, G.T.F. Raynal, *Histoire Philosophique des Deux Indes* [1772 edn], Geneva 1775, vol. 1, pp. 222–6.

26. Montesquieu, *The Spirit of the Laws*, translated by A.M. Cohler, B.C. Miller and H.S. Stone, Cambridge 1989, p. 37.

27. F. Diaz, *Dal Movimento dei Lumi al Movimento dei Popoli*, Bologna 1986, p. 516.

28. Chamfort, 'Sur les Mémoires de la Vie Privée de Benjamin Franklin', OC, vol. 3, p. 317; Condorcet, 'Vie de Voltaire', OC, vol. 4, pp. 157–8.

29. Turgot, letter to R. Price of 22 March 1778, in *Oeuvres de Turgot*, Paris 1923, vol. 5, pp. 534–5; also Paine, Condorcet, Mazzei and others in their circle.

30. Volney, 'Sur Gallipolis', OC, p. 702; compare Chamfort, *Maximes et Pensées*, OC, vol. 1, pp. 443–5.

31. Chateaubriand, *VA*, in ORV, vol. 1, p. 667.

32. M. Regard, ed., R.-F. de Chateaubriand, *Essai Historique, Politique et Morale sur les Révolutions Anciennes et Modernes* (henceforth *E*), Paris 1978, p. 330nA; Grosclaude, *Malesherbes*, pp. 463–97.

33. Chateaubriand, *E*, pp. 316–17.

34. Chateaubriand, *E*, pp. 422–3n.

35. F. Venturi, *L'Antichità Svelata e l'Idea del Progresso in N.A. Boulanger (1722–1759)*, Bari 1947, pp. 96–107.

36. Lafitau, *Customs of the American Indians compared with the Customs of Primitive Times* [1724], translated by W.N. Fenton and E.L. Moore, Toronto 1974, vol. 1, pp. 33, 46, 79–81.

37. D. Diderot, 'Chronologie Sacrée' [1752], in OC, vol. 6, ed. J. Lough and J. Proust, Paris 1976, pp. 437–60.

38. Volney, *Recherches Nouvelles sur l'Histoire Ancienne*, OC, pp. 310–11.

39. J. Morel, 'Recherches sur les Sources du Discours de l'Inégalité', AJJR, vol. 5, 1909, pp. 179–87.

40. Chateaubriand, *E*, p. 52nC; and see M. Bernal, *Black Athena: The Afro-Asiatic Roots of Classical Civilization*, vol. 1: *The Fabrication of Ancient Greece 1785–1985*, London 1987, pp. 109, 179–82.

41. Chateaubriand, *E*, p. 53nD.

42. R. Porter, *The Making of Geology: Earth Science in Britain 1660–1815*, Cambridge 1977, p. 11; and G.N. Cantor, 'Revelation and the Cyclical Cosmos of John Hutchinson', in L.J. Jordanova and R. Porter, eds., *Images of the Earth: Essays in the History of the Environmental Sciences*, Chalfont St Giles 1978, pp. 3–22.

43. R.-F. de Chateaubriand, *Le Génie du Christianisme*, Paris 1978, edited by M. Regard, p. 541; and R. Shackleton, 'Chateaubriand and the Eighteenth Century', in R. Switzler, ed., *Chateaubriand Today*, Madison, Milwaukee, London 1970, pp. 17–20.

44. Chateaubriand, *E*, p. 57n.

45. D. Outram, *Georges Cuvier: Vocation, Science and Authority in Post-Revolutionary France*, Manchester 1984.

46. Porter, *The Making of Geology*, p. 198, and see G. Cuvier, *Discours Préliminaire* to *Recherches sur les Ossemens Fossiles de Quadrupedes*, Paris 1812, vol. 1, pp. 85–106. Note, in addition, W. Jones, 'Ninth Anniversary Discourse' [23 February 1792], in *Works*, London 1807, vol. 3, pp. 192, 196.

47. G.R. Jameson, Preface to G. Cuvier, *Essay on the Theory of the Earth*, Edinburgh 1813, pp. v–ix.

48. W. Maturi, *Interpretazioni del Risorgimento*, Turin 1962, pp. 150–1.

49. S. Timpanaro, Introduction to English edn, *On Materialism*, translated by L. Garner, London 1975, pp. 19–20; R. Grant, 'Hutton's Theory of the Earth', in Jordanova and Porter, eds., *Images of the Earth*, pp. 25–6.

50. Raynal, *Histoire Philosophique*, vol. 3, p. 338. For a more jaundiced account of Pennsylvania, of William Penn and of the Quakers, see F. Mazzei, *Recherches Historiques et Politiques sur les Etats-Unis de l'Amérique Septentrionale*, Paris 1788, vol. 1, pp. 64–86; vol. 3, pp. 29–71.

51. Chateaubriand, *M*, vol. 1, p. 355.

52. Gordon Wood has chronicled the growing realization in the 1780s that the Thirteen Colonies were not, after all, havens of virtue (*The Creation of the American Republic 1776–1787*, Chapel Hill, North Carolina 1969, ch. 10), but there is no reason to suppose that a reader of Raynal or Mably should have marked this disillusion. For, as Pocock has argued in *The Machiavellian Moment* (Princeton 1975), virtue and corruption were ever solidary elements within the neo-Harringtonian or Old Whig sociology embraced so fully by the colonists.

53. Chateaubriand, *VA*, in ORV, vol. 1, p. 677; *M*, vol. 1, p. 356.

54. M. Lescarbot, *Histoire de la Nouvelle France*, translated by W.L. Grant, Toronto 1907–14.

55. Lafitau, *Customs*, vol. 1, pp. 27–8.

56. Chateaubriand, *M*, vol. 1, pp. 365–6; and Preface, *Atala* (henceforth *A*), ORV, vol. 1, p. 16.

57. J. Pommier, 'Le Cycle de Chactas', RLC, 1938, pp. 604–29.

58. Chateaubriand, *M*, vol. 1, pp. 368–9; *VA*, in ORV, vol. 1, p. 683; Volney, 'Sur Gallipolis', OC, p. 703.

59. Chateaubriand, *E*, p. 442.

60. J.-J. Rousseau, *A Discourse on the Origins of Inequality*, translated by M. Cranston, Harmondsworth 1984, p. 168; OC, vol. 3, p. 220.

61. Chateaubriand, *A*, in ORV, vol. 1, pp. 39–40.

62. Chateaubriand, *E*, pp. 438–9nA. Contrast Turgot's fears regarding a frontier infested with 'tribes' consisting of a mixture of political exiles, outlaws and 'savages', who might then ravage the consolidated, agrarian territories to the east (letter of 22 March 1778 to Price, p. 538). Raynal and Chamfort, however, both refer to the predicament of those who, having lived in the woods, found it impossible to return to society; see *Histoire Philosophique*, vol. 3, p. 128, and *Maximes et Pensées*, OC, vol. 1, p. 436.

63. Chateaubriand, Preface, *A*, in ORV, vol. 1, p. 19.

64. See, however, Pocock's criticism of the argument, advanced by Gordon Wood, that the conservative revolution of 1787 represented the 'end of classical politics' (*The Machiavellian Moment*, ch. 15). I consider the dispute between Federalists and anti-Federalists and, more generally, the question of confederation in chapter 6.

65. Chateaubriand, *E*, pp. 444–5.

66. Raynal, *Histoire Philosophique*, vol. 3, pp. 113–15.

67. Chateaubriand, *A*, in ORV, vol. 1, p. 99.

68. Chateaubriand, Preface, *A*, in ORV, vol. 1, p. 23.

69. See G. Chinard, Introduction, Chateaubriand, *Les Natchez*, (henceforth *LN*), Paris 1931, to which I am greatly indebted.

70. Christophorov, *Sur les Pas de Chateaubriand*, pp. 124–30.

71. Duchet, *Anthropologie*, p. 39. On sources for the early history of Louisiana, see J.R. Swanton, *Indian Tribes of the Lower Mississippi Valley and Adjacent Coast of Mexico*, Bureau of American Ethnology, No. 43, Washington 1911, p. 187, and Chinard, Introduction, *LN*, Paris 1931.

72. Chateaubriand, Preface, *A*, in ORV, vol. 1, p. 16.

73. Raynal, *Histoire Philosophique*, vol. 3, p. 191, drawing on Charlevoix.

74. Charlevoix, Le Page du Pratz, in Swanton, *Indian Tribes*, pp. 102, 106.

75. Chateaubriand, *LN*, in ORV, vol. 1, p. 256. In *The Machiavellian Moment*, pp. 467–9, Pocock remarks upon the six *Lettres Persanes* containing references to John Law's Mississippi schemes, a highly characteristic threat posed by financial speculation to republican virtue.

76. Swanton, *Indian Tribes*, pp. 107, 245–6.

77. Lafitau, *Customs*, vol. 1, p. 296; Chateaubriand, *A*, in ORV, vol. 1, pp. 49–50; *LN*, in ORV, vol. 1, p. 187.

78. F. Lanthénas, 'Bases Fondamentales de l'Instruction Publique et de Toute Constitution Libre', AP, vol. 64, p. 485n1; he refers to Carver, Charlevoix, and Le Page du Pratz, and quotes, quite as selectively as Chateaubriand, from Lafitau.

79. Chateaubriand, *LN*, in ORV, vol. 1, pp. 342, 367, 406.

80. Chateaubriand, *LN*, in ORV, vol. 1, pp. 167–8.

81. Wordsworth also used this passage from Bartram.

82. For his handling of sources, see Chinard, *L'Exotisme Américain dans l'Oeuvre de Chateaubriand*, Paris 1918.

83. Chateaubriand, *LN*, in ORV, vol. 1, pp. 170–2.

84. Chinard, ed., Chateaubriand, *LN*, Paris 1931, p. 519.

85. Chateaubriand, *LN*, in ORV, vol. 1, p. 182.

86. Raynal, *Histoire Philosophique*, vol. 3, p. 192.

87. Chateaubriand, *LN*, in ORV, vol. 1, pp. 477–90.

88. Chateaubriand, *LN*, in ORV, vol. 1, pp. 413–14.

89. Volney, *Tableau du Climat et du Sol des Etats-Unis*, OC, p. 630.

90. Volney, *Leçons d'Histoire*, OC, p. 586.

91. As did Jefferson, in his *Notes on the State of Virginia*, written in 1780–81, in response to a list of queries from the French government. The queries may have been drafted by Buffon; see W. Peden, ed., Jefferson, *Notes on the State of Virginia*, Chapel Hill 1955. For an account of Volney's friendship with Jefferson, see Chinard, *Volney et l'Amérique*, Paris and Baltimore 1923.

92. Volney, *Leçons d'Histoire*, OC, p. 586.

93. P.J.G. Cabanis, *Rapports du Physique et du Moral dans l'Homme*, OP, vol. 1, p. 461.

94. S. Moravia, *Il Pensiero degli Idéologues*, Florence 1974, pp. 599–601; P. Schouls, *The Imposition of Method: A Study of Descartes and Locke*, Oxford 1980.

95. See Chinard, Introduction, Chateaubriand, *LN*.

96. C.-F. de Volney, *Voyage en Syrie et en Egypte*, OC, pp. 115–16.

97. Volney, *Tableau*, OC, p. 631; see Jefferson, *Notes*, pp. 64, 83–5.

98. Cabanis, *Rapports*, OP, vol. 1, pp. 473–4.

99. Volney, 'Observations', OC, p. 710.

100. Moravia, *Il Pensiero degli Idéologues*, pp. 643–71.

101. Volney, 'Observations', OC, p. 710.

102. Volney, 'Observations', OC, pp. 716, 720, 726.

103. Volney, 'Observations', OC, p. 722.

104. C. Lévi-Strauss, 'Jean-Jacques Rousseau, Founder of the Sciences of Man', in *Structural Anthropology*, vol. 2, translated by M. Layton, London 1973, pp. 33–48.

105. Volney, *Leçons d'Histoire*, OC, p. 588.

106. See S. Moravia, *La Scienza dell'Uomo nel Settecento*, Bari 1970, pp. 108–9.

107. For example, Croce, *History of Europe in the Nineteenth Century*, [1932], translated by H. Furst, London 1934, p. 43.

108. Cabanis, *Rapports*, OP, vol. 1, p. 474.

109. Volney, 'Observations', OC, p. 711.

110. Volney, 'Observations', OC, p. 715.
111. Volney, *Leçons d'Histoire*, OC, pp. 562–5; J. Gaulmier, 'Volney et ses Leçons d'Histoire', HT, vol. 2, 1962, p. 54.
112. Moravia, *La Scienza dell'Uomo*, pp. 79–107, 223–38 and Appendices. Degérando's text was drafted for an expedition to the South Pacific, which Alexander von Humboldt had originally planned to join.
113. Volney, 'Observations', OC, p. 711.
114. Volney, 'Observations', OC, p. 727.
115. See Jefferson, *Notes*, pp. 101–2.

# Chapter 6 The Cities Eclipsed

1. See A.L.G. de Staël, letter of 10 August 1799 to D.J. Garat, CG, vol. 4, pt 1, pp. 220–3, and Garat, *Mémoires Historiques sur la Vie de Suard, sur ses Ecrits, et sur le XVIIIe Siècle*, Paris 1820, vol. 2, pp. 395–407.
2. A. de Tocqueville, *The European Revolution*, translated by J. Lukacs, New York 1959, pp. 140–2.
3. F. Picavet, *Les Idéologues*, Paris 1891, p. 221.
4. J.-J. Rousseau, *The Social Contract* (henceforth *SC*), translated by M. Cranston, Harmondsworth 1968, pp. 170–4; OC, vol. 3, pp. 455–8.
5. See M. Isnard, 10 May 1793, AP, vol. 64, p. 418.
6. J. Gaulmier, *L'Idéologue Volney (1757–1820): Contribution à l'Histoire de l'Orientalisme*, Beirut 1951, p. 412; on General Washington's earlier surrender of his military command, in 1783, and on the republican myths surrounding the event, see F. Venturi, *The End of the Old Regime in Europe, 1776–1789*, vol. 1: *The Great States of the West*, translated by R. Burr Lichfield, Princeton 1991, pp. 426–38, and in the final chapter of Carlo Botta, *Storia della Guerra dell'Independenza degli Stati Uniti d'America* [1811], Florence 1856, vol. 2, the altogether characteristic account of the General's desire to 'porre alcun termine all' appetito della gloria dell'armi', and to 'lasciare alla patria sua un utile esempio di temperanza cittadina'. For Botta, as for so many others, the Republic found its complete vindication in Washington's gesture. Jefferson, however, judged the proposal to create a dictator for the state of Virginia, first in 1776 and then again in 1781, wholly abhorrent; W. Peden, ed., T. Jefferson, *Notes on the State of Virginia*, Chapel Hill, North Carolina 1955, pp. 126–9 and 284–5n28.
7. On the Babouvists' conception of dictatorship, see A. Galante Garrone, *Buonarroti e Babeuf*, Turin 1948, pp. 203–14.
8. Picavet, *Les Idéologues*, p. 408.
9. S. Moravia, *Il Tramonto dell'Illuminismo*, Bari 1968, p. 308.
10. Moravia, *Il Tramonto dell'Illuminismo*, p. 310.
11. B. Constant, 'Fragments sur la France', in *Mélanges de Littérature et de Politique*, Paris 1829, p. 78.
12. Picavet, *Les Idéologues*, p. 223n1.
13. P. van Tieghem, ed., A.L.G. de Staël, *De la Littérature Considérée dans ses Rapports avec les Institutions Sociales*, Geneva and Paris 1959, vol. 2, pp. 403–19.
14. F. Engels and K. Marx, *The Holy Family*, CW, London and Moscow 1975, vol. 4, p. 123; and note A.L.G. de Staël, *Dix Années d'Exil*, Paris 1906, p. 217.
15. K. Marx, *The Eighteenth Brumaire of Louis Bonaparte*, CW, vol. 11, p. 104.
16. L. Colletti, 'Rousseau as Critic of Civil Society' in *From Rousseau to Lenin*, translated by L. Merrington and J. White, London 1972, pp. 185–93.
17. Livy, *Ab Urbe Condita*, 2.32–3, Loeb, vol. 1, pp. 320–9.
18. F. de Martino, *Storia della Costituzione Romana*, Naples 1951, vol. 1, ch. 13.
19. C. Nicolet, *The World of the Citizen in Republican Rome*, translated by P.S. Falla, London 1980, p. 321.
20. B.G. Niebuhr, *History of Rome* (henceforth *HR*), 2nd edn, translated by J.C. Hare and C. Thirlwall, London 1837, vol. 1, pp. 612–16, 625–6; T. Mommsen, *History of Rome*

(henceforth *HR*), London 1911, vol. 1, p. 271; Fustel de Coulanges, *La Cité Antique*, p. 351.

21. Rousseau, *SC*, Cranston, p. 139; OC, vol. 3, pp. 427–8.

22. Galante Garrone, *Buonarroti e Babeuf*, pp. 91–6; but note A. Saitta, *Filippo Buonarroti*, Rome 1972.

23. Galante Garrone, *Buonarroti e Babeuf*, p. 95n1.

24. A. Keaveney, 'The Three Gracchi: Tiberius, Caius and Babeuf', in *La Storia della Storiografia Europea sulla Rivoluzione Francese*, published by the Istituto Storico Italiano per l'Eta Moderna e Contemporanea, Rome 1990, pp. 417–32.

25. N. Machiavelli, *The Discourses* (henceforth *D*), translated by L.J. Walker, London 1950, vol. 1, p. 217.

26. Machiavelli, *D*, Walker, vol. 1, pp. 220–2.

27. Machiavelli, *D*, Walker, vol. 1, pp. 218–19.

28. Montesquieu, *Considerations on the Causes of the Greatness of the Romans and their Decline*, translated by D. Lowenthal, London and New York 1965, pp. 84–5.

29. Montesquieu, *The Spirit of the Laws* (henceforth *SL*), translated by A.M. Cohler, B.C. Miller and H.S. Stone, Cambridge 1989, p. 57.

30. Montesquieu, *SL*, bk 11, ch. 6.

31. Rousseau, *SC*, Cranston, p. 132; OC, vol. 3, p. 421n.

32. Rousseau, *SC*, Cranston, pp. 168–9; OC, vol. 3, p. 454.

33. Rousseau, *SC*, Cranston, p. 170; OC, vol. 3, pp. 454–5.

34. P. Catalano, *Tribunato e Resistenza*, Turin 1971, p. 44; a point confirmed by the case of Angelo Querini, in 1761–62, see F. Venturi, 'Venise et, par Occasion, de la Liberté', in A. Ryan, ed., *The Idea of Freedom*, Oxford 1979, p. 201.

35. Rousseau, *SC*, Cranston, p. 139; OC, vol. 3, pp. 427–8.

36. Catalano, *Tribunato*, p. 40.

37. Rousseau, *SC*, Cranston, p. 169; OC, vol. 3, p. 454.

38. P. Andrivet, 'Jean-Jacques Rousseau: Quelques Aperçus de son Discours Politique sur l'Antiquité Romaine', SVEC, vol. 151, 1976, p. 133.

39. Mommsen, *HR*, vol. 1, p. 233. Niebuhr's viewpoint was in this regard transitional, as I show in chapter 9.

40. Colletti, 'Rousseau'.

41. D. Diderot, 'Machiavélisme', OC, vol. 16, p. 33.

42. Rousseau, *SC*, Cranston, p. 118, translation modified; OC, vol. 3, p. 409.

43. M. Rosa, *Dispotismo e Libertà nel Settecento: Interpretazioni 'Repubblicane' di Machiavelli*, Bari 1964, p. 46; and G. Procacci, *Studi sulla Fortuna del Machiavelli*, Rome 1965, pp. 355–6.

44. Mazzei, who taught Gibbon Italian, and studied the *Discourses* and the *History of Florence* with him, could well have communicated this interpretation to his pupil, to judge by *Recherches Historiques et Politiques sur les Etats-Unis de l'Amérique Septentrionale*, Paris 1788, vol. 1, pp. 189–90.

45. Venturi, *The End of the Old Regime*, vol. 1, pp. 49–66; F. Diaz, *Dal Movimento dei Lumi al Movimento dei Popoli*, Bologna 1986, pp. 333–6; D. Carpanetto and G. Ricuperati, *Italy in the Age of Reason*, translated by C. Higgitt, London 1987, pp. 210–23.

46. Rosa, *Dispotismo e Libertà*, p. 70. One should be wary of depicting all Florentine interpretations of Machiavelli in this period as intrinsically radical; see G. Ricuperati, review of Rosa and Procacci, RSI, vol. 79.1, 1967, p. 256.

47. Rosa, *Dispotismo e Libertà*, p. 84; contrast Procacci, *Studi*, pp. 383–5.

48. Rosa, *Dispotismo e Libertà*, p. 84.

49. L. Omacini, ed., A.L.G. de Staël, *Des Circonstances Actuelles qui Peuvent Terminer la Révolution en France*, Geneva 1979, pp. 359–425.

50. M. Minerbi, ed., J.C.L. Simonde de Sismondi, *Recherches sur les Constitutions des Peuples Libres*, Geneva 1965, p. 316.

51. H.S. Harris, *Hegel's Development: Towards the Sunlight 1770–1801*, Oxford 1972, pp. 416–27.

52. G.W.F. Hegel, 'The German Constitution' [1799–1802], in *Hegel's Political Writings*, translated by T.M. Knox, Oxford 1964, pp. 143, 218–19.

53. Hegel, 'The German Constitution', pp. 188, 219.

54. Procacci, *Studi*, pp. 392–3, 396–7.

55. Rousseau, *SC*, Cranston, p. 118n; OC, vol. 3, p. 409.

56. H. Baron, 'Machiavelli: The Republican Citizen and the Author of the Prince', *EHR*, vol. 76, 1961, p. 220.

57. N. Machiavelli, *The Prince* (henceforth *P*), translated by R. Price, Cambridge 1988, p. 6.

58. Machiavelli, *D*, Walker, vol. 1, pp. 322–3.

59. F. Chabod, 'Del "Principe" di Niccolò Machiavelli', in *Scritti su Machiavelli*, Turin 1964, pp. 69–74.

60. Chabod, 'Del "Principe" ', pp. 74–80.

61. P. Anderson, *Lineages of the Absolutist State*, London 1974, pp. 150–3.

62. See V. Gerratana, ed., A. Gramsci, *Quaderni del Carcere*, Turin 1975, vol. 3, pp. 1555–61; vol. 4, pp. 2379, 2449.

63. But see Chabod's later essays, for example, 'Il Segretario Fiorentino', in *Scritti*, pp. 241–368.

64. Baron, 'Machiavelli', p. 222.

65. Machiavelli, *D*, bk 1, chs 29, 58; bk 2, ch. 2; bk 3, ch. 9.

66. Baron, 'Machiavelli', p. 223.

67. G. Sasso, 'Intorno a Due Capitoli dei Discorsi', *Studi su Machiavelli*, Naples 1967, pp. 111-60.

68. Baron, 'Machiavelli', pp. 231–5.

69. Baron, 'Machiavelli', p. 239.

70. Baron, 'Machiavelli', p. 243; and S. Bertelli, Introduction, N. Machiavelli, *Il Principe e Altri Scritti*, Bergamo 1975, pp. 15–16.

71. Baron, 'Machiavelli', pp. 237–44.

72. Baron, 'Machiavelli', pp. 236–7.

73. F. Gilbert, 'Bernardo Rucellai and the Orti Oricellari: A Study on the Origin of Modern Political Thought', JWCI, vol. 12, 1949, pp. 101–31.

74. Baron, 'Machiavelli', p. 249.

75. Baron, 'Machiavelli', pp. 250–1.

76. M. Viroli, *From Politics to Reason of State*, Cambridge 1992.

77. Q. Skinner, 'Machiavelli's *Discorsi* and the Pre-humanist Origins of Republican Ideas', in G. Bock, Q. Skinner and M. Viroli, eds., *Machiavelli and Republicanism*, Cambridge 1990, pp. 121–42.

78. B. Croce, 'Machiavelli e Vico – la Politica e l'Etica', *Etica e Politica*, Bari, 1945, p. 251.

79. Machiavelli, *P*, Price, p. 62; Q. Skinner, *The Foundations of Modern Political Thought*, Cambridge 1978, vol. 1, pp. 131–8; see also N. Bobbio, 'Etica e Politica', in W. Tega, ed., *Etica e Politica*, Parma 1984, pp. 7–17, for some insight into the subtitles of Croce's position.

80. Machiavelli, *P*, Price, p. 62.

81. See B. Croce, review of Chabod's edition of *The Prince*, *La Critica*, vol. 22, 1924, pp. 313–15.

82. J.G.A. Pocock, *The Machiavellian Moment*, Princeton 1975, p. 194.

83. Rousseau, *SC*, Cranston, pp. 85, 89; OC, vol. 3, pp. 382, 385.

84. F. Venturi, *Utopia and Reform in the Enlightenment*, Cambridge 1971, p. 21.

85. F. Venturi, *Settecento Riformatore*, vol. 1: *Da Muratori a Beccaria*, Turin 1969, pp. 215–54; *Utopia and Reform*, pp. 38–40.

86. See G.W. Bowersock, 'Gibbon on Civil War and Rebellion in the Decline of the Roman Empire', in G.W. Bowersock, J. Clive and S.R. Graubard, eds., *Edward Gibbon and the Decline and Fall of the Roman Empire*, Cambridge, Mass. 1977, pp. 32–3. For the response, in fact markedly similar, of Gabriel-François Coyer, on his visit to Italy, also in 1764, see F. Venturi, *Settecento Riformatore*, vol. 4: *La Caduta dell' Antico Regime, t. 2, Il Patriottismo Repubblicano e gli Imperi dell'Est*, Turin 1984, pp. 506–7.

87. Venturi, *Utopia and Reform*, p. 22.

88. See C.J.V.A. de Broglie, 'Etudes Diplomatiques. Fin du Ministère D'Argenson', RDM, vol. 96, 1889, pp. 721–50, and vol. 97, pp. 54–85.

89. Venturi, *Settecento Riformatore*, vol. 1, p. 252.

90. R. Tisserand, *Les Concurrents de Rousseau à l'Académie de Dijon*, Paris 1936, p. 123; also R.L. de Voyer, Marquis D'Argenson, *Considérations sur le Gouvernement Ancien et Présent de la France*, Amsterdam 1764, p. 13.

91. Tisserand, *Les Concurrents de Rousseau*, p. 132.

92. Tisserand, *Les Concurrents de Rousseau*, p. 128.

93. Rosa, *Dispotismo e Libertà*, p. 36n74.

94. Venturi, *Utopia and Reform*, p. 70.

95. J. Shklar, 'Montesquieu and the New Republicanism', in Bock, Skinner and Viroli, eds., *Machiavelli*, p. 266.

96. Shklar, 'Montesquieu', p. 267.

97. See P. Rétat, '1789: Montesquieu Aristocrate', and R. Barny, 'Montesquieu Patriote?', DHS, vol. 21, 1989, pp. 73–82, 83–95, and, in particular, the references to Bonneville (pp. 74, 77), Saint-Just (pp. 86–7) and Marat (pp. 88–91).

98. Venturi, *The End of the Old Regime*, vol. 1, p. 131; *Settecento Riformatore*, vol. 4, pt 2, p. 8.

99. Venturi, *The End of the Old Regime*, vol. 1, p. 198, and contrast Jean Fabre's exposition, paraphrased in chapter 3 of this volume .

100. Venturi, *The End of the Old Regime*, vol. 1, pp. xvi–xvii.

101. Venturi, *The End of the Old Regime*, vol. 1, p. 414.

102. Pocock, *The Machiavellian Moment*, p. 87, also p. 462.

103. For what is still, to my knowledge, the fullest treatment, see E.A. Freeman, *The History of Federal Government*, London 1863, vol. 1 (the second volume never appeared). Freeman, however, was not an advocate of confederated liberty, but a publicist of the tribe-nation. John Burrow has well described this deeply racist author's 'idea of the branching history of Aryan freedom; one, the classical line, leading up to the impasse of the city-state; the other, the Teutonic, leading directly from the village-community to tribalism and the nation-state and the invention of representative government'. See *A Liberal Descent: Victorian Historians and the English Past*, Cambridge 1981, p. 189.

104. Machiavelli, *D*, Walker, vol. 1, p. 372.

105. Montesquieu, *SL*, pp. 131–3.

106. Rosa, *Dispotismo e Libertà*, p. 38.

107. Carpanetto and Ricuperati, *Italy in the Age of Reason*, p. 216; E.R. Cochrane, *Tradition and Enlightenment in the Tuscan Academies, 1690–1800*, Rome 1961, pp. 216–17.

108. Rosa, *Dispotismo e Libertà*, p. 36n74.

109. Rosa, *Dispotismo e Libertà*, p. 43.

110. Montesquieu, *SL*, pp. 285–6.

111. Procacci, *Studi*, p. 355.

112. M. Forsyth, *Unions of States: The Theory and Practice of Confederation*, New York 1981, p. 6.

113. Forsyth, *Unions*, p. 4.

114. In G. Wood, *The Creation of the American Republic, 1776–1787*, Chapel Hill, North Carolina 1969, p. 128.

115. M. Jensen, *The Articles of Confederation*, Madison 1959, pp. 263–70.

116. Wood, *The Creation of the American Republic*, p. 354.

117. A. Aquarone, ed., F. Mazzei, *Memorie della Vita*, Milan 1970, vol. 1, pp. 257–8.

118. Wood, *The Creation of the American Republic*, ch. 10; Pocock, *The Machiavellian Moment*, p. 516.

119. Wood, *The Creation of the American Republic*, p. 164.

120. J. Madison, A. Hamilton and J. Jay, *The Federalist Papers*, London 1987, no. 10 [Madison], p. 127.

121. I. Kramnick, Introduction, *The Federalist Papers*, p. 75. Yet there were many references to the American experience in debates held during the year III in the Convention, and figures such as Gouverneur Morris had atended Staël's salon at the Rue du Bac.

122. Wood, *The Creation of the American Republic*, p. 161.

123. Kramnick, Introduction, *The Federalist Papers*, pp. 23–6.

124. Condorcet, Supplement to 'De l'Influence de la Révolution d'Amérique sur l'Europe', OC, vol. 8, pp. 43–9. On p. 47 there is a passage either borrowed from, or elaborated in conversation with Jefferson; see letter of 13 November 1787 to W. Smith, in J.P. Boyd, ed., *The Papers of Thomas Jefferson*, Princeton 1955, vol. 12, p. 356. See also Mazzei, *Recherches*, vol. 4, pp. 1–10.

125. T. Jefferson, letter of 16 January 1787 to E. Carrington, in Boyd, ed., *The Papers of Thomas Jefferson*, vol. 11, pp. 48–9.

126. A. Adams, letter of 29 January 1787 to Jefferson, in Boyd, ed., *The Papers of Thomas Jefferson*, vol. 11, pp. 86–7.

127. Jefferson, letter of 30 January 1787 to Madison, in Boyd, ed., *The Papers of Thomas Jefferson*, vol. 11, pp. 92–7.

128. W. Peden, ed., T. Jefferson, *Notes on the State of Virginia*, Chapel Hill, North Carolina 1955, pp. 117–29, especially p. 120, and see D. Malone, *Jefferson and his Time*, vol. 2: *Jefferson and the Rights of Man*, Boston 1951, ch. 9.

129. For a survey of the whole debate, R.B. Morris, 'The Confederation Period and the American Historian', WMQ, 3rd series, 13, 1956, pp. 139–56.

130. See *The Federalist Papers*, nos. 18–20.

131. Forsyth, *Unions of States*, pp. 3–4, 60–72.

132. Jefferson, *Notes*, pp. 164–5.

133. Pocock, *The Machiavellian Moment*, p. 535, also p. 539.

134. Pocock, *The Machiavellian Moment*, pp. 534–45.

135. See P.H. Thore, 'Fédérations et Projets de Fédérations dans la Région Toulousaine', AHRF, vol. 21, 1949, pp. 346–68.

136. A. Forrest, 'Federalism', in K.M. Baker, F. Furet and C. Lucas, eds., *The French Revolution and the Creation of Modern Political Culture*, in C. Lucas, ed., vol. 2, *The Political Culture of the French Revolution*, Oxford 1988, pp. 309–28.

137. J. Godechot, *La Grande Nation*, Paris 1956, pp. 238–44; R.R. Palmer, *The Age of the Democratic Revolution*, vol. 2, Princeton 1964, pp. 192–8.

138. F. Buonarroti, 'Riflessi sul Governo Federativo Applicato all' Italia' [1831], in F. della Peruta, ed., SP, Turin 1976, pp. 88–9.

139. Godechot, *La Grande Nation*, p. 235.

140. P. Grosclaude, *Malesherbes, Témoin et Interprète de son Temps*, Paris 1961, p. 652; and see R.R. Palmer, 'The Dubious Democrat: Thomas Jefferson in Bourbon France', PSQ, vol. 72, p. 393.

141. Venturi, 'L'Italia Fuori d'Italia', in R. Romano and C. Vivanti, eds., *Storia d'Italia*, vol. 3: *Dal Primo Settecento all'Unità*, Turin 1973, p. 1174.

142. On Botta, see W. Maturi, *Interpretazioni del Risorgimento*, Turin 1962, pp. 36–91.

143. C. Botta, 'Proposizione ai Lombardi di una Maniera di Governo', in A. Saitta, ed., *Alle Origini del Risorgimento: I Testi di un 'Celebre' Concorso (1796)*, Rome 1964, vol. 1, pp. 43–4.

144. Botta, 'Proposizione', p. 47.

145. Botta, 'Proposizione', pp. 50–1.

# Chapter 7 Crossing the Rhine

1. S. Balayé, ed., A.L.G. de Staël, *Corinne, ou l'Italie*, Paris 1985, p. 32.

2. S. Balayé, ed., A.L.G. de Staël, *Les Carnets de Voyage de Madame de Staël*, Geneva 1971, p. 29.

3. Balayé, ed., Staël, *Les Carnets de Voyage*, pp. 32, 33, 41, 62; contrast F. von Schlegel, 'Principles of Gothic Architecture', in AMW, translated by E.J. Millington, London 1849, pp. 149–99.

4. J. de Pange, ed., A.L.G. de Staël, *De l'Allemagne*, Paris 1958–60, vol. 1, pp. 230–2.

5. W.H. Bruford, *Culture and Society in Classical Weimar*, Cambridge 1962, pp. 137–42.

6. A. de Rivarol, 'De l'Universalité de la Langue Française', in *Oeuvres de Rivarol*, Paris 1857, p. 79.

7. V. Alfieri, *Memoirs*, London 1961, p. 155.

8. Rivarol, 'De l'Universalité de la Langue Française', pp. 88–9. The same view was expressed by Diderot in his article on the patois in the Encyclopédie.

9. Rivarol, 'De l'Universalité', pp. 120–1.

10. Rivarol, 'De l'Universalité', pp. 84, 88.

11. Rivarol, 'De l'Universalité', pp. 81, 84, 88.

12. Rivarol, 'De l'Universalité', pp. 81, 110–15; and see C. Lancelot and A. Arnauld, *Grammaire Générale et Raisonnée* [1660], Menston 1969, p. 147. On the history and nature of Provençal, see Jefferson, letter of 29 March 1787, written in Aix, to William Short, in J.P. Boyd, ed., *The Papers of Thomas Jefferson*, Princeton 1955, vol. 11, pp. 253–5.

13. In what follows, I owe a great debt to Hans Aarsleff, 'The Eighteenth Century, including Leibniz', in T.A. Sebeok, ed., *Current Trends in Linguistics*, The Hague and Paris 1975, vol. 13, pp. 383–479; also 'The Tradition of Condillac: The Problem of the Origin of Language in the Eighteenth Century and the Debate in the Berlin Academy before Herder', in D. Hymes, ed., *Studies in the History of Linguistics*, Bloomington, Indiana and London 1974, pp. 93–156; and Introduction to W. von Humboldt, *On Language: The Diversity of Human Language-Structure and its Influence on the Mental Development of Mankind*, translated by P. Heath, Cambridge 1988.

14. B. Barère, 8 Pluviôse year II, *Moniteur*, vol. 19, pp. 317–20; H. Grégoire, 'Rapport sur la Nécessité et les Moyens d'Anéantir les Patois, et d'Universaliser l'Usage de la Langue Française', in *Oeuvres de l'Abbé Grégoire*, Paris 1977, vol. 2, pp. 227–54.

15. Grégoire, 'Rapport', pp. 234–5.

16. Grégoire, 'Rapport', p. 236. One of the last to revive the question of linguistic reform, in November 1794, at a time when the democratic pedagogy of the Jacobins was in retreat, was Romme, a tireless advocate, as I noted in chapter 1, of technical manuals on farming.

17. Grégoire, 'Rapport', pp. 228, 238.

18. In contrast to my own position, see, for example, C. Rearick, *Beyond the Enlightenment: Historians and Folklore in Nineteenth-Century France*, Bloomington, Indiana 1974.

19. R.L. Meek, *Social Science and the Ignoble Savage*, Cambridge 1976, pp. 179–82.

20. See D. Forbes, 'The Rationalism of Walter Scott', CJ, October 1953, vol. 7, pp. 20–35, and P.H. Scott, *Walter Scott and Scotland*, Edinburgh 1981, ch. 6. Engels also viewed Scott's novels in this light; see *The Origin of the Family, Private Property and the State*, in Marx and Engels, SW, London 1968, p. 548.

21. D.J. Garat, *Mémoires Historiques sur la Vie de Suard, sur ses Ecrits, et sur le XVIIIe Siècle*, Paris 1820, vol. 1, p. 154.

22. A.C. Kors, *D'Holbach's Côterie: An Enlightenment in Paris*, Princeton 1976, p. 264.

23. For example, P. Gay, *The Enlightenment: An Interpretation*, vol. 1: *The Rise of Modern Paganism*, New York 1966, p. 17.

24. M. Löwy and R. Sayre, *La Révolte Mélancolique: Le Romanticisme à Contre-Courant de la Modernité*, Paris 1992.

25. R.J. Mackintosh, ed., J. Mackintosh, *Memoirs of the Life of the R.H. Sir James Mackintosh*, London 1835, vol. 1, p. 28.

26. J. Locke, *An Essay Concerning Human Understanding*, ed. by P.H. Nidditch, Oxford 1975, p. 81.

27. R. Mortier, 'Unité ou Scission du Siècle des Lumières?' and 'Madame de Staël', in *Clarté et Ombres du Siècle des Lumières*, Geneva 1969, pp. 123, 127, 131; ' "Sensibilité", "Néo-Classique", ou "Préromantisme" ', in P. Viallaneix, ed., *Le Préromantisme: Hypothèque ou Hypothèse*, Paris 1975, p. 310. Jean Fabre pioneered this line of argument.

28. Rivarol, 'De l'Universalité', p. 91.

29. Rivarol, 'De l'Universalité', p. 92.

30. D.J. Garat, review of Rivarol, 6 August 1785, MF, republished Geneva 1974, vol. 129, pp. 131–2. I owe this reference to Aarsleff.

31. Aarsleff, 'The Tradition of Condillac'; E. Bonnot de Condillac, *Essai sur l'Origine des Connoissances Humaines*, in G. le Roy, ed., *Oeuvres Philosophiques de Condillac*, Paris 1947, vol. 1, pp. 98–104.

32. J. Roussel, *Jean-Jacques Rousseau en France après la Révolution, 1795–1830*, Paris 1972, p. 29; but contrast La Harpe's retrospective account of Condillac.

33. See G. Galasso, ed., Croce, *Teoria e Storia della Storiografia* [1915], Milan 1989, pp. 269–316, and N. Bobbio, 'Benedetto Croce e il Liberalismo', in *La Politica e la Cultura*, Bari 1955, pp. 244–5, 253–7.

34. A.L.G. de Staël, letter of 18 March 1796 to Henri Meister, CG, vol. 3, pt 2, p. 160; more generally, see J. de Pange, *Auguste-Guillaume Schlegel et Madame de Staël*, Paris 1938, pp. 34–5.

35. A.L.G. de Staël, letter of 1 August 1802 to Charles de Villers, CG, vol. 4, pt 2, p. 541.

36. B. Constant, letter of 7 June 1794 to Isabelle de Charrière, OC, vol. 4, p. 458, in marked contrast to her 'Eloge de Rousseau', I. de Charrière, OC, vol. 10, pp. 576–82. See also P. Köhler, *Madame de Staël et la Suisse*, Lausanne and Paris 1916, pp. 564–9.

37. F. Baldensperger, *Le Mouvement des Idées dans l'Emigration Française*, Paris 1924, vol. 1, ch. 2.

38. E. Biré, ed., R.-F. de Chateaubriand, *Mémoires d'Outre-Tombe* (henceforth *M*), Paris 1880, vol. 2, p. 132.

39. J. Godechot, *La Grande Nation*, Paris 1956, p. 100.

40. Baldensperger, *Le Mouvement des Idées*, vol. 1, p. 140.

41. SN, January 1797, vol. 1, no. 1, p. 10.

42. Note the vacuous and sneering review of Staël's treatise on the passions, SN, vol. 1, no. 3, pp. 425–8.

43. On the more liberal aspects of emigré Hamburg, see Godechot, *La Grande Nation*, p. 103.

44. Köhler, *Madame de Staël*, p. 569.

45. SN, vol. 7, no. 1, pp. 9–15.

46. Villers, *Philosophie de Kant ou Principes Fondamentales de la Philosophie Transcendentale*, Metz 1801.

47. L. Wittmer, *Charles de Villers 1765–1815: Un Intermédiaire entre la France et l'Allemagne et un Précurseur de Madame de Staël*, Geneva and Paris 1908, p. 17.

48. J.G. Fichte, letter of April 1795 to Baggesen, in M. Guéroult, 'Fichte et la Révolution Française', *Etudes sur Fichte*, Hildesheim, New York 1974, pp. 152–3.

49. Wittmer, *Charles de Villers*, p. 102.

50. Garat, *Mémoires Historiques*, vol. 2, pp. 29–30.

51. P.R. Sweet, *Wilhelm von Humboldt: A Biography*, Volume 1: *1767–1808*, Ohio 1978, p. 220.

52. W. von Humboldt, letter of 26 October 1798 to F.H. Jacobi, in A. Leitzmann, ed., *Briefe von Wilhelm von Humboldt an Friedrich Heinrich Jacobi*, Halle 1892, pp. 64–5; M. Forsyth, *Reason and Revolution: The Political Thought of the Abbé Sieyes*, New York 1987, pp. 41–2.

53. Sweet, *Wilhelm von Humboldt*, pp. 182–5.

54. P. van Tieghem, ed., A.L.G. de Staël, *De La Littérature Considérée dans ses Rapports avec les Institutions Sociales* (henceforth *DLL*), Geneva and Paris 1959, vol. 1, p. 17.

55. Staël, *DLL*, vol. 1, pp. 42, 44–5, and Conclusion.

56. See P. van Tieghem, Introduction, Staël, *DLL*, pp. xliii–xlviii; Chateaubriand, *Lettre au Citoyen Fontanes* [December 1800], CG, Paris 1977, vol. 1, p. 107.

57. Condorcet, *Esquisse d'un Tableau Historique des Progrès de l'Esprit Humain*, OC, vol. 6, pp. 13, 21, 109–10, 92, 98, 102–3. On the Emperor Julian, contrast Gibbon's more nuanced position.

58. Condorcet, *Esquisse*, OC, vol. 6, pp. 112, 113, seventh epoch, 146, 129–31, 109–11; D. Droixhe, *La Linguistique et l'Appel de l'Histoire (1600-1800)*, Geneva 1978, pp. 362–6.

59. J.G.A. Pocock, *The Machiavellian Moment*, Princeton 1975, pp. 48–9.

60. W.K. Ferguson, *The Renaissance in Historical Thought*, New York 1948, p. 6.

61. Ferguson, *The Renaissance*, pp. 48–9.

62. Q. Skinner, *The Foundations of Modern Political Thought*, Cambridge 1978, vol. 1, p. 85.

63. T.E. Mommsen, 'Petrarch's Conception of the "Dark Ages" ', in E.F. Rice, ed., *Medieval and Renaissance Studies*, Ithaca 1959, pp. 106–29.

64. E.R. Cochrane, *Historians and Historiography in the Italian Renaissance*, Chicago and London 1981, pp. 36–7.

65. Staël, *DLL*, vol. 1, p. 130; F. Simone, 'La Littérature Italienne dans *Corinne*', in *Madame de Staël et l'Europe*, Colloque de Coppet 1966, Paris 1970, pp. 289–304.

66. Staël, *De la Littérature*, vol. 1, p. 128.

67. Momigliano, 'La Formazione della Moderna Storiografia sull'Impero Romano' [1936], *Contributo alla Storia degli Studi Classici*, Rome 1955, pp. 126–7; B. Croce, *Teoria e Storia della Storiografia*, pp. 284, 295.

68. Staël, *DLL*, vol. 1, pp. 131–2.

69. Staël, *DLL*, vol. 1, pp. 91–2.

70. J.B. Bury, ed., E. Gibbon, *The Decline and Fall of the Roman Empire* (henceforth *DF*), London 1930, 10th edn, vol. 1, ch. 9, and London 1935, 10th edn, vol. 2, chs 15 and 16.

71. Staël, *DLL*, vol. 1, pp. 135–7; vol. 2, pp. 287–8.

72. Van Tieghem, *Le Romantisme Français*, Paris 1944, pp. 6–7, 13–14.

73. Mortier, in Viallaneix, *Le Préromantisme*, pp. 621–3.

74. Mortier, 'Madame de Staël', p. 125; and see Balayé, 'A Propos du "Préromantisme": Continuité ou Rupture chez Mme de Staël', in Viallaneix, *Le Préromantisme*, pp. 153–68, and S. Moravia, *Il Tramonto dell'Illuminismo*, Bari 1968, pp. 462–79.

75. Mortier, 'Madame de Staël', pp. 128–30. I am not sure that Mortier gives due weight to the criticisms offered by Fauriel and Cabanis. A further difficulty arises with Turgot's orations, namely, the fact that he was constrained in 1749–51 by his post as *prieur* at the Sorbonne. No one has yet demonstrated that they constitute a theoretical unity, and it is interesting to note that R.L. Meek almost entirely neglected the first of them in *Social Science*, pp. 69–70.

76. See, however, R. Mortier, *Le 'Tableau Littéraire de la France au XVIIIe Siècle'*, Brussels 1972.

77. C. Fauriel, *Les Derniers Jours du Consulat*, ed. A. Lalanne, Paris 1886, p. 12.

78. Fauriel, *Les Derniers Jours*, p. 12.

79. Fauriel, *Les Derniers Jours*, p. 113.

80. Fauriel, *Les Derniers Jours*, p. 80.

81. Chateaubriand, *M*, vol. 2, pp. 400–2.

82. D. Lacroix, ed., A.L.G. de Staël, *Dix Années d'Exil*, Paris 1906, p. 287.

83. Staël, *Dix Années*, p. 288.

84. Staël, *Dix Années*, p. 289-90.

85. Fauriel, *Les Derniers Jours*, p. 204.

86. F.A. Mignet, *History of the French Revolution from 1789 to 1814*, London 1906, p. 378.

87. Garat, *Mémoires Historiques*, vol. 2, pp. 428–30.

88. P.J.G. Cabanis, letter of 6 June 1804 to C. Fauriel, in J.B. Galley, *Claude Fauriel: Membre de l'Institut 1722–1843*, Saint-Etienne 1909, p. 144.

89. See chapter 9.

# Chapter 8 Nations and Tribes

1. S. Bertelli, *Ribelli, Libertini e Ortodossi nella Storiografia Barocca*, Florence 1973, pp. xi–xiv.

2. L.W. Spitz, *The Religious Renaissance of the German Humanists*, Cambridge, Mass. 1963, p. 83.

3. G. Strauss, ed., *Manifestations of Discontent in Germany on the Eve of the Reformation*, Bloomington, Indiana 1971, p. xiv.

4. It would be an error, however, to claim that later versions of classical republicanism *necessarily* sustained the Machiavellian and Spinozist opposition between free city and Covenant; see, for example, T. Jefferson, *Notes on the State of Virginia*, Chapel Hill, North Carolina 1955, pp. 164–5, and, more generally, J.G.A. Pocock, *The Machiavellian Moment*, Princeton 1975, ch. 15.

5. I use J.G.C. Anderson, ed., Tacitus, *De Origine et Situ Germanorum* (henceforth *G*), Oxford 1938.

6. In J. Rudé, 'La Germania d'Enea Silvio Piccolomini et la "Réception" de Tacite en Allemagne', EG, vol. 19, 1964, p. 279.

7. L. Wittmer, *Charles de Villers, 1765–1815*, Geneva and Paris 1908, p. 15. Many parallels may be drawn between celebrations of a Teutonic liberty in Germany and in Victorian Britain; see, for example, J. Burrow, *A Liberal Descent: Victorian Historians and the English Past*, Cambridge 1981, chs 5–7 and, more particularly, for E.A. Freeman's reference to Arminius, p. 189.

8. For the 'fortunes' of Tacitus, see K.C. Schellhase, *Tacitus in Renaissance Political Thought*, Chicago 1976.

9. H. Holborn, *Ulrich von Hutten and the German Reformation*, London and New Haven 1937, pp. 5–6.

10. Schellhase, *Tacitus*, p. 9.

11. Schellhase, *Tacitus*, pp. 32–9.

12. Anderson, ed., Tacitus, *G*, p. ix.

13. Anderson, ed., Tacitus, *G*, p. 100; L. Musset, *The Germanic Invasions: The Making of Europe AD 400–600*, translated by E. and C. James, London 1975, p. 197. Note also how Gibbon underlined this point, J.B. Bury, ed., E. Gibbon, *The Decline and Fall of the Roman Empire*, London 1930, 10th edn, vol. 1, pp. 218–19.

14. Anderson, ed., Tacitus, *G*, p. x.

15. Anderson, ed., Tacitus, *G*, p. xxiv.

16. Anderson, ed., Tacitus, *G*, pp. xxv–xxvi; E.A. Thompson, *The Early Germans*, Oxford 1965, pp. 19–22; M. Todd, *The Northern Barbarians 100 BC–AD 300*, London 1975, p. 27.

17. E. Norden, *Die Germanische Urgeschichte in Tacitus Germania*, Berlin and Leipzig 1920, 3rd edn 1923, pp. 59–84.

18. Norden, *Die Germanische Urgeschichte*, p. ix.

19. In L. Canfora, 'Tacito e la "Riscoperta degli Antichi Germani": dal II al III Reich', in *Le Vie del Classicismo*, Bari 1989, pp. 32 and 32n11. See, more generally, E. Kedourie, *Nationalism*, London 1961, chs 4 and 5.

20. Wittmer, *Charles de Villers*, p. 62; H. Tronchon, *La Fortune Intellectuelle de Herder en France*, Paris 1920, p. 216.

21. Canfora, 'Tacito', p. 37.

22. Canfora, 'Tacito', p. 39.

23. Canfora, 'Tacito', p. 44.

24. Norden, *Die Germanische Urgeschichte*, pp. 105–15.

25. Norden, *Die Germanische Urgeschichte*, pp. 124–7.

26. Anderson, ed., Tacitus, *G*, p. xxxiii.

27. Compare Norden, *Die Germanische Urgeschichte*, pp. ix, 502n.

28. Thompson, *The Early Germans*, pp. vi–vii.

29. See J.J. Tierney, 'The Celtic Ethnography of Posidonius', PRIA, vol. 60C, 1960, pp. 211–24, where Caesar's reliance upon Posidonius is emphasized.

30. W. Jones, 'The Third Anniversary Discourse' [2 February 1786], *Works*, London 1807, vol. 3, p. 34.

31. Chateaubriand, *E*, p. 53; Cuvier, *Discours*, pp. 101–2; C.J.K. Bunsen, *The Life and Letters of Barthold Georg Niebuhr*, London 1852, vol. 1, p. 87.

32. J.B. Galley, *Claude Fauriel: Membre de l'Institut 1772–1843*, Saint-Etienne 1909, p. 190.

33. A.W. Schlegel, *A Course of Lectures on Dramatic Art and Literature*, translated by J. Black, London 1846, pp. 18, 340; 'Observations sur la Langue et la Littérature Provençale' [1818], ELH, Bonn 1842, p. 225; and see F. Schlegel, letter of May 1804 to Staël, in J. de Pange, *Auguste-Guillaume Schlegel et Madame de Staël*, Paris 1938, pp. 121–2.

34. A.W. Schlegel, 'Comparison entre la Phèdre de Racine et Celle d'Euripide' [1807], ELH, pp. 85–170.

35. F. Schlegel, *On the Indian Language, Literature and Philosophy* [1808], AMW, p. 425. Schlegel almost certainly had access, while in Paris, to drafts of the translation of the Asiatic Society of Calcutta's seven volumes, published as *Recherches Asiatiques*, Paris 1805, translated by A. Labaume, and massively annotated by Langlès, who knew Hamilton, and, to a lesser extent, by Cuvier, Lamarck and others. The *Recherches* include versions of the first seven of Jones's anniversary discourses.

36. S. Timpanaro, Introduction, F. Schlegel, *Ueber die Sprache und Die Weisheit der Indier*, Amsterdam 1977, pp. xviii–xix; K. Koerner, 'The Place of Friedrich Schlegel in the Development of Historical-Comparative Linguistics', in T. de Mauro and L. Formigari, eds., *Leibniz, Humboldt and the Origins of Comparativism*, Amsterdam and Philadelphia 1990, p. 244; and, more generally, M. Foucault, *The Order of Things*, London 1970, pp. 280–94.

37. F. Schlegel, *On the Indian Language*, AMW, p. 454; R. Schwab, *La Renaissance Orientale*, Paris 1950, pp. 33–35.

38. For example, G. Vico, *The Third New Science*, translated by T.G. Bergin and M.H. Fisch, Ithaca and London 1984, p. 129; and see G. Costa, 'Vico e il Settecento', FI, vol. 10, pp. 10–30; and S. Gensini, ' "Vulgaris Opinio Babelica": sui Fondamenti Storici-Teorici della Pluralità delle Lingue nel Pensiero di Leibniz', in Mauro and Formigari, eds., *Leibniz*, pp. 61–83.

39. Timpanaro, Introduction, Schlegel, *Ueber die Sprache*, p. xxiii.

40. For example, A.W. Schlegel, 'De l'Origine des Hindous', ELH, p. 474. For critical comment, see E. Sapir, *Language*, New York 1921, p. 124n2; S. Timpanaro, *On Materialism*, translated by L. Garner, London 1975, pp. 204–5; M. Bernal, *Black Athena: The Afro-Asiatic Roots of Classical Civilization*, vol. 1: *The Fabrication of Ancient Greece 1785–1985*, London 1987, pp. 230–3.

41. See criticisms of this model in C. Renfrew, *Archaeology and Language: The Puzzle of Indo-European Origins*, London 1987, ch. 5. I am not competent to assess the solution offered to the puzzle, which involves an Anatolian origin for Indo-European and which posits a gradual transfer of the languages through the spread, over more than three millennia, of Neolithic farming.

42. J. Fraser, 'Linguistic Evidence and Archaeological and Ethnological Facts', PBA, vol. 12, 1926, p. 272.

43. Renfrew, *Archaeology and Language*, pp. 104–5.

44. Timpanaro, *On Materialism*, p. 49n21.

45. A.W. Schlegel, 'De l'Origine des Hindous', ELH, p. 474; B.G. Niebuhr, *History of Rome*, 2nd edn, translated by J.C. Hare and C. Thirlwall, London 1837, vol. 1, pp. 82–3.

46. Bernal, *Black Athena*, vol. 1, pp. 226–7.

47. Renfrew, *Archaeology and Language*, pp. 14–15.

48. M. Todd, *The Northern Barbarians*, p. 20. On the use to which Kossinna's theories were put under the Nazi regime, see G.L. Mosse, *Toward the Final Solution*, London 1978, p. 45.

49. H. van de Weerd, review of Anderson, ed., *Tacitus*, G, in AC, 1938, p. 408. Grahame Clark condemned Kossinna's racism unequivocally in *Archaeology and Society*, London 1939, pp. 205–6.

50. G. Childe, *The Aryans*, London 1926, pp. 91–3, for illustration of the notion of the protolexicon, ch. 7 for an account of Kossinna's theories. Childe never referred to this book in later years, and regretted its publication. In Renfrew, *Archaeology and Language*, the final, disturbing sentence is, however, quoted in full. In order to counterbalance the

unfortunate effect of this quotation, consider the following passage, also from the *The Aryans*, pp. 163–4: 'The apotheosis of the Nordics has been linked with policies of imperialism and world domination: the word "Aryan" has become the watchword of dangerous factions and especially of the more brutal and blatant forms of anti-Semitism . . . the gravest objection to the word Aryan is its association with pogroms.'

51. C. Lévi-Strauss, 'Race and History' [1953], *Structural Anthropology*, translated by M. Layton, London 1977, vol. 2, p. 325.

52. Norden, *Die Germanische Urgeschichte*, pp. 379–96; for an elaboration of a similar point regarding the Celts, see Renfrew, *Archaeology and Language*, pp. 218–25.

53. R. Rosdolsky, *Engels and the 'Nonhistoric' Peoples: The National Question in the Revolution of 1848*, translated by J.-P. Himka, Glasgow 1987.

54. E. Gellner, 'Zeno of Cracow', *Culture, Identity and Politics*, Cambridge 1987, pp. 47–74.

55. E.R. Leach, *Political Systems of Highland Burma* [1954], London 1964, and M. Sahlins, 'The Segmentary Lineage: An Organisation of Predatory Expansion', AA, vol. 63, 1961, pp. 322–45.

56. E.R. Leach, *Rethinking Anthropology*, London 1961, ch. 1. Contrast A.R. Radcliffe-Brown, *A Natural Science of Society*, Glencoe, Illinois 1957.

57. E. Sapir, 'Do we Need a Superorganic?', AA, vol. 19, 1917, pp. 441–7; *Language*, pp. 207–20.

58. H. Hubert, *Les Germains*, Paris 1952, pp. 21, 33–4, 38–40, and chs 2 and 3. See also lectures from the same period on *Les Celtes*, Paris 1932, vol. 1, p. 57.

59. In addition to 'Race and History', see the UNESCO statement of July 1950, in which Lévi-Strauss had a hand, *Four Statements on the Race Question*, Paris 1969, pp. 30–5, and M. Leiris, *Race and Culture*, Paris 1951.

60. P. Anderson, 'Fernand Braudel', in *A Zone of Engagement*, London 1992, pp. 255–6.

61. S. Piggott, 'The Early Bronze Age in Wessex', PPS, vol. 4, 1938, pp. 52–106; Childe, *Prehistoric Communities of the British Isles*, London 1940, p. 91, also pp. 97, 110, 117, 119.

62. G. Clark, 'The Invasion Hypothesis in British Archaeology', A, vol. 40, 1966, p. 188.

63. Clark, 'The Invasion Hypothesis', pp. 172–73; see D. Mellor, ed., *A Paradise Lost: The Neo-Romantic Imagination in Britain 1935–55*, London 1987.

64. C. Renfrew and J.F. Cherry, eds., *Peer Polity Interaction and Socio-Political Change*, Cambridge 1986.

65. This section owes much to Q. Skinner, *The Foundations of Modern Political Thought*, Cambridge 1978, vol. 2, ch. 8.

66. Pocock, *The Ancient Constitution and the Feudal Law*, Cambridge 1957, p. 14.

67. Skinner, *The Foundations*, vol. 2, pp. 310–11.

68. J.H.E. Salmon and R.E. Giesey, eds., F. Hotman, *Francogallia*, Cambridge 1972, pp. 147, 155, 234–5, 238.

69. H. de Boulainvilliers, Count de Saint-Saire, *Histoire de l'Ancien Gouvernement de la France*, The Hague 1727, pp. 27, 33–4, 35–9.

70. J.B. du Bos, *Histoire Critique de l'Etablissement de la Monarchie Française dans les Gaules* [1734], 2nd edn, Paris 1742, vol. 1, pp. 10, 13–14, vol. 4, pp. 34–5.

71. Du Bos, *Histoire Critique*, vol. 4, pp. 287–8.

72. R.L. de Voyer, Marquis D'Argenson, *Considérations sur le Gouvernement Ancien et Présent de la France*, Amsterdam 1764, p. 123.

73. D' Argenson, *Considérations*, ch. 6.

74. Turgot, *Mémoire au Roi sur les Municipalités* [1775], in *Oeuvres de Turgot*, Paris 1809, vol. 7, pp. 386–484.

75. Montesquieu, *The Spirit of the Laws*, translated by A.M. Cohler, B.C. Miller and H.S. Stone, Cambridge 1989, pp. 627, 639, 659, 628, 663, 620–1, 166n10, 167, 536–7; and D'Argenson, *Considérations*, p. 122.

76. Chs 11 and 19 of the *Germania* would seem to have influenced Rousseau, and it is possible that his enthusiasm for the patron–client relation reflected an interest in the

*comitatus*, discussed in chs 13–15. More generally, see Mirabeau, *Essai sur le Despotisme*, London 1776, pp. 29–30.

77. D'Argenson, *Considérations*, pp. 13, 15, ch. 4. For quotations, see J.-J. Rousseau, *The Social Contract*, translated by M. Cranston, Harmondsworth 1968, pp. 51n, 73n, 185n; OC, vol. 3, pp. 353, 371, 467.

78. J.-J. Rousseau, *A Discourse on the Origins of Inequality*, translated by M. Cranston, Harmondsworth 1984, p. 106; OC, vol. 3, p. 162.

79. J.-J. Rousseau, *Emile*, OC, vol. 4, pp. 567–70.

80. Rousseau, *Emile*, OC, vol. 4, p. 608.

81. Rousseau, *Emile*, OC, vol. 4, p. 611.

82. B. Spinoza, *Theological–Political Treatise*, translated by R.H.M. Elwes, Toronto and London 1951, pp. 15, 21–5, 94.

83. Spinoza, *Theological–Political Treatise*, ch. 1.

84. Rousseau, *Emile*, OC, vol. 4, p. 612; compare Spinoza, *Theological–Political Treatise*, pp. 81–3, 85.

85. Rousseau, *Emile*, OC, vol. 4, pp. 622–4.

86. For example, C.-F. de Volney, *Les Ruines*, OC, p. 18.

87. M. Duchet, *Anthropologie et Histoire au Siècle des Lumières*, Paris 1978, p. 377.

88. G. Goggi, ed., D. Diderot, *Contributions à l'Histoire des Deux Indes*, Siena 1976–77, vol. 1, p. 163.

89. F. Venturi, *L'Antichità Svelata e l'Idea del Progresso in N.A Boulanger (1722–1759)*, Bari 1947, pp. 23–6, 51.

90. Venturi, *L'Antichità Svelata*, pp. 113–15; and Burrow, *A Liberal Descent*, p. 32.

91. J.B. Mably, *Observations sur l'Histoire de France*, 2nd edn, Paris 1788, vol. 1, pp. 219–20; vol. 1, pp. 244–5; vol. 2, pp. 5–6, 239–55; vol. 2, pp. 72–119.

92. J.N.A. Thierry, *Considérations sur l'Histoire de France* [1840], in *Récits des Temps Mérovingiennes*, Paris 1864, vol. 1, pp. 94–5.

93. E. Carcassonne, *Montesquieu et la Problème de la Constitution Française*, Paris 1927, pp. 198–9.

94. E. Sieyes, 'Qu'est-ce que le Tiers Etat?', *Oeuvres de Sieyes*, Paris 1989, vol. 1, pp. 10–11.

95. Contrast F. Furet and M. Ozouf, 'Deux Légitimations Historiques de la Société Française au XVIIIe Siècle: Mably et Boulainvilliers', AESC, vol. 34.1, 1979, p. 449.

96. N. de Bonneville, *De l'Esprit des Religions*, Paris 1791, pp. 53–7.

97. Bonneville, *De l'Esprit des Religions*, pp. 47, 57; Venturi, *L'Antichità Svelata*, p. 120n.

98. J.-Y. Guiomar, 'La Révolution Française et les Origines Celtiques de la France', AHRF, vol. 64, 1992, pp. 65–7.

## Chapter 9 The Tribe-nation

1. H. Heine, *The Romantic School*, translated and edited by H.M. Mustard, SW, New York 1973, p. 130.

2. J. de Pange, *Auguste-Guillaume Schlegel et Madame de Staël*, Paris 1938, p. 503.

3. Pange, *Auguste-Guillaume Schlegel*, pp. 221, 455.

4. Pange, *Auguste-Guillaume Schlegel*, p. 221; note his letter of 28 February 1814, pp. 489–91.

5. Pange, *Auguste-Guillaume Schlegel*, pp. 18–19, 233–34, 391, 456.

6. Pange, *Auguste-Guillaume Schlegel*, p. 387.

7. Pange, *Auguste-Guillaume Schlegel*, pp. 410, 447.

8. J. de Pange, ed., A.L.G. de Staël, *De l'Allemagne* (henceforth *DLA*), Paris 1958–60, vol. 1, pp. 52–5.

9. Staël, *DLA*, vol. 1, p. 10.

10. S. Moravia, *La Scienza dell'Uomo nel Settecento*, Bari 1970, pp. 191–2.

11. Moravia, *La Scienza dell'Uomo*, p. 192; Staël, *De l'Allemagne*, vol. 1, p. 10; vol. 3, pp. 314–15, 318.

12. As letters to Goethe and Jacobi in that year testify; see, for example, P.R. Sweet, *Wilhelm von Humboldt: A Biography*, vol. 1: *1767–1808*, Ohio 1978, vol. 1, p. 206.

13. W. von Humboldt, 'Plan einer Vergleichenden Anthropologie', GS, vol. 1, pp. 377–410; 'Das Achtzehnte Jahrhundert', GS, vol. 2, pp. 1–112.

14. As John Burrow does; see Introduction, W. von Humboldt, *The Limits of State Action*, Cambridge 1969, pp. xxvii–xxviii.

15. W. von Humboldt, letter of 26 October 1798 to Jacobi, in A. Leitzmann, ed., *Briefe von Wilhelm von Humboldt an Friedrich Heinrich Jacobi*, Halle 1892, pp. 60–74.

16. W. von Humboldt, 'Plan', GS, vol. 1, p. 379.

17. W. von Humboldt, 'Plan', GS, vol. 1, p. 379–80.

18. F. Meinecke, *Cosmopolitanism and the National State*, translated by F.B. Kimber, Princeton 1970, p. 45.

19. Sweet, *Wilhelm von Humboldt*, vol. 1, p. 420. Sieyes, however, was more responsive; M. Forsyth, *Reason and Revolution: The Political Thought of the Abbé Sieyes*, New York 1987, p. 42.

20. H. Aarsleff, Introduction, W. von Humboldt, *On Language: The Diversity of Human Language-Structure and its Influence on the Mental Development of Mankind*, translated by P. Heath, Cambridge 1988, pp. xxxiii–xxxiv.

21. H. Aarsleff, 'The Tradition of Condillac: The Problem of the Origin of Language in the Eighteenth Century and the Debate in the Berlin Academy before Herder', in D. Hymes, ed., *Studies in the History of Linguistics*, Bloomington, Indiana and London 1974, pp. 121–43. Such affinities between purportedly opposed traditions undermine many of the generally accepted accounts of Enlightenment thought, as Aarsleff observes, at greater length, in 'The Eighteenth Century; including Leibniz', in T.A. Sebeok, ed., *Current Trends in Linguistics*, The Hague and Paris 1975, vol. 13, pp. 383–479. Furthermore, Foucault's observations regarding a disjunction between general grammar and comparative philology are belied by the evident overlap in the case of both the Schlegels and Humboldt. See, for example, P.R. Sweet, *Wilhelm von Humboldt*, vol. 2, pp. 395–8. In *The Order of Things*, London 1970, p. 285, Foucault claims that comparative philology, by contrast with general grammar, had rendered all human languages equal. This generalization may apply to Bopp or Rask, but many passages in Humboldt, as in the Schlegels, appear to rank languages in a hierarchy. Aarsleff, Bernal and Sweet thus identify a strong element of racism in Humboldtian linguistics. Conversely, Donatella di Cesare insists that Humboldt's linguistic types are not classes; see 'The Philosophical and Anthropological Place of Wilhelm von Humboldt's Linguistic Typology: Linguistic Comparison as a Means to Compare the Different Processes of Human Thought', in T. de Mauro and L. Formigari, eds., *Leibniz, Humboldt and the Origins of Comparativism*, Amsterdam and Philadelphia 1990, pp. 172–3. Finally, I would add that Foucault's generalization also fails to do justice to the generally egalitarian approach of the *idéologues* to language. See, for example, C.-F. de Volney, 'Rapport', MAC, vol. 1, 1807, pp. 128–9, and V. Cuoco, in correspondence with Degérando, 'Giambattista Vico e lo Studio delle Lingue come Documenti Storici' [1804], SV, vol. 1, p. 79, and Moravia, *La Scienza dell'Uomo*, p. 437.

22. J.-F. La Harpe, *Du Fanatisme dans le Langage Révolutionnaire ou de la Persécution Suscitée par les Barbares du Dix-Huitième Siècle, Contre la Religion Chrétienne et ses Ministres*, Paris 1797, p. 5n.

23. R. Mortier, *Le 'Tableau Littéraire de la France au XVIIIe Siècle'*, Brussels 1972, p. 11; and, in particular, J.N.A. Thierry, 'Sur la Philosophie du XVIIIe Siècle et sur Celle du XIXe', a review of Garat's *Mémoires Historiques*, in *Dix Ans d'Etudes Historiques*, OC, vol. 3, Paris 1884, pp. 534–8.

24. For example, I. Berlin, *Vico and Herder*, London 1976, pp. 43, 167. Note Aarsleff, 'The Eighteenth Century', pp. 427–30, and M. Lilla, 'The Trouble with the Enlightenment', LRB, vol. 16, no. 1, 6 January 1994, pp. 12–13.

25. Staël, *DLA*, vol. 4, p. 38; see also her correspondence with Humboldt in 1801–2.

26. Staël, *DLA*, vol. 4, pp. 41–5; also B. Constant, *De la Religion*, Paris 1824, vol. 1, pp. 2–6, and C. de Villers, *Introduction à la Philosophie de Kant*, Metz 1801, vol. 2, p. 377n1.

27. C. Fauriel, in P. Déguise, *Benjamin Constant Méconnu*, Geneva 1966, p. 81; P.J.G. Cabanis, *Rapports du Physique et du Moral dans l'Homme*, OP, vol. 1, p. 510.

28. Staël, *DLA*, vol. 4, p. 21.

29. Staël, *DLA*, vol. 4, pp. 108–9.

30. Staël, *DLA*, vol. 4, pp. 121–3; Constant, journal entry for 7 August 1804, in A. Roulin and C. Roth, eds., *Journaux Intimes*, Paris 1952, p. 120.

31. Staël, *DLA*, vol. 4, pp. 116–18, 119, 123–4, 129, 130; Villers, *Introduction*, vol. 2, pp. 359–61.

32. Staël, *DLA*, vol. 4, p. 189.

33. Staël, *DLA*, vol. 4, pp. 193–4, 196, and note the comparison she draws between Schlegel's arguments and the earlier researches of Bailly, one of the epigones of Diderot mentioned by Franco Venturi.

34. Cabanis, *Rapports*, OP, vol. 1, p. 509; Constant, journal entries for 24 April, 17 May, 25 May, 2 October, 12 October, 13 October 1804, in Roulin and Roth, eds., *Journaux Intimes*, pp. 81, 88, 91, 145, 149.

35. In 293 AD, rule by two Emperors and two Caesars was introduced: Maximian in the West had Constantius as his Caesar (with particular responsibilities for Gaul and Britain); Galerius was Caesar to Diocletian.

36. R.-F. de Chateaubriand, *Les Martyrs* (henceforth *LM*), ORV, vol. 2, p. 29.

37. Chateaubriand, Preface, *LM*, 3rd edn, ORV, vol. 2, p. 73.

38. Chateaubriand, letter of 30 May 1809 to Guizot, CG, vol. 2, p. 47.

39. Boulainvilliers, *Histoire de l'Ancien Gouvernement de la France*, The Hague 1727, p. 7.

40. Chateaubriand, *LM*, in ORV, vol. 2, p. 1606.

41. Chateaubriand, *LM*, in ORV, vol. 2, p. 501.

42. Note Constant's scathing comments, letter of 22 March 1809 to Sismondi, RESS, vol. 18, 1980, p. 118.

43. Chateaubriand, *LM*, in ORV, vol. 2, p. 502.

44. Chateaubriand, *LM*, in ORV, vol. 2, p. 115.

45. Chateaubriand, *LM*, in ORV, vol. 2, p. 147.

46. Chateaubriand, Preface, *LM*, 3rd edn, ORV, vol. 2, pp. 79, 81.

47. Chateaubriand, *LM*, in ORV, vol. 2, p. 168.

48. C. Blennerhassett, *Madame de Staël*, London 1889, vol. 3, p. 209.

49. Blennerhassett, *Madame de Staël*, vol. 3, p. 210.

50. Chateaubriand, *LM*, in ORV, vol. 2, p. 167.

51. Lactantius, *De Mortibus Persecutorum*, edited and translated by J.L. Creed, Oxford 1984, pp. 24–5.

52. Chateaubriand, *LM*, in ORV, vol. 2, p. 399.

53. Chateaubriand, *LM*, in ORV, vol. 2, p. 239–41.

54. Thierry, Preface, *Récits des Temps Mérovingiennes*, Paris 1864, vol. 1, p. 12; see also S. Turner, *The History of the Anglo-Saxons*, London 1807, p. iv, for another historian's fascination with a northern song of death.

55. Moravia, *La Scienza dell'Uomo*, p. 206.

56. J. Lavallée, 'Discours Inaugurale', MAC, vol. 1, 1807, pp. 7–8. If such assertions are reminiscent of the philosophy of Nicholas de Bonneville, of some aspects of eighteenth-century deism, or even of theophilanthropy, this is no doubt because Lavallée, like Cambry, Mangourit and Lépeaux, had long been a member of one of the Breton Masonic Lodges; see J.-Y. Guiomar, 'La Révolution Française et les Origines Celtiques de la France', AHRF, vol. 64, 1992, pp. 76–7.

57. E. Johanneau, 'Discours d'Ouverture', MAC, vol. 1, pp. 38–40.

58. For example, A. Van Gennep, *Manuel de Folklore Français Contemporain*, Paris 1937, vol. 1, p. 32.

59. MAC, vol. 1, pp. 72–86.

60. M. Ozouf, 'L'Invention de l'Ethnographie Française: le Questionnaire de l'Académie Celtique', *L'Ecole de la France*, Paris 1984, p. 357.

61. See L.-M. La Revellière-Lépeaux, *Réflexions sur le Culte, sur les Cérémonies Civiles et sur les Fêtes Nationales*, Paris 1797, pp. 3–5, and, more generally, L. Sozzi, 'I Sepolchri e le Discussioni Francesi sulle Tombi negli Anni del Direttorio', GSLI, vol. 144, 1967, pp. 567–8.

62. M. Mangourit, 'Des Noms Propres', MAC, vol. 2, pp. 234, 253; E. Johanneau, 'Sur la Vie et les Oeuvres de Le Brigant', MAC, vol. 6, pp. 5–8.

63. F. Schlegel, *On the Indian Language*, AMW, p. 429; A.W. Schlegel, 'De l'Origine des Hindous', ELH, pp. 492–3.

64. For example, E. Kedourie, who likewise attributes the discovery of diversity as a value to Herder, *Nationalism*, London 1961, revised edn; contrast Guiomar, 'La Révolution Française', p. 84.

65. E. Boutroux, 'Germanisme et Humanité' [August 1915], in *Etudes d'Histoire de la Philosophie Allemande*, Paris 1926, p. 141.

66. Boutroux, 'L'Evolution de la Pensée Allemande' [May 1915], in *Etudes*, pp. 204–6.

67. Boutroux, 'L'Allemande et la Guerre' [September 1914], in *Etudes*, p. 134; see H. von Treitschke, *What we Demand of France*, London 1870.

68. T. Mommsen, *Agli Italiani*, Berlin 1870, p. 5.

69. Fustel de Coulanges, *L'Alsace est-elle Allemande ou Française? Réponse à M. Mommsen*, Paris 1870, p. 15, and 'De la Manière d'Ecrire l'Histoire en France et en Allemagne', RDM, vol. 101, 1872, pp. 241–51.

70. Boutroux, 'Germanisme', p. 151.

71. Léon, *Fichte et son Temps*, Paris 1927, vol. 2, pt 2, pp. 70–1n5.

72. J.G. Fichte, *Addresses to the German Nation*, ed. G.A. Kelly, New York and Evanston 1968, p. 45.

73. Fichte, *Addresses*, pp. 47, 58.

74. M. Guéroult, 'Fichte et Xavier Léon', in *Etudes sur Fichte*, Hildesheim, New York 1974, pp. 256–61.

75. Léon, *Fichte*, vol. 2, pt 1, pp. 422–62.

76. Léon, *Fichte*, vol. 2, pt 2, pp. 63–4, and see F. Schlegel, 'Principles of Gothic Architecture', AMW, pp. 156–7.

77. Léon, *Fichte*, vol. 2, pt 2, pp. 78ff.

78. Guéroult, 'Fichte et la Révolution Française' [1937], *Etudes*, pp. 230–46, and for the contrast with Friedrich Schlegel's later views, see Meinecke, *Cosmopolitanism*, pp. 65–7.

79. Fichte, *Addresses*, p. 75.

80. Guéroult, 'Fichte et la Révolution Française', p. 237.

81. Fichte, *Addresses*, p. 74.

82. Fichte, *Addresses*, p. 81–6.

83. Fichte, *Addresses*, p. 108.

84. G.A. Kelly, *Idealism, Politics and History: Sources of Hegelian Thought*, Cambridge 1969, p. 183.

85. Fichte, *Addresses*, pp. 100–1, 108.

86. Kelly, Introduction, Fichte, *Addresses*, p. xxx.

87. Fichte, *Addresses*, p. 108.

88. Moravia, *La Scienza dell'Uomo*, pp. 164–5.

89. See A. Momigliano, 'Lettere di B.G. Niebuhr su suoi Studi Orientalistici', RSI, vol. 72, 1960, pp. 336–47.

90. S. Rytkönen, *Barthold Georg Niebuhr als Politiker und Historiker*, Helsinki 1968, p. 34.

91. B.G. Niebuhr, *History of Rome* (henceforth HR), 1st edn, translated by F.A. Walter, London 1827, vol. 1, p. 269, also pp. 338–9.

92. Niebuhr, *HR*, 1st edn, vol. 1, p. 269.

93. Niebuhr, *HR*, 1st edn, vol. 1, p. 398, and Preface, *HR*, 2nd edn, vol. 1, p. xiii.

94. Niebuhr, Preface, *HR*, 2nd edn, vol. 1, p. xxii.

95. Momigliano, 'Alle Origini dell'Interesse di Niebuhr su Roma Arcaica e l'India', RSI, vol. 92, 1980, pp. 361–71.

96. Niebuhr, letter of 21 May 1804 to A. Moltke, in K. Christ, *Vom Gibbon zu Rostoevtseff*, Darmstadt 1972, p. 31.

97. Rytkönen, *Georg Barthold Niebuhr*, p. 76, and see pp. 74–9.

98. P. Catalano, *Populus Romanus Quirites*, Turin 1974, pp. 21–6.

99. Niebuhr, *HR*, 1st edn, vol. 1, p. 242.

100. Niebuhr, *HR*, 1st edn, vol. 1, p. 252.

101. Niebuhr, *HR*, 1st edn, vol. 1, p. 271.

102. Niebuhr, *HR*, 1st edn, vol. 1, p. 269, and *HR*, 2nd edn, vol. 1, pp. 486–7.

103. For the whole argument, see Z. Yavetz, 'Why Rome? Zeitgeist and Ancient Historians in Early 19th Century Germany', AJP, vol. 97, 1976, pp. 276–96.

104. See F.W. Maitland, Introduction to O. Gierke, *Political Theories of the Middle Age*, Cambridge 1900, pp. vii–xlv.

105. Niebuhr, *HR*, 2nd edn, vol. 1, pp. 314–15.

106. Meinecke, *Cosmopolitanism*, pp. 91–2.

107. Momigliano, 'Perizonius, Niebuhr and the Character of Early Roman Tradition', in *Essays on Ancient and Modern Historiography*, Oxford 1977, pp. 323–53.

108. B. Doer, 'Livy and the Germans', in T.A. Dorey, ed., *Livy*, London and Toronto 1971, pp. 97–117.

109. Niebuhr, *HR*, 1st edn, vol. 1, p. xxix.

110. Niebuhr, *HR*, 1st edn, vol. 1, p. 6.

111. Niebuhr, *HR*, 1st edn, vol. 1, pp. xxx–xxxi.

112. Niebuhr, *HR*, 1st edn, vol. 1, p. xxxi.

113. Meinecke, *Cosmopolitanism*, pp. 154–5n15, and see Pange, *Auguste-Guillaume Schlegel*, pp. 198–204. Contrast, however, W. von Humboldt, 'Plan', GS, vol. 1, pp. 379–80.

# Chapter 10 A Postscript from Milan

1. L. di Breme, letter of 25 May 1816 to L. Stolberg, in P. Camporesi, ed., L. di Breme, *Lettere*, Turin 1966, p. 325.

2. Breme, letter of 14 July 1814 to T. Valperga di Caluso, in Camporesi, ed., Breme, *Lettere*, p. 239.

3. Beyle (Stendhal), *Rome, Naples et Florence* (1826, 3rd edn), entry for 15 December 1816, in V. Del Letto, ed., *Voyages en Italie*, Paris 1973, p. 378.

4. S. Moravia, Introduction, G.D. Romagnosi, SF, Florence 1974, vol. 1, p. 27.

5. G. Moget, 'En Marge du Bi-Centenaire de Madame de Staël: Classiques et Romantiques à Milan en 1816', LP, vol. 131, February 1967, p. 48.

6. C. Capra, 'Italian Jacobins and the French Revolution', NASMI, 17, Spring 1990, pp. 6–7.

7. J. de Pange, ed., A.L.G. de Staël, *De l'Allemagne*, Paris 1958–60, vol. 3, p. 352.

8. Staël, 'Su la Maniera e l'Utilità delle Traduzioni', 1 January 1816, in E. Bellorini, ed., *Discussioni e Polemiche sul Romanticismo*, Bari 1943, vol. 1, p. 4.

9. S. Balayé, ed., *Les Carnets de Voyage de Madame de Staël*, Geneva 1971, p. 120.

10. Staël, 'Su la Maniera', pp. 5–6; P.J.G. Cabanis, 'Lettre à M. T[huriot] sur les Poèmes de Homère', OC, vol. 5, pp. 286–7.

11. Staël, 'Su la Maniera', p. 7.

12. Camporesi, ed., Breme, *Lettere*, p. 379.

13. PLV, April 1816, Bellorini, ed., *Discussioni*, vol. 1, pp. 10–15; in the same vein, Carlo Botta, letter of 17 November 1826 to L. Cibrario, in W. Maturi, *Interpretazioni del Risorgimento*, Turin 1962, pp. 42–3.

14. P. Giordani, April 1816, Bellorini, ed., *Discussioni*, vol. 1, p. 18.

15. Timpanaro, *Classicismo e Illuminismo nell'Ottocento Italiano*, Pisa 1969, 2nd, revised edn, pp. 46–7.

16. Giordani, April 1816, Bellorini, ed., *Discussioni*, vol. 1, p. 22.

17. Giordani, April 1816, Bellorini, ed., *Discussioni*, vol. 1, p. 23.

18. Breme, 1 June 1816, Bellorini, ed., *Discussioni*, vol. 1, pp. 29, 39, where the names of Bacon, Locke, Condillac, Smith, Genovesi, Soave, Dugald Stewart, Degérando and Tracy feature. The tributes paid to Kant, Jacobi and Fichte would seem to be a direct reflection of *De l'Allemagne*, vol. 4. See also Beyle (Stendhal), *Rome, Naples et Florence* (1826), in *Voyages en Italie*, pp. 342–4.

19. Breme, 1 June 1816, Bellorini, ed., *Discussioni*, vol. 1, p. 27, a point of view shared by Stendhal.

20. G. Leopardi, 18 July 1816, E. Mazzali, ed., Leopardi, *Discorso di un Italiano Intorno Alla Poesia Romantica*, 1970, p. 124; F. Flora, ed., Leopardi, *Zibaldone*, Milan 1983, vol. 1, p. 25; compare Cabanis, 'Lettre à M. T[huriot]', OC, vol. 5, pp. 282–6.

21. Leopardi, *Discorso*, pp. 123–4.

22. Leopardi, *Discorso*, pp. 126–7.

23. Leopardi, *Discorso*, pp. 8–9.

24. Leopardi, *Zibaldone*, p. 26.

25. Leopardi, *Discorso*, p. 16.

26. Timpanaro, *Classicismo*, p. xvi.

27. G.D. Romagnosi, *Assunto Primo della Scienza del Diritto Naturale* [1820], in A. de Georgi, ed., *Opere di G.D. Romagnosi*, Milan 1844, vol. 3, pt 1, pp. 581–2.

28. Romagnosi, *Della Ragione Civile delle Acque nella Rurale Economia*, Milan 1835; also C. Cattaneo, *Notizie Naturali e Civili su la Lombardia* [1844], in E. Sestan, ed., *Opere di Romagnosi, Cattaneo, Ferrari*, Milan and Naples 1957, pp. 771–3.

29. Romagnosi, 'Dell'Origine e dei Progressi della Civile Jurisprudenza' [1826], *Opere di G.D. Romagnosi*, vol. 2, pt 1, pp. 385–6.

30. S. Pellico, letter to U. Foscolo, in V. Branca, ed., *Il Conciliatore*, Florence 1948, vol. 1, p. xxii.

31. Romagnosi, 'Della Poesia Considerata Rispetto alle Diverse Età delle Nazione', *Il Conciliatore*, vol. 1, p. 55.

32. Staël, *De l'Allemagne*, vol. 2, pp. 127–9.

33. Romagnosi, 'Della Poesia', p. 58.

34. Romagnosi, 'Della Poesia', p. 60.

35. Branca, ed., *Il Conciliatore*, vol. 1, p. 59n.

36. In Timpanaro's view, a reference was intended to *Verona Illustrata* [1727], a book in which Scipione Maffei had argued that the Lombards had been far less numerous than had commonly been supposed; *Classicismo*, p. 244.

37. Romagnosi, 'Delle Fonti della Coltura Italiana', *Il Conciliatore*, vol. 1, pp. 201–2.

38. Moravia, 'Vichismo e "Idéologie" nella Cultura Italiana del Primo Ottocento', in *Omaggio a Vico*, Naples 1968, pp. 419–38.

39. G. Vico, *The Third New Science* (henceforth *TNS*), translated by T.G. Bergin and M.H. Fisch, Ithaca and London 1984, p. 397.

40. Vico, *TNS*, p. 414.

41. Romagnosi, 'Delle Fonti', p. 203.

42. A. Momigliano, 'Gibbon from an Italian Point of View', in G.W. Bowersock, J. Clive and S.R. Graubard, eds., *Edward Gibbon and the Decline and Fall of the Roman Empire*, Cambridge, Mass. 1977, p. 83.

43. Momigliano, 'La Formazione della Moderna Storiografia sull' "Impero Romano" ', *Contributo alla Storia degli Studi Classici*, Rome 1955, pp. 126–7; and 'Christianity and the Decline of the Roman Empire', *Terzo Contributo agli Studi Classici*, Rome 1966, vol. 1, pp. 69–86.

44. Vico, *TNS*, p. 400.

45. J.B. Bury, ed., E. Gibbon, *The Decline and Fall of the Roman Empire* (henceforth *DF*), London 1930, 10th edn, vol. 1, p. 76.

46. Gibbon, *DF*, vol. 1, pp. 9–10, 59.

47. Gibbon, *DF*, vol. 1, p. 64.

48. Momigliano, 'La Formazione', p. 125.

49. Gibbon, *DF*, vol. 1, p. 1.

50. Gibbon, *DF*, vol. 1, p. 67.

51. Gibbon, *DF*, vol. 1, pp. 53–4.

52. D. Forbes, *Hume's Philosophical Politics*, Cambridge 1976, ch. 5.

53. Forbes, *Hume's Philosophical Politics*, pp. 150–2.

54. J.G.A. Pocock, *The Machiavellian Moment*, Princeton 1975, pp. 498–504.

55. Pocock, 'Between Machiavelli and Hume: Gibbon as Civic Humanist and Philosophic Historian', in Bowersock, *et al.*, eds., *Edward Gibbon*, pp. 105–6.

56. Gibbon, *DF*, vol. 1, pp. 9–10, 9n32, 40–1.

57. Pocock, 'Between Machiavelli and Hume', p. 105.

58. Pocock, 'Between Machiavelli and Hume', p. 106.

59. Romagnosi, *Dell'Indole e dei Fattori dell'Incivilmento con Esempio del suo Risorgimento in Italia* [1829–32], in Sestan, ed., *Opere*, p. 153.

60. Romagnosi, *Dell'Indole*, p. 155.

61. Romagnosi, *Dell'Indole*, p. 178. See also G. Falco, 'La Questione Longobarda e la Moderna Storiografia Italiana', RSI, vol. 63, 1951, pp. 270–2.

62. Romagnosi, *Dell'Indole*, pp. 179n1, 185–6.

63. Romagnosi, *Dell'Indole*, p. 184n1.

64. A. de Gubernatis, *Il Manzoni e il Fauriel*, Rome 1880.

65. F.-D. de Reynaud, Count of Montlosier, *De la Monarchie Française depuis son Etablissement jusqu'à nos Jours*, Paris 1814, vol. 1, pp. 32–42, 106–7.

66. Montlosier, *De la Monarchie Française*, vol. 1, pp. 12, 18–19, 20–1, 24–5.

67. Montlosier, *De la Monarchie Française*, vol. 1, pp. 135–6.

68. S. Mellon, *The Political Uses of History*, Stanford, California 1958, ch. 2, and J.N.A. Thierry, 'Sur l'Antipathie de Races qui Divise la Nation Française' [2 April 1820], *Dix Ans d'Etudes Historiques*, Paris 1884, OC, vol. 3, p. 543.

69. Thierry, 'Sur la Conquête de l'Angleterre par les Normands; A Propos du Roman d'Ivanhoe' [27 May 1820], *Dix Ans*, OC, vol. 3, p. 441.

70. Thierry, Préface [1834], *Dix Ans*, OC, vol. 3, p. 345.

71. Thierry, 'Sur l'Affranchissement des Communes' [13 October 1820], *Dix Ans*, OC, vol. 3, pp. 572–3.

72. Thierry, 'Sur l'Affranchissement des Communes', OC, vol. 3, pp. 575.

73. F. Guizot, letter of 25 October 1820 to C. Fauriel, J.B. Galley, *Claude Fauriel: Membre de l'Institut 1772–1843*, Saint-Etienne 1909, p. 238.

74. Galley, *Claude Fauriel*, pp. 403–20.

75. A. Manzoni, letter of 17 October 1820 to Fauriel, in Manzoni, TO, vol. 7, p. 215.

76. C. de Sainte-Beuve, 'Claude Fauriel', *Portraits Contemporains*, Paris 1870, vol. 4, pp. 217–20.

77. Manzoni, letters to G. Cattaneo, TO, vol. 7, pp. 219, 220, 221, 235–6.

78. Manzoni, *Discorso Storico sulla Storia Longobarda* [1822], TO, vol. 4, pp. 222–3, quoting the *Third New Science*.

79. Manzoni, *Discorso Storico* [1822] TO, vol. 4, p. 194.

80. Manzoni, *Discorso Storico* [1822] TO, vol. 4, p. 44.

81. B. Croce, *Storia della Storiografia Italiana nel Secolo Decimonono*, Bari 1921, vol. 1, pp. 188–9.

82. Manzoni, *Discorso Storico* [1845] TO, vol. 4, p. 94–113.

83. Thierry, 'Sur les Libertés Locales et Municipales' [2 February 1820], OC, vol. 3, pp. 523–7.

84. Manzoni, *Discorso Storico* [1845] TO, vol. 4, p. 35n.

85. B. Constant, *De la Religion*, Paris 1824, vol. 2, pp. 211, 220–1, 238–9.

86. Manzoni, *Sulla Morale Cattolica – Osservazioni* [1819], TO, vol. 3, p. 304.

87. Manzoni, *Del Romanzo Storico* [conceived in 1828–29 as a letter to Goethe, drafted *c.* 1851], R. Bacchelli, ed., Manzoni, *Opere*, Milan and Naples 1953, pp. 1079–89.

88. D. Forgacs and G. Nowell-Smith, eds., Gramsci, *Selections from Cultural Writings*, translated by W. Boelhower, London 1985, pp. 287–97.

89. M. Pavan, 'La Fine dell'Impero Romano e il Manzoni', RSI, vol. 70, 1958, pp. 169–87.

90. F. Ulivi, *Manzoni, Storia e Providenza*, Rome 1974, p. 262.

91. N. Machiavelli, *The History of Florence*, New York 1960, and *The Discourses*, translated by L.J. Walker, London 1950, vol. 1, p. 245.

92. Manzoni, *Discorso Storico* [1845], TO, vol. 4, p. 111.

93. Ulivi, *Manzoni*, pp. 163–232.

94. Manzoni, *Sulla Morale Cattolica*, TO, vol. 3, pp. 484–5.

95. In B. Croce, *Alessandro Manzoni*, 6th edn, Bari 1969, pp. 7–8.

96. H. Heine, *The Romantic School*, translated and edited by H.M. Mustard, SW, New York 1973, p. 132.

97. See, in fact, the crucial remarks by Timpanaro, *Classicismo*, pp. 369–70.

98. Manzoni, *Sentir Messa, Libro della Lingua d'Italia* [1824], Milan 1923; A. Rosmini Serbati, *The Origin of Ideas* [1830], London 1886, vol. 1, pp. 97–113; V. Gioberti, *Del Primato Morale e Civile degli Italiani* [1843], Turin 1932, vol. 1, pp. 12–13. Conversely, note Cattaneo, 'Delle Dottrine di Romagnosi' [1836], SF, vol. 1, p. 40, and 'Carlo Cattaneo a Don Serbati Rosmini' [1836], SF, vol. 1, p. 82.

99. Manzoni, *Pensieri Religiosi e Vari* [1834?], TO, vol. 3, p. 784.

100. Romagnosi, 'Alcuni Pensieri sopra un Ultra-Metafisica Filosofia della Storia', SF, vol. 2, p. 65.

101. B. Croce, *Storia della Storiografia Italiana nel Secolo Decimonono*, Bari 1921, vol. 1, p. 23.

102. C.-F. de Volney, *Leçons d'Histoire*, OC, p. 595.

103. Cattaneo, 'Istoria Universale di Heinrich Leo' [1840], in L. Ambrosoli, ed., *'Il Politecnico' 1839–44*, Turin 1989, vol. 1, p. 469, and 'Frammenti d'Istoria Universale' [1846], in Sestan, ed., *Opere*, p. 841.

104. See, for example, Gioberti, *Del Primato Civile*, pp. 31–3, 46–7. In neo-Guelph historiography, a hostility towards Islam is generally complemented by a readiness to celebrate the ancient wisdom of India. As Edward Said has argued, Romantic conceptions of Christian Europe appeared to rest upon a division, crystallized in comparative philology, between a near and a distant Orient, or between the Semitic and the Indo-Germanic; *Orientalism*, London 1978, for example, pp. 78–9, 120–2, 137–9. A distinction should, however, be made between a hostility that is primary, as in the case of Chateaubriand, Gioberti or Balbo, and a Volneyan critique of a despotism which was accidentally, not essentially, associated with Islam.

105. Cattaneo, 'Filosofia della Rivoluzione' [1851], SF, vol. 1, p. 280.

106. Cattaneo, 'Su la "Scienza Nuova" di Vico' [1839], SF, vol. 1, pp. 99, 101–3.

107. Cattaneo, 'Su la "Scienza Nuova" ', SF, vol. 1, pp. 122–3; 'Sul Principio della Filosofia' [1844], in Ambrosoli, ed., *'Il Politecnico'*, vol. 2, pp. 1401–2, 1404.

108. Cattaneo, 'Su la "Scienza Nuova" ', SF, vol. 1, pp. 120.

109. Cattaneo, 'Frammenti', in Sestan, ed., *Opere*, pp. 834–5.

110. Croce, *Storia della Storiografia Italiana*, vol. 1, pp. 22–3, vol. 2, p. 9.

111. Bobbio, *La Filosofia è una Milizia*, Turin 1970, pp. 182–3.

112. Croce, *Storia della Storiografia Italiana*, vol. 1, p. 22.

113. Romagnosi, 'Cenni su i Limiti e su la Direzione degli Studi Storici' [1832], SF, vol. 2, pp. 55–6.

114. Croce, *Storia della Storiografia Italiana*, vol. 1, pp. 54–7, 151–2.

115. In support of Croce's case, however, compare Romagnosi, 'Esame della Storia degli Antichi Popoli Italiani di Giuseppe Micali', *Opere*, vol. 2, pt 1, p. 438 with Gioberti, *Del Primato Civile*, vol. 1, pp. 42–7.

116. Moravia, 'Vichismo e "Idéologie" '; F. Tessitore, 'Vincenzo Cuoco e il Liberalismo "Moderato" ', in G. Cherubini, F. Della Peruta, E. Lepore, G. Mori, G. Procacci and R. Villari, eds., *Storia della Società Italiana*, pt 4, vol. 13, *L'Italia Giacobina e Napoleonica*, Milan 1985, pp. 329–69.

117. Cattaneo, 'Su la "Scienza Nuova" ', pp. 116–17; 'Frammenti', p. 826.

118. Cattaneo, 'Su la "Scienza Nuova" ', pp. 116–18.

119. Cattaneo, 'Frammenti', p. 836.

120. Ambrosoli, *La Formazione di Carlo Cattaneo*, pp. 13–18.

121. Cattaneo, 'Influenza della Gran Transmigrazione di Barbari sulla Lingua Italiana', in P. Trèves, ed., Cattaneo, SL, Florence 1981, vol. 2, pp. 21–8.

122. Cattaneo, 'Della Conquista d'Inghilterra pei Normanni' [1839, 1846], in Sestan, ed., *Opere*, p. 576.

123. Cattaneo, 'Vita di Dante di Cesare Balbo', in Ambrosoli, ed., *'Il Politecnico'*, vol. 1, p. 201; 'Della Conquista', p. 575; 'Su la Lingua e le Leggi dei Celti' [1844], SL, vol. 1, pp. 210, 213–4; 'Tipi del Genere Humano' [1862], in D. Castelnuovo Frigessi, ed., C. Cattaneo, OS, Turin 1972, p. 376.

124. Cattaneo, 'Vita di Dante', pp. 191, 200; 'La Città Considerata come Principio Ideale delle Istorie Italiane', [1858], OS, vol. 4, p. 86.

125. Timpanaro, *Classicismo*, pp. 249–52.

126. Timpanaro, *Classicismo*, pp. 253–8; C. Tagliavini, *Le Origini delle Lingue Neolatine*, 3rd edn, Bologna 1959, pp. 10–11.

127. F. Schlegel, *On the Indian Language, Literature and Philosophy*, AMW, pp. 460, 502–7.

128. Cattaneo, 'Sul Principio Storico', p. 170; 'Su la Lingua e le Leggi dei Celti', pp. 209–10; 'Frammenti', pp. 829–31.

129. Cattaneo, 'Sul Principio Storico', p. 167.

130. Cattaneo, 'Su la Lingua e le Leggi dei Celti', p. 214.

131. Cattaneo, 'Sul Principio della Filosofia', pp. 1404–5.

132. Cattaneo, 'Notizie Naturali e Civili su la Lombardia' [1844], in Sestan, ed., *Opere*, pp. 716–18.

133. Note, in particular, the critique of Niebuhr, in 'Notizie', pp. 717–18.

134. Cattaneo, 'La Città', pp. 80–6, 120. I would add that a proper understanding of Cattaneo's political thought could only be achieved by placing it in its immediate historical context, and by contrasting it with the neo-Guelph schemes of confederation expounded by Gioberti and Balbo. Studies by Bobbio, Timpanaro, Moravia and others have rescued Cattaneo from the neglect he suffered when neo-idealist philosophy was in the ascendancy in Italy, but there is still, so far as I know, no rounded picture of this remarkable polymath. I am not in a position to comment upon the effect that the rise of the Lega Lombarda and the Lega Nord in the 1990s has had upon the interpretation of Cattaneo's thought, but the racist tone of some of their pronouncements leads me to fear the worst.

135. J.N.A. Thierry, *Politique des Nations et de leurs Rapports Mutuels* (henceforth *PN*), in *Oeuvres de Saint-Simon et d'Enfantin*, Paris 1868, pp. 20–2.

136. Thierry, *PN*, ch. 8.

137. Thierry, *PN*, pp. 37–8.

138. Thierry, 'Première Lettre', *Dix Ans*, p. 560.

139. Thierry, *PN*, p. 20n.

140. Thierry, 'Sur l'Affranchissement des Communes', *Dix Ans*, p. 572.

141. Marx, letter of 27 July 1854 to Engels, in CW, vol. 39, pp. 472–6; Cattaneo, 'Della Formazione e del Progresso del Terzo Stato' [15 February 1854], a review of the book to which Marx was referring, now in OS, vol. 4, pp. 18–19.

142. L. Gossman, 'Augustin Thierry and Liberal Historiography', in *History and Theory: Studies in the Philosophy of History*, Beiheft 15, no. 4, Middletown 1976, p. 29.

143. Gramsci, *Selections from the Prison Notebooks*, edited and translated by Q. Hoare and G. Nowell-Smith, London 1971, pp. 118–20.

144. N. Bobbio, 'Benedetto Croce e il Liberalismo', in *La Politica e la Cultura*, Bari 1955, pp. 244–9, 253–7; Bobbio, *Liberalism and Democracy*, translated by M. Ryle and K. Soper, London 1990, ch. 2.

# Index